TORONTO MEDIEVAL TEXTS AND TRA

THE BEGINNINGS OF ENGLISH LAW

The laws of Æthelberht of Kent (ca. 600), Hloþhere and Eadric (685x686), and Wihtred (695) are the earliest laws from Anglo-Saxon England, and the first Germanic laws written in the vernacular. They are of unique importance as the only extant early medieval English laws that delineate the progress of law and legal language in the early days of the conversion to Christianity. Æthelberht's laws, the closest existing equivalent to Germanic law as it was transmitted in a pre-literate period, contrast with Hloþhere and Eadric's expanded laws, which concentrate on legal procedure and process, and contrast again with the laws of Wihtred, which demonstrate how the new religion of Christianity adapted and changed the law to conform to changing social mores.

This volume updates previous works with current scholarship in the fields of linguistics and social and legal history to present new editions and translations of these three Kentish pre-Alfredian laws. Each body of law is situated within its historical, literary, and legal context, annotated, and provided with facing-page translation.

(Toronto Medieval Texts in Translation)

LISI OLIVER is an associate professor in the Department of English at Louisiana State University.

LISI OLIVER

The Beginnings of English Law

UNIVERSITY OF TORONTO PRESS
Toronto Buffalo London

© University of Toronto Press 2002
Toronto Buffalo London
Printed in the U.S.A.

Reprinted in paperback 2012

ISBN 0-8020-3535-3 (cloth)
ISBN 978-1-4426-1483-3 (paper)

∞

Printed on acid-free paper

National Library of Canada Cataloguing in Publication Data

Oliver, Lisi
    The beginnings of English law

(Toronto medieval texts and translations, 14)
Annotated edition of the early Kentish laws, with facing page translation and commentary.
Includes bibliographical references and index.
ISBN 0-8020-3535-3 (bound). – ISBN 978-1-4426-1483-3 (pbk.)

1. Law, Anglo-Saxon – Translations into English. 2. Law – Great Britain – Early works to 1800. 3. Law – Great Britain – History – Sources. 4. Law – England – Kent – History – Sources. 5. Common law – History – Sources. 6. Christianity and law. 7. English language – Old English, ca. 450–1100 – Texts. 8. Anglo-Saxons – Kings and rulers. 9. Manuscripts, English (Old). I. Title. II. Series.

    KD542.O45 2002   349.42'09'021   C2002-900153-6

University of Toronto Press acknowledges the financial assistance to its publishing program of the Canda Council for the Arts and the Ontario Arts Council.

    Canada Council **Conseil des Arts**   **ONTARIO ARTS COUNCIL**
    for the Arts   **du Canada**   **CONSEIL DES ARTS DE L'ONTARIO**

University of Toronto Press acknowledges the financial support for its publishing activities of the Government of Canada though the Canada Book Fund.

*In memory of
William Alfred
who taught me Old English,
I offer, in his own words,
'these bare and patient bones of language
on which we build this petulant flesh of empire.'*

Contents

Preface xi

Acknowledgments xiii

Map of early Anglo-Saxon England 2

1 **Background** 3
   An outline of the history leading up to Æthelberht's reign 3
   Historical background to Æthelberht's laws 8
      Æthelberht, Augustine, and the conversion of Kent 8
      The role of kingship and Christianity in the promulgation
      of law 14
   The manuscript 20
   Archaic traces in the language of the laws 25
      Orthography 26
      Phonology 27
      Morphology 29
      Syntax 30
      Word division 34
   The question of dating 34
      Remnants of oral transmission 34
      Chronological layering of Æthelberht's laws 41

2 **The Laws of Æthelberht** 52
   Notes on the edition 52

Editorial conventions 53
Edition and translation 59
Commentary 82
　Monetary system 82
　Rubric 83
　The church and the public assembly 83
　The king 85
　Fines payable to an *eorl* 89
　Fines payable to a freeman 89
　Freedmen 91
　Theft 93
　Killing 96
　Rihthamscyld 97
　Personal injury 99
　Women and children 105
　　Maidens 106
　　Women 109
　　Widows 111
　Servants 114
　Slaves 116

3　**The Laws of Hloþhere & Eadric** 117
Historical background 117
Some notes on the language 120
　Archaisms 121
　Modernizations 122
　Dialect features 122
　Abbreviations 123
Edition and translation 125
Commentary 134
　Rubric and prologue 134
　Fines 135
　Legal responsibilities in hospitality 138
　The process of bringing a charge 139
　The regulation of commerce 141
　Oath supporters 144

4　**The Laws of Wihtred** 147
　Historical background 147

Some notes on the language   148
  Archaisms   148
  Modernizations   149
  Dialect features   149
Edition and translation   151
Commentary   164
  Rubric and prologue   164
  Rights of the church   166
  Unlawful matrimony   167
  Abuses by ecclesiastics   168
  Manumission   169
  Transgressing the laws of the church   170
  Exculpation   174
  Theft   177
Conclusion   180

Appendix I: Diplomatic Transcription   181

Appendix II: Comparison of Restitution According to Amount in Æthelberht   195

Appendix III: Comparison of Restitution According to Status in Æthelberht   199

Appendix IV: Payment to the King for Disturbance of the Peace   201

Notes   203

Glossary   235

Concordance of proper names   249

Previous editions and translations of the Kentish laws   251

Bibliography   257

Index   277

Preface

This volume contains new editions and facing-page translations of the three Kentish pre-Alfredian laws: those of Æthelberht (ca. 600), Hloþhere & Eadric (sometime between 685 and 686) and Wihtred (695). These are the earliest Anglo-Saxon laws to have survived, and the first Germanic laws written in the vernacular. The text of Æthelberht is the closest extant equivalent to Germanic law as it was transmitted in a preliterate period, while the laws of Hloþhere & Eadric and Wihtred testify to the expansion of customary law when laws were first cast in the medium of writing. The text of Hloþhere & Eadric concentrates on legal procedure and process, discussion of which is almost entirely lacking in the tersely worded clauses of Æthelberht. The laws of Wihtred subsequently reveal the way in which the new religion of Christianity adapted and altered the law to reflect changing social mores. It must be kept in mind that Anglo-Saxon England in this period was not a single entity, but rather a cluster of seven or more individual kingdoms, of which Kent was only one. But the other early legal text we have – that of the West Saxon king Ine – was drafted at roughly the same time as the last of the three Kentish texts, and the next laws to be written – those of Ine's descendent Alfred the Great – date from almost two centuries later. The trio of texts contained in this volume, then, is of unique importance to legal, historical, and linguistic scholars. Together they delineate the progress of law and legal language in the early days of the conversion to Christianity in the only territory of Anglo-Saxon England for which we have any evidence.

Both editions and translations draw on the work of previous interpreters but update their analyses to reflect current scholarship in the fields of linguistics and social and legal history. The texts are annotated with interpretation of individual clauses, while commentary following each body of laws discusses the legal implications of related sections. Each body of law is situated within its historical and legal context. A diplomatic transcription is provided in an appendix.

It is hoped that this volume will serve the needs of readers in a variety of disciplines. Legal scholars can use it as a springboard for investigation of the historical development of the modern Anglo-American legal system. For the scholar of medieval history, it provides evidence of the evolution of Anglo-Saxon law and society during the early stages of the transition from paganism to Christianity. The diplomatic transcription provides historical linguists with an accessible reproduction of three of our earliest Old English texts, allowing analysis of the early development of the Anglo-Saxon language. And for students of Old English literature, these laws provide a further example of the balance of pagan and Christian elements found in such literary works as *Beowulf* and *The Seafarer*.

Finally, one must always bear in mind that the nature of the material is such that interpretation of the text often raises more questions than are answered. It is, however, precisely in the raising of such questions that scholarly discourse advances.

Acknowledgments

The springboard for this book was my doctoral dissertation; my dissertation director Calvert Watkins and advisers Dan Donoghue and Charlie Donahue have been of tremendous assistance both then and since. I can overstate neither their intellectual nor their moral support, and I am greatly indebted to them. I would also like to thank Patrick Wormald, who has generously and graciously given of his time to read and respond not only to my dissertation but also to many subsequent papers that were absorbed into this volume. Thanks also to John Fischer, Ben Fortson, Jesse Gellrich, Ben Guelfo, Mark Hale, Kent Hare, Michael Hegarty, Dominique Homberger, and Joshua Katz, who have kindly read parts of drafts at various periods, and to Kathryn MacDonald and Judy Kemerait, who helped with bibliographic research. The comments on earlier drafts made by the University of Toronto Press's anonymous readers have immeasurably improved this book; I only regret that their anonymity makes it impossible to thank them personally. But above all, I would like to thank Stephanie Jamison, my first linguistics teacher; apart from being my most assiduous reader, she also taught me – at least to the best of my ability – how to be a scholarly writer. Any errors or stylistic infelicities remaining are solely my own responsibility.

I would also like to acknowledge those who facilitated the process of bringing this project to completion. Canon Armson of Rochester Cathedral permitted me to view the manuscript of the *Textus Roffensis* in the Kent County Archives. The Whiting Foundation provided generous financial support during the final year of my dissertation process. Louisiana State University granted me a semester of research leave, and the Linguistics Department at Harvard University gave me a home during this period. Maranda Cardinale and Brent Barnard undertook much of the tedious work of proofreading and Kristen Pedersen and Barbara Porter patiently saw the manuscript through to publication.

Finally, I owe a special debt of gratitude to my parents for their unwavering and unstinting encouragement and assistance.

THE BEGINNINGS OF ENGLISH LAW

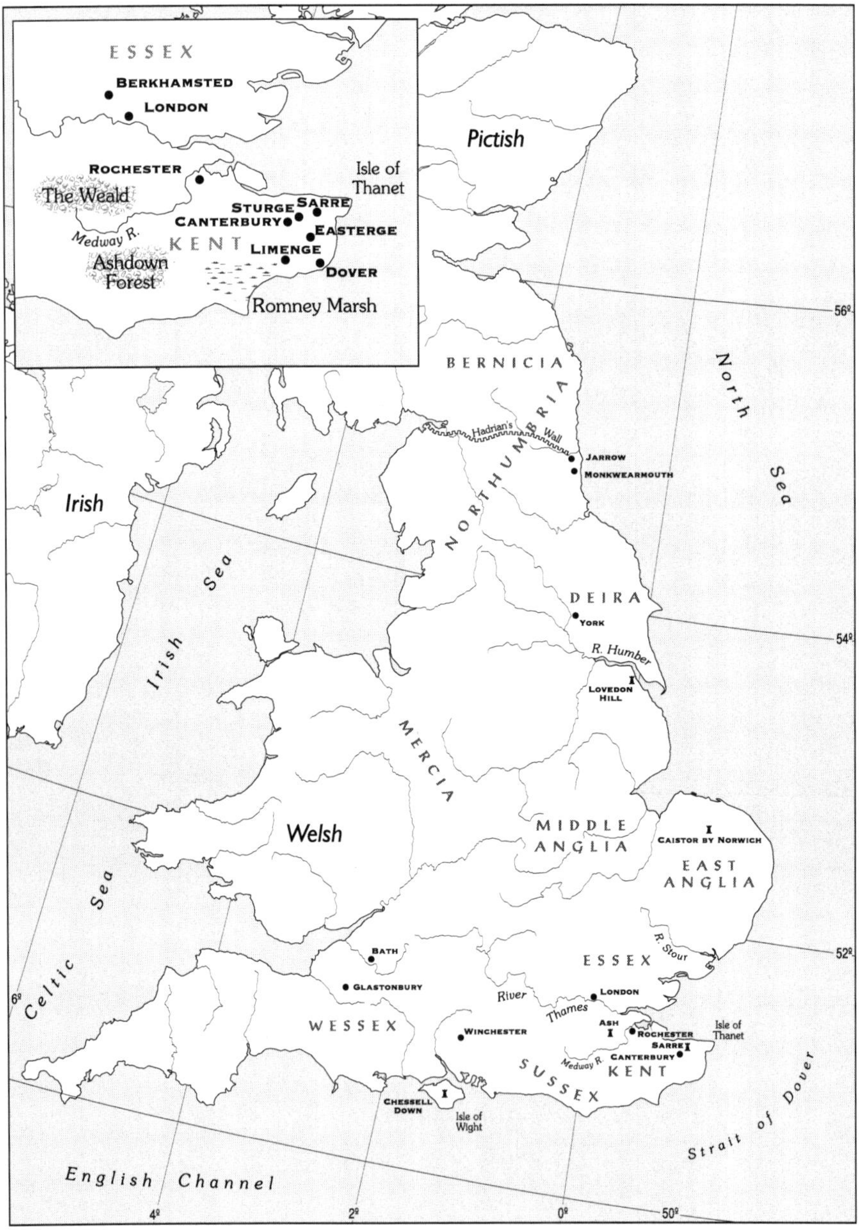
ESSEX
BERKHAMSTED
LONDON
ROCHESTER
The Weald
Isle of Thanet
STURGE
SARRE
CANTERBURY
EASTERGE
Medway R.
KENT
LIMENGE
Ashdown Forest
DOVER
Romney Marsh
Pictish
56º
BERNICIA
North Sea
NORTHUMBRIA
Hadrian's Wall
JARROW
MONKWEARMOUTH
Irish
Irish Sea
DEIRA
YORK
R. Humber
54º
LOVEDON HILL
MERCIA
Welsh
MIDDLE ANGLIA
CAISTOR BY NORWICH
EAST ANGLIA
Celtic Sea
R. Stour
52º
BATH
ESSEX
GLASTONBURY
River Thames
LONDON
6º
WESSEX
WINCHESTER
ASH
ROCHESTER
Isle of Thanet
SARRE
Medway R.
CANTERBURY
SUSSEX
KENT
CHESSELL DOWN
Isle of Wight
Strait of Dover
English Channel
4º
2º
0º
50º

1
Background

An outline of the history leading up to Æthelberht's reign[1]

'The island of Britain is 800 miles long and 200 miles broad, and here in the island there are five languages, English, British, Scottish [=Irish], Pictish and Latin.'[2] Thus begins the preface to the *Anglo-Saxon Chronicle*, paraphrasing the opening to Bede's famous *Ecclesiastical History of the English People*. The linguistic diversity to which it refers reflects the early history of the island. Celtic, which would produce British (or Welsh) and Irish, spread from the mainland well before the Christian era.[3] Whether Pictish was a language spoken by indigenous peoples or a collateral branch of Celtic is a much-studied question which the paucity of linguistic remains makes difficult to resolve.[4] Latin was first introduced when Julius Caesar invaded in 55 BC; Britain subsequently became the western outpost of the Roman Empire. The northern boundary was marked by Hadrian's Wall, which served to keep the savage Picts from northern and lowland Britain, while in the central and southern part of the fertile island, Romans and Roman mercenaries built villas, churches, and towns and for the most part settled amicably with the indigenous Britons. By some estimations, the population of Roman London could have been as high as 30,000, a level that would not be reached again until the later medieval period.[5]

But as the Roman Empire started to collapse in upon itself, barbarian warbands began to harry its European borders. On the last day of 406, unusually cold weather caused the Rhine to freeze and troops of barbarians seized the opportunity to cross it and attack Gaul. In the same year the Britons raised the first of three rival emperors. Britain itself came under attack from the pagan Saxons: Bede i.12 tells us that around 410 'the Romans informed the Britons that they could no longer be burdened with such troublesome expeditions for their defence; they advised them to take up arms themselves and make an effort to oppose their foes, who would prove too powerful for them only if they themselves were weakened by sloth.'[6] Thus the Roman Empire effectively sloughed off Britain as its westernmost territory[7] and the island entered a period of turmoil, for which we can only piece together the history from later (and sometimes questionable) sources.[8]

The Britons became subject to attack from marauding bands of Picts and Irish, and from Saxon raiders from across the Channel. Sometime before 441 they wrote to Aetius, the Roman consul, for help in a letter preserved (or perhaps recreated) in §20 of *De Excidio Britanniae*, written by the early medieval Welsh historian, Gildas.[9] This letter is quoted in Bede i.13: 'The barbarians drive us to the sea: the sea drives us back on the barbarians; between them two kinds of death face us: we are either slaughtered or drowned.'[10] Aetius was unable to answer their pleas as the Romans themselves were occupied in staving off the attacks of Atilla, the leader of the Huns. In §23 of *De Excidio*, Gildas tells us that a 'proud tyrant,' to whom Bede i.14 gives the name Vortigern, asked Germanic mercenaries to come across the channel to the aid of the Britons. These warriors were famous for their size and ferocity throughout the Middle Ages – Dante describes the giant Nimrod as so huge that three champions from the Germanic territory of Frisia could not reach from his waist to his hair.[11] But the Germans gave Vortigern more than he had bargained for.[12]

Gildas §23 goes on to tell us that 'a pack of cubs burst forth from the lair of the barbarian lioness, coming in three *keels*, as they call warships in their language.'[13] Although three ships may not seem like a very substantial fleet, the longboat recently excavated in Roskilde, Denmark, is over 30 metres long and could have accommodated a crew of over a hundred men. If we take Gildas literally, the number of initial recruits would likely have been between one and two hundred, perhaps even as many as three hundred, depending on the size of the ships – no mean force for those days.[14] Even if we don't question Gildas's account, the number of warriors who landed was probably not much greater, as Vortigern was unlikely to accept large hordes of Saxons descending on his territory. Once there, the Saxons sent home for reinforcements and fellow settlers: the archaeological record shows a partial abandonment of parts of the northern continental shoreline at this time.[15] Bede i.15 sets the date between 449 and 455. For a brief period, peace reigned. But then the Germans, complaining of insufficient food and other grievances, rose in rebellion against their erstwhile employers. British efforts to fight back were unsuccessful – perhaps the Britons had been weakened by their *Romanitas* – and the sixth and seventh centuries saw a gradual takeover of many of the southern parts of the island. Some territories remained Celtic holdouts; many were overcome by the military strength of the Germanic warriors; and others no doubt assimilated in the process of more peaceful settlement. The archaeological record often shows a high degree of continuity between the late Roman and early Anglo-Saxon landscapes.[16] The Germanic warrior band was founded on the *comitatus*, according to whose ethos a leader gave his followers armour and treasure in return for their support in battle. Gradually, it seems, some of these warrior chieftains assumed the role of king. They may even have modelled themselves according to the example of kingship provided by the Celts.[17]

Ironically, those who had been summoned to help stayed to colonize. According to Bede i.15, the foreign settlers consisted of Angles (who settled in the northern territories), Saxons (in the east), and Jutes (in the south). This tripartite division is now seen as overly simplistic: not only were the territorial boundaries not so clear-cut, but Frisians were surely involved. Warriors may even have come from as far away as Sweden, and the Angles themselves constituted a plurality of peoples.[18] All of the Germans were pagan and their settlements subordinated the Christian religion, although it is possible that some pockets still remained. St Martin's Church near Canterbury, for one, may have maintained an ongoing tradition.[19] It is in this ancient settlement of Canterbury that the recording of Anglo-Saxon law was inaugurated.

Located at the centre of the Roman southeastern road system, Canterbury had, under Roman rule, been the principal city of Kent. But when the area was taken over by the Jutish settlers, the city was temporarily abandoned: Germanic tribes typically built in wood and mud, and they did not have the technology to maintain the old stone walls.[20] Kent had been a principality long before the arrival of the Jutes, an Iron Age Celtic settlement giving way to the Romano-British *civitas*. While the names of other southern Anglo-Saxon kingdoms are typically derived from their Germanic settlers (Sussex, Essex, Wessex from the Saxons, Anglia from the Angles), *Cantium* was known to Julius Caesar, and there is evidence that the name – at least as it applies to a geographical territory – probably predates him by at least two centuries.[21]

6 The Beginnings of English Law

Bede claims that the Jutes settled Kent and the Isle of Wight. Archaeological evidence, however, shows predominantly Saxon settlement in western Kent beyond the Weald (a large forested territory). It seems likely, then, that the focus of the Jutish settlement lay in the east, and that the west was annexed later, leaving the kingdom with two distinct regions: eastern Kent and western Kent (which may well never have been a part of *Cantium* as Caesar knew it).[22] This distinction, both regal and ecclesiastical, continued into the Anglo-Saxon period. Kent was often subject to joint rule, with the junior king having his main court in Rochester.[23] A second bishopric was also established at Rochester in 604, although no other Anglo-Saxon kingdom had two episcopal sees until the 670s. Both the bishops of Canterbury and Rochester are named in the prologue to the early eighth-century laws of Wihtred. The very location of eastern Kent helped to distinguish it from the rest of the southern mainland: it is a virtual island, bounded on the north by the Thames estuary, on the east and south-east by the English channel, on the south by the forest of the Weald and Romney Marsh, and to the west by the Medway River and Ashdown Forest.

Geographically isolated, the people of Kent, speaking in their Jutish-influenced dialect, lived in a kingdom very different from other parts of the country. At some point in the prehistoric period the kingdom was divided into 'lathes,' or territories, each containing a royal vill which could house the peripatetic king on his travels, and from which he could administer law. Although their number is uncertain, we can be fairly sure of at least four: *Stūr-gē*, 'Stour district capital' (modern Sturry); *Easter-gē*, 'the eastern district capital' (modern Eastry); *Limen-gē*, 'the Limen district capital' (modern Lyminge),[24] and Wester Linton, perhaps the western district capital.[25] The forest belonging to these lathes consisted not only of royal holdings but also of common territory. As certain peasants repeatedly allowed their swine to graze for acorns in specific areas in the common forest, over time they were perceived as having the right to use that particular area; this right would later develop into the exclusively Kentish system of 'denns.' Also unique to the Kentish people was the process of inheritance known as 'gavelkind,' which 'substituted for the normal rule of primogeniture the equal division of land between surviving sons (or daughters if there were no sons), the youngest making the division and retaining the ancestral hearth and the eldest having first choice among the portions.'[26] As overseas commerce expanded, Kentish jewellers seem to have been importing silver rather than using that obtained from melting down Roman objects, as was the practice elsewhere in England.[27] In fact, the degree of difference in the amount of trade Kent undertook with the Continent compared to other early, less well-developed Anglo-Saxon kingdoms has led to the postulation that the Kentings – with the help of their cousins on the strategically located Isle of Wight – may actually have deterred trade in the west by naval blockade.[28] The Renaissance poet Sir Thomas Wyatt satirizes an old proverb that encompasses activities 'in Kent or in Christendom,' neatly distinguishing the former from the latter.[29] Twentieth-century historian G.O. Sayles likewise argues that 'Kent has always seemed to be a district apart, and its inhabitants a peculiar people.'[30]

Who were the early rulers of this peculiar people? 'The leaders of the first Germanic invaders,' Bede i.15 tells us, 'are said to have been two brothers, Hengist and Horsa ... They were the sons of Wihtgisl, son of Witta, son of Wecta, son of Woden, from whose stock the royal families of many kingdoms claimed their descent."[31] Here we may move into the realm of foundation myth: according to Bede, the race owes its origin to two brothers of godly ancestry whose names would be translated in modern terms as 'stallion' and 'horse.' (Compare the story of the founding of Rome by Romulus and Remus.) Wallace-Hadrill claims that 'neither their duality nor their curious names compel us to dismiss them as fiction: dual, and even triple rule was not unknown to the continental Germans, and there were certainly names as implausible as theirs. Moreover, there was a continental Hengest, of the Danish tribe of the Eota, according to *Beowulf.*'[32] Although there seem to be good grounds for believing in the existence of Hengist, it is possible that Horsa was, in fact, a later addition designed to invoke the traditional dualism of foundation mythology. Interesting that Hengist and Horsa should be the ancestors of a kingdom which was itself often subject to dual kingship! The successor to the Jutish Hengist in Bede's genealogy bears the northern name of Oeric (Eric), but with an unlikely surname of Oisc, if we take the latter as cognate to Old Norse *Áss*, 'god.' The *Anglo-Saxon Chronicle*, recording the event approximately four hundred years later, puts his year of accession at 488 and says he ruled for twenty-four years.[33]

It is around 500 that Frankish influence becomes evident in the archaeological remains in eastern Kent. Trade between the Kentish peninsula – the nearest landfall to the continent – and the Germanic tribes across the channel began to increase, and the small kingdom soon became a wealthy and cosmopolitan centre. The flow of commerce appears to have extended from southwest Gaul to southern Scandinavia, but the majority of the goods found in archaeological digs are from Francia.[34] Frankish influence does not seem to have been limited to the field of trade, however. The king who succeeded Oeric's son Octa bore the Frankish name of Eormenric, although history has not preserved for us the reason. Eormenric would be the last pre-Christian ruler of Kent. But pride in the ancient tradition of the house remained strong, even after the conversion of Eormenric's son Æthelberht, for Bede ii.5 gives us his genealogy in much the same form as it must often have been sung in the halls of Kent: 'Now Æthelberht was the son of Eormenric, the son of Octa, the son of Oeric, whose surname was Oisc, whence the kings of Kent were known as *oiscingas*. Oisc's father was Hengist who with his son Oisc first entered Britain at the invitation of Vortigern.'[35]

Historical background to Æthelberht's laws

Æthelberht, Augustine, and the conversion of Kent

Despite his importance to both the religious and legal history of England, we know very little about Æthelberht. Even his dates are difficult to establish with any precision.[36] Bede ii.5 begins as follows: 'In the year of our Lord 616, the twenty-first year after Augustine and his companions had been sent to preach to the English nation, King Æthelberht of Kent, after ruling his temporal kingdom gloriously for fifty-six years, entered upon the eternal joys of the heavenly kingdom. He was the third English king to rule over all the southern kingdoms, which are divided from the north by the river Humber and the surrounding territory; but he was the first to enter the kingdom of heaven.'[37] But Bede contradicts himself later in the same chapter, when he states that Æthelberht died twenty-one years after his conversion in 597; this would put his date of death at 618 rather than 616.[38] Calculating according to Bede, the beginning of Æthelberht's reign should be dated 560x2 ('x' is used throughout to indicate 'sometime between'). But Bede's reckoning may be doubtful; as Nicholas Brooks points out, 'fifty-six years would indeed be a reign of unusual length, some fifteen years more than the longest Anglo-Saxon reign otherwise known, that of Æthelbald of Mercia (716–57). Indeed it would be longer than that of any other English rulers apart from George III (1760–1820) and Victoria (1837–1901).'[39]

Gregory of Tours's *History of the Franks*, an important contemporary continental source, provides competing information in a glancing reference. Æthelberht took as his wife Bertha, daughter of the Frankish king Charibert, the grandson of the powerful king Clovis who had been the first of the Frankish kings to accept Christianity. The lives of Æthelberht's in-laws across the channel, as chronicled by Gregory, may thus provide further clues to the dates of Æthelberht's reign.

Book Four of Gregory's history has been tentatively dated to 573x575 or 576x580.[40] In this book Gregory states that 'King Charibert married a woman called Ingoberg. He had by her a daughter, who eventually married a man from Kent and went to live there.'[41] If Gregory could still refer to Æthelberht as a 'man from Kent' either as early as 573 or as late as 580, it is clear that by that time Æthelberht had not yet taken the kingship.[42] Perhaps Bede, working through a Kentish informant more than a century later, misinterpreted his source; in any event, 560x2 is in fact more likely to be the date of Æthelberht's birth, not his accession. As 580 is the *terminus post quem non* for Gregory's Book IV, Æthelberht and Bertha's marriage cannot postdate that year. Fifteen was the age of majority, so it is conceivable that Æthelberht married Bertha as early as 575. Her father, Charibert I, had died in 567, and his territory was divided among his three brothers, Bertha's uncles. Bertha's marriage to a prince across the Channel may have been seen as an advantageous way of providing for a princess whose position in the new kingdoms might well be awkward: not only had her father's royal line become defunct, but Bertha was the daughter of Charibert's first wife, whom he discarded to take the second of three (or possibly four) wives. The alliance cannot, therefore, have brought much political power to the Kentish prince Æthelberht, but he may have considered it prestigious to have allied himself, however distantly, with the ruling family of Gaul.[43]

The *Anglo-Saxon Chronicle* implies that Æthelberht was already an important military ruler in Kent by 568: the entry for that year states that '[i]n this year Ceawlin and Cutha [of Wessex] fought against Ethelberht, and drove him in flight into Kent, and killed two ealdormen, Oslaf and Cnebba, at *Wibbandum*.'[44] But the dating of this entry would make Æthelberht a mere eight years old, if we accept 560 as the date of his birth rather than the beginning of his reign. However, since the Chronicle was not begun until the end of the ninth century, the entries for the early dates must often be looked at with a critical eye.

Probably more reliable in determining the date of Æthelberht's succession to the kingship of Kent is Book Nine of Gregory, written 587x90,[45] in which he states of Queen Ingoberg that 'she left a daughter, who had married the son of a king of Kent.'[46] Clearly Æthelberht could not have become king until after the completion of Gregory's book, so we must assume a date for Æthelberht's accession of after 587x90. The *Anglo-Saxon Chronicle* tells us that in the year 592 'there occurred a great slaughter at "Woden's barrow", and Ceawlin [king of the West Saxons] was driven out.'[47] Ceawlin's defeat opened the way for Æthelberht to become the dominant ruler in the south of England.

Bede i.25 tells us that by the time Pope Gregory I dispatched his evangelizing deputation to England in 595, 'Æthelberht, king of Kent, was a very powerful monarch. The lands over which he exercised his suzerainity stretched as far as the great river Humber, which divides the northern from the southern Angles.'[48] It seems that Æthelberht was already recognized as *imperator*[49] or overlord of the southern kingdoms when he received the Christianizing mission headed by Augustine, who arrived in Kent in the spring of 597. Augustine settled in Canterbury, where Æthelberht subsequently accepted Christianity as (?one of) the chief religion(s) of the Kentish people. Augustine's epitaph tells us that he died on 26 May, but it does not specify the year. In 604, he consecrated Mellitus as bishop of London and Justus as bishop of Rochester, so he must still have been alive at this time. On 27 February 610, however, it was Mellitus who attended Pope Boniface V's synod in Rome. The date of Augustine's death must therefore lie somewhere between 604 and early in 610.[50]

We can thus postulate the following time line for Æthelberht:

560x2	Birth of Æthelberht
ca.580	Marriage to Bertha
587x90	Æthelberht succeeded to Kentish kingdom
prior to 595	Æthelberht became overlord
597	Arrival of Augustinian mission
604x10	Death of Augustine
616x18	Death of Æthelberht

If we were to believe an almost certainly apocryphal story related in Bede ii.1, the conversion of Anglo-Saxon England began with three of the worst puns in history. Gregory, in the days before he became pope, was wandering one day in the market place of Rome:

> As well as other merchandise he saw some boys put up for sale, with fair complexions, handsome faces and lovely hair. On seeing them, he asked, so it is said, from what region or land they had been brought. He was told that they came from the island of Britain, whose inhabitants were like that in appearance. He asked again whether these islanders

were Christians or still entangled in the errors of heathenism. He was told that they were heathen. Then with a deep-drawn sigh he said, 'Alas that the author of darkness should have men so bright of face in his grip, and that minds devoid of inward grace should bear so graceful an outward form.' Again he asked for the name of the race. He was told that they were called *Angli*. 'Good,' he said, 'they have the face of angels, and such men should be fellow-heirs of the angels in heaven.' 'What is the name,' he asked, 'of the kingdom from which they have been brought?' He was told that the men of the kingdom were called *Deiri* [men of Deira, a Northumbrian kingdom]. '*Deiri*,' he replied, '*De ira*! [From wrath!] good! snatched from the wrath of Christ and called to his mercy. And what is the name of the king of the land?' He was told that it was Ælle; and playing on the name, he said, 'Allelulia! the praise of God the Creator must be sung in those parts.'[51]

As David Pelteret observes, 'In defence of Pope Gregory, it is not inapposite to note that this story appears in Anglo-Saxon sources and not in Gregory's own correspondence. It is evident that the Englishman's penchant for puns has a long ancestry.'[52] Bede himself seems to have regarded this colourful story as questionable: he prefaces it with the disclaimer that 'it has come down to us as a tradition of our forefathers' and in the same passage carefully distinguishes oral tradition from authorial voice with the phrase 'so it is said.' Nonetheless, pagan slaves were, in fact, sold in the Roman markets, and such an encounter may well have provided Gregory with his introduction to the Anglo-Saxon peoples and planted the seeds of his future mission of conversion. Gregory instructed his administrator in charge of the church's lands in Provence to buy English boys seventeen or eighteen years old for education in monasteries.[53]

In 590 Gregory was elected pope; history has justly given him the sobriquet 'the Great.' Gregory was a highly literate man passionately committed to the preaching of the gospel, and his *Pastoral Care*, an essay of instruction as to how a priest should govern his flock, was one of the most widely read works of the Middle Ages. Myriad manuscripts of this work survive in several languages including Old English: in his campaign to re-establish literacy in the Anglo-Saxon territories after the Viking depredations, King Alfred the Great himself translated it in the late ninth century. Although we have no direct evidence of Gregory's motivation for dispatching the evangelizing mission to the remote island of Britain, Henry Mayr-Harting suggests three possible reasons.[54] First, Anglo-Saxon England was the only outpost of the former Roman Empire that remained pagan, and Gregory, himself a former prefect of the City of Rome, may have wished to re-establish these boundaries for the Christian rule of the Holy City. Second, several territories of the earlier Empire had converted to Arian Christianity, a doctrine perceived by its opponents as denying the divinity of Christ. Worse than remaining in a state of paganism would be succumbing to the Arian heresy. Finally, the kingdom of Kent had close political contacts through Æthelberht's marriage to the powerful kingdom of the Franks across the channel; Gregory may well have learned of Æthelberht's accession to the overlordship of the southern regions from his Frankish subjects. Perhaps the establishment of a Christian Kentish territory, with its political ties to Frankish Gaul, might give the papacy a foothold from which to undertake a reform of Gaulish Christianity, which had fallen prey to worldliness and simony (the selling of religious offices). Interestingly, letters written by Gregory to the leaders of Frankish territories commending Augustine to their care imply that the English had already sought conversion, but that the neighbouring bishops (by which he almost surely means bishops from Francia) had not responded.[55]

Whatever Gregory's motivations, in 595 he dispatched a Roman mission of forty monks headed by the cleric Augustine to the Anglo-Saxon territories. We can trace its route through Gaul fairly precisely by means of letters of introduction Gregory wrote for Augustine to various bishops along the route.[56] This rather undistinguished monk may seem a strange choice to lead such an important expedition; '[t]here were indeed plenty of able clergy in Rome on whom Gregory's choice might have fallen, but perhaps they would not exactly have leapt at the opportunity to come to this island, ridden as it was with fogs, swamps, forests and kings with unpronounceable names.'[57] But in Gregory's view, Augustine may have seemed especially qualified for the mission by his biblical scholarship, for the bringing of the Bible's message to the Germanic pagans was the core of Gregory's purpose.[58] Biblical scholarship did not, however, prepare Augustine for the rigours of his mission. According to Bede i.23, shortly into the journey Augustine and his companion monks were 'paralyzed with terror. They began to contemplate returning home rather than going to a barbarous, fierce and unbelieving nation whose language they did not even understand.'[59] An encouraging letter from Gregory persuaded them to continue, and the tired mission finally arrived on the Isle of Thanet, on the eastern shore of Kent, in 597.

Augustine sent from Thanet to announce his arrival to Æthelberht, who ordered the mission to remain there while he decided how to proceed. Bede i.25 relates that '[s]ome days afterwards the king came to the island and, sitting in the open air, commanded Augustine and his comrades to come thither to talk with him. He took care that they should not meet in any building, for he held the traditional superstition that, if they practised any magic art, they might deceive him and get the better of him as soon as he entered.'[60] The implication that Æthelberht was afraid of the powerful magic the new religion might work indoors is suspect. Æthelberht's wife Bertha was a Christian when they were married, and she brought with her to the pagan Anglo-Saxon kingdom her chaplain Liudhard.[61] Christian mass had been celebrated by the Frankish contingent in Canterbury from the time of their marriage in ca. 580. Surely Æthelberht was aware that no evil magic resided in this religion: he had been in marital contact with it for close to twenty years, even though he himself had probably remained pagan. (Since Bede never tells us specifically that Æthelberht himself was converted, it is even not impossible that his conversion had taken place before the arrival of the Augustinian delegation.) Æthelberht may have been acting on behalf of his followers, who lacked his familiarity with the Christian religion, and thus might look upon its god with suspicion. Drawing on much earlier evidence from the Roman historian Tacitus, we know that in any event the Germanic peoples did not customarily worship in enclosed spaces.[62] It is also possible that at this first meeting Æthelberht had not yet been informed of the precise nature of the goal of this large party of foreigners, and that he did not identify their missionary quest with the religion of his wife.[63]

Æthelberht allotted to the Roman delegation a dwelling in Canterbury, and it was probably the need for an urban centre to house the new episcopal see that instigated the rebuilding of the old Roman city after its abandonment by the Jutish invaders.[64] Augustine's first masses were held in the Church of St Martin, which still stands outside the walls of Canterbury, where he converted some of the people of Kent. In a letter to the Patriarch of Alexandria written in June 598, Pope Gregory claims that on Christmas day of 597 Augustine baptized more than 10,000 converts. Although we might take this figure with a grain of salt, it seems clear that Æthelberht himself had accepted baptism by this date, and a recent royal conversion provided the impetus for his followers to adopt the new religion.[65]

A final question to be considered is why the conversion of Kent was delayed until the Roman mission, when Christianity had already been practised by Bertha and her fellow Franks for nearly two decades. Disregarding any spiritual motivation, the political advantage of conversion was obvious: it would ally Kent directly with the politically and economically important centre of culture in Rome.[66] The acceptance of a mission sent directly from Rome gave Æthelberht an importance and independence that would not have been his had he received baptism at the hands of a priest delegated by his powerful Frankish in-laws. Furthermore, a monotheistic religion would only support the secular idea of a centralized monarchial figure.[67] The concept of a strong, independent ruler turning his country from a pagan backwater into a Christian kingdom independently allied with Rome may have laid the groundwork for the first recording of a uniquely Anglo-Saxon text of law.

The role of kingship and Christianity in the promulgation of law

The only extant copy of Æthelberht's laws is preceded by a rubric which states: 'These are the decrees which King Æthelberht set in Augustine's time.' There are four possibilities with respect to the actual date of the recording of these laws. A literal interpretation of the heading, that the laws were written *on Agustinus dæge* 'in Augustine's time,' would set the parameters of 597x609 – between Æthelberht's conversion and Augustine's death – for their composition, while a more liberal interpretation would be something like 'in the days in which the influence of Augustine was strongly felt.' But clearly Æthelberht's laws must have been written during Æthelberht's reign: otherwise they would be someone else's. The second interpretation then pushes the *terminus post quem non* beyond the death of Augustine to the death of Æthelberht in 616x18. Of course, the verb *asette*, 'set' may refer not to the recording on parchment of the laws but to the oral establishment of these judgments, which were then committed to writing at a subsequent date. Given the archaic shape of much of the language, however, this possibility seems unlikely.

The final option is that some parts of the laws could have been recorded before the arrival of Augustine.[68] If so, these laws would represent pre-conversion literacy in the Anglo-Saxon territories. There seems good evidence that some, at least, of the Celtic peoples were literate in the vernacular. The shape of the orthography of early Brythonic languages – in particular Old Welsh – implies that this system was developed at the time of the conversion of the Welsh to Christianity in the sixth century, considerably before the Germanic settlers in the east embraced the new religion.[69] Furthermore, it has recently been argued that both inscriptions and written manuscripts were almost certainly generated in pre-Christian Ireland.[70] Either of these practices could have left traces in early Kent: palaeographic comparison indicates that our received copy of Æthelberht's laws exhibits certain orthographic usages that parallel early British or Old Irish usage, but which are otherwise unattested in the pre-Alfredian laws copied by the same scribe.[71] Linguistically closer to home, most of the extant early insular Germanic runic inscriptions come from Kent and the surrounding regions, and at least five of them in all likelihood predate the arrival of Augustine: the deer-bone – perhaps a game piece – from Caistor-by-Norwich, the cremation urn from Lovedon Hill, the scabbard plate from Chessel Down, and the sword pommels from Sarre and Ash/Gilton (all of which present such difficulties in interpretation that I refer the reader elsewhere for discussion).[72] Finally, Æthelberht's wife Bertha was herself learned in letters,[73] and her chaplain Liudhard, as a cleric, was surely literate at least in Latin; he may perhaps even have tried his hand in the recording of the Anglo-Saxon language, so closely related to his own native Frankish tongue.

The possibility of pre-conversion literacy in Kent pushes back the *terminus ante quem non* for the recording of these laws to Æthelberht's accession to the kingship (587x590) or, more likely, to his overlordship (sometime before 595). Richardson and Sayles argue on the basis of content and the similarity to the Germanic laws that Æthelberht's laws were written before his conversion (which, in fact, they question ever occurred). They go even further to postulate that there may have been written Anglo-Saxon laws before those of Æthelberht.[74]

Evidence that might be offered against pre-Christian recording is the fact that Æthelberht's laws begin with a discussion of restitution for theft from the clergy. We know that these clauses must have been in place at the time of Bede, for he states in ii.5 that 'among [Æthelberht's laws] he set down first of all what restitution must be made by anyone who steals anything belonging to the church or the bishop or the clergy.'[75] This first group of clauses, however, differs stylistically from those that follow; furthermore, the amounts of restitution specified do not accord with instructions sent by Pope Gregory to Augustine (see discussion below under 'Chronological layering').[76] This first section looks, therefore, very much like a later accretion, and thus the laws dealing with the church must be disallowed as evidence for dating the remainder of the laws.[77]

Most modern scholars agree that Æthelberht's conversion to Christianity provided the impetus for the recording of these laws, although they differ as to specific motivations. Pollock and Maitland argue that Augustine taught Æthelberht that 'new law can be made by the issue of commands,'[78] and J.M. Wallace-Hadrill supports the hypothesis that the Augustinian mission is primarily responsible for persuading Æthelberht to write down laws: '[The text] strikes me as a coherent and well-ordered document, such as might be expected from the entourage of Augustine ... What is new is that the king, by causing them to be written, makes them his own. Lawgiving is a royal function; it is something that the emperors, through the Church, can give kings. It comes with Christianity.'[79]

Although A.W.B. Simpson questions the influence of Augustine on Æthelberht's laws, he agrees that the recording of the text was due to the arrival of Christianity, given that 'what Ethelberht's laws were plainly concerned with was to provide, in the form of fixed money payments, an alternative to retaliation and the feud ... We can see in the laws the attempt inspired by the church to introduce a new and merciful alternative to the tradition of retaliation.'[80]

Winfred Lehman attributes the impetus to Æthelberht himself,[81] claiming that the breakup of old Germanic kinship groups in the move to the British Isles meant that 'kings became participants in settlement of feuds.' Expanding Simpson's argument, he links the writing of the laws to the fact that 'gold coins were, after nearly two centuries, again minted in England,' which facilitated an 'ordered conversion to money wergild [man-price], ... a conscious adjustment of the compensation system.'[82] This hypothesis is difficult to reconcile with the fact that Æthelberht did not mint his own coins. Although there were in England a few imitations of coins copied from Roman or continental models, Philip Grierson claims that 'in no case do they seem to have been intended to serve any economic purpose.'[83]

Patrick Wormald had already refuted Lehman's view: 'given the evidence of Tacitus that such compensation were established among the Germans of the first century AD, we should never have needed anthropologists to demonstrate that the principle of compensation is an inherent part of any feuding system, and cannot represent an innovation by christianized authority.' Instead, he ties the recording of Æthelberht's (and other) Germanic laws to the 'Romano-Christian image of the legislating monarch.' This does not, however, presuppose the Christianization of Germanic law. 'St. Augustine may well have wished to see King Æthelberht equipped with a written law code, but both its content and its language argue that Æthelberht's code was the work of the king and his *sapientes* [counsellors], not of the Roman missionaries.'[84]

In a more recent publication, Patrizia Lendinara argues that the laws were based on a Latin model and even raises the supposition that they were translated from an original Latin text.[85] Her second postulation can be ruled out on the basis of vocabulary: if the text were translated from Latin, we would expect to find numerous borrowings in the lexicon. In fact, Latinized terms occur only in the Christian denominations in the church laws (which we have reason to believe were a later addition in any case) and in the term *ynce*, 'inch,' used for measuring the width of wounds (see discussion below under 'Chronological layering'). As to Lendinara's first hypothesis, while there is a clear influence of Roman law on the Latinized text of the Franks, no such influence appears in the laws of Æthelberht. Although Christianity may have provided the impetus for recording the laws, the Church does not seem to have provided a model or lent its language for this purpose.

Accepting that Christianity was the catalyst for the recording of the laws, whether before or after Augustine's mission, we are still left with the question of why Æthelberht should have committed these decrees to writing, rather than using the time-honoured technique of oral transmission. To determine the answer, we must return to Æthelberht's place within early Anglo-Saxon societies. Bede ii.5 claims that Æthelberht is only the third king to rule (*imperauit*) over the southern territories: 'The first king to hold the like sovereignty was Ælle, king of the South Saxons; the second was Cælin, king of the West Saxons, known in their own language as Ceawlin; the third ... was Æthelberht, king of Kent.'[86] But we have no corroboratory evidence that Ælle or Ceawlin ever styled themselves as *imperators*; in fact, it is even possible that the overkingship of Southumbria was invented by Æthelberht.[87] It may be that the attribution of the post of *imperator* to these figures who had achieved near-mythical status was part of a political manoeuvre to link Æthelberht with heroes from the past. In a similar fashion, Bede's listing of Æthelberht's genealogy, cited previously, traces the king's lineage back through his ancestor Oisc to the Germanic warrior Hengist, who is himself purported to be descended from Woden. Oisc may in fact have been one of the war leaders who subsequently founded a dynasty of kings (similar to

Wuffa of the Wuffingas kings of East Anglia), although this is mere surmise.[88] But by linking Æthelberht to Hengist, one of the two leaders of the original migration, the genealogy implies that the ancestors of the Kentish kings were descended from the leaders who headed the mercenary forces, thus supporting Kentish claims to hegemony over all the Anglo-Saxon territories.[89] Given his alleged offspring, it is not surprising that one of Woden's great talents is his ability to shade the truth! The proposed line of Æthelberht's descent, according to Nicholas Brooks, 'can ... be seen to be a fiction of epic heroes, gods and demi-gods and of eponymous but invented Wight-men. It is likely to reflect the stories that were cultivated at the royal court of Kent by English court poets (*scopas*) in the early eighth century and which were passed on to Bede by his informant on Kentish matters, abbot Albinus of St Augustine's.'[90]

It is tempting to hypothesize that Æthelberht, tracing his political heritage to the great ruler Ælle and his genealogy to the near-mythological warrior Hengist (and hence back to Woden), positioned himself in a tradition of great Indo-European lawgivers such as Solon in Greece and Manu in India. However, Wormald convincingly demonstrates that 'ancient Germanic kingship as such was not closely associated with the "finding," promulgation or enforcement of law.'[91] The issue here may be one rather of preservation of law in the new medium of writing. Bede ii.5 claims that Æthelberht wrote his laws *iuxta exempla Romanorum*, 'according to the examples of the Romans'; as stated previously, there is no influence of Roman legislation in the text of Æthelberht. Wormald has argued persuasively that Bede meant precisely that the laws were *committed to writing* after the manner of the kings of the federated nations of the Roman Empire.[92]

What may have been the significance to Æthelberht of the use of the new technology of writing in the transmission of his laws? An interesting question in this regard is why there is so little recorded evidence of the Pictish language.[93] The Picts were a people living in what is now Scotland, and their language comes to us in a very few inscriptional texts. Perhaps the Picts felt that writing was an inferior method of transmission: important texts are committed to memory. As a modern parallel, consider the Lord's Prayer in Christian communities: how many who have grown up in a Christian environment learned this prayer other than by rote, or have ever actually written it out? Similarly, those brought up in the Jewish faith, particularly in modern times, can generally recite the Shabbat prayers before they can read or write a word of Hebrew. Religious invocations tend to be passed on orally by parents or by the elders of the church, and they will probably continue to be thus handed down to later generations.

In fact, written records of many early societies support an hypothesis that writing was often used to record trivial fact rather than philosophy or myth. As an example, much of our knowledge of Gaulish (an early Celtic language) comes from inventory tablets preserved due to a fire in an old pottery factory, or from graffiti, often scatological, scratched onto spindle whorls. Similarly, the majority of attested examples of Mycenean Greek are records of palace possessions. To return to the earlier analogy, while most who grew up in the Christian church can remember the Lord's Prayer, few would be able to enumerate accurately the number, fabric, and colour of the shirts that they sent to the dry-cleaner. The prayers can be recalled by memory; the laundry list is more surely committed to writing.

This thesis, however, overlooks another important function of writing in early times: that is, monumental self-immortalization. Very common, for example, are funereal inscriptions: the recording of a man's name in stone to last for all time. Similarly the great carvings in Old Persian preserve for eternity (albeit not always with a high veracity content) the conquests of Darius, Xerxes, and their offspring. To return to law texts, perhaps the best example of 'monumental' employment of legal writing was created by the Babylonian king Hammurabi around 2100 BC. His laws were engraved on a stone column about seven and a half feet tall set on a three foot base. Were they meant to provide an easy reference source? Only for someone who comes equipped with a stepladder as well as a knowledge of cuneiform writing.

Recall that Æthelberht was not merely a local king, but king of all the territories south of the Humber, and that his genealogy links him to the greatest warrior kings of the Germanic past, back to the god Woden himself. In addition to aligning himself with the great figures of the past, Æthelberht ensured his own position in future remembrance by being the first of the Anglo-Saxon kings to accept the new religion of Christianity. Wallace-Hadrill points out that for the recorded laws of the early Germanic kings, 'the fact of their existence as books was what mattered most. They recorded customs that were old and new, and sometimes contradictory. Carried about from court to court as a corpus of texts, they must first and foremost have struck their readers as a form of kingly literature ... A royal book is made, to be stored, it may be, with the books of the Bible – not inappropriately, since the Bible, too, was a repository of law.'[94] Just as Æthelberht tied his connection to the past using the technology of the past, adding his name to the orally preserved lists of great rulers and conquerors, it would not be at all surprising if he wished to ensure his importance to the future by means of a permanent memorial in the technology of the future, that is, writing. These laws of the Kentish people may well have been intended not as a record of legislation, but rather as a monument to the king: by committing their laws to writing, the people of Kent had joined the ranks of the civilized peoples of Europe.[95] Not only did Æthelberht employ for his legal monument the new technology of writing, he also had it adapted from a system designed for the Latin language to one which could serve for the Anglo-Saxon tongue, thus providing a foundation for all future writing in the English language. Wallace-Hadrill claims that 'it was a good gamble, at least.'[96] It was better than that: in immortalizing his laws in this new technology, Æthelberht did, in fact, succeed in immortalizing himself.

The manuscript[97]

The only copies of the Kentish laws are contained in the twelfth-century compilation of Anglo-Saxon law known as the *Textus Roffensis*, literally, the 'Rochester text,' which Mary P. Richards calls, with some justice, 'the single most important manuscript produced at Rochester.'[98] The *Textus Roffensis* belongs to the collection of the Rochester Cathedral Library, catalogued as ms. A. 3. 5, and is currently stored in the Kent County Archives in Maidstone. Folios 1–118 are a collection of Anglo-Saxon laws from Æthelberht to Henry I; folios 119–235 contain charters of the Rochester Cathedral priory. Peter Sawyer argues persuasively that the two halves, the laws and the cartulary, were originally separate volumes, and only later bound together.[99] The manuscript is vellum, ca. 225 x 155 mm (8 7/8" x 6 1/8"). The leaves have clearly been cut, as shown by the prickings (incisions made down the sides of the page at regular intervals to allow the scribe to inscribe lines across the page to keep his writing straight), but it is hard to say by how much as this does not impinge on the text itself. A water stain can be seen on all the pages due to the misfortune that the volume was dropped into the Thames in the eighteenth century (see discussion below), but folios 103–16 suffered the most. The Kentish laws, contained on folios 1–6, remain clearly legible; the water stain, quite obvious in the manuscript itself, is barely apparent in the facsimile.

The laws contained in the first part of the *Textus Roffensis* are all written in the same hand. We have several Latin manuscripts by this scribe, but no others in Old English.[100] The scribe employed different

Table 1.1
Emendations by Main Scribe

	Æthelberht
1ᵛ5	ðeowan has -n# added higher and later in different ink
1ᵛ10	si changed to sy
1ᵛ15	leo_d with erasure underlined to indicate single word
1ᵛ19	scH added above line in different ink
2ʳ12	nowiht changed to nawiht
2ʳ13	o of weorð over erasure
2ʳ16	u– added higher and later to scillingum [101]
2ᵛ2	ond changed to and
2ᵛ11	litlan changed to lytlan
2ᵛ15	as 2ᵛ2
3ʳ6	gy changed to gyfe (f in space before next word, e added above o of following ofer; same hand)
3ʳ9–10	micle changed to mycle
3ʳ16	y of sy over erasure
3ʳ20	As 3ʳ16
	mon changed to man
3ʳ21	As 3ʳ16
3ᵛ4	–mon changed to –man
3ᵛ6	As 3ʳ16
3ᵛ7	gan changed to gang; g added as later interpolation
3ᵛ8	oþerne added later above line
	Hloþhere & Eadric
3ᵛ16	as of cyningas written above insertion mark
3ᵛ23	æ of æwdum written on erasure
4ʳ17	þane changed to þone
4ʳ19	mannan written above insertion mark
4ʳ20	ea of byrigean on erasure
4ʳ21	y of awyrce on erasure
4ᵛ7	nille changed to nylle
5ʳ13	n of agend added above insertion mark
	Wihtred
5ᵛ5	weorþige_n with erasure between e and n
5ᵛ14	ne of dryhtne on erasure
6ʳ1	þina changed to hina
6ʳ	omitted phrases added at bottom of page
6ᵛ4	gemange tithe run together; separated by point
6ᵛ7	n of godne added above insertion mark
6ᵛ15	2nd þ of oþþe added above insertion mark
6ᵛ16	selle of geselle added in margin

characters in his Old English hand from those he used when writing Latin, in addition to the specifically Old English ð (eth) and runic þ (thorn) and ƿ (wynn). Whereas his Latin manuscripts exhibit only caroline and rounded s, the Old English text also contains insular s.

Greater difference is shown in the shape of the r: Latin texts contain a caroline r and a variant shaped like a 2, which occurs after o, while the *Textus Roffensis* contains insular and, up to folio 37, uncial r. Folio 1ᵛ3 exhibits the scribe's sole use in Old English of the character ę (for æ), which is common in his Latin script.

In the *Textus Roffensis*, the scribe used three forms of y. In Æthelberht's laws, the most common draws the right branch as a long, single stroke containing the tail while in the second most common the tail is incorporated into the left branch; in both instances the character is dotted. The third and least common form looks like a slanted f, with the left branch incorporating both the tail and the dot. (Lines 3ʳ6 and 3ʳ7 double-mark this by adding a second dot.) The only form used in the Latin manuscripts is that in which the right branch and tail are made in a single stroke with the dot separate. The other two types are employed in the Old English text only up to folio 37, after which the Latin type predominates.

That the *Textus Roffensis* scribe is a careful copyist can be seen from the fact that he often emends the text when he catches himself modernizing. Æthelberht's laws alone contain twenty erasures or additions that appear to have been made by the main scribe. Table 1.1 lists the emendations by the main scribe in the Kentish laws.

Linguistic emendation and orthographic variation continue until folio 37 (the laws of Æthelstan, 925x ca. 935); up to this point the scribe appears to have been meticulous in preserving elements of the exemplars which seemed to him archaic. The language of the post-Æthelstan laws was almost surely closer to West-Saxon Old English, the literary koiné most likely to have been known by the *Textus Roffensis* scribe. Note that folio 37 is also where the orthographic shape of the y changes, which may imply that the scribe was copying from a different set of manuscripts. It is also possible that the scribe may have become less careful about emending his copy to match its exemplar(s) as the work progressed.[102]

On the bottom of folio 1 is an *ex libris* written in a hand not that of the scribe of the manuscript proper:

Textus de ecclesia Roffensi per Ernulfum episcopum
Text of the bishopric of Rochester according to Bishop Ernulf.

Ernulf was bishop of Rochester from 1115 to 1124, and that he might have instigated the recording of the laws is consistent with what we know of his character: he was a judge, a scholar of canon law, and a writer of Latin. As prior of Canterbury Cathedral and later as abbot at Peterborough, he assigned to his monks the task of continuing the recording of the Anglo-Saxon annals.[103]

The scribe included on folio 110^v a list of archbishops of Canterbury. Here he recorded the death of Rodulfus (Ralf d'Escures) in 1122, so he cannot have completed his work on the manuscript before that time. On 18 February 1123, Ralf's successor William de Corbeil was consecrated, and this fact is recorded in a different hand, which may – but does not necessarily – imply that the main scribe had finished by the time the succession was chronicled. Felix Liebermann considers the script to be more typical of mid-century practice and suggests that the scribe may have begun the work on a commission from Ernulf and completed it under a later bishop, which would extend the period of compilation by an additional two decades. But neither Peter Sawyer nor Neil Ker mention this possibility, and – unlike Liebermann – they take into consideration other manuscripts copied in the same hand. Furthermore, the catalogue of the Rochester library listed by this scribe at the end of the *Textus Roffensis* contains no manuscript that appears to have been written later than about 1130. 1130 thus seems to be a plausible *terminus ad quem non* for the compilation, although we must then assume that the inscription for William's consecration was written considerably after the actual occurrence, or that for reasons obscured by time a different scribe was assigned to record this particular event.[104]

It is surely more than coincidence that the Kentish laws are contained in a collection made in a Kentish scriptorium, for where else would the exemplars more likely have been cherished and preserved? Furthermore, the *Textus Roffensis* was produced specifically at the *Rochester* scriptorium; according to Bede ii.3, Æthelberht himself founded Rochester in 604. As Richards points out: 'just as the Canterbury monks tried to preserve, and even revive, the legends of local saints in the post-Conquest years, and other monasteries turned to Bede's *Historia* to increase their prestige, so the Rochester monks may have hoped to preserve the Anglo-Saxon laws in such a way as to glorify the heritage of their own episcopal foundation.'[105]

Liebermann, whose monumental *Die Gesetze der Angelsachsen* has set a standard for all medieval legal scholars, writes that 'the history of the *Textus Roffensis* is almost the history of Anglo-Saxon studies in general,'[106] and an adventurous, if not at times actually disreputable, history it is. Generations of Anglo-Saxon philologists have used this compilation.[107] In 1573 William Lambard, the first editor of the Anglo-Saxon laws, recorded the fact of his study in an initialled note on folio 1 (he did not make use of this manuscript in his *Archaionomia*, which had already been published in 1568). In 1589, Francis Tate made the first transcript to have survived (preserved as British Museum ms. Cotton Julius CII); Liebermann relies on Tate for his restoration of *mæthlfrith* on folio 1ʳ6, of which the -*aeth*- is no longer legible except for an upper hook which appears to be from the *h*.[108] In 1631 the manuscript was 'acquired' by Dr Thomas Leonard. Samuel Pegge suggests that the acquisition may have occurred under shady circumstances: 'One Leonard, a doctor of physick, had got it into his hands, and kept it two years; but the dean, Walter Balcanqual, and the chaplain, getting scent of the purloiner, bestirred themselves, and at last recovered their MS, but not without a bill in chancery.'[109] The story of the recovery is told (in Latin) on folio ii and copied on folio iii: 'This venerable monument of antiquity, [which was] sought for an entire two years, the thief finally having been found but strenuously refusing its return: Walter Balcanqual, Dean of this Church, recovered [it] by Decree of the Highest Curia, which they call the Chancellery, at no small expense to this Church, [and] took care that [it] be returned to its previous owners. In the year 1633 after the Incarnate Birth.'[110]

During the tumultuous period of Cromwell's interregnum the manuscript was given for safekeeping to Sir Roger Twysden, who was a legal historian. In 1712 the *Textus* was in London, at which time 'Mr William Elstob and his sister Mrs Elizabeth Elstob employed one James Smith, a boy of ten years old, to make a transcript for them, in folio, of such parts of the manuscript as had not before been published. This transcript ... was finished X kal June, or 23 May, 1712, being fairly written in three months' time; and a very extraordinary performance it is for such a boy.'[111] Elizabeth Elstob herself copied some of the text onto vellum, and Sawyer considers her probably responsible for the list of 'Saxon Characters' on folio iiiᵛ of the *Textus* initialled EE, which seems a reasonable supposition: she was the first to write an analysis, *The Rudiments of Grammar for the English-Saxon Tongue* (published in 1715), and the eighteenth-century scholar Thoresby designated her the 'justly celebrated Saxon nymph.'[112] Elstob was unable to continue with her research after her brother's death: 'a stop was ... put to her progress for a time, through a vulgar, mistaken notion of her guardian, that one Tongue was enough for a woman.'[113]

Pegge reports that at some point between 1712 and 1720, 'being carried by water from Rochester to London, and back again, the book by some means or other fell in its return into the water, but was happily recovered, and without much damage; for when I saw it, about the year 1742, by the favour of the late archbishop Herring, who was then bishop of Bangor and dean of Rochester, it was in very good condition, being a small quarto on vellum, bound in red. The book has been in perils both by land and water, and I presume this last escape will prove a sufficient warning to the dean and chapter, not to suffer it to go any more out of their custody.'[114] This does, in fact, seem to have been the end of its travels. In 1937 Charles Lamacraft rebound the manuscript in red leather and removed from the vellum the salt remaining from its immersion in the Thames. It has been transferred from the Cathedral library to protected storage in the Kent County Archives.

In 1957 an excellent facsimile of the collection of laws was produced as volume 7 of the series Early English Manuscripts in Facsimile;[115] although the waterstain and certain erasures are less obvious than in the original, the reproduction is otherwise very faithful to the manuscript in its current state.

Archaic traces in the language of the laws

Our only copies of the laws of early Kent are contained in the *Textus Roffensis*, which was compiled roughly six centuries after the date assigned to the text ascribed to Æthelberht. Two Anglo-Saxon sources provide corroboration that an early text of Æthelberht's laws did exist. First, Bede, who completed his *Historia Ecclesiastica Gentis Anglorum* in 731, more than a century after Æthelberht's reign, says of Æthelberht: 'among other benefits which he conferred upon the race under his care, he established with the advice of his counselors a code of laws after the Roman manner. These are *written in English* [emphasis added] and are still kept and observed by the people.'[116] Second, Alfred, who ruled from 871 to 899, some three centuries after Æthelberht, mentions in the introduction to his own laws that the laws of Æthelberht were among those he consulted.[117]

If the text of Æthelberht's laws genuinely reflects a late-sixth-/early-seventh-century original, then it constitutes (albeit much changed by centuries of scribal modernization and error) the earliest Old English text available to us. Furthermore, these would be the first Germanic laws recorded in the vernacular, rather than in Latin, as was the practice on the Continent. But all we have is a copy made several centuries later; proof of the antiquity of the laws of early Kent must therefore be sought in the shape of the language itself. Traces of archaic spellings, words, or sentence formation might authenticate the antiquity of the

26　The Beginnings of English Law

original text: such evidence provides a type of linguistic carbon-dating. The linguistic analysis found below focuses on archaism of the text first in its orthography (or writing system), then in its phonology (or representation of sounds) and morphology (word formation), and finally in the structure of phrases and sentences.[118]

In the discussion that follows, I use the following conventions:

[ ] represents sound
< > represents orthographic practice
boldface represents agreement between phonetic sound and orthographic practice
represents word or morpheme boundary
? marks a word or phrase of uncertain meaning
Æbt = laws of Æthelberht, ca. 600
H & E = laws of Hloþhere & Eadric, 679x86
W = laws of Wihtred, 695

Where I refer to 'Classical Old English,' I mean the West Saxon employed at the time of Alfred (r. 871–899) that has come to be regarded as a grammatical norm.[119] Differences between Classical Old English and the form(s) under consideration that could or should be attributed not to archaism but to dialectal variation (as the Kentish dialect differs in certain features from that of the West Saxons) are discussed in the analysis.

Orthography

The indication of vowel length by doubling is restricted in the *Textus Roffensis* to three words in Æthelberht's laws: *laadrinc mannan*, '?herald/guide' (§13, 1ʳ15),[120] *taan*, 'toe' (§71, 3ʳ12), and *foot*, 'foot' (§80, 3ᵛ9).[121] Doubling was common throughout the languages of the British Isles in the early period; however, it also persisted sporadically into later Old English. Considering that Æthelberht's laws contain the sole instances of doubling in the *Textus Roffensis*, it seems likely that the usage reflects an archaic exemplar.

In the *Textus Roffensis* the dental fricative is overwhelmingly represented by the Anglo-Saxon <ð> and the runic <þ>. However, there are sporadic uses of <th> and <d>: *mæthl* for *meðle*, 'public assembly' (Æbt §7, 1ʳ6),[122] and *æltheodige* for *ælðeodige*, 'foreign' (W §3.1, 5ᵛ8); *widobane* for *wiðobane*, 'collarbone' (Æbt §50, 2ᵛ3/4); *medle* for *meðle*, 'public assembly' (H & E §6, 4ʳ19); *hwæder* for *hwæðer*, 'whether' (H & E

§6.2, 4ᵛ6); *gehwæder* for *gehwæðer*, 'each of the two' (W §4.1, 5ᵛ16). These uses reflect archaic orthographic practice: <d> was the preferred spelling in Kent until ca. 725, after which it quickly became obsolete, with <th> always a less-used alternative.[123] They are replaced by <ð> and <þ> in the eighth and ninth centuries respectively.[124] The use of <d> in the early Kentish laws preserved in the *Textus Roffensis* probably points towards a southeastern, perhaps specifically Kentish, pre-725 provenance of the original exemplar. It must be remarked, however, that Northumbrian scribes continued to use <d> throughout the eighth century; this practice in the Kentish laws could therefore be due to an early Northumbrian copy (such as Bede might have seen).[125]

The last of the orthographic archaisms is the representation of [æ] twice as a digraph in the majuscule <Ae> at the beginning of the word *Aet* in Æbt §21.1 and §21.2 (1ʳ4 and 1ᵛ5) and the miniscule at the beginning of *aende* 'and' in W §7 (5ᵛ24); this use of the digraph is a common feature of early Anglo-Saxon texts. Elsewhere in the *Textus Roffensis* the majuscule form shows two variations: <Æ> or <Aᵉ>.

Phonology

Several words in the Kentish laws exhibit the archaic genitive singular -æs# of Germanic masculine a-stems, which becomes -es# in Classical Old English. Compare *ceorlæs*, 'ceorl's' (Æbt §26, 1ᵛ17–18) to *ceorles* (Æbt §20, 1ᵛ1–2); the former appears to adhere to an archaic exemplar, whereas the latter shows a modernized version. The older form is also seen in *lyswæs/leswæs*, 'of serious dishonesty,'[126] in Æbt §9 (1ʳ9)/§72 (3ʳ15), respectively, and in Æbt §82 (3ᵛ11–12) *Ðeowæs*, 'Of a slave'; in H & E §11.1 (5ʳ6) *cyngæs*, 'of the king'; and in W §3.2 (5ᵛ10) *ciriclicæs gemanan*, 'of churchly company,' §4 (5ᵛ13) *cyngæs*, 'of the king,' and §14 (6ʳ18) *sylfæs*, 'of himself.' That the genitive -æ# must have already been obsolescent in the south by the time of Wihtred is shown by charter S19, dated by Peter Sawyer to 697,[127] which twice contains the new genitive in the compound place-name *Wieghelmestun*, 'the *tun* of Wieghelm.'

A similar retention of æ in unstressed syllables is found once in the dative singular ending of *þegnunæ*, 'from service,' in W §5 (5ᵛ16–19). This is the only appearance of a dative -æ# in the Kentish laws. Elsewhere the case-form appears as -e#, as in *mid hreowe*, 'with remorse,' in the previous clause in Wihtred.

Eduard Sievers cites the use of æ in H & E §7 (4ᵛ10) *bismærwordum*, 'with mocking words,' as archaic; the first element of the compound is commonly written as *bismer*, 'mock.'[128] There are only four other attestations of *bismær*, one of them on the Ruthwell Cross, the other three all post-Conquest. Two of these three later manuscript attestations can be attributed to the Rochester scriptorium, and the scribe of the third may also have trained there. It is thus uncertain whether to attribute this usage to archaism or later Kentish scriptorial practice.[129]

Æbt §76 (3ʳ20–1) contains the word *ceapi*, 'with a price,' which exhibits an archaic instrumental singular in -i#. This ending did not survive far into the seventh century; the instrumental singular was quickly subsumed by the dative with its -e# ending, thus providing a grammatical parallel to the plural -um#, which represents both dative and instrumental. Sievers lists *folcy*, 'with the populace,' from the prologue to Withred's laws as another example of an archaic instrumental singular with <y> substituted for <i>.[130] Karl Brunner, however, takes the -y# to be a hypercorrection for the later Kentish practice of writing <e> for <y>,[131] which seems a reasonable hypothesis given the spellings of *wyrgelde*, 'with a manprice,' in W §20 (6ᵛ12) and the doublet in *lyswæs/leswæs* in Æbt §§9 and 72 mentioned above.[132]

In both Æthelberht and Wihtred we find instances in which the Classical Old English diphthong -eo- appears as the archaic -eu- (which can be found sporadically in Kent until the middle of the eighth century): Æbt §15 (1ʳ17) *freum*, 'from a freeman'; Æbt §64 (2ᵛ24) *leudgeldum*, 'with person-prices'; W §10 (6ʳ12), §19 (6ᵛ4), and §22 (6ᵛ17) *þeuw(ne)*, 'slave;' and W §20 (6ᵛ11) *leud*, 'person.' The preservation of this diphthong is unambiguous, if inconsistent, in the stems *þeuw-* 'slave' and *leud-* 'person.' The digraph in *freum*, 'from a freeman,' occurs across a morpheme boundary, and could simply represent the scribe's adding the dative ending *-um* directly to the stem *freo(h)*. But if -eu- were later regularly retained across a morpheme boundary we would not have H & E §1 (3ᵛ20) *þreom*, 'with three,' which illustrates a similar bimorphemic form with a more modern phonological adaption.

Æbt §76.1 (3ʳ6) begins with *Gyfe*, 'if;' throughout the rest of Æthelberht, the initial conjunction is spelled *gif*. This particular instance seems to have been vexing for the scribe, as the **gy-** follows the normal copying practice, whereas the **-fe** is added later in a different ink. The etymology of *gif* is problematic. On the basis of the Gothic cognate *jabai*, it appears that there was a final vowel in the Proto-Germanic form. An archaic *gife* is what one might expect in early Old English, and this instance may indeed represent a hapax whose unusual form caused trouble for the twelfth-century scribe.

W §7 (5ᵛ24) shows another retention of a final -e# in the form *aende*, 'and.'[133] Forms of this conjunction in other Germanic languages overwhelmingly contain a final vowel (usually -i#). Whereas this is the only disyllabic attestation in Old English. I have argued elsewhere that the form has been retained in a fixed oath formulation used in the manumission process, and may already have been perceived as archaic when Wihtred's laws were compiled.[134] Note that this form also preserves the digraph **ae** discussed above.

It is worth noting that the phonology transcribed in the laws of Hloþhere & Eadric indicates that the exemplar was more modernized than that for either Æthelberht or Wihtred. The only unambiguous example of phonological archaism in Hloþhere & Eadric is the single retention of the archaic genitive *cyngæs*, 'of the king.' This usage implies that either the scribe of the *Textus Roffensis* or a previous scribe compiling Kentish laws was working from at least two exemplars: more archaic forms of the language remained in the manuscript(s) for Æthelberht and Wihtred than for that of Hloþhere & Eadric. (See discussion in chapter 3 under 'Some notes on the language.')

Morphology

Several terms used in Æthelberht's laws appear otherwise either rarely or not at all in the corpus of Old English: *mæthlfrith*, 'assembly peace' (§7, 1^{r}6);[135] *drihtinbeage*, 'lord-payment' (§12, 1^{r}14); *laadrinc-mannan*, '?guide' (§13, 1^{r}15); *leodgeld/leudgeld*, 'person-price' (§13, 1^{r}15; §24, 1^{v}12–13; §64, 2^{v}24); *bebyreþ*, 'provides' (§23, 1^{v}8); *weg-reaf*, 'highway robbery' (§23.1, 1^{v}10; §82, 3^{v}13); *hlaf-ætan*, 'loaf-eater' (§26, 1^{v}18); *riht-ham-scyld*, '?' (§32, 2^{r}5); *feaxfang*, 'seizing of hair' (§33, 2^{r}6); *cearwund*, '?grievously wounded' (§63, 2^{v}23); *wælt-wund*, '?welt-wound' (§68, 3^{r}8, if this is in fact a compound);[136] *friwif*, 'free woman' (§72, 3^{r}14); *locbore*, '?in charge of the locks/?bearing locks'[137] (§72, 3^{r}14); *mægðbot*, 'compensation for a maiden' (§73, 3^{r}15); *mægþman*, 'maiden' (§77, 3^{v}4); and *gæn-gan*, '?return'[138] (§77.2, 3^{v}7). Fewer hapax compounds are found in Hloþhere & Eadric and Wihtred (although the texts are much shorter), and none of them are particularly opaque. The one exception is *æwda(mann)*, 'oath-helper' (H & E §§1.1, 3^{v}23; 2.1, 4^{v}5; 3, 4^{v}8), in which the first element is clearly *æ*, 'law,' but the second is unclear. (Perhaps *wed-* 'pledge,' with syncope of the second syllable; see note to translation of §2 in chapter 3.) Given the fecundity of compounding in Old English, such hapaxes may not reflect archaic usage: they could easily be *sui generis*.[139]

The non-compounded hapaxes in Æthelberht's laws are as follows: *fedesl*, 'feeding' (§17, 1^{r}21); *læt*, 'designation of subordinate rank' (§27,

1ᵛ19); *hion*, '?skull' (§36, 2ʳ9); *lærest*, 'least' (§60, 2ᵛ13); and *wælt*, '?welt' (§68, 3ʳ8). The monomorphemic words defy analysis pending viable etymologies, which have so far proven elusive. I discuss possible interpretations under the relevant sections in the Commentary to chapter 2.[140] The bimorphemic words, however, deserve consideration.

An unambiguous archaism is demonstrated by the form *fedesl*. In Classical Old English, the *-isl-* suffix regularly metathesizes in trisyllabic stems, as shown by the doublet Old Saxon *rādislo* and Old English *raedels*, 'riddle.' This usage is part of a more general rule in Old English, whereby following weakly stressed or unstressed syllables *-sl#*, *-fl#*, and *-þl#* (or *-dl#* from *-þl#*) become *-ls#*, *-lf#*, and *-ld#*, respectively.[141] In more modern phonological terms, the language has developed the constraint that decreasing sonority must hold in the coda of a weakly stressed or unstressed syllable when the coda is [+cont, -back, -son] followed by [l]. Although we can find a few other examples of non-metathesized forms, none of them, except where retained in foreign names, postdate the middle of the eighth century.[142]

In Æbt §60 (2ᵛ13/14) we find the superlative *lærestan*, 'least' (cognate with Old Frisian *lerest*); the word otherwise appears in Old English as *læs(es)t* (cognate with Old Frisian *lest*).[143] Spirants in Gothic follow a rule of voicing dissimilation across an unstressed vowel: if the first spirant is voiced, the second will be unvoiced, whereas if the first spirant is unvoiced, the next will be voiced. Assuming the Gothic rule to hold true for Old English, in the case of the comparative from the Proto-Germanic *láisizon (which becomes Old English *læssa*) the spirant is voiced by rule because of the preceding unvoiced [s]. As Antoine Meillet noted, in the case of the Proto-Germanic superlative *láiziston, the voicing of the second [s] is blocked by the dental cluster [st]. The dissimilation must therefore work backwards, voicing the first [s]; the [z] that would result from this recessive voicing dissimilation would then rhotacize to [r], giving the attested forms in Old English and Old Frisian.[144] The paradigmatic spread of the [s] from the comparative to the superlative giving Old English *læsest* must have occurred very early, as this is the only example we have of the form *lærest*.

Syntax[145]

The following analyses address the question of syntactic archaism from two perspectives. The first is one of pure grammaticality: if a formulation employed in Æthelberht has become impermissible by the rules of Classical Old English syntax, the usage can clearly be ascribed to archaism. The second approach is one of style: even if the configuration remains grammatical, if it is no longer employed in the context of Classical legal writing it can be taken to represent archaic usage within this genre.

Lack of univerbation in the participial compound *of-aslagen*
Æbt §39 (2ʳ13) begins *Gif eare of weorð aslagen* ... 'If an ear off is struck ...' and similarly Æbt §80 (3ᵛ10/11), *Gif esnes eage ꝺ foot of weorðeþ aslagen* ... 'If a servant's eye or foot off is struck ...' In both cases the preverb *of-* and the participle *aslagen* are divided by the finite verb *weorð(eþ)*. The same usage can be found in later West Saxon, for example, John 18:26: *þæs eare sloh Petrus of* 'his ear struck Peter off.'[146] In law texts, however, by the time of Alfred, this is already univerbated as in §56: *Gif se þuma bið ofaslægen* ... 'If the thumb is struck off ...' Separation of preverb and verb (or here the verbal participial form) is typical of an older stage of syntax (dating back to Proto-Indo-European),[147] and in Anglo-Saxon legal writing can be found only in the earliest laws.

Verb-final main clause
In the apodosis (or 'then' clause) in Æthelberht, the verb is always in final position, which is consistent with what has been reconstructed as the unmarked position in Germanic and Indo-European.[148] But the laws of Hloþhere & Eadric contain, in addition to structures in which the main clause is verb-final, unambiguously verb-initial clauses and clauses that, on the surface, are verb-second. This variation is repeated in the laws of Wihtred.[149] The later laws of Kent demonstrate that the placement of the jussive subjunctive in the apodosis was changing within the genre of legal writing. In the Classical Old English laws of Alfred the verb appears only in initial position in the apodosis. Although the clause-final position of the jussive subjunctive in Æthelberht's laws remains grammatical under the general rules of Classical Old English syntax, this stylistic choice is an archaism within the language of law.

Auxiliary of the passive
Passive clauses in Æthelberht use forms of the auxiliary *weorðan*, as does the only passive in Hloþhere & Eadric (§9.1, 4ᵛ19); there are no passives in Wihtred. (Stative clauses in all three texts use forms of *beon*.) Passives in the laws of Alfred, however, always employ forms of

beon. Both *weorðan* and *beon* passives remain grammatical throughout Classical Old English – Alfred himself used *weorðan* passives in his translation of Boethius's *Consolation of Philosophy* – but once again, there is a distinction between the practice of legal writing in Kent and the syntax of Alfred's laws, which became the standard for the West-Saxon–influenced Classical Old English formal legal phraseology. The change is already evident in the laws of Alfred's predecessor Ine, which never employ a *weorðan* passive.

In the laws of Æthelberht, forms of *weorðan* are always in the indicative, whereas forms of *beon* are almost invariably in the subjunctive. The indicative verb *weorþ* establishes the situation (a person has struck a blow); the subjunctive *sie*, by contrast, adds an extra ramification to this condition (not only has a blow been struck, but there is also a bruise as a result). This usage is demonstrated by the following group of clauses in the personal injury laws:

§44. Gif nasu ðyrel weorð, VIIII scillingum gebete.
If a nose becomes pierced, let him pay with 9 shillings.
§44.1. Gif hit sio an hleore, III scill gebete.
If it [i.e., the piercing] should be on the cheek, let him pay [with] 3 shillings.
§44.2. Gif butu ðyrele sien, VI scill gebete.
If both [cheeks] should be pierced, let him pay [with] 6 shillings.

The initial clause establishes that the offence to be considered is piercing; the second elaborates on the fine should the location of the piercing be the cheek rather than the nose, and the third discusses further the ramifications if both cheeks are pierced rather than merely one. This indicative/subjunctive formulation with the change of verb appears to be unique to Æthelberht.

Dative of Quantity
In the clauses of restitution in Æthelberht, the stem *scilling-* can appear in the direct case (i.e., nominative/accusative *scillingas*), and in the oblique dative (*scillingum*) and genitive (*scillinga*). As a standard in Old English grammar, nominative/accusative is employed for numbers under twenty, while for numbers twenty or greater a partitive genitive is used. What I will term the 'dative of quantity' is an instrumental use of the dative, where X *scillingum* translates 'with x shillings.' This collocation does not appear elsewhere in Old English, although it is a perfectly acceptable construct of any other West Germanic language.

Table 1.2
Case Use in Individual Sections of the Laws

§§	Content of Laws	Direct case	Genitive	Dative
§§1–7	Offences against church/public assembly			
§§8–11	Offences against king		1x	
§§12–17	Offences against king's household	1x	4x	
§§18–19	Offences against nobles			
§§20–32	Offences against freemen	2x	4x	9x
§§33–71	Personal injury [150]	6x	2x	11x
§§72–77	Offences against women		3x	
§§78–81	Offences against servants			
§§82–83	Offences against slaves	1x		

Crucially, it is restricted in Æthelberht's laws according not to amount but to content, as demonstrated in Table 1.2. For many of the laws, only the abbreviations *scll'* and *scill'* are used. Due to the ambiguity of expansion, these have been excluded from this discussion. This accounts for the seeming underrepresentation in certain portions of this tabulation. It is striking that the dative of quantity is limited to paragraphs either referring to offences against freemen or setting recompense for personal injury.

Similarities among the personal injury sections in various Germanic laws are too strong to be merely coincidental.[151] I do not subscribe to an hypothesis of a common written source or shared written sources for the Germanic personal injury laws for two reasons: first, this would imply a widespread dissemination of written texts in a largely illiterate era, and second, early laws in all languages overwhelmingly include compensation for personal injury. That such a ruling would have been introduced with, or substantially changed by, the technology of writing in the Germanic territories seems to me highly improbable. It seems more likely that, at least in the majority of cases, these laws are brought from an era of oral transmission into the written law: thus the phraseology might well exhibit traces of an older stage of the language frozen in the memorized sequence. And in fact, the archaic – for Old English – use of the dative case in these sections of Æthelberht's laws provides linguistic confirmation of this hypothesis. I would thus assign the clauses containing the dative of quantity to the oldest stratum in the compilation – these would include the personal injury laws and those dealing with freemen. The only other use of the dative of quantity occurs in H & E §2.1 (4ʳ3–4), *twam manwyrþum*, 'with two man-worths.' Wormald suggests that the first clauses in Hloþhere & Eadric serve the function of filling gaps left in the recorded laws of Æthelberht and thus may still show oral traits; this archaic retention gives support to his theory.[152]

Word division

In the manuscript of Æthelberht's laws, prosodic indications are given by word-grouping:[152] certain prepositions are written with the following nouns, the abbreviation ꝥ, 'and,' is usually written with the following word, and in one instance the copula is written with the preceding word (§75, 3ʳ15–16). Further, the negative and the deictic (or definite article) are optionally written with the next word, while preverbs are often separated from their verbs and the individual elements of compounds frequently stand alone. All of these usages are common in medieval practice; in any case, as word division may well be the first sphere in which scribal modernization occurs, it is possible that the document as we have it reflects the practice not of the original compilation but of a later copy.

The question of dating

Remnants of oral transmission

'We find among the *Saxons*, the Example and the Reason why our Common Law was … an unwritten law. They were originally a *Grecian* Colony coming out of *Lacedæmon* and the territory of *Sparta*, where *Lycurgus* being sometime King and Author of their Law, among other of his Decrees … ordained this for one, that their Laws should not be written, because he would have every Man to fix them in his Memory, and for that purpose made them short and summary, after the manner of our Maxims.'[154] From the first studies of Æthelberht's laws, scholars have remarked that the text may well represent the closest written version that we have of Germanic laws as they were orally preserved. The interest in this possibility has not been restricted to earlier scholars of Anglo-Saxon law such as Sir Henry Spelman (whose historical analysis, although picturesque, has long since been superseded). Wormald, for example, has raised it several times, pointing out that 'Æthelberht's code looks "primitive" by almost any test that can be devised: neat system, simple syntax, lack of procedural knots, and skimpy Christian influence fits in with this.'[155]

That Germanic law must have been passed down orally in the preliterate era is inferable from several indicators. First, both common sense and anthropological parallels in other illiterate societies dictate that law is not an invention introduced concomitantly with literacy.[156] Second, the early Germanic laws recorded in Latin contain certain similarities – particularly in the personal injury sections discussed above – that, on the basis of content (as the wording of the vernacular is no longer recoverable),[157] may be attributed to a common source. And third, we find throughout the Germanic territories a figure whose job was the oral proclamation of law. Medieval Iceland had an elected official known as the lǫgsǫgumaðr, 'Lawspeaker,' whose primary function was to recite Icelandic law over the course of three summer parliaments.[158] Similar terms can be found elsewhere in Germanic: the northern Swedish laghsaga and western Old High German/Old Saxon êosago. (Although the function of the official may have changed; for example, in Old Saxon the term refers to a scribe who knows Jewish law.)[159] The figure in preliterate times whose job was the memorization and accurate transmission of customary law is, unsurprisingly, not limited to the Germanic tribes: a far earlier counterpart can be found in the fifth-century BC Cretan law-court official mnāmōn, whose job it was to 'remember' the laws.[160] Although there is no evidence that such an official position existed in the Anglo-Saxon territories, the Exeter book poem *The Gifts of Men* twice mentions those who are endowed by the Lord with the faculty of knowing the law: *Sum in mæðle mægmodsnottera folcrædenne forð gehycgan*, 'A certain person can in the assembly of wise men determine the custom of the people,' and *Sum domas con, þær dryhtguman ræd eahtiað*, 'A certain person knows the laws, where men deliberate.'[161]

Assuming, then, that the laws of the preliterate Germanic kingdoms were preserved by a tradition of oral transmission, we must turn back to an issue discussed at length by Wormald:[162] what exactly does Bede mean when he says that Æthelberht wrote his laws *iuxta exempla Romanorum*, 'according to the examples of the Romans'? There is no influence of Roman legislation in the text of Æthelberht. Wormald concludes that Bede's 'Roman example' meant precisely that the laws were *committed to writing* after the manner of the kings of the *fœderati*, 'federated nations' of the Roman Empire. Elsewhere in the Germanic territories German law was being written in Latin under Roman or sub-Roman administration, using the Latin language of the government. As Rosamund McKitterick points out, '[t]he written word was accommodated within Frankish society not only through the influence of the Christian church and its promotion of a "religion of the book," but also through the secular law and administration.'[163]

The crucial distinction between the laws of the Anglo-Saxons and those of their Continental cousins is that the latter are in Latin, whereas the former are in Old English. If we assume, based on the linguistic evidence previously discussed, that the text of Æthelberht does in fact represent a record of archaic Anglo-Saxon laws, they are the first Germanic laws to be recorded in the vernacular.[164] As such they stand boldly at the watershed between orality and literacy in the Anglo-Saxon legal tradition. If we assign them to this position, then they should show traces of their spoken past as they move into the literate future.

The overall structure of Æthelberht's laws can be laid out as follows:

§§1–7	Offences against the church and public assembly
§§8–17	Offences against the king and his household
§§18–19	Offences against *eorlas*, 'noblemen'
§§20–32	Offences against *ceorlas*, 'freemen'
§§33–71	Personal injury laws
§§72–7	Offences against (and rights of) women
§§78–81	Offences against *esnas* (a rank with a legal status intermediate between freeman and slave)
§§81–3	Offences against *þeowas*, 'slaves'

Excluding the first provisions dealing with the church and public assembly, these are presented in a top-to-bottom order. They deal first with the king, then move to his household, to his nobles, and finally turn to the freemen of the land. Then follow the personal injury laws, and finally the laws regarding those whose status differs from that of freemen: women, *esnas* or servants, and slaves.

The personal injury laws illustrate a head-to-toe mnemonic similar to the top-to-bottom ordering of the text as a whole. This section consists of thirty-nine clauses (§§33–71) laid out in order from the top of the head to the ripping off of the big toenail. At periodic points there is a pause to enumerate particulars:

53. *If [a person] strikes off a thumb, 20 shillings.*
54. *If a thumbnail becomes off, let him pay [with] 3 shillings.*
55. *If a person strikes off a shooting finger [=forefinger], let him pay [with] 9 shillings.*

Background 37

56. *If a person strikes off a middle finger, let him pay [with] 4 shillings.*
57. *If a person strikes off a goldfinger [i.e., ringfinger], let him pay [with] 6 shillings.*
58. *If a person strikes off the little finger, let him pay [with] 11 shillings.*

Æthelberht's personal injury laws follow what Mary Carruthers terms the 'architectural mnemonic':[165] one in which the memory can associate with a familiar physical structure. This same mnemonic applies to the text as a whole: as the personal injury laws move from head to toe according to physiology, so the entire body of the laws moves from top to bottom according to status. Such a physiological model would seem natural, and, indeed, almost necessary for a sequence committed to memory rather than parchment. An excellent modern parallel is provided by a biographical sketch in *Time* entitled 'Jackie Can!': 'Some movie stars measure their worth by how many millions of dollars they make. Jackie Chan, Asian action-star extraordinaire, measures his by how many of his bones he has fractured. Let him count the breaks: "My skull, my eyes, my nose three times, my jaw, my shoulder, my chest, two fingers, a knee – everything from the top of my head to the bottom of my feet."'[166] Chan's enumeration is based on the mnemonic of mentally tracing down his body, the identical aid to memory we witness in Æthelberht.

One might argue that the methodological arrangement of Æthelberht's personal injury block, rather than being the echo of a mnemonic from the days of oral transmission, simply reflects a logical and natural way of ordering this group of laws. This common-sense arrangement, however, is not a regular feature of *written* personal injury sections in other ancient laws. For purposes of comparison, Table 1.3 lays out the personal injury sequence as presented in several other legal texts. The laws of the Merovingian Franks (Capitulum 17) and the Old Frisian *Brokmer* laws (§§177–204) represent the Germanic territories; the Hittite sequence (Table 1, §§7–17) presents another Indo-European system; finally the laws of Hammurabi (§§196–209) provide a non-Indo-European comparandum.[167] Surprisingly, the head-to-toe layout occurs in none of these texts; clearly, albeit unexpectedly, this progression is not typical when laws are committed to writing.

An interesting bifurcation is demonstrated by the laws of Alfred. His personal injury laws fall into two basic sections, the first exhibiting a top-to-bottom succession as in the laws of Æthelberht, and the second displaying an apparently randomly ordered set of addenda.

38   The Beginnings of English Law

Table 1.3
Sequence of Personal Injury Laws in Selected Texts

Frankish	Frisian	Hittite	Hammurabi
extremity	head	blinding/tooth	eye
hand	tongue	head	bone
thumb/toe	speech/hearing	sick-maintenance	teeth
2nd finger	foot/hand	hand/foot	body
3rd finger	eye	nose	fetus
4th finger	thumb/lip/ear/nose	ear	
5th finger	eye	fetus	
2 fingers	thumb/lip/ear		
foot	'?' wound		
eye	open wound		
nose	tooth		
ear	fingers		
tongue	fingernails		
tooth	toes		
penis	thumb/nose		
	knuckles/palm		
	ribs/fingers/toes		
	arms/legs/jaw/shoulderblade/upper arm		
	shoulder sinew		
	muscle in back		
	arm		

The two sequences are given in Table 1.4. That the first section resembles that of Æthelberht is probably more than coincidence: Alfred states in his prologue that the laws of Æthelberht were among those he consulted in compiling his own. Nowhere else in Alfred can we detect any apparent influence of his predecessor's laws; however, the close similarity of Alfred's first group of personal injury laws to the block found in Æthelberht makes it likely that the early Kentish laws here provided a model. The second section, however, shows no such clear progression. One possible mnemonic might appear to be that of a warrior walking across a battlefield randomly strewn with body parts.[168] In a more serious vein, if we assume that Alfred's first section deliberately copies the older, orally based ordering of Æthelberht, the second section can be taken to represent the written addenda to the original core. The technology of writing has obviated the need for a pattern easily retained in the mind's eye.

One final, albeit highly speculative, point must be addressed with respect to possibly oral elements in the personal injury section. Traces

Table 1.4
Sequence of Personal Injury Laws in Alfred

Section One: §§44–64	Section Two: §§65–77
head	scrotum
ear	lower arm
eye	visible wound
nose	loins
tooth	shoulder
cheek	hand
jaw	rib
windpipe	skin-break
tongue	eye/hand/foot
shoulder	calf
arm	shoulders
armbone	'large' sinew
thumb	'small' sinew
nail	?spine
shooting finger	
middle finger	
goldfinger	
little finger	
stomach	
thigh	
shank	
big toe	
second toe	
middle toe	
little toe	

may remain of the alliteration typical of Old English, and indeed Germanic, poetry.

§66. Gif **rib** forbrocen weorð, III scill' gebete.
If a rib becomes broken, let him pay 3 shillings.
§67. Gif man þeoh ðurhstingþ, stice gehwilce VI scillingas.
If a person stabs through a thigh, for each thrust 6 shillings.
§68. Gif wælt wund weorðeþ, III scillingas gebete.
If a 'welt-wound' occurs, let him pay 3 shillings.

Arguably, §66 shows consonance of **r-b/br**, while §§67 and 68 alliterate þ and w respectively. Conceivably what we are seeing here is a remnant of law couched, not in poetry, but in an elevated prose style employing the poetic device of alliteration.[169] As Dorothy Bethurum points out, '[t]he large numbers of legal formulas, many of them alliterative, many of them rhymed, which repeat themselves throughout the decrees of the Old English and Old Frisian laws, the Sachsenspiegel, and the Old Norse laws, lend some probability to the hypothesis of an original poetic form for the Germanic laws.'[170]

Parallels can be found in other Indo-European languages of the mnemonic of poetry used to preserve legal tradition, especially in the Old Irish laws. For example, we find the following gloss to §46 of the *False Judgments of Caratnia*:[171]

fortoing airm ł aimseir	*It is sworn by place or time*
ł meid ł messair	*or weight or measure*
ł laid ł litteir	*or song or letter*
ł crich ł coirthe	*or border or (boundary) stake*
ł thoraid ł thunide	*or profit or ownership.*

Each pair alliterates, and the metric scheme for each is monosyllable/disyllable except for the last pair, where the scheme is disyllable/trisyllable. This excerpt is in typical Old Irish verse form, that is, alliterative and syllable-counting. The Sanskrit *Laws of Manu*, for their part, are cast in the Indic poetic *śloka*, an octosyllabic line in which the last four syllables are regulated as to length. Similarly the section from Æthelberht's laws may illustrate the alliteration typical of Germanic poetry as incorporated into the legal prose. Each of these societies has adapted the techniques of transmission to its poetic norm.

The efficacy of the poetic transmission of law can be seen by the glancing references to the Old Irish oath cited above made elsewhere in the legal corpus:

CIH 983.31ff: Fortoing airem ł aimsir ⁊rl-.
 It is sworn by place or time and the rest ...
CIH 2143.18ff: FORTOING AIREM NO AIMSER.
 It is sworn by place or time.

The citation of the first line is clearly sufficient to evoke the entire poetic sequence: this presupposes that the reader knows it by heart.

It is not surprising to find such formulas in an Old Irish text, because Irish practice represents another vernacular tradition of secular legal writing in the early Middle Ages: parallel to Anglo-Saxon law, the oral tradition was incorporated into the later written texts. But even the earliest of these written texts probably postdates that of Æthelberht; it seems likely that Irish secular law was not written down until about the middle of the seventh century.[172] The first extant Welsh laws are attributed to the tenth-century king Hwyel Dda, although the earliest manuscripts date from the last quarter of the twelfth century. The tradition of vernacular legal texts was strong throughout the British Isles, but the earliest written text we have is that of Æthelberht.[173]

In summation, there are stylistic elements in the laws of Æthelberht that seem to hark back to a preliterate version. As Patrick Wormald points out, 'It is impossible to demonstrate that any law existed in an oral version exactly corresponding to its written form; oral versions are by definition irrecoverable.'[174] But although we cannot claim that the text which survives is a transcription of what was spoken, we can point to certain mnemonics that accord well with what we might expect for laws preserved by oral transmission. First, the physiological ordering of the personal injury laws, as shown above, is not a common feature of written legal texts. Second, the overall structure moves from top to bottom according to status, following the head-to-toe pattern of the personal injury laws. Finally, there may be traces of an elevated prose style, using the poetic device of alliteration as an aid to memory. Never again in Old English law will we see a system laid out so clearly: the technology of writing changed forever the way in which law was transmitted. The Anglo-Saxon territories demonstrate in this regard a shift that was taking place throughout medieval Europe. This change was exemplified in the kingdom of their Frankish cousins across the channel, as described by McKitterick: 'If it be correct to understand Frankish society before the late fifth century as pre-literate, the process of expansion, political assertion and social integration in sub-Roman and Merovingian Gaul meant that legal norms gradually ceased to reside in the memory of each man in the community, but instead were recorded in writing and preserved, and thus given a new character.'[175]

Chronological layering of Æthelberht's laws

A collation of laws such as that represented by Æthelberht's text is not created as a unit, but is rather the result of accretion and change over time. As Henry Spelman points out, this is true not only of preliterate law but of legal practice to the present day: 'To tell the Government of *England* under the old *Saxon* laws, seemeth an Utopia to us present; strange and uncouth: yet can there be no period assign'd, wherein either the frame of those laws was abolished, or this of ours entertained; but as Day and Night creep insensibly, one upon the other, so hath this Alteration grown upon us insensibly, every age altering something, and no age seeing more than what themselves are Actors in, not thinking it to have been otherwise than as themselves discover it by the present.'[176] During a period of literacy it is easy to recover the stages by which new law is added to the old. This identification might seem impossible for laws dating from a preliterate period, but certain indicators within the language of the laws may allow us to deduce at least some relative chronology within the text of Æthelberht. In some cases this deduction represents near-certainty; in others it is no more than informed speculation.

The first, and surest, group to consider is the body of laws containing the archaic 'dative of quantity' discussed above: laws dealing with the *ceorl*, 'freeman,' and the personal injury laws. These sections contain an obsolete syntactic construction in which the amount of restitution is expressed by the independent instrumental dative phrase:

(*numeral*) *scillingum* '(with) # shillings.'

This usage is conspicuously absent in the rest of the laws, and we can thus with a fair amount of certainty postulate that the laws employing this syntagm represent the oldest stratum in the laws of Æthelberht.

The 'dative of quantity' appears only once after Æthelberht, namely in the following sequence from Hloþhere & Eadric:

§2: Gif mannes esne frigne mannan ofslæhð ... se agend þone banan agefe ⁊ oþer manwyrð þær to.
If a person's servant kills a free man ... the owner should give up that killer and another man-worth in addition.
§2.1: Gif bana oþbyrste, twam manwyrþum hine man forgelde
...
If the killer should escape, [the owner] should compensate him with two man-prices ...

The *bana*, 'killer,' of §2.1 refers to the *mannes esne* 'person's servant' of §2; it is interesting that the dative of quantity is used here in a provision concerning the lower rank of *esne* or servant. Perhaps the laws in Æthelberht dealing with the *esne* were also part of the older, central core dealing with freemen and personal injury: that is, §§78–81 have been displaced by the insertion of the laws dealing with women. Support for this theory is provided by §78:

Gif man mid esnes cwynan geligeþ be cwicum ceorle, II gebete.
If a person lies with a servant's (esne's) wife while the husband (ceorl) is alive, let him pay 2[-fold what he would have paid were she unmarried].

The word *ceorl* can mean 'husband' or 'freeman,' and it is possible that the former meaning alone is intended here; however, elsewhere in Æthelberht the word refers specifically to freemen. Accepting the latter definition (or, more likely, the possibility that *both* meanings are intended here) would provide a clear association of the word *esne* with the word *ceorl*, 'freeman.' If we then suppose that the laws of the *esne* also formed part of the earliest block, we would expect to find the archaic dative of quantity in this section in Æthelberht. But only one of the laws in §§78–81 actually lists an amount of reparation, and in this instance, the abbreviation *sciłł* is used. Hloþhere & Eadric §2.1, however, provides a clear syntactic link between the two ranks semantically linked by §70. I would thus assign the laws dealing with the *esne* to the earliest temporal stratum, which can then be defined as laws dealing with *ceorlas*, personal injury laws, and laws dealing with *esnas*. Liebermann points out that any inherited remnants cannot predate Æthelberht by very much, as only a few generations before 600 Germanic peoples reckoned wealth in chattel rather than coins.[177]

Within this oldest section, the vocabulary is predominantly Germanic in origin. The one salient exception is found in the clauses dealing with the depth of thigh wounds:

§67. Gif man þeoh ðurhstingþ, stice gehwilce VI scillingas.
 §67.1. Gyfe ofer ynce, scilling.
 §67.2. Æt twam yncum, twegen.
 §67.3. Ofer þry, III scłł.

§67. *If a person stabs through a thigh: for each thrust 6 shillings.*
 §67.1. *If [the width of the wound] is over an inch: a shilling.*
 §67.2. *For two inches: two [shillings].*
 §67.3. *Over three [inches]: 3 shillings.*

The term *ynce* is a borrowing into Old English from the Latin *uncia*, 'a twelfth part'; the [i] has palatalized the [k] and fronted the [u] to [y]. It must have been a fairly recent addition to the terminology of the personal injury laws, as the term is unique to Old English among the Germanic languages. Interestingly, certain clauses in the eighth-century (and in parts earlier) Old Irish law of injuries, *Bretha*

Déin Chécht, employ *uinge*, similarly borrowed from the Latin *uncia*, to discuss the depth of wounds. But the preceding clauses use the native term *grainne*, 'grain,' of various cereals and legumes in ascending size, which may represent an older system of measurement.[178] We seem to witness here an early stylistic borrowing shared by the legal vocabulary of at least two of the languages of the British Isles. The phonological form shows, however, that the term was borrowed independently into the insular languages. It is possible that the subclauses to §67 were a late addition incorporating the newly borrowed legal terminology; conversely, the clauses may be original with only the term of measurement modernized at a later time. Finally, *ynce* could actually represent an archaic, pre-Christian borrowing. There is nothing in the linguistic form of the word to give preference to any of these hypotheses, but since the laws exhibit no other pre-Christian borrowings from Latin, either of the first two possibilities seems historically more likely than the third.

The second most surely datable of the temporal strata within the text of Æthelberht's laws is the most recent, namely, the laws dealing with the church. From the first reprint of these laws by George Hickes,[179] editorial practice has lumped the provisions concerning the church in a single clause, although there are actually seven separate provisions. These deal with property belonging to God and the church; property belonging to a bishop, a priest, a deacon, or a cleric, respectively; restitution for violation of the church's peace; and restitution for violation of public assembly:

§1: Godes feoh ⁊ ciricean XII gylde.
God's property and the church's [is to be compensated] with 12[-fold] compensation.

§2: Biscopes feoh XI gylde.
A bishop's property [is to be compensated] with 11[-fold] compensation.

§3: Preostes feoh IX gylde.
A priest's property [is to be compensated] with 9[-fold] compensation.

§4: Diacones feoh VI gylde.
A deacon's property [is to be compensated] with 6[-fold] compensation.

§5: Cleoroces feoh III gylde.
A cleric's property [is to be compensated] with 3[-fold] compensation.

§6: Ciricfriþ II gylde.
[Violation of] church peace [is to be compensated] with 2[-fold] compensation.

§7: Mæthlfriþ II gylde.
[Violation of] assembly peace [is to be compensated] with 2[-fold] compensation.

Each of these clauses follows a simple template.

[Property/peace] Y *gylde.*

The syntax of the provisions dealing with the church and public assembly is unique in Æthelberht's laws. It presupposes one of two things: either a deleted verb of restitution without an immediately preceding model on which to restore the deleted verb, or copula deletion with a finite sum of restitution.[180] Neither of these options appears elsewhere in the laws.[181] On linguistic grounds then, we can differentiate them from the rest of the text.

The content itself provides a compelling argument for assuming that at least the first six of these laws represent an addition to the original core. First is the obvious fact that they must postdate Æthelberht's acceptance of Christianity. But were they added at the time of the original recording of Æthelberht's laws, or were they appended in a later copy or revision? Two issues arise in this consideration.

First, we must take into account the amount of restitution due for theft from the king compared to that demanded for robbing the clergy. The first three provisions state:

§1. Godes feoh ⁊ ciricean, XII gylde.
God's property and the church's [is to be compensated with] 12[-fold] compensation.
§2. Biscopes feoh, XI gylde.
A bishop's property [is to be compensated with] 11[-fold] compensation.
§3. Preostes feoh, IX gylde.
A priest's property [is to be compensated with] 9[-fold] compensation.

Compare these to §10, which deals with theft from the king:

Gif frigman cyninge stele, IX gylde forgylde.
If a freeman should steal from the king, let him compensate with 9[-fold] compensation.

Although it is possible that Æthelberht, in an excess of Christian humility, might have placed himself on the same plane as a bishop with his elevenfold compensation, it seems unlikely that he would have equated himself with a priest in his ninefold compensation. But ninefold is the degree of compensation due to a king of the Visigoths, so perhaps the sum represents the traditional amount due to a Germanic king; it is likewise conceivable that elevenfold similarly echoes the ancient recompense due a pagan high priest.[182] That a newly converted Anglo-Saxon king could consider himself subservient to a Christian bishop is demonstrated by a story about King Oswine of Northumbria and his bishop Aidan. Oswine had given Aidan a horse, which Aidan passed on to a beggar asking for alms. The king's anger at the reallocation of the royal gift was dispelled by Aidan's query: 'Surely the son of a mare is not dearer to you than the son of God?"[183] In Wallace-Hadrill's interpretation: 'The gifts of a good king, then, will be lavished as his bishop chooses, and not otherwise; he will owe to his bishop neither more nor less than obedience. Royal humility is obedience to the church.'[184] The early eighth-century Old Irish law of status, *Críth Gablach*, ends by addressing the question of relative status:

§137. Which is higher in dignity, a king or a bishop? A bishop is higher, since a king rises to salute him because of religion. A bishop, too, raises his knee to salute a king.[185]

Finally, the prologue to Wihtred's laws lists the archbishop of Britain before the king, although this is not surprising in a text in which the law has been so thoroughly Christianized. (Note, however, that W §2 equates the fine for violation of the king's protection to that of the church.) Any or all of these parallels may help to explain why Æthelberht decrees the amount of restitution for a king to be less than that owing for a bishop, but leaves unresolved the question of why he places himself on parity with a priest (although that equation might be attributable to the humility of the newly converted). Patrick Wormald offers a resolution in pointing out that *Lex Alamanni* xi 'left episcopal compensations open to negotiations.' He speculates that 'the Kentish Church negotiated itself into a position of unparalleled strength, or else that the bishop's place was at first equal to a priest's (and king's) and was revised upwards at a later date when kings of Kent were weak (or absent) but its prelates remained strong.'[186] Whatever the reason for this imbalance, by the time of Alfred, the proportional restitutions for church and king were inverted – the ratio there is set at twelve to nine in favor of the king.[187]

The second discrepancy arises between the laws dealing with the church and Gregory's instructions to Augustine, as recorded in Bede i.27:[188]

Augustine's third question. I beg you to tell me how one who robs a church should be punished.

Gregory answered: My brother, you must judge from the thief's circumstances what punishment he ought to have. For there are some who commit theft though they have resources, while others transgress in this matter through poverty. So some must be punished by fines, some by a flogging, some severely and others more leniently. And when the punishment is more severe, it must be administered in love and not in anger, for it is bestowed on the one who is punished so that he shall not be delivered up to hell fire. We ought to maintain discipline among the faithful as good fathers do with their children according to the flesh; they beat them with stripes for their faults and yet the very ones they chastise, they intend to make their heirs; and they keep whatever they possess for those whom they appear to persecute in their anger. So we must always keep love in mind and love must dictate the method of correction, so that we do not decide on anything unreasonable. You should also add that they ought to restore whatever they have stolen from a church. But God forbid that the Church should make a profit out of the earthly things it seems to lose and so seek to gain from such [fines].[189]

Not only is there no mention in the provisions in Æthelberht of distinguishing according to the circumstances of the thief (as opposed to the rank of the victim), but the stipulation that the church's property should be recompensed twelvefold seems to be in direct contradiction to Gregory's instruction that the church should make no profit from theft. (The late seventh-century penitentials attributed to Theodore of Tarsus, archbishop of Canterbury, stipulate that 'money stolen or robbed from churches is to be restored four-fold,'[190] which lies unambiguously closer to Gregory than to Æthelberht.) Wallace-Hadrill, in explaining this discrepancy, assumes that Gregory's letter of instruction postdates the recording of the clauses dealing with the church: 'Later, when the pope heard about them, he insisted that simple restitution was all that should be claimed.'[191] But we do not have the wording of Augustine's question, and there is no mention of an existing law text in the reply of Gregory. The issue here is the chronological relationship of the recording of the church clauses in Æthelberht to Augustine's query and Gregory's response. If Augustine wrote Gregory for *validation* of the breakdown as presented in the laws then being recorded, Gregory's response was in the nature of correction. But if Augustine wrote for *instruction*, and that instruction was received before the recording of the laws, the ordinances dealing with the church in Æthelberht's laws must postdate the Augustinian period, if we can assume that Augustine followed Gregory's direction in advising Æthelberht. In that case, we must assume that the clauses were added by a later redactor (or, less likely, that Augustine and Æthelberht ignored the instructions from the pope). The *terminus post quem non* for a postulated addition of these laws is provided by Bede's *Ecclesiastical History* of 731, as he states in ii.5: 'among [Æthelberht's laws] he set down first of all what restitution must be made by anyone who steals anything belonging to the church or the bishop or the clergy.'[192] In summation, the church laws must postdate Æthelberht's (?public) acceptance of Christianity (sometime after 597), but predate Bede, who refers to them in his *Ecclesiastical History* (731) as part of the law text attributed to Æthelberht.[193]

It is interesting that the law about disturbing the public assembly was added at this time, if we can assume this to be an addition on the basis of the parallelism of the unique syntactic structure discussed earlier. The earliest extant Welsh laws – those of the tenth-century king Hywel Dda – stipulate a double penalty for disturbing the king's court or the church; it is conceivable (although in my opinion, unlikely) that these last two clauses were added according to an early indigenous Welsh model.[194]

It is more difficult to establish a chronology for the laws that belong neither to the most recent addition nor to the oldest core. The discussion that follows, therefore, moves into the realm of speculation.

As a first consideration, it is interesting that alliteration in the clause of restitution occurs only three times in the text, and two of these occurrences are found in contiguous provisions.[195]

§9: Gif cyning æt mannes ham drincæþ, ꝛ ðær man lyswhæs hwæt gedo, twibote gebete.
If the king drinks at a person's home, and a person should do anything seriously dishonest there, let him pay two[-fold] restitution.

§10: Gif frigman cyninge stele, IX gylde forgylde.
If a freeman should steal from the king, let him compensate with 9[-fold] compensation.

The only other time we find this alliterative turn of phrase in the apodosis is in another of the laws dealing with the king:

§13: Gif cyninges ambiht smið oþþe laadrinc mannan ofslehð, medumanleod gelde forgelde.
If [a person] kills the king's official [?,] smith or ?herald/guide, let him pay an ordinary person-price.

Not only do these laws use alliteration, but they are all *figurae etymologicae*: that is, the noun and verb are derived from the same root. Nowhere else in Æthelberht's laws or in the succeeding laws of Kent do we find this construction. The stylistic link raises the possibility that at least these three clauses concerning the king were added simultaneously to the older central core. Another possibility is that §§9 and 10 were incorporated at the same time, and that §13 was added later using the stylistic device of alliteration as a model.

Turning to the final consideration, we must remember that the laws of Æthelberht deal with substance, but virtually never with process. There are, however, two instances in which we can find traces of procedural ruling. The first of these to be addressed is contained within the personal injury section:

§65: Gif þeoh gebrocen weorðeþ, XII scillingum gebete.
If a thigh becomes broken, let him pay with 12 shillings.
§65.1: Gif he healt weorð, þær motan freond seman.
If he becomes lame, then friends[196] must arbitrate.

The second clause may mean that if the lamed man is physically unable to bring his case to justice (presumably at the *mæthl*, 'public assembly'), he can depute representatives. It may also mean that the matter goes to arbitration, as the fine must depend on the degree of disability. The fact that this stipulation applies only to laming of the thigh might be adduced as an argument that the clause was inserted to address a particular instance. On the other hand, it has procedural overtones reminiscent of the scene in the Old Norse *Hrafnkels Saga* in which Sám arrives at the legal convocation to present his suit, accompanied by his gang of supporters. If this type of process is in fact typical of Germanic legal procedure, then it is possible that §65.1 dates back as far as the oldest layering.

Wormald has postulated that a second instance of procedure appears in §§24–24.2, which describe the process of paying *wergild*:

§24: Gif man mannan ofslæhð, medume leodgeld C scillinga gebete.
If a person kills someone, let him pay an ordinary person-price, 100 shillings.
§24.1: Gif man mannan ofslæhð æt openum græfe, XX scillinga forgelde ⁊ in XL nihta ealne leod forgelde.
If a person kills someone, let him pay 20 shillings at the open grave, and let him pay the entire person[-price] in 40 nights.

§24.2: Gif bana of lande gewiteþ, ða magas healfne leod forgelden.
If the killer departs from the land, let his kinsmen pay a half person [-price].

Clause 24.1 is unique in Æthelberht, in that it elaborates as to where and when the penalty shall be paid; §24.2 further defines the recourse if the payment is not rendered by the party responsible for the killing. Wormald argues that 'the instruction that kins pay half a wergild on behalf of an absconding member is sufficiently odd, when the essence of feud was that kins were liable for *whatever* fell due from a member's misdeeds, to look like a special measure prompted by a particular case. This would then be the nearest that Æthelberht gets to the sort of "*Satzung*" which Beyerle discovered amidst the "*Weistümer*" of Frankish and Lombard law.'[197] Accepting Wormald's hypothesis, we might assign this clause to the most recent stratum; if it is in fact a *Satzung*, 'ordinance,' then it must have been added at some point to the inherited core of law. Another possible interpretation arises upon comparison with the first clauses of the laws of Hloþhere & Eadric, discussed earlier.

§1. Gif mannes esne eorlcundne mannan ofslæhð, þane ðe sio þreom hundum scill gylde, se agend þone banan agefe ⁊ do þær þrio manwyrð to.
If a person's servant kills a man of noble birth, who should be compensated for with three hundred shillings, the owner should give up that killer and add three man-worths.

§1.1. Gif se bane oþbyrste, feorþe manwyrð he to gedo ⁊ hine gecænne mid godum æwdum þæt he þane banan begeten ne mihte.
If the killer should escape, he should add a fourth man-worth and clear himself with good oath-helpers that he was not able to seize the killer.

§2. Gif mannes esne frigne mannan ofslæhð, þane þe sie hund scillinga gelde, se agend þone banan agefe ⁊ oþer manwyrð þær tó.
If a person's servant kills a free man, who should be compensated for with a hundred shillings, the owner should give up that killer and another man-worth in addition.

§2.1. Gif bana oþbyrste, twam manwyrþum hine man forgelde ⁊ hine gecænne mid godum æwdum, þæt he þane banan begeten ne mihte.
If the killer should escape, [the owner] should compensate him with

> *two man-worths, and clear himself with good oath-helpers that he was not able to seize the killer.*

In these clauses, the unfree killer is himself part of the payment. Should he escape, the owner must pay for him with equal value. The parallel of the escaping freeman killer raises the question of whether the payment in Æthelberht may be for *additional* restitution, either to prove that there was no collusion among the kin-group or simply to fine them for not keeping their kinsman under control. If we accept the argument that the use of the archaic dative of quantity indicates that §§1 and 2 in Hloþhere & Eadric belong to the oldest layer, it seems reasonable to postulate the same dating for the similar stricture in Æthelberht.

Although we can distinguish both the very earliest materials and the very latest, a precise chronology for the intermediate additions in Æthelberht's laws lies beyond our grasp. The oldest section, set off by its use of the archaic dative of quantity, seems to have contained the laws dealing with *ceorlas*, the personal injury laws, and possibly the laws dealing with *esnas* (as a subset of *ceorlas*). The provision in §65.1 with respect to sending representatives to plead one's case may always have belonged to this earliest section; while there is no direct linguistic evidence to prove or disprove this possibility, parallels can be found in Germanic literature outside the Anglo-Saxon territories attesting to such a procedure. The subclauses in §67 use the term *ynce*, borrowed from Latin, to measure the depth of wounds, and thus were either added fairly late to the personal injury laws or demonstrate a later terminological replacement. Clause 24.2 deals with an absconding killer and may or may not have been added in response to a specific case. Clauses 9, 10, and 13 share the stylistic feature of the *figura etymologica* in the apodosis, which suggests that §§9 and 10 at least may have been added by the same compiler. Finally, the laws dealing with the church were appended to the older laws, perhaps at the time of their first writing or perhaps afterwards, but certainly no later than 731 when Bede comments upon them in his *Ecclesiastical History*.

2

The Laws of Æthelberht

Notes on the edition

The text of Æthelberht's laws is presented in a facing-page edition, with the original text positioned beside the translation. Footnotes to the text itself comment on manuscript reading; footnotes to the translation deal with interpretation. The format and application of editorial conventions applied here is followed for the laws of Hloþhere & Eadric and Wihtred.

An important innovation in this edition is the badly needed revision of the clause breakdown. The manuscript itself is written continuously and the choice of clause numeration thus depends on the editor. All previous editions are based on that of Johan de Laet in 1620, with only minor changes made by subsequent editors in the arrangement. Linguistic clues such as stipulative subjunctives and referential pronouns, however, suggest a more complex legal structure than that which may be inferred from de Laet's layout.

Four criteria govern my numeration:

1. A clause with a subjunctive *sie* in the protasis represents an additional stipulation to the preceding law, and is numbered as a subclause.
    §23. *If a person provides someone with weapons where strife arises, but he does no harm, let him pay 6 shillings.*
    23.1. *If highway robbery should be done (sy), let him [i.e., the one who provided the weapons] pay 6 shillings.*
2. A clause that contains a pronoun or other referent to the preceding law is numbered as a subclause.
    §16. *If a man lies with the king's maiden, let him pay 50 shillings.*

16.1. *If she (hio) should be a 'grinding' slave, let him pay 25 shillings.*

16.2. *If she should be (sio) [of the] third [rank], 12 shillings.*

3   A clause in which the subject is the same as that of the previous clause is numbered as a subclause.

§24. *If a person kills someone, let him pay an ordinary person-price, 100 shillings.*

24.1. *If a person kills someone, let him pay 20 shillings at the open grave, and let him pay the entire person[-price] in 40 nights.*

24.2. *If the killer departs from the land, let his kinsmen pay a half person[-price].*

4   A clause whose meaning is dependent on the preceding clause is numbered as a sub-clause.

§77. *If a person takes a maiden by force ...*

77.2. *If return [of the stolen maiden] occurs, 35 shillings and 15 shillings to the king.*

A final consideration is that editorial practice has hitherto been to group the church and public assembly clauses under one number, even though they represent seven independent clauses. This decision seems to have been guided by their close similarity in style and content, and the general supposition that these laws represent an addition to a pre-existing body of law (see discussion under 'Chronological layering' in chapter 1). While there is little doubt that at least the stipulations dealing with the church represent the most recent addition to the compilation of laws, I have chosen to enumerate clauses based solely on discernible linguistic clues.

As most previous discussions refer to Liebermann's clause breakdown, his numeration is given in square brackets on the right-hand side of the edition page.

Editorial conventions

The þ and ð (with its capital Đ) both stand for the sounds represented by the modern English 'th';[1] I have followed the manuscript practice in their representation. Although ƿ is used throughout the manuscript, I have replaced it with the modern English equivalent, 'w,' for easier reading. The scribe occasionally but inconsistently marks long vowels with an accent; I have left these where they occur in the manuscript.

Medieval punctuation was far less elaborate than that of today and a raised dot (called a 'point') served where we would use a comma, semi-colon, colon, or period. The text is also pointed in places in which we would use no punctuation at all; for instance, numerals are typically set off by a point on either side. In editing the text, I have adopted modern punctuation practice. The reader should bear in mind that this necessarily imposes an interpretation on the clause structure that may not have been intended by the medieval scribe. The original pointing is reproduced in the diplomatic transcription in Appendix One. Following a period, I have changed lower-case characters to upper-case when necessary (e.g., Æbt §§74.2, 76.1; H & E §§11.1, 11.2, 11.3). Capitals that exist in the manuscript are printed in bold-face; newly created capitals are not.

There is no consistency in the medieval text in the practice of word (or morpheme) division: for example, sometimes the bound prefix *ge-* is written with its verbal stem, and sometimes it stands alone (Æbt §19, 1ᵛ2 *geligeþ*, 'lies,' versus Æbt §21, 1ᵛ4 *ge ligeþ*). Although the partition or fusion of morphemes in the manuscript can in some cases provide linguists with prosodic clues (for example, the clitic status of the demonstrative may be indicated by the lack of separation in *seman*, 'the man,' in Æbt §28, 1 1ᵛ2), I have chosen to normalize morpheme division throughout. The original spacing is reproduced in the diplomatic transcription in Appendix One. As there is some evidence that the preverb and verb could still be separated at the time of Æthelberht (see discussion under 'Chronological layering' in chapter 1), I have preserved the manuscript distinctions. Where contiguous but separated words seem unambiguously to form a compound, I have written them together (thus *cicfriþ*, 'church peace,' Æbt §6, 1ʳ5 and *wegreaf*, 'highway robbery,' Æbt §23.1, 1ᵛ10); where there is ambiguity about whether to interpret such elements as a compound, I have left them separate and discussed the alternatives in the footnotes (thus *ambiht smið*, either 'official smith' or 'official (and) smith,' Æbt §13, 1ʳ14, and *hrif wund*, either 'abdominal wound' or 'abdomen (becomes) wounded,' Æbt §62, 2ᵛ20).

Where I have emended the text or restored illegible readings, the supplementary or changed characters are enclosed in square brackets. Thus *M[æthl]frith* indicates that the **æthl** represents editorial emendation or (in this case) restoration of letters which are no longer legible in the manuscript; similarly *ge[s]elle* indicates that the s represents an editorial change from the manuscript reading of *gefelle*. Where I have emended the text by deletion, the characters I consider to be superfluous are enclosed in round brackets: thus *forgelde(n)* indicates that the manuscript reading of *forgelden* would be better emended to *forgelde*. These editorial choices are discussed in the footnotes.

There is little scribal abbreviation except in the text of Hloþhere & Eadric. Where there is no ambiguity, I have expanded abbreviations and indicated the expansion with italic characters. For example, þon*ne* means that while þon appears in the manuscript, ne was originally represented by a scribal abbreviation (the form in fact looks something like þoñ).

I have not expanded the symbol ⁊ (the medieval equivalent of the modern &). It would appear that although the exemplar for Æthelberht contained the form **and** when the conjunction was written out, the scribe of the *Textus Roffensis* was more comfortable with the dialectal alternative **ond**: twice (§§48.3 and 60.1) he corrects the latter form to match the former, presumably bringing the copy into line with the exemplar.[2] One might, for uniformity, expand all ⁊s in Æthelberht to **and**; however, this task is not so easy for either Hloþhere & Eadric or Wihtred. It would create a false sense of dialectal consistency to simply match the expansions of Æthelberht, and in one instance at least, it is actually wrong: Wihtred §7 has *ænde* for the first conjunction and ⁊ for the second, which is almost surely to be expanded as the first. Although this form can be attributed to archaic retention (see discussion under 'Manumission' in chapter 4), it seems possible that the phonological shape of the other conjunctions in Wihtred was **end**, a form typical of later Kentish.[3] There is no evidence at all on which to postulate the original form used in Hloþhere & Eadric. Furthermore, the phonology of the scribe(s) of the exemplars may well have differed from that of the scribe of the *Textus Roffensis*: whose version should the expansion match? Finally, as a feature of Early Old English, the conjunction **and** can serve as the conjunctive 'and' or the adversative 'or.' It functions as an adversative, for example, in Æbt §80: Gif esnes eage ⁊ foot of weorðeþ aslagen ... '*If a servant's eye or foot becomes struck off ...*' Further examples are to be found in Æbt §§15, 23, and 30, in H & E §9, and in W §§8.2, 9. For the reader less versed in early Old English, it might be confusing to see **and** in the Old English text rendered as 'or' in the translation. For all these reasons, I have found it more prudent to leave the symbol ⁊ unexpanded. Where the meaning is adversative, it is thus translated, and discussed in the footnotes.

The other abbreviations left unexpanded are those representing the terms for shillings: *scill*, *scill*, and *scll*. In Classical Old English[4] these expansions would be straightforward: *scillingas* if the number is under twenty, and *scillinga* if the number is twenty or greater. But both Æthelberht and Hloþhere & Eadric also employ an archaic dative *scillingum* in some clauses; I have argued under 'Chronological layering' in chapter 1 that the sections employing this syntagm represent the oldest section of the text, which centres on Æthelberht's personal injury laws. But even here, the usage is not consistent in this manuscript. For example, Æbt §34 specifies restitution of III *scillingum*, as we might predict. But §60 stipulates a payment of III *scillingas*: either the clause is a later addition or – more likely – the archaic case usage has been modernized. Which model should one then follow in expanding the III *scill* of §40? Assuming the section was part of the original group of personal injury laws, the original form would have been the dative *scillingum*. However, this form was certainly obsolete in the language of the *Textus Roffensis* scribe, and it could have been modernized to *scillingas* at any time in the several intervening centuries. As there is no evidence to enable a disambiguation of this expansion, I have left the abbreviations as they appear in the text: they can be considered the equivalent of the U.S. $ sign, namely, symbols that indicate meaning but do not commit to any phonological realization. Where the dative *scillingum* appears in the text, I have translated it 'with shillings.' Where the form is abbreviated I use [with] in the personal injury clauses following the hypothesis that these instances would originally also have been in the dative case.

In readings of characters written on erasure I defer to Liebermann unless otherwise noted. These readings are not always obvious in the facsimile, as erasure can often best be detected or verified by holding the parchment up to a light source.

For easy reference to the diplomatic transcription, page breaks are indicated between slashes: /1r/ stands for 1 *recto* (the 'front' side) and /1v/ stands for 1 *verso* (the 'back' side). Found in Appendix One, the diplomatic transcription reproduces as nearly as possible the spacing, pointing (punctuation), and line breaks of the original manuscript.

In the translation, a ? indicates that the meaning of the term following is uncertain. Square brackets surround words that do not appear in the original but have been inserted into the translation for the sake of grammar or clarity, as demonstrated by the following clauses:

74. Mund   þare betstan widuwan eorlcundre,   L scillinga gebete.
    Protection of the foremost widow   of noble rank,   50 shillings let him pay.

74.1. Ðare oþre,   XX scḦ.
Of the second, 20 shillings.

74. [*For violation of*] *protection of the foremost widow of noble rank, let him pay 50 shillings.*

74.1. [*For a widow*] *of the second* [*rank*], *20 shillings.*

The fact that the fine in §74 is for violation of protection is implicit in the original but requires amplification in translation. The interpolations in §74.1 are added for the sake of clarity in the Modern English reading.

EDITION AND TRANSLATION

Þis syndon þa domas þe Æðelbirht cyning asette on ᴀGustinus dæge

1. Godes feoh ⁊ ciricean XII gylde. [1]
2. Biscopes feoh XI gylde.
3. Preostes feoh IX gylde.
4. Diacones feoh VI gylde.
5. Cleroces feoh III gylde.
6. Ciricfriþ II gylde.
7. M[æthl]friþ^b II gylde.

---

a This text appears in red ink, rather than the black of the text proper. The diphthong in Latin 'Augustinus' is anglicized to a monophthong.
b Only a hook from what could have been the t remains legible in the manuscript. The restoration is based on the transcription made by Francis Tate in 1589.

These are the decrees which King Æthelberht set in Augustine's time.

1. God's property and the church's [is to be compensated] with 12[-fold] compensation.[a]
2. A bishop's property [is to be compensated] with 11[-fold] compensation.
3. A priest's property [is to be compensated] with 9[-fold] compensation.
4. A deacon's property [is to be compensated] with 6[-fold] compensation.
5. A cleric's property [is to be compensated] with 3[-fold] compensation.
6. [Violation of] church peace [is to be compensated] with 2[-fold] compensation.
7. [Violation of] assembly peace [is to be compensated] with 2[-fold] compensation.

---

a As discussed in chapter 1, the block of church laws almost certainly represents the final addition to the body of laws; previous editions have therefore grouped them under a single number. The first seven clauses are syntactically ambiguous, as *gylde* can be translated technically as a dative/instrumental noun (*with compensation*) or as a subjunctive verb (*let him compensate*). This block of laws could thus also be translated along the template: *[For] God's property and the church, let him pay 12[-fold compensation]*. Other than in these clauses, *gelde* appears in the text four times with a nominal reading (§§10, 28.1, 75, 83) and twice with a verbal reading (§§30, 70.1). Felix Liebermann, *Die Gesetze der Angelsachsen* (Halle: M. Niemeyer, 1847–1916), 3:4 argues for a nominal reading on the basis of other Germanic parallels, where, for example, the term *angylde*, '[with] single compensation,' is attested; in his Glossary (*Gesetze*, 2:103) he enters these terms as compounds, such as *siexg-*, 'six-fold compensation,' or *nigong-*, 'nine-fold compensation.' This could be an instrumental use of the dative, or a denominal adverbial suffix, as in *twibote* in §§8 and 9 (*Gesetze*, 2:216). Since comparative evidence disambiguates the Old English grammatically ambiguous structure, I have followed Liebermann's lead in translating *gylde* as a noun.

8. Gif cyning his leode to him gehateþ ⁊ heom mon þær yfel [2]
   gedo, II bóte, ⁊ cyninge L scillinga.
9. Gif cyning mannes ham drincæþ ⁊ ðær man lyswæs hwæt [3]
   gedo, twibote gebete.
10. Gif frigman cyninge stele, IX gylde forgylde. [4]
11. Gif in cyninges tune man mannan of slea, L scill gebete. [5]
12. Gif man frigne mannan of sleahþ, cyninge L scill to [6]
    drihtinbeage.

8. If the king summons his people[a] to him and a person does any harm to them there, 2[-fold] restitution and 50 shillings to the king.
9. If the king drinks at a person's home, and a person should do anything seriously dishonest[b] there, let him pay two[-fold] restitution.
10. If a freeman should steal from the king, let him compensate with 9[-fold] compensation.
11. If a person should kill someone in the king's dwelling,[c] let him pay 50 shillings.
12. If a person kills a free man, 50 shillings to the king as lord-payment.

---

a According to J.M. Wallace-Hadrill, *Early Germanic Kingship in England and on the Continent* (Oxford: Clarendon Press, 1971), 38, the term *leod*, with its Frankish equivalent *leudes*, 'may reveal a social rank common to Franks and Kentings; or just possibly one of Augustine's Frankish interpreters may have had a hand in writing down the Kentish vernacular and used an English verbal equivalent of something he was familiar with at home.' But the Germanic term is derived from an Indo-European root, *leudh- 'offspring, people' (see Julius Pokorny, *Indogermanisches etymologisches Wörterbuch* [Bern: Francke, 1989], 684), and therefore its appearance in written records of the Franks and the Kents could simply reflect a common retention unattested in other remaining Germanic texts. Given the skimpy records which have come down to us in the early West-Germanic vernaculars, I would hesitate to place too much reliance on this term to argue strongly for a Frankish/Kentish connection here.
b See Christine Fell, 'A "friwif locbore" Revisited,' *Anglo-Saxon England* 13 (1984): 157–66 for the interpretation of *lyswæs* as 'seriously dishonest.'
c Dorothy Whitelock, *English Historical Documents, Volume 1: c. 500–1042* (London: Eyre & Spottiswood, 1979) translates *tun* as 'estate'; see, however, discussion in Commentary under 'Theft.'

13. Gif cyninges ambiht smið oþþe laadrincmannan ofslehð, [med]uman[a] leodgelde forgelde. [7]
14. Cyninges mundbyrd, L scillinga. [8]
15. Gif frigman freum stelþ, III gebete, ⁊ cyning age þæt wite ⁊ ealle þa æhtan. [9]
16. Gif man wið cyninges mægdenman geligeþ, L scillinga gebete. [10]
    16.1. Gif hio grindende þeowa sio, XXV scillinga gebete. [11]
    16.2. Sio þridde, XII scillingas.
17. Cyninges fedesl, XX scillinga forgelde. [12]

---

[a] Thus restored by Liebermann, presumably on the model of §24. The lower part of the d in [med] is still legible in the manuscript.

13. If [a person] kills the king's official [?,] smith or ?herald/guide, let him pay an ordinary person-price.[b]
14. [For violation of] the king's protection, 50 shillings.[c]
15. If a freeman steals from a freeman, let him pay 3[-fold], and the king obtains that fine or all the possessions.[d]
16. If a man lies with the king's maiden, let him pay 50 shillings.
    16.1. If she should be a 'grinding' slave, let him pay 25 shillings.[e]
    16.2. [If] she should be [of the] third [rank], 12 shillings.[f]
17. [For] feeding of the king, let him pay 20 shillings.[g]

---

a Liebermann takes *ambiht smið* as a compound meaning 'official smith'; as in other medieval manuscripts, the scribe often leaves a space between the component elements of compounds. The manuscript break between the two elements could, however, represent a word boundary, giving the meaning of 'official [or] smith.' Whether *laadrinc man* should be interpreted as 'lead-warrior man [=guide]' or 'bringing-warrior-man [=herald/messenger]' is unclear, although Old Norse parallels seem to give preference to the latter possibility. See discussion in Commentary under 'King.'

b 'Person-price' provides a literal – if somewhat inelegant – translation of the Kentish *leodgeld*. Unlike the *wergild*, 'man-price,' of §31, the first component of this compound is gender neutral. I think it is likely that the two are, in fact, synonyms, but maintain the distinction in translations to preserve the terminological difference in the manuscript.

c The 'king's protection' is the right to peace for members of the king's household, retinue, and guests. Injury or damage done to any of these constitutes a violation of protection.

d Bill Griffiths, *An Introduction to Early English Law* (Norfolk: Anglo-Saxon Books, 1995), 33, translates: 'the king shall take the fine and all the [stolen] goods.' But it makes no sense to assume that the stolen goods would not be returned to the original owner. Following Liebermann and Whitelock, I take the second ⁊ here to be the adversative 'or' rather than the conjunctive 'and.' See parallels in §§23, 30, 80.

e The 'grinding slave' is responsible for the production of meal from grain; see discussion in Commentary under 'King.'

f *sio* can either be a third person singular subjunctive or a feminine demonstrative modifying *þridde*. In the latter case, the clause would read '[For] the third [rank] ...' I have chosen the former, as it parallels the use of *sio* in §16.1.

g The term *fedesl*, 'feeding,' probably refers to the responsibility of the king's subjects to provide him with sustenance: the *feorm* of later texts. Should a person default that duty or wish to commute it to a monetary payment, he owes 20 shillings. See Lisi Oliver, '*Cyninges fedesl*: The Feeding of the King in Æthelberht ch. 12,' *Anglo-Saxon England* 27 (1998): 59–75, and references therein.

18. Gif on eorles tune man mannan /1v/^a ofslæhþ, XII scill [13]
    gebete.
19. Gif wið eorles birele man geligeþ, XII scill gebete. [14]
20. Ceorles mundbyrd, VI scillingas. [15]
21. Gif wið ceorles birelan man geligeþ, VI scillingu*m*^b gebete. [16]
    21.1. Aet þære oþere ðeowan,^c L scætta.
    21.2. Aet þare þriddan, XXX scætta.
22. Gif man in mannes tún ærest geirneþ, VI scillingu*m* [17]
    gebete.
    22.1. Se þe æfter irneþ, III scillingas.
    22.2. Siððan gehwylc scilling.
23. Gif man mannan wæpnum bebyreþ ðær ceas weorð, [18]
    ⁊ man nænig yfel ne gedeþ, VI scillingum gebete.
    23.1. Gif wegreaf sy^d gedón, VI scillingum gebete. [19]
    23.2. Gif man þone man of slæhð, XX scillingu*m* gebete. [20]
24. Gif man mannan ofslæhð, medume leodgeld C scillinga [21]
    gebete.
    24.1. Gif man mannan ofslæhð, æt openum græfe, XX [22]
          scillinga forgelde, ⁊ in XL nihta ealne leod^e forgelde.
    24.2. Gif bana of lande gewiteþ, ða magas healfne leod [23]
          forgelden.
25. Gif man frigne man geb[inde]þ,^f XX scill gebete. [24]

---

a There is a space here roughly equal to the length of the verb *of slæhþ*.
b Nasal extension line above u. This is the first use of the archaic dative of quantity; see the discussion in chapter 1.
c n added later above **a**.
d i changed to y by scribe.
e Manuscript reads *leo_d*.
f Thus restored by Liebermann, presumably on the model of §81. The lower part of all characters is still visible.

18. If a person kills someone in a nobleman's dwelling, let him pay 12 shillings.
19. If a person lies with a nobleman's cupbearer,[a] let him pay 12 shillings.
20. [For violation of] a freeman's protection, 6 shillings.[b]
21. If a person lies with a freeman's cupbearer,[c] let him pay with 6 shillings.
    21.1. For that second [rank of female slave], 50 sceattas.[d]
    21.2. For that third [rank], 30 sceattas.
22. If a person breaks [as the] first into someone's dwelling, let him pay with 6 shillings.
    22.1. He who breaks in next, 3 shillings.
    22.2. Afterwards, each a shilling.
23. If a person provides someone with weapons where strife arises, but[e] he does no harm, let him pay with 6 shillings.
    23.1. If highway robbery should be done, let him [i.e., the one who provided the weapons] pay with 6 shillings.
    23.2. If a person kills that man [who is being robbed] let him [i.e., the one who provided the weapons] pay with 20 shillings.
24. If a person kills someone, let him pay an ordinary person-price, 100 shillings.
    24.1. If a person kills someone, let him pay 20 shillings at the open grave, and let him pay the entire person[-price] in 40 nights.
    24.2. If the killer departs from the land, let his kinsmen pay a half person[-price].
25. If a person binds a freeman, let him pay [with] 20 shillings.

---

a This figure is a woman: the noun is feminine.
b Whitelock, *English Historical Documents*, 392 states that the sense of *ceorl*, which I translate as 'freeman' throughout, is 'peasant proprietor.'
c See parallel in §19.
d The Kentish *shilling* was a gold piece containing 20 *sceattas*; the *sceatta* was a smaller gold piece equal in weight to a grain of barley. See discussion in Commentary under 'Monetary system.'
e Another adversative use of ꝼ 'and'; see parallels in §§15, 30, and 80.

26. Gif man ceorlæs hlafætan ofslæhð, VI scillingum gebete. [25]
27. Gif læt ofslæhð, þone selestan LXXX scll^a forgelde. [26]
   27.1. Gif þane oþerne ofslæhð, LX scillingum forgelde.
   27.2. Ðane þriddan, XL scilling*um* forgelde(n).[b]
28. Gif friman edorbrecþe gedeþ, VI scillingum gebete. [27]
   28.1. Gif man inne feoh genimeþ, se man III gelde gebete. [28]
29. Gif friman edor gegangeð, IIII scillingum gebete. /2r/ [29]
30. Gif man mannan ofslea, agene scætte ⁊ unfacne feo gehwilce gelde. [30]
31. Gif friman wið fries mannes wif geligeþ, his wergilde abicge, ⁊ oðer wif his agen*um* scætte begete ⁊ ðæm oðrum æt þam[c] gebrenge. [31]

---

a Added later above the last x of numeral.
b I follow Liebermann in emending this to the singular *forgelde*.
c Liebermann suggests emending this to *ham*, 'home'; see note f to translation.

26. If a person kills a freeman's loaf-eater,[a] let him pay with 6 shillings.
27. If [a person] kills a freedman[b] of the first rank, let him pay [with] 80 shillings.
    27.1. If he kills [one of] that second [rank], let him pay with 60 shillings.
    27.2. [For one of] that third [rank], let him pay with 40 shillings.
28. If a freeman breaks into an enclosure,[c] let him pay with 6 shillings.
    28.1. If a person takes property therein, let that man pay 3[-fold] as compensation.
29. If a freeman enters an enclosure [?with intention to rob], let him pay with 4 shillings.
30. If a person should kill someone, let him pay [with] his own money or[d] unblemished property, whichever.
31. If a freeman lies with a free man's wife, let him buy [him/her] off [with] his/her *wergild*[e] and obtain another wife [for the husband] [with] his own money and bring her to the other man at home.[f]

---

a Etymologically, the members of the household centre themselves on the *hlaf*, 'loaf': the *hlaford*, 'lord' (< guardian of the loaf), the *hlæfdige*, 'lady' (< shaper of the loaf), and the *hlafæta*, 'dependent' (< eater of the loaf).

b The exact ramifications of the rank *læt* are unclear, as the term occurs nowhere else in Old English; this designation may also include indigenous Welshmen. See discussion in Commentary under 'Freedman.'

c *edorbrycþ* literally means 'hedge-breaking'; that is, breaking through the hedge surrounding an enclosure, thereby violating the security of the property (and it is thus translated by Liebermann, *Gesetze*, 2:60). See discussion in Commentary under 'Theft.'

d Another example of the adversative ʒ; see parallels in §§15, 23, 80.

e As *wif* is neuter and the possessive pronoun *his* can be masculine or neuter, whether the *wergild* is that of the man or the woman is grammatically ambiguous.

f As stated in note c to the Old English text, Liebermann suggests an emendation to *ham*, 'home.' I am not convinced this is necessary. Modern German still retains the idiom 'bei ihm,' which is more familiar perhaps in the French 'chez lui,' but both instances mean roughly 'at his home.' Although we do not find this idiom elsewhere in English, as we have no text that predates this one, I would not rule out the possibility that we are seeing here the remnants of an idiomatic use of the pronoun that does not survive long in the Anglo-Saxon territories. The choice of one interpretation over the other does not materially affect the translation.

70 The Beginnings of English Law

32. Gif man rihthamscyld þurh stinð, mid weorðe forgelde. [32]
33. Gif feaxfang geweorð, L sceatta to bote. [33]
34. Gif banes blice weorðeþ, III scillingum gebete. [34]
35. Gif banes bite weorð, IIII scillingum gebete. [35]
36. Gif sio uterre hion gebrocen weorðeþ, X scillingum gebete. [36]
    36.1. Gif butu sien, XX scillingum gebete. [37]
37. Gif eaxle gelæmed weorþeð, XXX scill gebete. [38]
38. Gif oþer eare nawiht[a] gehereð, XXV scill gebete. [39]
39. Gif eare of weorð[b] aslagen, XII scill gebete. [40]
40. Gif eare þirel weorðeþ, III scill gebete. [41]
41. Gif eare sceard weorðeþ, VI scill gebete. [42]
42. Gif eage of weorð, L scillingum[c] gebete. [43]
43. Gif muð oþþe eage woh weorðeþ, XII scill gebete. [44]
44. Gif nasu ðyrel weorð, VIIII scillingum gebete. [45]
    44.1. Gif hit sio an hleore, III scill gebete. [46]
    44.2. Gif butu ðyrele sien, VI scill gebete. [47]
45. Gif nasu ælcor sceard weorð, gehwylc VI scill gebete. [48]
46. Gif ðirel weorþ, VI scill gebete.[d] [49]
47. Se þe cinban forslæhð, mid XX scillingum forgelde. [50]
48. Æt þam feower toðum fyrestum, æt gehwylcum VI scillingas. [51]
    48.1. Se toþ se þanne /2v/ bi standeþ, IIII scill.
    48.2. Se þe ðonne bi ðam standeþ, III scill.
    48.3. And[e] þonne siþþan gehwylc, scilling.
49. Gif spræc awyrd weorþ, XII scillingas. [52]
50. Gif widobane gebroce[n][f] weorðeþ, VI scill gebete [52.1]

---

a Changed from *nowiht* by scribe.
b o on erasure.
c There is a character above the line that Liebermann reads as an open [a], and thus renders the term *scillinga*. However, the scribe never uses such a character elsewhere; furthermore, this ascription cannot account for the long tail off the a. It seems far more likely that the character is a u with an appended nasal suspension stroke, giving a dative plural *scillingum*; note that this character appears within the section in which the dative of quantity is used. (See discussion in chapter 1 under 'Chronological layering.')
d Liebermann postulates that a word may be missing from this clause. This seems likely, as §44 has already dealt with the piercing of the nose, and the amounts of restitution are different in the two clauses.
e Changed from *ond* by scribe.
f Manuscript reads *gebroced*.

32. If a person pierces through the *rihthamscyld*,[a] let him pay with [its] worth.
33. If seizing of hair occurs, 50 sceattas as restitution.
34. If exposure of a bone occurs, let him pay with 3 shillings.
35. If cutting of a bone occurs, let him pay with 4 shillings.
36. If the outer hion [?=covering of the skull][b] becomes broken, let him pay with 10 shillings.
    36.1. If both [?outer covering and skull] should be [broken], let him pay with 20 shillings.
37. If a shoulder becomes lamed, let him pay [with] 30 shillings.
38. If either ear hears nothing, let him pay [with] 25 shillings.
39. If an ear becomes struck off, let him pay [with] 12 shillings.
40. If an ear becomes pierced, let him pay [with] 3 shillings.
41. If an ear becomes gashed, let him pay [with] 6 shillings.
42. If an eye becomes gouged out, let him pay [with] 50 shillings.
43. If mouth or eye becomes damaged, let him pay [with] 12 shillings.
44. If a nose becomes pierced, let him pay with 9 shillings.
    44.1. If it [i.e., the piercing] should be on the cheek, let him pay [with] 3 shillings.
    44.2. If both [cheeks] should be pierced, let him pay [with] 6 shillings.
45. If a nose becomes gashed otherwise, let him pay [with] 6 shillings for each [gash].
46. If [?it][c] becomes pierced, let him pay [with] 6 shillings.
47. He who breaks a jawbone, let him pay with 20 shillings.
48. For the foremost four teeth, for each 6 shillings.
    48.1. [For] that tooth which is beside there, 4 shillings.
    48.2. [For] that [tooth] which is beside that one, 3 shillings.
    48.3. And [for] each of the others, a shilling.
49. If speech becomes damaged, 12 shillings.
50. If a collarbone becomes damaged, let him pay [with] 6 shillings.

---

a This word appears nowhere else in Old English, and its meaning is uncertain. See discussion in Commentary under 'Rihthamscyld.'

b The term *hion* appears nowhere else in Old English, and its meaning is uncertain. See discussion in Commentary under 'Personal injury.'

c See note d to §46 in the Old English text. On the basis of other Germanic parallels, Liebermann suggests that the word *þrotu*, 'throat,' may have been inadvertently omitted by the scribe because of the þ of the following *þirel*. See Liebermann, *Gesetze*, 3:11.

72 The Beginnings of English Law

51. Se þe earm þurh stinð, VI scillingum gebete. [53]
52. Gif earm forbrocen weorð, VI scill gebete. [53.1]
53. Gif þuman of aslæhð, XX scill. [54]
54. .Gif ðuman nægl of weorðeþ, III scill gebete. [54.1]
55. Gif man scytefinger of aslæhð, VIIII scill gebete. [54.2]
56. Gif man middelfinger of aslæhð, IIII scill gebete. [54.3]
57. Gif man goldfinger of aslæhð, VI scill gebete. [54.4]
58. Gif man þone[a] lytlan[b] finger of aslæhð, XI scill gebete. [54.5]
59. Æt þam neglum gehwylcum, scilling. [55]
60. Æt þam lærestan wlitewamme, III scillingas. [56]
    60.1. And[c] æt þam maran, VI scill.
61. Gif man oþerne mid fyste in naso slæhð, III scill. [57]
    61.1. Gif dynt sie, scilling. [58]
    61.2. Gif he heahre handa dyntes onfehð, scill forgelde. [58.1]
    61.3. Gif dynt sweart sie buton wædum, XXX scætta gebete. [59]
    61.4. Gif hit sie binnan wædum, gehwylc XX scætta gebete. [60]

---

a The demonstrative here serves to close the section enumerating damage to the fingers.
b i made into y by scribe.
c Changed from *ond* by scribe.

51. He who stabs through an arm, let him pay with 6 shillings.
52. If an arm becomes broken, let him pay [with] 6 shillings.
53. If [a person] strikes off a thumb, 20 shillings.
54. If a thumbnail becomes off, let him pay [with] 3 shillings.
55. If a person strikes off a shooting finger [=forefinger], let him pay [with] 9 shillings.
56. If a person strikes off a middle finger, let him pay [with] 4 shillings.
57. If a person strikes off a goldfinger [i.e., ringfinger], let him pay [with] 6 shillings.
58. If a person strikes off the little finger, let him pay [with] 11 shillings.
59. For each of the nails, a shilling.
60. For the least disfigurement of the appearance, 3 shillings.
    60.1. And for the greater, 6 shillings.
61. If a person strikes another in the nose with [his] fist, 3 shillings.
    61.1. If it should be a blow, a shilling.
    61.2. If he receives a blow [from] a raised hand, let him [who struck the blow] pay a shilling.[a]
    61.3. If the [bruise which arises from the] blow should be black outside the clothing, let him pay 30 sceattas [in addition].
    61.4. If it should be inside the clothing, let him pay 20 sceattas [in addition] for each [bruise].

---

a It is not clear what distinguishes these different types of blow. I am tempted to take §61.1 as the same as §61.2, inserted by scribal oversight; note that the amounts of restitution are identical. Then the crucial distinction would be between §§61 and 61.2. Liebermann suggests that the blow in §61.2 may be struck with the open hand as opposed to a fist. It is also possible that the difference lies between a right-handed and a left-handed blow: Grimm claims that the Norse cognate of *heah* was used to distinguish the right hand. See Jacob Grimm, 'Review Ancient Laws,' in *Kleinere Schrifte* (Hildesheim: Olms, 1991), 318–19. But I think the interpretation is likely more straightforward: a blow delivered with a raised hand is restituted by a(n additional) shilling because the windup literally allows it to deliver more punch.

62. Gif hrif wund^a weorðeþ, XII scill gebete. [61]
    62.1. Gif he þurhðirel weorðeþ, XX scill gebete. [61.1]
63. Gif man gegemed weorðeþ, XXX scill gebete. [62]
    63.1. Gif man cearwund sie, XXX scill gebete. [63]
64. Gif man gekyndelice lim awyrdeþ, þrym leudgeldum hine [64]
/3r/ man forgelde.
    64.1. Gif he þurhstinð, VI scill gebete. [64.1]
    64.2. Gif man inbestinð, VI scill gebete. [64.2]
65. Gif þeoh gebrocen weorðeþ, XII scillingum gebete. [65]
    65.1. Gif he healt weorð, þær motan freond seman. [65.1]

---

a Either *hrif* is the subject of the verb with *wund* serving as predicate, or the two form a compound subject; see parallel §68 and note a to translation.

62. If an abdominal wound occurs, let him pay [with] 12 shillings.[a]
   62.1. If he becomes pierced through, let him pay [with] 20 shillings.[b]
63. If a person becomes cured [after having been wounded], let him [i.e., the person who caused the wound] pay [with] 30 shillings.
   63.1. If a person should be grievously wounded, let him pay [with] 30 shillings.[c]
64. If a person damages the genital organ, let him pay him with three person-prices.
   64.1. If he stabs through [it], let him pay [with] 6 shillings.
   64.2. If a person stabs into [it], let him pay [with] 6 shillings.[d]
65. If a thigh becomes broken, let him pay with 12 shillings.
   65.1 If he becomes lame, then friends[e] must arbitrate.

---

a This could also be translated: 'If an abdomen becomes wounded ...' Indeed, *hrif* occurs only rarely as the first element of a compound in Old English. But the *Lex Alamannorum* (written sometime between 584 and 629) has *hreuouunt* (*hreuo* - *hrif* + *wunt* - *wund*), which also served as the model for *hreuauunt* in *Lex Bavariorum* (see Georg Baesecke, 'Die deutschen Worte der germanischen Gesetze,' *Beiträge zur Geschichte der deutschen Sprache und Literatur* 59 [1935]: 1–101 at 19). Comparative evidence would thus suggest interpreting the Old English similarly as a compound.

b That is, the wound goes right through the injured man: *he* cannot refer to either the stomach (*hrif*, neuter) or the wound (*wund*, feminine).

c See discussion of these clauses in Commentary under 'Personal injury.'

d Liebermann, *Gesetze*, 3:13, points out that these sums seem remarkably small compared to the fine stipulated for damage to the penis and speculates that perhaps §§64.1 and 64.2 refer to another body part which has been omitted in the copying. But one could also interpret them as referring to the scrotum as a whole; this eliminates the discrepancy, since the scrotum can be pierced without impairing the ability to engender children.

e The term *freond* can mean either 'friends' or 'kinsmen.' Note, however, that elsewhere in the text 'kinsmen' is rendered by *mægas*. Although D.H. Green, *Language and History in the Early Germanic World* (Cambridge and New York: Cambridge University Press, 1998), 57, claims that 'the meaning "kinsman" is clear when frēond is employed in a legal context,' all his examples are from a later date. Alexander C. Murray, *Germanic Kinship Structure: Studies in Law and Society in Antiquity and the Early Middle Ages* (Toronto: Pontifical Institute of Medieval Studies, 1983), 136, suggests that *freond* should be seen as 'not a strict kin group at all, but as a kindred-based group composed of interested relatives, friends and dependents'; Thomas Charles-Edwards makes a similar suggestion in 'Anglo-Saxon Kinship Revisited,' in John Hines, ed., *The Anglo-Saxons from the Migration Period to the Eighth Century: An Ethnographic Perspective* (Woodbridge: Boydell, 1997), 180. It is not clear whether §65.1 refers to friends of the injured man or to representatives chosen by both parties. See discussion in chapter 1 under 'Chronological layering.'

66. Gif rib forbrocen weorð, III scill gebete. [66]
67. Gif man þeoh ðurhstingþ, stice gehwilce VI scillingas. [67]
    67.1. Gyfe[a] ofer ynce, scilling. [67.1]
    67.2. Æt twam yncum, twegen.
    67.3. Ofer þry, III scll.
68. Gif wælt[-]wund[b] weorðeþ, III scillingas gebete. [68]
69. Gif fot of weorðeþ, L scillingum forgelde(n).[c] [69]
70. Gif seo micle[d] ta of weorðeþ, X scll forgelde(n).[e] [70]
    70.1. Æt þam oðrum taum gehwilcum, healf gelde [71]
    ealswa æt þam fingrum ys cwiden.
71. Gif þare mycclan taan næge of weorþeð, XXX scætta to bote. [72]
    71.1. Æt þam oþrum gehwilcum, X scættas gebete. [72.1]
72. Gif friwif locbore leswæs hwæt gedeþ, XXX scill gebete. [73]
73. Mægþbot sy[f] swa friges mannes. [74]
74. Mund þare betstan widuwan eorlcundre, L scillinga [75]
gebete.
    74.1. Ðare oþre, XX scll. [75.1]
    74.2. Ðare þriddan, XII scll.
    74.3. Þare feorðan, VI scll.
75. Gif man widuwan unagne genimeþ, II gelde seo mund sy.[g] [76]

---

a The f is added later in the space following gy, and the e is then written above the o of *ofer*.
b Either *wælt* is the subject of the verb with *wund* serving as predicate, or the two form a compound subject; see §§62 and 63.1, both of which contain similar ambiguities.
c I follow Liebermann's suggestion that *forgelden* should be emended to the singular *forgelde*; see §27.2.
d Changed from *mycle* by scribe.
e I follow Liebermann's suggestion that *forgelden* should be emended to the singular *forgelde*; see §§27.2 and 69.
f There is a point added later in a different ink to separate *mægþbot* from *sy*. Liebermann says the y is on an erasure.
g y on an erasure.

66. If a rib becomes broken, let him pay [with] 3 shillings.[a]
67. If a person stabs through a thigh, for each thrust 6 shillings.
   67.1. If [the width of the wound] is over an inch,[b] a shilling.
   67.2. For two inches, two [shillings].
   67.3. Over three [inches], 3 shillings.
68. If a 'welt-wound' occurs, let him pay 3 shillings.[c]
69. If a foot becomes [struck] off, let him pay with 50 shillings.
70. If the big toe becomes [struck] off, let him pay [with] 10 shillings.
   70.1. For each of the other toes let him pay half the amount already discussed for the fingers.
71. If the big toenail becomes [struck] off, 30 sceattas as restitution.[d]
   71.1. For each of the others, let him pay 10 sceattas.
72. If a free woman in charge of the locks does anything seriously dishonest,[e] let her pay 30 shillings.
73. Compensation for [injury to/offence against] a maiden shall be as for a free man.
74. [For violation of] protection of the foremost widow of noble rank, let him pay 50 shillings.
   74.1. [For a widow] of the second [rank], 20 shillings.
   74.2. [For a widow] of the third [rank], 12 shillings.
   74.3. [For a widow] of the fourth [rank], 6 shillings.
75. If a person takes a widow who does not belong to him, the [payment for violation of] protection shall be 2[-fold] as compensation.

---

a §66 seems to have been displaced in the usual top-to-bottom enumeration of the personal injury laws: note that it comes between two clauses concerning injury to the thigh.

b A term similarly borrowed from Latin *uncia* 'one-twelfth' is used for measuring the width of wounds in Old Irish law; see discussion in chapter 1 under 'Chronological layering.'

c Previous editors translate this clause along the lines of 'If a sinew becomes wounded ...'; see discussion in Commentary under 'Personal injury.'

d At 20 *sceattas* to the shilling, this represents half the sum for the 3-shilling thumbnail.

e Translation of this passage taken from Fell, 'The "friwif locbore" Revisited.' See discussion in Commentary under 'Women and children.'

76. Gif man[a] mægþ gebigeð[b] ceapi, geceapod sy[c] gif hit [77]
unfacne is.
 76.1. Gif hit þonne facne is, ef[t][d] þær æt ham gebrenge, [77.1]
 ⁊ him man his scæt agefe.
 76.2. Gif hio cwic bearn gebyreþ, healfne scæt age gif [78]
 ceorl ær swylteþ. /3v/
 76.3. Gif mid bearnum bugan wille, healfne scæt age. [79]
 76.4. Gif ceorl agan wile, swa an bearn. [80]
 76.5. Gif hio bearn ne gebyreþ, fæderingmagas fioh agan [81]
 ⁊ morgengyfe.
77. Gif man mægþman[e] nede genimeþ, ðam agende L scillinga, [82]
⁊ eft æt þam agende sinne willan ætgebicge.
 77.1. Gif hio oþrum mæn in sceat bewyddod sy,[f] XX [83]
 scillinga gebete.
 77.2. Gif gængang[g] geweorðeþ, XXXV scill ⁊ cyninge XV [84]
 scillingas.
78. Gif man mid esnes cwynan geligeþ be cwicum ceorle, II [85]
gebete.
79. Gif esne oþerne[h] ofslea unsynningne, ealne weorðe [86]
forgelde.

---

a Changed from *mon* by scribe.
b Liebermann reads this character as a barred **d**; both in the manuscript and in the facsimile it looks to me like any other **ð** written by this scribe.
c **y** on an erasure.
d I follow Liebermann's suggestion in emending the manuscript reading of *ef* to *eft*.
e **a** is a correction for **o**.
f **y** is on an erasure.
g Deformed **g** here looks like a later interpolation; it is on an erasure.
h Written above following words.

76. If a person buys a maiden with a [bride-]price, let the bargain be [valid], if there is no deception.
   76.1. If there is deception, afterwards let him bring [her to her] home, and let him be given his money.
   76.2. If she bears a living child, let her obtain half the goods [belonging to the household] if the husband dies first.
   76.3. If she should wish to dwell with the children, let her obtain half the goods [of the household].[a]
   76.4. If she should wish to take a man [i.e., another husband], provision as for one child [i.e., the inheritance is split equally between the mother and each of the children].
   76.5. If she does not bear a child, her paternal kin should obtain [her] property and the morning-gift.[b]
77. If a person takes a maiden by force: to the owner [of her protection] 50 shillings, and afterwards let him buy from the owner his consent [to marry her].
   77.1. If she should be betrothed to another man by goods [i.e., the bride-price has been paid], let him pay 20 shillings [to that man as well].
   77.2. If return [of the stolen maiden] occurs, 35 shillings and 15 shillings to the king.
78. If a person lies with a servant's[c] wife while the husband[d] is alive, let him pay 2[-fold what he would have paid were she unmarried].
79. If a servant should kill another [who is] guiltless, let him pay [the dead man's master] the entire worth.

---

a For translation of this and the following clause, see Carole A. Hough, 'The Early Kentish "Divorce Laws": A Reconsideration of Æthelberht, chs. 79 and 80,' *Anglo-Saxon England* 23 (1994): 19–34.
b See discussion of these clauses in Commentary under 'Women and children.'
c The *esne* – here translated as 'servant' – 'was probably a poor freeman from whom a certain portion of labour could be demanded in consideration of his holdings, or a certain rent ... reserved out of the produce of the hives, flocks or herds committed to his care. He was a poor mercenary, serving for hire, or for his land, but was not of so low a rank as the þeow or wealh.' See Joseph Bosworth, *An Anglo-Saxon Dictionary* (Oxford: Clarendon Press, 1898). F.L. Attenborough, ed., *The Laws of the Earliest English Kings* (Cambridge: Cambridge University Press, 1922), 178, points out that the original meaning 'appears to have been "harvester" (cf. Gothic *asans*, "harvest").'
d The term *ceorl* can mean 'man,' 'freeman,' or 'husband,' although the primary sense here is clearly 'husband.'

80 The Beginnings of English Law

80. Gif esnes eage ⁊ foot of weorðeþ aslagen, ealne weorðe hine forgelde. [87]
81. Gif man mannes esne gebindeþ, VI scill[a] gebete. [88]
82. Ðeowæs wegreaf se III scillingas. [89]
83. Gif þeow[b] steleþ, II gelde gebete. [90]

---

a As discussed in chapter 1, I would expand *scill* as the dative *scillingum* and connect chronologically the section of the text concerning the *esne* with those sections dealing with the *ceorl* and personal injuries.
b w written in another hand.

80. If a servant's eye or foot becomes struck off, let him pay him [i.e., the servant's master] the entire worth.[a]
81. If a person binds a person's servant, let him pay [with] 6 shillings.
82. A slave's highway robbery shall be [paid for with] 3 shillings.
83. If a slave steals, let him pay 2[-fold] as compensation.

---

a ⁊ can mean either 'and' or 'or'; the latter seems more likely here, but see discussion in Commentary under 'Servants.' Other adversative uses of this ligature can be found in §§15, 23, 30.

Commentary

With the exception of a discussion on the monetary system, which is relevant to the understanding of all the laws, the commentary found below essentially follows the layout of the text itself. Thus the first sections address the prologue, the church laws, and laws dealing with king, *eorl*, freeman, and freedman. At this point I have inserted discussion of issues that affect all of the above ranks: namely, theft and killing. I then return to the order of the text to consider the personal injury laws, women and children, servant and slave.

Monetary system[5]

The two monetary units mentioned in these texts are the shilling and the *sceatt*. The term *shilling* comes from the Germanic verb *skil-, which originally meant 'to divide,' and once referred to a piece cut from a golden ring. Throughout the Germanic territories treasure was commonly counted in rings, as discussed under 'King' below. (Compare the American phrase 'two bits' used for a quarter, which originated from the custom of dividing Spanish dollars into eight parts, each of which was called a 'bit.' Devotees of pirate literature recognize these bits as 'pieces of eight.')[6] The term *sceatt* literally means 'wealth' or 'property' (compare Modern German *Schatz*). At the time of Æthelberht it referred to a small unit of gold whose weight equalled that of a grain of barley corn;[7] in the Kentish territories at this time there were 20 *sceattas* to the shilling.[8] That the two represented weights of gold, of which one was a multiple of the other, can be seen in an early Old English poem, in which Widsið tells of having been rewarded with a ring

> ... on þam siex hund wæs smætes gold
> gescyred sceatta, scillingrime. (91–2)[9]

> ... *in which by shilling count was reckoned 600 sceattas of pure gold.*

Using the value of the Roman *solidus* as a comparison, H. Munro Chadwick suggests that the Kentish shilling might be equated in worth to one ox.[10]

Although the early kings of Kent did not mint their own coins, from about 575 on Anglo-Saxons used Merovingian gold coins imported from the Frankish territories.[11] Several early Anglo-Saxon coins copied

The Laws of Æthelberht 83

Merovingian designs, and one of the earliest seems to have been made in Canterbury by a Frankish moneyer named Eusebius in the first part of the seventh century.[12] Gold coins were struck in Kent – probably in Canterbury – from the turn of the seventh century, but until about 630 coining was only sporadic.[13] The earliest gold coin with a royal name found south of the Humber bears the name of Æthelberht's son Eadbald; comparative evidence leads numismatists to believe that it was minted in London.[14] Mints were in operation in Kent and London throughout the period of Kentish independence. By the last quarter of the seventh century, these centres also produced silver coins, which rapidly became far more common than the gold coins of the earlier period. The mints in London and Kent continued in operation under the later overlordship of the kings of Mercia, although by that time they were primarily turning out the new-style penny.[15]

Rubric

These are the decrees which King Æthelberht set in Augustine's time.

The rubric is written in red ink and does not belong to the text proper; it matches those preceding the prologues to the laws of Hloþhere & Eadric and Wihtred. Liebermann, arguing on the basis of later Anglo-Saxon laws, postulates that traces of an original prologue may be contained in this rubric, and in Bede's statement that Æthelberht established these laws 'with the advice of his counselors'[16] (see the parallel in Wihtred's prologue). J.M. Wallace-Hadrill draws a similar conclusion through a comparison with Continental laws. He also postulates that the lost introduction to the Kentish laws may have contained a king-list, such as is common in their Continental analogues.[17]

The text of this rubric must predate 747. By this time Augustine was beatified and would have been referred to as a saint, as he is in the decree of the Council of Clofeshoh which states that the day of deposition *Sancti Augustini Archiepiscopi* (and, coincidentally, the birthday of Pope Gregory) should be henceforward kept as a feast day.[18]

The church and the public assembly

1. God's property and the church's [is to be compensated] with 12-fold compensation.
2. A bishop's property [is to be compensated] with 11-fold compensation.

3. A priest's property [is to be compensated] with 9-fold compensation.
4. A deacon's property [is to be compensated] with 6-fold compensation.
5. A cleric's property [is to be compensated] with 3-fold compensation.
6. [Violation of] church peace [is to be compensated] with 2-fold compensation.
7. [Violation of] assembly peace [is to be compensated] with 2-fold compensation.

The ecclesiastical laws open with a reference to 'God and the church,' which represents a fixed collocation; charters often donate land *Deo et ecclesiae*, 'to God and the church.'[19] These laws deal with two issues: theft and disturbance of the peace. Recompense for theft is made in multiples of the value of the goods stolen. The first and highest fine attaches to theft from the church itself; this is the stiffest fine imposed in all of Æthelberht's laws. Fines for theft from various ranks of clergymen are based on status, moving from the highest-ranking bishop to the priest, deacon, and finally to clerics, or lower ranks of churchmen. The sixth-century Roman laws of Justinian include under the rubric *'clerici' Presbyteros, Subdiaconos, Lectores, et Cantores*, 'priests, sub-deacons, readers, and cantors'; the seventh-century scholar and bishop Isidore of Seville defines *clerici* as including the *ostiarius, psalmista, lector, exorcista, acolythus, subdiaconus, diaconus, presbyter, episcopus*, 'doorkeeper, psalmist, reader, exorcist, acolyte, subdeacon, deacon, priest, bishop,' apparently roughly in reverse order of status.[20] This hierarchical structure echoes that of Rome, and may well have been brought by the entourage of Augustine. It is also possible that such elaboration did not exist in the early stages of conversion in Kent, and that these clauses are predictive of an anticipated ecclesiastical hierarchy modelled on that of Rome.[21]

Restitution for theft from a priest is the same as that required for theft from a king by §10;[22] similarly, the degrees of restitution are the same for a cleric as those later stipulated in §15 for a freeman. The last two clauses concern violation of the *friþ*, 'peace' of the church and the public assembly. Since these clauses do not involve theft, the twofold compensation must mean that whatever the usual fine is for the offence committed, it is doubled when the transgression takes place in church or in the *mæþl*, 'public assembly.'[23] In other words, whereas the normal fine for striking off a thumb is 20 shillings (§53), the amount is raised to 40 shillings when the action takes place in a religious or other public gathering. We find a similar ruling elsewhere in the British Isles: the earliest extant Welsh laws, attributed to the tenth-century king Hywel Dda, rule 'It is right that there be double [penalty] in court and in church,' although the 'court' referred to here is specifically the king's gathering.[24] A cross-cultural influence between these laws is not out of the question, but it seems more likely that each society independently doubled the fine for an offence that simultaneously impinges on individual rights and public peace.

The king

8. *If the king summons his people to him and a person does any harm to them there, 2[-fold] restitution and 50 shillings to the king.*
9. *If the king drinks at a person's home, and a person should do anything seriously dishonest there, let him pay two[-fold] restitution.*
10. *If a freeman should steal from the king, let him compensate with 9[-fold] compensation.*
11. *If a person should kill someone in the king's dwelling, let him pay 50 shillings.*
12. *If a person kills a free man, 50 shillings to the king as lord-payment.*
13. *If [a person] kills the king's official [?,] smith or ?herald/guide, let him pay an ordinary person-price.*
14. *[For violation of] the king's protection, 50 shillings.*
15. *If a freeman steals from a freeman, let him pay 3[-fold], and the king obtains that fine or all the possessions.*
16. *If a man lies with the king's maiden, let him pay 50 shillings.*
    16.1. *If she should be a 'grinding' slave, let him pay 25 shillings.*
    16.2. *If she should be [of the] third [rank], 12 shillings.*
17. *[For] feeding of the king, let him pay 20 shillings.*

In addition to the twofold fine, a man disturbing a public assembly called by the king owes a supplementary 50 shillings to the king. The same fine is imposed for violation of the king's protection (i.e., creating a disturbance or causing injury within the area or circle for which the king is directly responsible).[25] In some sense, all public assemblies stand under the king's protection. Similar is the stipulation that the king receives 50 shillings if a person kills a freeman (as all freemen are in some respect under the king's protection) or another person in the king's dwelling. If §11 is interpreted so that the killing of *any person* (i.e., slave, servant, or freedman) in the king's dwelling draws a fine of 50 shillings, then logically §12 would imply that if a person kills a *freeman* in the king's dwelling, the fine to the king would total 100 shillings (50 for the slaying, and 50 for the breach of protection of the king's dwelling). The use of the term *drihtenbeag*, literally 'lord-ring' (here translated as 'lord-payment'), refers to the practice of giving rings as a form of reward or payment, an enduring custom of the Germanic peoples. The *Beowulf* poet calls Scyld Sceafing, the mythical ancestor of the Danes, *beaga bryttan*, 'distributor of rings' (l. 35), and Beowulf applies the same epithet to the king Hroþgar (l. 352). In the Old High German *Hildebrandslied*, the warrior chief Hildebrand offers his son Haðubrand *wuntana baugas*, 'wound rings,' although Haðubrand rejects them in distrust. Anglo-Saxon references to payments in rings continue in wills as late as the eleventh century.[26]

The term *fedesl* in §17 has proven problematic, as it appears only rarely elsewhere (crucially in a slightly different, linguistically later, morphological form), and then only with the meaning 'fatted beast.' That it does not refer to an individual of the king's household can be deduced from the overwhelmingly instrumental function of the suffix *-sl. The cognate Old High German compound is glossed by Latin *pastus*, which has the specialized meaning in legal texts of 'food render': the responsibility for providing support for the king and his retainers. The king's household had no fixed location, but travelled from place to place, as in Duncan's visit to Macbeth's court. Even those who did not have responsibility for housing the court would have been responsible for 'food render,' that is, for supplying a certain amount of food for the 'king's feeding.' The practice was common elsewhere in the British Isles in this period and well documented in later Anglo-Saxon England.[27] If we accept this interpretation of the term *fedesl*, then provision of 'food render' (presumably for some understood period, such as a single day)[28] could be substituted by monetary payment of 20 shillings.

On the basis of certain Old Norse parallels, Renato Gendre argues that the 'drinking' in §9 refers to a quasi-judicial gathering, and not just a banquet.[29] The same interpretation would presumably have to hold true for H & E §§8 and 9, both of which discuss the penalties applied for a person who causes a disturbance 'where men are drinking.' The twofold restitution equals that for violating the peace of the public assembly stipulated in Æbt §7, which might be used to substantiate Gendre's hypothesis. However, early Welsh law distinguishes between two forms of providing food render for the king: one could provide either the wherewithal to allow the king to stay in his own royal hall (which included a man to kindle the fire in the hall), or the *gwestfa*, by which one fed the king in one's own house.[30] I think it is more likely that Æbt §9 refers to that latter type of formal visit addressed again in §17, which deals specifically with the (official) feeding of the king. It is conceivable that H & E §§8 and 9 also take place during the provision of food render. However, since the payments to the king could easily be invoked in absentia, it is also possible that these latter clauses merely refer to any private gathering.

The laws give a very incomplete picture of the composition of the king's household. Whether the word *ambiht*, 'official' or 'servant,' is a noun or the first element in a compound modifying the smith (and possibly the *lādrincman*) is as ambiguous in Old English as it is in the Modern English translation. We do get the compounds *ambiht-hera*, 'obedient minister'; *-scealc*, 'official servant'; *-secg*, 'official man, messenger'; *-þegen*, 'attendant thegn.' Presumably the interpretation of *ambiht* as 'servant' influences Liebermann's and Whitelock's interpretation that the figures referred to in these clauses are unfree.

Attending on the king are his *lādrincman*, '?herald/guide,' and his smith. That the smith is an important figure is unsurprising in a culture in which weapons are highly valued and either passed on as heirlooms or returned to the donor at the death of the warrior. The smith of Germanic legend appears as Vǫlundr in the Old Norse *Poetic Edda*, and Beowulf wears chain mail made by Wēland, to give the smith his Old English name.

The *lādrincman*, 'lead-warrior' or 'lead-man,' could be interpreted as a guide or a herald. Dorothy Whitelock rejects a possible Anglo-Saxon parallel in 'the official called in *Beowulf ar* "herald, messenger", who escorts strangers into the king's presence' precisely because 'he is of noble rank.'[31] Her objection stems from the fact that (following Liebermann) she assumes that what is meant in §13 is that the king's unfree servant, due to his position, is restituted with a *wergild* identical to that of an ordinary freeman. She supports her analysis with the parallel of §33 from the laws of Ine (although one must remember that these are West-Saxon not Kentish laws, and they were written a century later): 'The king's *horswealh*, who can carry messages for him [?=Æthelberht's *lādrincman*], his wergild is 200 shillings.' As Whitelock points out, 'the term *wealh* is ambiguous in Old English, meaning either a "Welshman" or a "slave."' (It can also mean a foreigner of any sort.) She goes on to say, 'From the context, I assume the former meaning here, the king's service raising the status of the Welshman so that he is entitled to the wergild of an English freeman. By itself, the law could mean that an unfree horse-servant in the king's service was to be paid for as a freeman, which would then remind us of [the clause in] Ethelbert.'[32]

I am not convinced, however, that §13 in Æthelberht in fact refers to raising the *wergild* for unfree servants of the king. For one thing, the preceding and following clauses specify payment to the king *over and above* restitution for the offence itself: in §12, the king receives 50 shillings (half a *wergild*) on top of the *wergild* paid to the relatives of a slain freeman; in §14, the king similarly receives a half-*wergild* payment for violation of his protection in addition to whatever sum might be due to the injured party. It seems likely that §13 is doubling the additional fine payable to the king if the slain man was one of his personal retainers.[33] But in this case, there is nothing to imply that the servant was not a free man. Consider further that the violation of a noble's protection is worth twice that of a freeman (see below under 'Eorl' and 'Freeman'). Could it then be possible that the king's servant is even of noble rank?

Heralds, in particular, often have special status in Germanic literature. Closest in time and space to these laws is the *ar* of *Beowulf* mentioned above. Ranging further afield, in the Middle High German *Nibelungenlied* it is the hero Siegfried who is sent to announce the Burgundian victory over the Saxons. Furthermore, parallels to both the smith and the *lādrincman* occur in Karl von Amira's list of nobles who served the king in late twelfth-century Norway: namely, the goldsmith and the *merkismaðr*, whose job it was to carry the standard.[34] Admittedly, these latter examples are widely separated in time and space. But the placement of §13 in the sequence of rulings implies that the payment of a 'medium *wergild*' is due to the king over and above the payment to the family of the slain man. If we take the king's servant to be a freeman, then the amount of the fine is doubled because this man was serving the king, which seems a perfectly plausible explanation. But considering first, that noblemen might serve the king in other Germanic cultures (including that depicted in *Beowulf*) and second, that a nobleman's restitution is otherwise double that for an ordinary freeman, I do not believe we can rule out the possibility that the king's servants referred to in this clause are of noble birth.

Three ranks of women are protected in the king's household. Whether the top rank is a free woman servant or a slave is not clearly defined; this is the position described as *birele*, 'cupbearer,' for both nobleman and freeman, although there is no such clear definition for the first rank of the king's women. It is interesting to note that in *Beowulf* it is the queen Wealhþēow who serves drink to the heroes in the mead-hall: her name is a compound of *wealh*, 'foreign' and *þēow*, 'slave.' The two last ranks in §16 are certainly slaves. The second group, described as 'grinding slaves,' are women whose job it was to grind corn into meal in the days before the more efficient water mill came into use.[35] It seems possible that the first two ranks are valued more highly than the third because they had responsibilities in the area of food and drink,[36] which would require slaves not only with certain skills but also with a high degree of trustworthiness, since poison would constantly have been feared as a method of assassination. The third rank, then, would be assigned more menial chores.

Fines payable to an eorl

18. *If a person kills someone in a nobleman's dwelling, let him pay 12 shillings.*
19. *If a person lies with a nobleman's cupbearer, let him pay 12 shillings.*

Æthelberht's laws tell us even less about the household of the *eorl* or nobleman than they do about the household of the king. The term *eorl* may once have referred to a member of the *comitatus* (war band) – Wulfgar refers to the troop surrounding Hroþgar in Heorot as *eorlas*[37] – but in these laws it probably means either a retainer to the king, or one who has been awarded land in return for service.[38] An *eorl*'s restitution is roughly 25 per cent of that due to the king for like offences: both for killing someone in his dwelling and violation of his (top-ranked?) female slave, 12 versus 50 shillings. (In the case of someone committing manslaughter in an *eorl*'s dwelling, the payment to the nobleman would, of course, be in addition to the *wergild* the killer owed the slain man's kin.) Only one member of the *eorl*'s household is mentioned: the *birele,* 'cupbearer.' Although this term is generally masculine in later Old English it must be feminine here, as it is used to describe the first-ranking of the freeman's female slaves in §21. By extrapolation, it is fairly certain that the *mund* or protection of a nobleman was also worth 12 shillings. (See also the discussion of widows' restitution under 'Women and children' below.) H & E §1 tells us that the *wergild* for a nobleman was 300 shillings.

Fines payable to a freeman

20. *[For violation of] a freeman's protection, 6 shillings.*
21. *If a person lies with a freeman's cupbearer, let him pay with 6 shillings.*
    21.1. *For that second [rank of female slave], 50 sceattas.*
    21.2. *For that third [rank], 30 sceattas.*
25. *If a person binds a freeman, let him pay [with] 20 shillings.*

26. *If a person kills a freeman's loaf-eater, let him pay with 6 shillings.*
31. *If a freeman lies with a free man's wife, let him buy [him/her] off [with] his/her* wergild *and obtain another wife [for the husband] [with] his own money and bring her to the other man at home.*

A freeman's protection is 6 shillings to the king's 50; similarly, the killing of a freeman's loaf-eater (= dependent) also demands a fine of 6 shillings (presumably payable to the freeman, over and above the *wergild* due for the slain person if he/she is free), whereas the killing of a man in the king's dwelling draws a 50-shilling fine. The amount of restitution a freeman receives for the violation of his *birele* is half that owed to a nobleman, namely 6 versus 12 shillings. Where restitution to an *eorl* is roughly 25 per cent of what it is for the king, restitution for a freeman is half that accorded to the *eorl*.[39]

The freeman had not only his loaf-eaters, but also three ranks of female slaves, as did the king; it seems a safe assumption that the same was true for the *eorl*, although these slaves are not specifically mentioned. Like the king's, the freeman's third rank of slave is worth 25 per cent of the first. But while the king's second rank of slave is worth 50 per cent of the first, the freeman's second rank is valued at slightly less (since 50 sceattas would be 2 1/2 shillings, compared to the 6 shillings for the freeman's top-ranked *birele*).

In §31 we find for the first time reference to family: if a freeman lies with another's wife, he must pay either the husband's or the wife's *wergild* (the masculine/neuter possessive *his* is grammatically ambiguous, as *wif* is a neuter noun) and provide the man with a new wife. (See discussion below under 'Women and children.') In this instance the *wergild* would seem to recompense both damage and honour. That *wergild* is not reserved solely for restitution for murder is additionally demonstrated by the fine of three *wergilds* for damage to a man's penis, rendering the injured man incapable of producing offspring (although this injury could be seen as a type of prospective murder).

The binding of a freeman carries a fine of 20 shillings. Liebermann asserts that it is legal to bind a man who is guilty of a crime, but the binding of an innocent man must be recompensed.[40] This fine can thus be seen as a recompense for damage to honour; additional examples of an 'honour-payment' are demonstrated in the personal injury laws (discussed below).

Fines payable by (as opposed to due to) a freeman are discussed below under 'Theft' and 'Killing.'

Freedmen

27. *If [a person] kills a freedman of the first rank, let him pay [with] 80 shillings.*
   27.1. *If he kills [one of] that second [rank], let him pay with 60 shillings.*
   27.2. *[For one of] that third [rank], let him pay with 40 shillings.*

The term *læt*, here translated 'freedman,' is a hapax in Old English – that is, it only occurs once – and the etymology is vexed. Although most scholars have taken *læt* and its Germanic cognates from the verb that in Old English gives *lǽtan*, 'to release,' this should regularly give us *lāt* in Old English.[41] But instead we have *læt*, if we assume the vowel, which is unmarked in the manuscript, to be long. In late Latin we find, borrowed from Germanic, the term *laetus*, 'a foreign bondsman who received a piece of land to cultivate, for which he paid tribute to his master; a serf';[42] the shape of the borrowing would imply a long vowel. Another problem with the etymology is the fact that when the noun appears in compounds, the compounds are always weak, such as the Corpus Glossary *frioleta* (with its typically Kentish raising to e) or Ælfric's *freolaeta*.[43] In consideration of these problems, Brunner takes the vowel to be short and allies the group to the word that gives us the Old English adjective *læt*, 'late, slow, sluggish, tardy.'[44] Less satisfying semantically, this does account for the phonology; however, such an alliance dissociates the word from the Latin *laetus*, which is unfortunate. I prefer to align myself with those who connect *læt* to the verb meaning 'release,' with the caveat that the phonological derivation remains unexplained.

The tripartite division indicated in this clause probably represents a class growing through three generations from a servile status towards the class of freemen, becoming fully free in the fourth generation. This evolution has counterparts throughout early medieval Europe.[45] In Frankish territories, we have records of people accused of servile status on the basis of allegations that their grandparents were slaves;[46] such a reckoning never extends to the great-grandparents, so presumably in the fourth generation you have grown free from the servile origins of your kin. Early Welsh law states that: 'A man becomes a *priodor* [one who enjoys the fullest right to land] when he is the fourth man, his father and his grandfather and his great-grandfather and himself as fourth.'[47] The loss of position similarly occurs over a four-generational span. This exactly parallels certain eighth-century Old Irish laws, in which servile status can be acquired or lost over

92 The Beginnings of English Law

Table 2.1
Restitution

Rank	Æthelberht	Ine
Lowest rank	40	60
Middle rank	60	80
Highest rank	80	120
Freeman	100	200

four generations.[48] Counting the kin-group unto the fourth generation can be found in legal contexts in Greek and Sanskrit as well, so this reckoning may be dated back to Indo-European.

It seems likely that the *læt* only appears in the earliest Kentish laws because the ancient system of growing towards freedom was replaced with the advent of Christianity by the *manumissio in ecclesia*, in which the slave was immediately transformed in status to freedman.[49] This procedure is already in place in §7 of the late seventh-century laws of Wihtred, which mandates the freeing of a slave at the altar. It appears that the replacement of the older legal process has eliminated the ranks of 'partially free.'

A clause in the late seventh-century West-Saxon laws of Ine provides a much-discussed parallel threefold distinction:[50]

> §32: If a Welshman (*Wilisc man*) has a hide of land, his *wergild* is 120 shillings; if, however, he has a half hide, 80 shillings; if he has none, 60 shillings.[51]

Elsewhere in the same text, §§23.3 and 74 set the value of a Welsh slave's life at 60 shillings; we may be presented here with three classes of which the lowest is servile while the higher two are landowners. Liebermann, however, points out that the *Norðleod* states that this clause intends precisely to distinguish a landless free Welshman from a slave.[52] Ine §32 may simply be incorporating the Welsh *priodor* into the West Saxon legal system: the lowest rank would then be the newly freed slave, whose kin is now set on the path to becoming *priodor*. If this is the case, not only does the future *priodor's* right to landholding increase with each generation, so too does the amount of land he may own. The question is how or if this relates to the Kentish *læt*. The first thing to be noted is that the amounts of restitution do not match in terms of proportion, as seen in Table 2.1. While the second class of *læt* is recompensed at a rate falling exactly between the highest and lowest, the *wergild* for the middle rank of Welshman is closer to the lowest than the highest. This assignment is particularly odd if we interpret the lowest rank as slave and the upper two as free, and might serve as further evidence that we are concerned in Ine's laws with the freedman whose kin will become *priodor* only two generations later. Nor do the percentages match: whereas Æthelberht's highest ranking *læt* has a *wergild* 80 per cent of the 100 shillings of a Kentish freeman, Ine's highest ranking Welshman has a *wergild* only 60 per cent of the West Saxon freeman's 200 shillings. The discrepancy does not rule out the possibility that Ine §32 is regulating ranks of freedmen in the same fashion as Æbt §27. The different territories might well have determined different amounts of compensation; further, Ine's clause specifically deals with non-West-Saxon Welshmen, while Æthelberht's gives no indication that the *lætas* are not, in fact, of Kentish origin.

Sir Frank Stenton, following the analysis of nineteenth-century predecessors, claims that the Kentish *læts* 'seem to represent a British peasantry, surviving under Jutish rule,'[53] which would connect them to both Ine's *Wilisc* man and the *laetus* of the late Roman Empire. It is true that cognate terms in Germanic law can encompass subjected peoples, who have the same legal rights as manumitted slaves; it is also true that the Old English term *wealh* came to mean both 'Welsh'/'foreign' and 'slave.' But the threefold division of recompense is difficult to explain unless there is some kind of hierarchy as we find already in place in the Frankish and Welsh generational count by which an individual grows free of kinship origins. It certainly seems likely that many Welshmen were, in fact, enslaved during the Anglo-Saxon takeovers, and they would presumably be subject to the same Kentish law as any other freedmen. Unfortunately, Æbt §§27–27.2 alone do not provide sufficient information to allow us to determine whether the term *læt* in Kentish law similarly equated the legal rights of *all* members of the indigenous population with those of freed slaves.[54]

Theft

10. *If a freeman should steal from the king, let him compensate with 9[-fold] compensation.*
15. *If a freeman steals from a freeman, let him pay 3[-fold], and the king obtains that fine or all the possessions.*
82. *A slave's highway robbery shall be [paid for with] 3 shillings.*
83. *If a slave steals, let him pay 2[-fold] as compensation.*

Theft is recompensed by a multiple of the worth of the goods, as also stated for the church in §§1–5: ninefold if stolen from the king, threefold if from a freeman. If the freeman is unable to pay the full

94 The Beginnings of English Law

amount, he must render all that he does own. Logically, unless his kin supports him, he must now bind himself to another (as *esne*, 'servant' or slave)[55] until he has the wherewithal to support himself. There is no indication as to the fine due for stealing from a nobleman. Note, however, that between the ninefold restitution for a priest, which equals that allotted for the king, and the threefold restitution for a cleric, which equals that for a freeman, lies the sixfold restitution for the deacon, which may perhaps have equalled the restitution for a nobleman. The fact that a nobleman's restitution is double that of a freeman parallels the difference in protection (12 shillings versus 6).

If a slave commits robbery, the goods are recompensed at twice the value, and an additional fine of 3 shillings is levied if he commits highway robbery (i.e., robbery on the open road with concomitant assault). From W §10, we know that a slave could be fined 6 shillings for 'offering to devils,' that is, making sacrifice to pagan idols. This implies that a slave, although unfree, could own property and be held responsible for his own fine. However, the first of the two Æthelberht slave clauses has no agent, and the second has no overt subject for the verb of recompense: it was perhaps axiomatic that the one who pays is the master and not the slave. (See parallel under 'Servants' below.)

22. *If a person breaks [as the] first into someone's dwelling, let him pay with 6 shillings.*
    22.1. *He who breaks in next, 3 shillings.*
    22.2. *Afterwards, each a shilling.*
28. *If a freeman breaks into an enclosure, let him pay with 6 shillings.*
    28.1. *If a person takes property therein, let that man pay 3[-fold] as compensation.*
29. *If a freeman enters an enclosure [?with intention to rob], let him pay with 4 shillings.*
23. *If a person provides someone with weapons where strife arises, but he does no harm, let him pay with 6 shillings.*
    23.1. *If highway robbery should be done, let him [i.e., the one who provided the weapons] pay with 6 shillings.*
    23.2. *If a person kills that man [who is being robbed] let him [i.e., the one who provided the weapons] pay with 20 shillings.*

Breaking and entering carry penalties additional to those for theft alone; Liebermann claims that those committing *edorbrycþ* may be doing so as a first step towards an illegal search or assault on the householder rather than for the specific purpose of robbery.[56] The first to break into a man's dwelling, the ringleader, incurs the largest fine; his lieutenant, who comes second, pays only half; and their followers get away with a fine of a shilling apiece. How we are to distinguish between the 'breaking into a man's dwelling' (*tun*) of §22 and the 'breaking into an enclosure' (*eodor*; literally *hedge*, although later used primarily with symbolic meanings ranging from 'enclosure' to 'prince')[57] of §28 is unclear; note that the fine for the ringleader of the group robbery is the same as for the 'hedge'-breaker. It seems likely that the two clauses describe the different acts of breaking into a man's *house* and breaking into a man's *homestead*; Alfred's laws use both *burgbryce* and *eodorbryce*.[58] This seems to equate the fine for stealing possessions from inside a building with that for rustling livestock or stealing other goods from a person's exterior property. This analysis demands an interpretation, at least in this instance, of *tun*, 'dwelling,' specifically as 'house.' The term occurs twice otherwise in Æthelberht's laws: in §11 (the payment required for killing a person in a king's *tun*), and in §18 (the fine for a killing committed in an *eorl's tun*). Although the word commonly means landed property, it can also denote a building. Similar provisions in Hloþhere & Eadric §§7, 8 and 9 use the term *flet*, which usually refers to a structure. Modern British English retains the meaning in the term 'flat,' for which Americans use 'apartment.'

Parenthetically, the *Beowulf* poet links *flet* and *eodor* when Hrothgar presents Beowulf with his reward for driving off the mortally-wounded Grendel:

Heht ða eorla hleo   eahta mearas
fætedhleore   on *flet* teon
in under *eodoras*.   1035–8

Then the protector of warriors commanded   that eight mares
with plated bridles   be led into the dwelling
into the enclosure.

The use of the appositive implies that *flet* and *eoderas* function to some extent as synonyms. Stylistically, however, there is no problem with looser variants, such as if the first referred to the hall itself and the second to the enclosure surrounding the hall.[59] (If we accept this interpretation, the reversal of the logical sequence of entry must be seen as driven by alliterative requirements.)

I think it likely that no real distinction is being made in this text. Since the mention of breaking and entering in §22 is followed by discussion of other offences committed by and against freemen, and of the killing of a freedman, perhaps §28 merely reiterates the fine already established in §22 for the act of breaking in to provide a background for the stipulation of recompense due for robbery within. In other words, §28 might simply function as a resumptive clause to reintroduce the topic of breaking and entering. The fine, whether for burglary or for rustling, is the same as for robbery of any kind from a freeman, previously established in §15: that is, threefold. The prospective robber is liable for the action of breaking and entering whether or not he successfully purloins goods; the fine for theft is additional. Calling on a Danish comparison, Liebermann suggests that crossing over a hedge may represent the work of a single perpetrator rather than a gang. But it seems to me that §29 implies rather that climbing over a hedge or enclosure without causing damage (i.e., entering without breaking) carries a lower fine than breaking through a hedge.[60]

Clause 23 shows that the instigator of a crime is liable, even if he himself did not carry it out. A provider of weapons must pay 6 shillings in the case of assault, an additional 6 if robbery is successfully performed using the weapons, and a further (?or perhaps this sum overrides the other penalties) 20 shillings if the man being robbed is killed. Perhaps this means that the killer pays the entire *wergild* and the 20 shillings from the arms provider goes to the king as additional payment for disturbance of the peace. This distribution would match the fine levied for defaulting the responsibility of food render, but the two offences are hardly comparable. Liebermann assumes that the payment goes to the kin of the slain man, and that the killer is responsible for the remainder of the *wergild*;[61] this analysis seems more attractive given the parallel in §24.1 (discussed below).

Killing

24. *If a person kills someone, let him pay an ordinary person-price, 100 shillings.*
    24.1. *If a person kills someone, let him pay 20 shillings at the open grave, and let him pay the entire person[-price] in 40 nights.*
    24.2. *If the killer departs from the land, let his kinsmen pay a half person [-price].*
30. *If a person should kill someone, let him pay [with] his own money or unblemished property, whichever.*

The *wergild* for a freeman is 100 shillings, payable in two instalments: 20 shillings at the open grave and the remaining 80 within forty days.[62] The open grave would be the location in which a blood feud would most likely break out: the payment of the first instalment here may have been intended precisely to avoid such an outbreak. Reinhold Schmid points out that the Frisian custom was to pronounce the accusation of murder at the open grave, and Liebermann adds that payment was made here to put the soul to rest.[63] Patrick Wormald hypothesizes that the stipulation that the kin is responsible for only half the *wergild* should the killer escape may have been inserted to address a particular case. Germanic law generally holds the kin fully responsible for offences committed by one of its members.[64] But I think a more likely reading is that a supplementary fine is added to the *wergild* if the killer escapes, as proof that the kin group has not supported him in his actions (see discussion under 'Chronological layering' in chapter 1).

An additional payment of 50 shillings to the king or 6 shillings to a freeman is mandated, depending on whose protection the slain man was under (see discussion in respective sections under 'The king' and 'Freeman' above). Clause 30 states that payment could be made in money or in goods. Wallace-Hadrill sees the word 'own' here as crucial: 'his kin was not merely exempted but actually forbidden to intervene, at least as bankers.'[65] But since (as stated above) one of the functions of the kin group was to share responsibility precisely for such duties as payment of *wergild*, I find Wallace-Hadrill's analysis unpersuasive.[66]

Rihthamscyld

> 32. *If a person pierces through the* rihthamscyld, *let him pay with [its] worth.*

I have not, as yet, arrived at a satisfactory interpretation of *rihthamscyld*; most translators, struggling with the same problem, leave the Old English term untranslated. Liebermann renders it morpheme-for-morpheme as 'den rechten Heimschild' (which doesn't actually mean anything), and understands the concept as a whole to mean something like 'disturbance of the homestead.' He interprets *ham* as 'home,' and compares *scyld* to the Frisian *skul*, 'covering,' thus taking the compound to refer to the wooden door protecting the house.[67] Following his analysis, this law refers to an attack on a homestead, and should be included among the laws on breaking and entering. It might then be related to the *burg-bryce* '[fine for] breaking into a dwelling' of later West-Saxon laws. How Liebermann would incorporate the adjective *riht*, 'legal, right, proper,' is not clear; surely *any* door is a legal or proper barrier. Attenborough renders the phrase, 'If anyone damages the enclosure of a dwelling ...,' thus essentially following Liebermann. He notes, however, his lack of 'confidence as to the translation of this passage.'[68]

Toller, in the *Supplement* to Bosworth's *Dictionary of Anglo-Saxon*, on the basis of a parallel in the *Lex Saxonum*, emends the phrase to *Gif man on unriht ham oðð̄e scyld [þurhstinð]* ..., 'if a person unjustly stabs through a garment or shield ...' The emendation seems somewhat severe to me, as no other clause, on the face of it, demonstrates corruption in the transmission to this degree. Jakob Grimm's suggestion that this might mean the right shoulderblade is followed by a very appropriate question mark. Such a translation would considerably disrupt the head-to-toe enumeration of body parts, even if we were to have reason to believe that *hamscyld* meant 'shoulderblade' (which we don't).[69]

Under any of the foregoing analyses, it is unclear as to what the *weorð*, 'worth,' of such a violation might be.

I am more inclined to accept a possible connection to the term *rihthæmed*, 'legitimate matrimony'; compare, for example *unrihthæmed(e)*, 'in an unlawful union' in W §§3 and 4.[70] This interpretation would then connect the clause to the preceding stipulation concerning the taking of another man's legal or proper wife. A somewhat similar stricture can be found in the 'Pentitentials of Theodore,' attributed to the famous archbishop of Canterbury, who postdates Æthelberht by almost a century:

12.7. A legal marriage may not be broken without the consent of both parties.[71]

We must approach this rather remote parallel with caution, given the difference in time, and the fact that one stems from secular practice and the other from canon law. But if we were to analyse *rihthæmscyld* along these lines, interpreting it as 'the protection of legal marriage,' then the perpetrator of the offence should be one of the two parties to the disruption of the marriage. This would connect the clause to the preceding §31, which addresses penalties for a man sleeping with another's wife: he is liable for a *wergild* and the payment of a brideprice for a second wife for the husband. Perhaps §32 augments the penalty by stipulating that the bride-price and/or morning-gift (the 'worth' of the marriage) must also be repaid. Given the ambiguity in gender of the indefinite pronoun *man*, this might even mean that the woman is responsible for returning the bride-price if she has been complicit in the adultery.

Personal injury[72]

> *Personal injury laws are too numerous to reiterate here: see §§33–71 in foregoing translation.*

The personal injury laws are, with a few exceptions, laid out in top-to-bottom order. They rank restitution according to two principles: the value in physiological terms of the wounded part and the degree to which the damage is visible, thus adding insult to injury.

Not surprisingly, the highest fine is reserved for serious damage to the penis. Although a man can live and function without a penis, the three-*wergild* fine recompenses the injured man for lack of future children. The fines stipulated for piercing or stabbing through the 'genital organ' probably refer to the scrotum rather than specifically to the penis: not only is the fine low for damage to the penis, but it is difficult to conceive of a blow so delicately delivered that it pierces into but not through the penis itself!

The next highest fine is the 50 shillings prescribed for striking off a foot or gouging out an eye: note that the sum of the two equals a freeman's *wergild*. It is curious that no fine is stipulated for striking off a hand; the laws dealing with the servant similarly refer to the eye and foot, but omit the hand. However, here as elsewhere in Germanic law, the sum for striking off all the fingers on one hand is, in fact, 50 shillings or 1/2 *wergild*,[73] equivalent to the sum for striking off a foot. The aggregate sum for striking off all the toes is 25 shillings, which means that striking off the stump of the foot incurs an additional 25-shilling fine.[74] But a man can at least hobble on a toeless foot, whereas a fingerless hand is not of much use. The Anglo-Saxon awareness of this disparity is even more obvious when we take into account that the fingers are fined at twice the value of the toes. If we were to assume that the value of the hand were similarly twice that of the foot, then the fine would be 100 shillings, or the price of a man's *wergild*, which would be exorbitant. Clearly the hand is seen as an aggregate of its fingers.

Similarly, a lamed shoulder is worth 30 shillings, while a lamed thigh goes to arbitration – the only instance of mediation found in

Æthelberht.[75] Damage to one arm incapacitates only that arm, whereas damage to the leg may require the use of a crutch and thus tie up an arm as well as the leg.[76] The 6-shilling fine for damaging a collarbone compared to the 30-shilling fine for a lamed shoulder demonstrates an awareness that only in the former case would the wounded person retain the use of his arm (although that use would be painful). A comparable understanding of the recuperative power of the body is reflected in the fact that a broken rib is recompensed at 3 shillings, the same rate legislated for striking off a molar tooth or a thumbnail. If anything, one might expect the fines for the last two injuries to be higher. The rib will heal with no lasting result, whereas a lost tooth or thumbnail torn out by the roots cannot be replaced.

A wound that causes not only damage but also loss of sensory perception is accorded a higher fine than one that does not. Striking off an ear, which lessens the acuteness of hearing (as it eliminates the reverse megaphone that drew in sound) attracts a fine of 12 shillings where a person who causes actual loss of hearing must pay 25 shillings. Clearly early Anglo-Saxon medical knowledge recognized that the external ear assists in, but is not integral to, the hearing process. Damage to speech (presumably from a blow to the jaw, as this clause follows those dealing with the jawbone) is fined 12 shillings; perhaps causing total loss of speech would also draw the higher fine of 25. Sense of smell seems not to be valued so highly: a pierced nose, which might deviate the septum and cause both damage to the olfactory sense (with a concomitant loss of taste sensation) and difficulty in breathing, is recompensed by a mere 9 shillings, as opposed to 6 shillings if the nose is simply slashed.

As stated earlier, some fines are assessed on the basis of the visibility of the damage. For example, a blow draws a 20-sceattas fine if it causes a bruise that can be covered by clothing, but 30 if the bruise cannot be concealed. In disfigurement of the appearance, degree is taken into consideration: greater disfigurement costs twice what less apparent damage does. Knocking out a front tooth draws the same fine (6 shillings) as breaking an arm; the latter is a payment for physical damage, whereas the former can be seen as restitution for the permanently visible injury to honour. The farther back in the mouth the lost tooth, the lower the fine. This attribution is in direct contradiction to the physiological value. The incisors (front teeth) are used for cutting or ripping, but this function could be fulfilled by a knife, whereas the molars (back teeth) are irreplaceable for chewing food. The discrepancy between utility and amount of restitution required presents another example of an increased fine for greater visible damage. Similarly, the difference in price between the 3-shilling ear-piercing and the 9-shilling nose-piercing probably reflects the fact that an injury to the nose is more immediately apparent than one to the ear. This concern for physical appearance is not unique to Anglo-Saxon law: in early Old Irish law, for example, a blemished man is considered ineligible for kingship.[77]

The fingers are valued individually. Not surprisingly, the most expensive is the thumb, valued at 20 shillings: this is the digit that allows a man to use a tool effectively. In terms of pure physiological function, the next in worth should be the middle finger, and yet the second most highly valued is in fact the little finger. On the surface the choice seems surprising, as the little finger is functionally of very little use. However, in a world in which the handspan may serve as a measuring device, the loss of this digit becomes obvious whenever a measurement must be made; the seemingly arbitrary high value may be an instance of retribution for visual damage.[78] Next in worth is the forefinger, designated as the 'shooting finger': this is the finger that allows a man to shoot an arrow from a bow, and its value is obvious. Greater recompense for more visible damage probably underlies the difference between the 6-shilling ringfinger and the 4-shilling middle finger, as the only obvious advantage of the *goldfinger* or ringfinger is precisely its function as the bearer of the ring.

Liebermann indicates that it is difficult to imagine that a thumbnail could be struck off with barbarian weapons without damaging the flesh, and therefore claims that the ruling about 'offing' a thumbnail may belong to the realm of juristic theory.[79] Note, however, that the law does not state that the thumbnail is *struck* off, merely that it *becomes* off. The tearing out of either a thumbnail or fingernail was then and remains now an effective torture. It involves not only immediate pain, but also a degree of permanent damage: if a nail is pulled out by the root, it will not grow back. It then becomes more difficult to use the affected digit: not only is the fleshy stump unprotected, but the grasping power provided by the fingernail is lost.

The interpretation of certain clauses in these laws remains uncertain: they contain words whose meanings are obscure, because they neither appear elsewhere in the corpus of Old English nor have any unambiguous cognates. The first of these is found in §36: '*If the outer hion [?covering of the skull] becomes broken, let him pay with ten shillings.*' This clause appears as the fourth in the personal injury section: it follows the stipulation about pulling of hair (on which see below), and the two clauses dealing with recompense for exposing or cutting into a bone, which presumably lead the enumeration of body parts because they are concerned with any bone thus affected, rather than with a specific body part. We know from the article and adjective that *hion* is feminine: that it is a bone might be inferred from the use of the participle *gebrocen*, 'broken,' which is used elsewhere only for bones. The adjective *uterre*, 'outer,' implies that there is also an *innere*, 'inner,' which should be an aid to interpretation. Unfortunately the Old English collocations that contain both terms overwhelmingly refer to the 'outer' and 'inner' man (primarily in religious texts) or to property boundaries. I have found no parallel that seems apposite to this text.[80] On the basis of comparison with Continental Germanic laws, Liebermann compares *hion* to Modern German *Hirn* 'skull.'[81] Under this reading, cracking the 'outer' skull as opposed to the 'inner' membrane that encloses the brain would draw a fine of 12 shillings. The difficulty arises when this analysis is extended to the connected §36.1: 'If both [?outer covering and skull] should be [broken], let him pay 20 shillings.' First, the *dura mater*, or 'inner' membrane that surrounds the brain, is a rubbery, flexible substance that might be torn or pierced, but not broken (although Liebermann cites a parallel in the laws of Alfred in which *hyd*, 'skin,' is broken).[82] More crucially, it is almost impossible to damage the *dura mater* without causing injury to the brain, and it is difficult to believe that the fine for brain damage is less than that for laming a shoulder. Almost certainly mistaken is Liebermann's alternative association of the 'outer' and 'inner' *hion* with the *dura mater* and *pia mater*. The latter is a very thin membrane that surrounds the brain itself, and is barely apparent unless pointed out. Even if the Anglo-Saxons were aware of the existence of the *pia mater*, to wound this membrane and not cause massive cerebral damage is almost impossible.[83]

I prefer to return to the Continental parallels for a model. The Salic laws distinguish three types of blow to the head: one which causes blood to flow, one which lays bare the skull, and one which fractures the skull.[84] The penalty for the last injury is 30 shillings in relation to a *wergild* of 200 shillings, which is an even lower percentage (15 per cent) than a fine of 20 shillings in relation to a *wergild* of 100 shillings (20 per cent). Given the parallel in Alfred in which skin is broken, I would interpret *uterre hion* as the skin surrounding the skull, and the *innere* as the skull itself.

The second problematic term occurs in §68, which states in the Old English: '*Gif wælt wund weorðeþ, iii scillingas gebete.*' Here again, the difficulty is that *wælt* occurs nowhere else in the language. The first clause could be translated either 'if a *wælt* becomes wounded' or 'if a *wælt*-wound occurs.' Compare §62 *gif hrif wund weorðeþ*, which could be either 'if an abdomen becomes wounded' or 'if an abdominal wound occurs'; both §68 and §62 are grammatically ambiguous. Elsewhere in Germanic personal injury laws we find the compounds *hreuouunt* (in *Lex Alamannorum*; *hreuo ~ hrif + uunt ~ wund*) and *hreuauunt* (in *Lex Bavariorum*); it thus seems more prudent to translate these as elements of a compound in §62. But pre-Liebermann editors have tended to translate this clause with *hrif* as the subject and *wund* as the predicate.[85] This same interpretation was invoked for §68 on the assumption that *wælt* is the subject of the verb, with *wund* as the predicate adjective. But what body part should *wælt* represent? Old Frisian contains the compound *waldsine*, which Holthausen translates as *spina dorsa*.[86] However, a 3-shilling fine can in no way serve to recompense damage to the spinal column. The second element of the Frisian compound is related to the English 'sinew,' and Liebermann thus assumes, since the clause lies between one dealing with the thigh and one concerning the foot, that the postulated sinew is one in the leg. But the half of the compound that might be related to the Old English term is *wald*, 'back,' not *sine*, 'sinew.' Further, damage to a sinew of the leg almost invariably results in laming, and Æthelberht already deals with this issue in §65. Lastly, the fine of 3 shillings remains much too low for an injury of this nature.

The alternative is to translate *wælt-wund* as a compound. Taking this path, Jacob Grimm associates *wælt* with the root that gives us Old English *wealte*, 'ring,' and German *wälzen*, 'to turn,' assuming that the 'turning' in question was that of a needle used to sew up the wound. He thus interprets the phrase as 'a wound that can be stitched.'[87] Although the semantic connection is something of a stretch, this analysis would at least be consistent with the fine assigned. Even more directly, the first element of the compound could simply be the ancestor of the Modern English term 'welt.'[88] This allows for various interpretations. The *Oxford English Dictionary*'s definition 1 is 'a strip of leather placed between and sewn to the edge of the sole and the turned-in edge of the upper in soling a boot or shoe'; following this one might construe the compound as 'a wound that detaches a strip of skin.' The same dictionary's definition 6 is 'a stroke with a lash or pliant stick,' which might align the clause to §17.8 of the Salic laws: 'If a freeman strikes a freeman with a stick, so that no blood comes out, by *mallberg* called *wadfalt*, let him pay for each blow ... 3 shillings.' Note the parallelism in the amount of the fine.[89] Under any of these analyses, the clause would seem to be out of order in the head-to-toe enumeration.

The more attractive option in my opinion is to link the term to a meaning of 'welt' such as provided in OED definition 4c, 'a ridge on the flesh, especially the mark of a healed wound.' This would give rise to the interpretation, 'a wound which raises a welt/a wound which leaves a scar.' A welt left by such an injury would be a visible reminder not only of the physical damage but also of the offence to the wounded man's honour. The welt might be raised by a blow such as that described in the Frankish law cited above. It is also possible that the fine in this clause applies additionally to any of the wounds discussed in the foregoing clauses: if a clearly evident scar remains, a subsidiary payment of 3 shillings is assessed, paralleling, for example, the relative fines assessed for various teeth and fingers depending on their prominence. The three personal injury clauses following this stipulation refer respectively to the striking-off of feet, toes, or toenails; since a body part that has been forcibly removed is no longer available to show a welt, this assessment would be irrelevant to them.

We have no Anglo-Saxon attestations of *any* of the meanings of 'welt' discussed above, despite the fact that the verb *wyltan/wealtan*, 'to roll,' from which it derives is not uncommon. I hesitate to defer to an argument from silence in defining this term, given the lack of any more likely etymology. It is not impossible (or even implausible) that the noun existed in the Anglo-Saxon period but never elsewhere made its way into recorded texts.

A compound similarly ending in *-wund* can be found in the *cearwund*, 'grievously wounded' of §63.1.[90] This and the preceding clause seem to be inserted within the enumeration of fines due for wounding body parts, as they deal with the method and duration of a cure.

> 63. *If a person becomes cured [after having been wounded], let him [i.e., the person who caused the wound] pay [with] 30 shillings.*
> 63.1 *If a person should be grievously wounded, let him pay [with] 30 shillings.*

These clauses concern the law of sick maintenance: namely, the responsibility of a person towards another whom he has wounded if the injury disables the injured man so that he is unable to perform his work. If the wounded man incurs medical fees, the man who wounded him is liable for 30 shillings. Further, if the man should be disabled for a period of time, the perpetrator owes an additional 30-shilling fine. Parallels to these laws are not uncommon cross-culturally: they can be found, for example, in *Exodus* 21:18: '... he shall pay for the loss of his time, and shall cause him to be thoroughly healed.' Drawing on comparative evidence from Hittite and Old Irish sources, Calvert Watkins has postulated a law of sick maintenance for the Indo-European world.[91] The three basic tenets are that the perpetrator pay medical fees, and a recompense for the time lost at work, and that he provide someone to work in the place of the injured person. The stipulations in Æthelberht lack the crucial third provision that would unambiguously allow us to link these clauses to the Indo-European tradition. It is possible that they represent an ancient inheritance; alternatively, however, they may simply reflect a legal universal that can arise in any society at any time.[92] In Old Irish law of the eighth century, the practice of sick maintenance is already being replaced by monetary restitution, and we may be seeing a similar substitution in the Anglo-Saxon laws.[93]

Finally, I would like to return to the very first of the personal injury laws, which deals with *feaxfang*, 'the seizing of hair.' E.G. Stanley proposes an emendation of line 1537 of *Beowulf*, in which Beowulf's struggle with Grendel's mother begins. In Klaeber's edition, the line reads *Gefēng þā be eaxle – nalas for fǣhðe mearn*,[94] 'he seized her by the shoulder, not at all was he anxious about the feud.' Stanley suggests changing *eaxle*, 'by the shoulder,' to *feaxe*, 'by the hair,' thus both improving the alliterative structure and relating the action to §33 in Æthelberht. The first seems a more persuasive argument in favour of the alteration than the second. If one accepts Stanley's emendation the fight in fact begins with Beowulf seizing Grendel's mother by the hair and thereby dragging her to the floor. In the same manuscript, the eponymous heroine of *Judith* similarly drags the drunken Holofernus to the floor *be feaxe*, 'by the hair,' before chopping his head off.[95] The symbolic value of the seizing of hair would not be inapposite to these epic confrontations, as is shown in numerous cross-cultural examples. The biblical hero Samson, for example, is deprived of his strength when shorn of his hair and the evil magician Tschernamor in Pushkin's *Ruslan and Ludmilla* loses his magic power when his beard is chopped off. Closer to hand, the royal status of the Merovingian kings is demonstrated by their uncut hair.

Women and children

Women in this text appear in three categories: widows, maidens, and the *frīwīf locbore*, 'free woman in charge of the locks,' of §72. I will consider these laws in the order in which they may have affected a woman over the course of her lifetime, beginning with clauses dealing with maidens and marriage, then turning to those concerning women, and concluding with the stipulations about legal rights of widows. The laws of children are discussed in relationship to the status of their mother.

Maidens

> 73. *Compensation for [injury to/offense against] a maiden shall be as for a free man.*

Although Æthelberht's laws primarily consider maidens in the context of the marriage contract, we are told here that a maiden's compensation is the same as for a free man: this ruling probably refers not only to the price due to her kinsmen if she is slain, but also to compensation for injury or theft. This clause might be taken to refer solely to virgins, but in poetic texts *mægð* can also mean 'woman.' There is no ruling specifically stipulating the amount of restitution due to a married woman; it is likely, although not certain, that §73 simply equates women with men in terms of the amount of restitution due them for offence.

> 76. *If a person buys a maiden with a [bride-]price, let the bargain be [valid], if there is no deception.*
> 76.1 *If there is deception, afterwards let him bring [her to her] home, and let him be given his money.*

Whether the institution of marriage by purchase existed in Anglo-Saxon England has been a much-addressed question. The phrase *gif man mægþ gebigeð ceapi*, 'if a man buys a maid with a price,' is grammatically similar to H & E §11.2, *he þæt feoh ... ceape in wic gebohte*, 'he bought that animal ... with a price in the town.' A similar collocation appears in *Maxims* I, 81–2: *cyning sceal mid ceape cwene gebicgan, bunum ond beagum*, 'the king shall pay with a price for a queen, with goblets and rings,'[96] and in *Maxims* II, 44–5, it is stated that a woman must resort to secret crafts in seeking out her lover *gif heo nelle ... þæt hi man beagum gebicge*, 'if she does not wish ... that one should pay for her with rings.'[97] But the idea that a woman was merely transferred as chattel contradicts our knowledge of the strong position of women in Anglo-Saxon society.[98] Possibly the compound *bicgan*, 'to buy,' prefixed by the intensifier *ge-*, signifies in this context specifically the exchange of money to seal the marriage contract: what in later years would come to be known as a dower.

Christine Fell identifies this transfer of money with the *morgengifu*, 'morning-gift,' and claims that 'it is paid not to the father or kin, but to the woman herself. She then has personal control over it, to give away, to sell or to bequeath as she chooses.'[99] I am not convinced that the dower and the morning-gift are identical in this period: traditionally, the morning-gift is given by a husband to his wife on the morning after the marriage is consummated (hence the name). The earliest Old Irish legal practice seems to have differentiated between the *tindscra*, or bride-price, and the *coibche*, which is given to the woman once she has successfully given birth to a son.[100]

Clearly in fairy tale rather than philology mode, Jacob Grimm interprets the formalities of betrothal differently, reading *in sceat* (translated here as 'with a [bride-]price') as 'in the lap,' and comparing a custom discussed in Norse folksongs in which a betrothal is formally sealed by the groom's taking the bride onto his lap.[101] Opera fans may see a parallel in Baron Ochs's treatment of Sophie in the second act of *Der Rosenkavalier*. Grimm's interpretation of this clause in Æthelberht seems indeed closer to comic opera than to legal verity.

> 76.5 *If she does not bear a child, her paternal kin should obtain [her] property and the morning-gift.*

Æthelberht §76.5 states that on the death of a childless widow, both her property and the morning-gift return to her family. The distinction here is probably between property she brought into the marriage and that which her husband gave her: the crucial fact is that during her lifetime the woman retains possession of her morning-gift. Later Anglo-Saxon wills show women bequeathing the land they had received as their morning-gift, and this tradition is continued in some place names. In Sussex, for instance, plots called Morgay Farm and Morgay Wood retain a first element that comes from the word *morgengifu*.[102]

A man who legitimately seals a marriage contract with a bride-price obtains a money-back guarantee that the bargain will contain no deceit: this almost surely refers to the certainty that he is marrying a virgin, although other forms of deception may also have been contemplated. In Sanskrit law, for example, a blind girl may have been passed off without disclosing the flaw.[103] Certainly virginity is important to establish the legitimacy of the line of succession and to ensure that the children a man raises are, in fact, his own. If the intended wife is not a virgin she can be returned, and the bride-price is refunded. Laws permitting the return of non-virginal spouses are found throughout the Indo-European world. The early Welsh laws of Hywel Dda even stipulate how this is to be proven: 'If immediately after he finds her to be corrupted he rises to the wedding guests with his penis erect, and testifies to them that he found her corrupted, and he does not sleep with her until the morrow, she is not entitled on the morrow to anything from him.'[104]

> 77. If a person takes a maiden by force: to the owner [of her protection] 50 shillings, and afterwards let him buy from the owner his consent [to marry her].
> 77.1. If she should be betrothed to another man by goods [i.e., the bride-price has been paid], let him pay 20 shillings [to that man as well].
> 77.2. If return [of the stolen maiden] occurs, 35 shillings and 15 shillings to the king.

The institution of marriage by capture can probably be dated back to Indo-European, as we find it in both Greek and Sanskrit;[105] the alliteration in *nede genimeþ*, 'takes by force,' in §77 may be an archaic remnant from Germanic legal poetic prose.[106] One who abducts (or rapes?) a maiden must pay the owner of her protection 50 shillings; only the highest rank of widow is compensated for abduction as highly. The fine is not the end of the matter, for the man must then negotiate a bride-price with the owner of the maiden's protection. If a marriage contract with another man has already been made, the abductor must pay that man another 20 shillings. The total fine is then 70 shillings, plus the bride-price if the abductor marries the girl. For this sum, you could cut off someone's foot *and* break his (or her) jawbone – and this doesn't even include the bride-price!

Clause 77.2 has recently come under considerable scrutiny, due to new interpretations of the otherwise unattested *gængang*. Certainly, as Fell points out, the constitutents of the compound 'are neither etymologically nor lexically opaque.'[107] The first element, *gæn*, is cognate with German *gegen*, 'against,' and in Old English can mean either 'opposition' or 'return.' The second element, *gang*, means 'path' or 'journey.' Liebermann interprets the whole along the lines of 'journey of return'; according to his interpretation, if the marriage by abduction is thwarted in time and the abductor returns the stolen maiden to her home still in a virginal state, he must pay 35 shillings to the owner of the maiden's protection, and a further 15 shillings to the king. These fines represent an allocation of the 50-shilling total discussed in §77.[108]

The Laws of Æthelberht 109

Carole Hough finds it odd that a fine should be payable to the king for this particular offence. Elsewhere in Æthelberht fines are payable to the king for more public delicts, such as defaulting the responsibility for feeding the king, disturbance of the peace, killing a person, or abetting robbery. Hough thus translates the first element as per German *gegen*, 'against,' and interprets the term along the lines of 'a going against.' She argues that *gængang* could refer to a hostile attack upon a woman, comparing it to clauses in Continental laws in which an attack on a woman on the road is fined more heavily than a similar attack against a man. This clause might then be interpreted as independent of the laws dealing with marriage by abduction. Conversely, it could be that an additional fine is levied if the abduction is achieved by violent attack.[109] Fell adds another possible interpretation to Hough's reading: namely, that the abductor and the man to whom the woman was betrothed came to blows (a 'going against'). She herself admits that it is difficult to determine under this reading why the fine has been reduced, and to whom the 35 shillings is payable, but argues correctly for the necessity of keeping an open mind when addressing any of these hapax words.

While I agree with Fell in general, in this instance I think comparative evidence overrides these new analyses. Several Continental laws contain clauses concerning the return of the abducted woman.[110] To cite merely one, §12.2 of the late sixth-century Burgundian law begins: *Si vero puella, quae rapta est, incorrupta redierit ad parentes* ... 'If indeed the girl, who has been abducted, returns uncorrupted to her parents ...'[111] Furthermore, the payment to the king could be seen as a type of payment for robbery, for which there are parallels elsewhere in Æthelberht's laws (see Appendix 3 and discussion under 'Theft' above).

Women

31. *If a freeman lies with a free man's wife, let him pay recompense [with] his/her wergild and obtain another wife [for the husband] [with] his own money and bring her to the other man at home.*

While abducting a maiden draws a 50-shilling fine, sleeping with a married woman is twice as costly, as it is fined with one *wergild*, or 100 shillings (see §24). Whether this is the man's or woman's *wergild* is grammatically ambiguous, and I know of no comparative evidence that would illuminate the issue. But if we accept §73 as reading that a woman's compensation is equal to a man's, the ambiguity does not affect the amount.[112] The husband has a right to divorce.[113] Just as in the case of the blemished virgin (discussed above), he now has damaged goods. It is not clear whether the woman is complicit in this affair or not (although if she is, clearly the *wergild* must go to her husband); nor is there any indication of what happens to the ex-wife afterwards. Roughly contemporary canon laws state that a wife guilty of adultery can be driven from the house[114] – presumably with the choice of returning to her parental kin or allying herself with her guilty partner. It is the responsibility of the adulterous man to provide the injured husband with a new wife. Attenborough points out that '[i]t would seem that the injured husband in Kent was not difficult to please, unless we are to suppose, with Liebermann, that his consent in regard to the choice of the lady was secured beforehand – but the law, at all events, gives no hint of such a stipulation.'[115]

72. *If a free woman in charge of the locks does anything seriously dishonest, let her pay 30 shillings.*

Until recently, the term *frīwīf locbore* has been translated along the lines of 'freewoman bearing locks.' All translators assumed that the locks in question referred to a hair style that distinguished a married woman from an unmarried one, or a free woman from a slave, or even a virtuous woman from a licentious one.[116] The first possibility seems the strongest, since the Lombard laws distinguish between married women and women *in capillo/capillis*, 'with hair,' which seems to mark the latter as unmarried. Further, from the Lombard territories we have a ninth-century relief in the church of S Maria della Valle in Cividale which shows veiled women and women with free-flowing locks. Giorgio Ausenda assumes that 'a maiden's misconduct was economically more damaging than that of a married woman, because the unmarried girl, as long as she was a real or presumed virgin, could be "bought" and given a considerable *morgengifu* which could potentially benefit her agnatic relatives in case of inheritance."[117] Certainly the economic argument seems valid; however, all of these analyses must remain speculative, as we possess no definite knowledge of coiffure styles for Anglo-Saxon women.

As the basis for an alternative hypothesis, Christine Fell adduces from much closer to hand the archaeological evidence of the key-shaped objects called 'girdle-hangers' (as they hang from the belt) found in several early women's graves, citing Hawkes's report on a cemetery at Polhill: 'Anglo-Saxon women were frequently buried with one or more keys or latch-lifters. At Polhill, the large specimens ... are likely to have been door keys, either for house or store-room. They must surely indicate that the women who carried them occupied a position of domestic responsibility in the community, and it is interesting to note that these were not the women buried with jewellery. It looks, therefore, as if the female grave-goods reflect some class distinction, and that the key-bearer was not the lady of the house but the housekeeper.'[118] Fell thus argues that the locks referred to here are of the type opened with keys, and relates -*bore* to its alternative meaning 'in charge of' (as opposed to 'bearing'), giving a translation of 'free woman in charge of the locks.' She assumes, then, that the woman under discussion is the one charged with maintaining the household; §72 represents a fine for embezzlement on the job.[119] Henrietta Leyser does not so categorically divide housekeeper and wife, suggesting rather that the keys simply provide a physical token of the role of guardian of a household and its contents.[120] It is hard, however, under this interpretaton, to account for the separation between graves containing keys and those containing jewellery. But given the archaeological evidence of the girdle-hangers and keys, the argument that §72 refers to a woman in charge of a household seems plausible.

The nature of the woman's dishonesty is difficult to determine. Since the keys give her access to locked treasure, it seems that the crime should be theft. Elsewhere in the laws, however, theft is always fined as a multiple of the value stolen. (Perhaps she is the inside contact for robbers from without?) It seems clear that the dishonesty in which she engages does not represent adultery, as this offence is already covered in §31.

Widows

> 74. *[For violation of] protection of the foremost widow of noble rank, let him pay 50 shillings.*
> 74.1. *[For a widow] of the second [rank], 20 shillings.*
> 74.2. *[For a widow] of the third [rank], 12 shillings.*
> 74.3. *[For a widow] of the fourth [rank], 6 shillings.*
> 75. *If a person takes a widow who does not belong to him, the [payment for violation of] protection shall be 2[-fold] as compensation.*

Widows are divided into four ranks. The protection for the lowest is the same as that for a freeman (6 shillings), for the second-lowest, the same as that accorded to a nobleman (12 shillings). There are two higher ranks, whose protection is 20 shillings and 50 shillings respectively: the latter amount equals the king's protection. It seems reasonable to assume that the ranking is dependent on whose protection the widow is under (i.e., who could bestow her hand and marriage portion on one of his dependents). A widow of lowest rank, then, is presumably under the protection of a freeman, one of the next rank under the protection of a nobleman, and the two higher under the protection of the king himself; the division at this level could be between non-related noble widows under the direct protection of the king and widows of the royal family.

Throughout the Middle Ages, widows were valuable commodities if they inherited property from their husbands. After Æthelberht died, his second wife was claimed by his son, and, towards the end of the Anglo-Saxon period, King Cnut married the widow of Æthelred II; both were manoeuvres to secure the kingship.[121] The term *unagen*, 'unowned,' in §75 probably means that the widow has no kin to protect her. If she is thus vulnerable, the recompense for a violation of her protection is twice what it would be otherwise.[122]

> 76.2 *If she [=a wife] bears a living child, let her obtain half the goods [belonging to the household] if the husband dies first.*

This ruling is augmented by Hloþhere & Eadric §4. '*If a freeman should die with a living wife and child, it is right that it, that child, should be under the protection of the mother, and one should give for him one among his father's kin who willingly gives surety to maintain his property, until he should be 10 years old.*' Clause 76.2 from Æthelberht directly follows the stipulations about the undeceptive marriage discussed above, but focuses on what happens to the widow and her children if her husband should die before she does. A woman who has borne a child receives half the property of the household should her husband predecease her; this property remains hers as long as she lives with the child(ren). Hloþhere & Eadric §4 tells us that the child of a deceased father should follow its mother, allowing her the option of returning to her own kin group. (Clause 38 in the late seventh-century West Saxon laws of Ine similarly stipulates that the child should remain with its mother.)[123] Meanwhile, a member of the paternal kin group is made responsible for protecting the child's property until he reaches ten years of age, the legal age of inheritance. (By comparison, fifteen was the age of majority, and a child as young as seven could be given to a monastery for upbringing.)

The next two clauses have recently been given a new interpretation by Carole Hough;[124] her translation is given below, with the newly analysed words underlined.

> 76.3 If she should wish to dwell with the children, let her obtain half the goods [of the household].
>
> 76.4 If she should wish to take a man [i.e., another husband], provision as for one child [i.e., the inheritance is split equally between the mother and each of the children].

The contested word in §76.3 is *bugan*, which has various meanings (from two different etymological sources), among them 'to turn, change direction' or 'to dwell, inhabit.' Previous translators have all followed the first option. Whitelock, for example, renders the clause: 'If she wishes to go away with the children ...'[125] This rendering has sparked reams of discussion about early Anglo-Saxon 'divorce laws,' for which there is no other real evidence. Hough chooses rather to translate *bugan* as 'dwell,' with the interpretation that as long as a widow lives with her children, she retains use of half the goods of the marital household. This concept of child support is well-attested throughout Continental laws.

Hough's interpretation crucially ties §76.3 to the next one. Here the phrase in question is *Gif ceorl agan wile, swa an bearn*. In this instance the ambiguity is grammatical rather than lexical. While the term *ceorl* can mean 'man,' 'freeman,' or 'husband' in this context it must clearly be taken as husband. In form, it can be either nominative or accusative: that is, it can serve as the subject or object of the verb *wille*, 'should wish to.' All previous translators have chosen to take it as the subject, with the children of the divorce the implied object. Thus Whitelock renders the clause: 'If the husband wishes to keep [the children], [she is to have the same share] as a child.'[126] But if, as Hough argues, there has been no divorce, this interpretation makes no sense. Hough chooses a perfectly acceptable alternative translation of *agan* as 'take,' and assumes that the implied subject is the widowed woman, with a new husband as the object, and translates the phrase: 'If she wishes to take [another] husband ...' That is, if the widow takes a second husband, she is no longer entitled to half the household property for child support, but inherits 'as one child': namely, the inheritance is split equally between the wife and each of the children. (This is the first reference to the Kentish practice of gavelkind, by which the oldest child is not the sole heir, but rather the inheritance is divided among the children.

The youngest decides the portions and keeps the hearth; the oldest gets first choice.)[127] Whether the children go with her or remain to be raised by their fathers' kin is not addressed, although parallels from Continental law would imply the latter. The parallels Hough adduces both from Continental Germanic laws and from later Anglo-Saxon laws and wills present a thoroughly convincing case according to which the 'Anglo-Saxon divorce laws' should now be abandoned.

Servants

78. *If a person lies with a servant's wife while the husband is alive, let him pay 2[-fold what he would have paid were she unmarried].*
79. *If a servant should kill another [who is] guiltless, let him pay [the dead man's master] the entire worth.*
80. *If servant's eye or foot becomes struck off, let him pay him [i.e., the servant's master] the entire worth.*
81. *If a person binds a person's servant, let him pay [with] 6 shillings.*

(Consider here also these first clauses from Hloþhere & Eadric.)

1. *If a person's servant kills a man of noble birth, who should be compensated for with three hundred shillings, the owner should give up that killer and add three man-worths.*
   1.1. *If the killer should escape, he should add a fourth man-worth and clear himself with good oath-helpers, that he was not able to seize the killer.*
2. *If a person's servant kills a free man, who should be compensated for with a hundred shillings, the owner should give up that killer and another man-worth in addition.*
   2.1. *If the killer should escape, [the owner] should compensate him with two man-worths, and clear himself with good oath-helpers, that he was not able to seize the killer.*

The term translated here as 'servant' is the Old English *esne*. An *esne* was probably a labourer: either a hired hand, or one who owed part of his produce to a master (see note c to §78 in translation). This rank had intermediate status between a freeman and a slave. The clause about sleeping with an *esne*'s wife uses the term *ceorl*, which elsewhere in the laws can mean 'man,' 'husband,' or 'freeman,' although the last meaning predominates in these texts. This linking of both terms in one phrase may imply that there is at least semantically a connection between the *esne* and the freeman. However, the fine for killing an *esne* is not referred to in terms of a freeman's *wergild*, but of 'entire worth.' As he is not a freeman, his recompense is reckoned by his value as a labourer. Furthermore, in Hloþhere & Eadric, the *esne* has an *agend*, 'owner,' which implies a non-free status for this rank.

The interpretation of §80 is ambiguous, since ⁊ can stand for either 'and' or 'or'; I have translated it as the latter, as it seems odd that someone should destroy both a foot *and* an eye. The parallel with the biblical collocation of 'the halt and the blind' is interesting, but since there is no other biblical reference in this text of which I am aware, I hesitate to make much of it.

The fine for binding a servant is only 6 shillings as compared to the freeman's 20. Although the offence is the same, the insult factor is less for a man who is already bound in another sense.

The first clauses in Hloþhere & Eadric state unambiguously that a master is responsible for the fines incurred if his servant kills a freeman or noble. Æthelbert §79 implies that it is the servant who pays the fine if he kills another of his own rank, and the later laws of Wihtred indicate that even slaves might own money. It is, however, possible that the understood subject of the verb is the servant's master rather than the servant himself (see the parallel for slaves discussed under 'Theft' above). In Hloþhere & Eadric, if the servant can be caught, the owner turns him over to the kin of the slain person and adds, in the case of a nobleman, three man-worths (i.e., the *weorþ*, 'worth,' of an unfree servant, not the *wergild*, 'manprice,' paid for a freeman), in the case of a freeman, one man-worth. In other words, a slain noble's family receives the equivalent of four servants, whereas a slain freeman's family receives the equivalent of two. If the servant escapes, the owner substitutes for him his value and must also give his oath that he was unable to catch the killer (presumably to prove that the owner was not complicit in the killing).

Liebermann assumes that the term *esne* in these clauses should be taken to include all unfree men, including the *þeow*, or slave.[128] Perhaps Æbt §§78–81, which specifically mention *esnas*, also pertain to the rank of *þeow*, the final two clauses then adding stipulations specific to slaves. Although Hloþhere & Eadric's laws never use the word *þeow*, there is no question but that the rank of slave existed during their reign. Wihtred's text uses both terms. The similarity between the two positions is demonstrated by the fact that both *esne* and *þeow* are subject to flogging as punishment, as shown in W §§8.1 and 10 respectively. On the other hand, W §8 stipulates the fine for an *esne* who performs *þeowweorc,* 'slave work,' on Sunday. Presumably such work is in contradiction to work the *esne* perfoms for his own benefit. Wihtred §18 refers to a *þeowne esne,* 'unfree *esne,*' although this would appear to be at least a partial redundancy.

Slaves

> 82. *A slave's highway robbery shall be [paid for with] 3 shillings.*
> 83. *If a slave steals, let him pay 2[-fold] as compensation.*

Both of the laws dealing with slaves concern restitution for theft and are discussed above under 'Theft.'

As observed above, in the absence of an epilogue, there is no way of telling whether the text is complete as we have it; it is also possible that internal sections or clauses have been omitted in the extant copy.[129]

3

The Laws of Hloþhere & Eadric

Historical background

Under Æthelberht's reign, Christianity had spread to the neighbouring kingdom of Essex, which was ruled by his nephew Sæberht. As *imperator* of all the territories south of the Humber, Æthelberht would have been overlord as well as uncle to Sæberht. (It was during Sæberht's reign that Æthelberht established the church of St Paul in London, the seat of the bishopric.) Further, Rædwald, king of the East Angles, was converted at Æthelberht's court, but his conversion seems to have been at best half-hearted,[1] for Bede ii.15 tells us that '[o]n his return home, he was seduced by his wife and by certain evil teachers and perverted from the sincerity of his faith, so that his last state was worse than the first. After the manner of the ancient Samaritans [who had a tendency to adopt the gods of other nations], he seemed to be serving both Christ and the gods he had previously served; in the same temple he had one altar for the Christian sacrifice and another small altar on which to offer victims to devils.'[2] The tenuous position of Christianity is demonstrated by the fact that both Æthelberht and Sæberht were succeeded by sons who had never professed the new religion.[3] Æthelberht's son Eadbald, who ruled until 640, was a pagan at the time of his accession and married his stepmother, Æthelberht's second wife, in a time-honoured Germanic method of consolidating power.[4] Bede does not conceal his horror as he goes on to say that the beginning of Eadbald's rule caused: 'a severe setback to the tender growth of the Church. Not only had he refused to receive the faith of Christ, but he was polluted with such fornication as the apostle declares to have been not so much as named among the Gentiles, in that he took his father's wife. By both of these crimes he gave the occasion to return to their own vomit to those who had accepted the laws of faith and continence during his father's reign.'[5]

The reversion to heathenism spread to the East Saxons when Sæberht's three sons took over the kingdom upon his death. Having apparently renounced paganism during their father's reign, they now allowed their subjects to worship pagan gods openly, and drove out Mellitus, the bishop of London. He fled to join Justus and Laurence, his fellow bishops in Kent, and the three ecclesiastics decided to abandon the island kingdoms in the throes of pagan reversion and return to a more civilized Gaul. Mellitus and Justus went first, leaving Laurence to follow. Bede ii.6 tells us that it was only by a miracle that the future of Christianity was ensured in the southern English kingdoms:

> As [Laurence] slept the blessed prince of the apostles appeared to him and in the dead of night scourged him hard and long. Then St. Peter asked him with apostolic severity why he had left the flock which he himself had entrusted to him; or to what shepherd he would commit the sheep of Christ when he ran away and left them in the midst of wolves ... Deeply moved by the scourgings and exhortations of St. Peter, Christ's servant Laurence went to the king [Eadbald] as soon as morning had come, drew back his robe and showed him the marks of his stripes. The king was amazed and asked who had dared to inflict such injuries on so great a man. When he heard that it was for the sake of his salvation that the bishop had suffered such torments and wounds at the hands of the apostle of Christ, he was greatly afraid. So he banned all idolatrous worship, gave up his unlawful wife, accepted the Christian faith, and was baptized; and thereafter he promoted and furthered the interests of the Church to the best of his ability.[6]

For many reasons, it is difficult to give this story much credence; the fact that the events take place in the monastery of St Augustine's in Canterbury gives rise to the supposition that it represents part of the hagiographical legend growing up around Augustine. More likely the true motivation for Laurence's decision to stay was a papal admonishment.[7] But there may also have been some Frankish pressure on Eadbald to renounce paganism: once he had converted, he repudiated the stepmother he had taken as his wife and married a Frankish princess who was, of course, already Christian.[8] The Frankish connection through marriage, as between Æthelberht and Bertha, was thus reaffirmed. Eadbald certainly did his part in promoting the new religion when he refused to allow Edwin, king of Northumbria, to marry Æthelberht's daughter Æthelburh (who went by the somewhat unusual nickname of *Tate*, 'the Merry')[9] until he converted to Christianity.[10]

At Eadbald's death in 640 the throne passed to his son Eorcenberht;[11] it was he, according to Bede iii.8, who 'was the first English king to order idols to be abandoned and destroyed throughout the whole kingdom.'[12] As discussed below, isolated pockets of paganism must have remained in Kent at least until the reign of Wihtred. But the prevalence of 'idols' in the early days of the reign of Eorcenberht casts an interesting light on the nature of Æthelberht's conversion. Wallace-Hadrill speculates that 'it may have been under his pagan gods that he won military overlordship throughout central and southern England, and held it, at least till the rise of Rædwald in East Anglia. His ultimate conversion, by missionaries who were neither Frankish nor British, but Roman, may perhaps betray some waning of his star, though not his abandonment of all that he understood by paganism. In general, Germanic conversions of this period signified not total abandonment of the pagan gods but acceptance of an additional god.'[13]

Bede claims that Eorcenberht, in addition to destroying the idols, 'also ordered the forty days fast of Lent to be observed by royal authority. And so that his commands might not be too lightly neglected, he prescribed suitably heavy punishments for offenders.'[14] Liebermann and Stubbs both postulate that Bede's reference may allude to a written body of laws that has not come down to us.[15]

In 664 there was a solar eclipse, followed by a plague, of which Eorcenberht died. He was succeeded by his eldest son, Egbert; it was in the latter's reign that Theodore of Tarsus became archbishop of Canterbury and established that town as a great centre of learning. Egbert – following a cross-culturally popular method of ensuring familial succession – had his two nephews put to death to prevent their later contending for the throne.[16] But when Egbert died unexpectedly in 673 his own sons were still children and the rule thus passed to his brother, Hloþhere. The *Anglo-Saxon Chronicle* tells us that in 678 'the star "comet" appeared in August, and shone every morning for three months, like a sunbeam';[17] this may actually have been a bad omen for Hloþhere's reign. In 679 a charter granting land to Abbot Beorhtwald names Eadric, son of Egbert, together with Hloþhere. Joint rule was not unusual in Kent, with the senior king presiding at Canterbury, and the junior ruling from Rochester.[18] This charter implies that Hloþhere had probably already designated Eadric as heir and also acknowledged

120 The Beginnings of English Law

him as co-ruler.[19] Unfortunately for Hloþhere, this proved to be a poor choice. In 684 Eadric conspired with an army from Sussex to invade Kent, and in February of the following year, Hloþhere died of wounds received in battle. Eadric ruled alone until his death in 686. As S.E. Kelly points out, 'Eadric's position was probably insecure, and it seems significant that a charter in his name in St. Augustine's archive (7) includes a statement of his legitimacy, such as is found in the charters of the slightly later usurper Oswine.'[20] Following a period of external incursions on the kingship (discussed in chapter 4), Eadric was succeeded by his brother Wihtred.

The laws of Hloþhere & Eadric need not necessarily be dated to the period of their brief joint rule between 679 and 685. Although the rubric attributes the text to both kings, it is possible that what remains to us actually represents a conflation of laws separately issued by the two kings, or that Eadric may have confirmed the laws of his uncle in an attempt to shore up his own tenuous hold on the kingship.[21] A sure *terminus post quem non* for this compilation is Eadric's death in 686. Liebermann points out that an indirect argument for the authenticity of the text is provided by the lack of fame attached to either of these rulers. Who, he asks, ever thought about them again after their deaths, and what later forger would choose these two kings with whom to associate this text?[22]

The direct time line for the genealogical succession of line of Æthelberht in Kent can be set up as follows:[23]

Æthelberht (r. 587/90x3–616x18)
|
Eadbald (r. 616x18–640)
|
Eorcenberht (r. 640-664)
|
Egbert (r. 664-673) — Hloþhere (r. 673-685)
|
Eadric (r. ca. 679-686) — Wihtred (r. 690-725)

Some notes on the language

The striking trait of the laws of Hloþhere & Eadric is that the language of the text as it appears in the *Textus Roffensis* (the only copy remaining to us) is more modern than that employed in the existing copy of either Æthelberht or Wihtred. There are both fewer archaic elements and more late Old English features. Furthermore, the laws differ in scribal style from those of the other two texts in that they employ abbreviation much more frequently. While we do not have access to any of the earlier manuscripts of Kentish law used by the *Textus Roffensis* scribe in making his compilation, it is clear that even if Æthelberht's and Wihtred's texts had followed the same route of transmission – and there is nothing to argue for or against this possibility – the manuscript of Hloþhere & Eadric ultimately arrived at the desk of the *Textus Roffensis* compiler by a different course, during the process of which the language was updated by an intermediate scribe to a greater extent than was the case for the other Kentish laws that have come down to us. (Whether the texts were ultimately reunited before or at the time of the compilation of the *Textus Roffensis* is impossible to determine.) One might hypothesize that the procedural rulings of Hloþhere & Eadric remained relevant longer than the stipulations laid out in the other laws, causing them to be recopied later and linguistically modernized in the process. This is a dangerous argument from silence, however, because there may also have been more modernized copies of the others for which we have simply lost any evidence.

The syntax of the laws of Hloþhere & Eadric is more involved than that displayed in Æthelberht's rulings. The relative complexity might be attributed in part to the fact that, while the laws of Æthelberht seem to be largely based on an oral original,[24] those of Hloþhere & Eadric were (at least to an extent) probably first cast in the medium of writing (see discussion below under 'Rubric and prologue' in Commentary).

Archaisms

As discussed in chapter 1, there are only a few traces of archaic linguistic structures to be found in Hloþhere & Eadric. These are as follows:

1. The representation of the dental fricative as d in *medle* for *meðle*, 'public assembly' (§6), and *hwæder* for *hwæðer*, 'whether' (§6.2).
2. The archaic genitive singular in -æs, retained only once, in *cyngæs*, 'of the king' (§11.1), although the middle syllable has been syncopated, as it is in the more modern genitive *cynges* (§5). The trisyllabic form is retained in the dative *cyninge* (§7).
3. The use of the archaic dative of quantity in *twam manwyrþum*, 'with two man-worths' (§2.1).
4. Although Eduard Sievers claims that *bismærwordum*, 'with mocking words' (§7), demonstrates an archaic use of æ,[25] this spelling is also typical of scriptorial practice in Kent at roughly the time the manuscript was compiled.[26]

Modernizations

There are far more modern features in the copy we have of the laws of Hloþhere & Eadric than appear in either Æthelberht or Wihtred. By 'modern' I mean specifically elements that indicate that the grammar of Old English was already beginning to lose certain distinctions of case (for nouns) and tense or mood (for verbs), particularly as unstressed vowels began to merge into schwa, and thus lose their identity. This development is typical of later stages of both the Kentish dialect and the West-Saxon literary koiné which is considered 'Classical' Old English.[27] As the distinctions of case and tense or mood would have been more strictly maintained at the time of the initial recording of these laws (they are, in fact, preserved, at least in part, in the copies we have of the other Kentish laws), the instances in which we find syncretism atypical of the late seventh century can be seen as modernizations made by a later copyist.

The use of e in place of Classical Old English a occurs in *seþ* for the third person plural indicative *sægaþ*, 'they say' (Prologue); *bane* for the nominative singular *bana*, 'killer' (§1.1; note that the correct form appears in §2.1); *þare* for the genitive plural demonstrative *þara* 'their' (§3); *begeten* for the infinitive *begetan*, 'seize' (§§1.1 and 2.1); and *gebrengen* for the infinitive *gebrengan*, 'bring' (§11.1). Conversely, the use of a in place of Classical Old English e occurs in *cuma* for the third person singular subjunctive *cume*, 'will come' (§3) and – even more tellingly for the breakdown of unstressed vowels – *cumin* for the past participle *cumen*, 'come' (§10). And æ replaces e once, in *gesecæn* for the third person plural present subjunctive *gesecen*, 'let them seek.'

There is similar confusion of the stressed vowel in the word *þane* for the accusative singular masculine demonstrative *þone*, 'that,' in which we find the replacement of o by a (§§1, 1.1, 2, 2.1, 6, 11.1), a frequent occurrence in later manuscripts.[28] Note, however, that the o is retained in §§1 and 2, which is interesting given that these are the same clauses that exhibit the archaic syntactic case use of the dative of quantity. Clauses 11.2 and 11.3 similarly give us *ðanne/þanne*, 'then,' where elsewhere we see *þonne* (cf. §§10, 11).

Dialect features

The laws of Hloþhere & Eadric demonstrate a mixture of dialect forms, which might be attributed to a series of copies emanating from scriptoria of different dialect regions.

Both the dative singular and nominative plural of *man* regularly appear as *mæn* (§§5, 8, 9, 9.1, 10, 11.1 [2x]), with the vowel exhibiting an intermediate form of the i-mutation of a (which Campbell says remains to Middle English in 'a limited south-eastern area, including Essex, but not Kent').[29] In one instance, the dative is preceded by the demonstrative *þem* for *þam*, a typically Kentish form.[30] Similarly we once get *wes* for *wæs*, 'was' (§6.1), and there is the rather odd *medder*, 'mother,' in §4, in place of the more usual accusative singular *modor*.

The form *sio* appears several times for the third person singular subjunctive *sie* 'let it be' (§§1, 6.1, 6.2 [2x], 10, although *sie* is used in §§2, 4). The only other uses Campbell cites of this form are found in the Kentish Glosses and in Kentish charters,[31] although Brunner claims that it also appears in eleventh-century West-Saxon texts.[32] *Sio* is also used for the feminine singular demonstrative, which is more usually *seo*. Campbell cites West-Saxon and Northumbrian forms, but none from Kent;[33] Sisam claims that these *io* forms are 'usually associated with South-Eastern dialects,' citing also the dative plural third-person pronoun *hiom*, which we find here in §§6 and 6.2.[34] If indeed the *eo* and *io* forms are confused 'in Kentish ... from the early-ninth century onwards, and *io* for *eo* is characteristic of Kentish at the end of the tenth century,'[35] this may give us some indication as to the age of the exemplar from which the scribe of the *Textus Roffensis* was copying. The usage is not consistent, however: W §21 uses the form *heom*, which first appears in the tenth century Rushworth Gospels and becomes a common feature of eleventh-century West Saxon.[36]

Substitutions of y for e are typical in the Kentish Glosses[37] and are in fact a common feature of Kentish from the tenth century on.[38] There are several examples in evidence here: *hyr*, 'here' (Prologue), *gylde*, 'should be compensated for with' (§1, vs. *gelde* §3), *acwyle*, 'he should die' (§4), and *agylde*, 'let him pay' (§6.1). We also find y replacing the diphthong eo in *manwyrð*, 'man-worth' (§§1.1, 2.1, vs. *weorð* §11.2).[39]

Abbreviations

While the texts of neither Æthelberht nor Wihtred make much use of abbreviation beyond the standard ⁊ for 'and' or 'or,' the copy of Hloþhere & Eadric often employs þ̄ for *þæt*, 'that,' and þoñ for *þonne*, 'then.'

EDITION AND TRANSLATION

þis syndon þa domas ðe Hloþhære ⁊ Eadric Cantwara cyningas asetton.[a]

Hloþhære ⁊ Eadric, Cantwara cyningas,[b] ecton þa æ þa ðe heora aldoras ær geworhton[c] ðyssum domum, þe hyr efter sægeþ.
1. Gif mannes esne eorlcundne mannan ofslæhð, þane ðe sio [1]
þreom hundum scill gylde, se agend þone banan agefe ⁊ do þær þrio manwyrð to.
    1.1. Gif se bane oþbyrste, feorþe manwyrð he to gedo ⁊ [2]
    hine gecænne mid godum æwdum[d] þæt he þane banan begeten ne mihte.
2. Gif mannes esne /4r/ frigne mannan ofslæhð, þane þe sie [3]
hund scillinga gelde, se agend þone banan agefe ⁊ oþer manwyrð þær tó.
    2.1. Gif bana oþbyrste, twam manwyrþum hine man [4]
    forgelde ⁊ hine gecænne mid godum æwdum, þæt he þane banan begeten ne mihte.

---

a N is stretched to fill end of line.
b as written above insertion mark.
c N is stretched to fill end of line.
d æ on erasure. See note b to translation on *æwdum*.

The Laws of Hloþhere & Eadric

These are the decrees which Hloþhere and Eadric, kings of the Kentish people, set.

Hloþhere and Eadric, kings of the people of Kent, added to the laws that their ancestors made before with these decrees, which are stated hereafter.

1. If a person's servant kills a man of noble birth, who should be compensated for with three hundred shillings,[a] the owner should give up that killer and add three man-worths.
    1.1. If the killer should escape, he should add a fourth man-worth and clear himself with good oath-helpers[b] that he was not able to seize the killer.
2. If a person's servant kills a free man, who should be compensated for with a hundred shillings,[c] the owner should give up that killer and another man-worth in addition.
    2.1. If the killer should escape, [the owner] should compensate him with two man-worths, and clear himself with good oath-helpers that he was not able to seize the killer.

---

a That is, his *wergild* is 300 shillings.

b The term *æwda(mann)* does not occur outside the Kentish laws. The first element is obviously connected to *æw* 'law,' but the etymology of the remainder is obscure. An attractive suggestion, proposed by an anonymous reader of this manuscript, is that it may be connected with *wed-* 'pledge, security,' giving an original **æwwedum* with subsequent syncopy of the second syllable. This syncope would have to have occurred by the time of the exemplar, as the syncopated form is consistently rendered by the careful copyist of the *Textus Roffensis*. Previous editors translate *æwdum* along the lines of 'oath-helpers,' presumably taking as a model the *æwdamann* of §3. There is nothing in the term as it stands here to imply that the owner does not clear himself with his own oaths. However, as W §16.2 requires that four men stand with a freeman in an oath of exculpation, it seems preferable to follow that pattern here also.

c That is, his *wergild* is 100 shillings.

3. ᵃGif frigman mannan forstele, gif he eft cuma stermelda, [5]
secge an andweardne. Gecænne hine gif he mæge; hæbbe
þare freora rim æwdamanna ⁊ ænne mid in aþe æghwilc man
æt þam tune þe he tohyre.
   3.1. Gifᵇ he þæt ne mæge, gelde swa he gonoh áge.ᶜ
4. Gif ceorl acwyle be libbendum wife ⁊ bearne,ᵈ riht is þæt [6]
hit, þæt bearn, medder folgige, ⁊ him man an his
fæderingmagum wilsumne berigean ge[s]elleᵉ his feoh to
healdenne, oþ þæt he X wintra sie.
5. ᶠGif man oþrum mæn feoh forstele, ⁊ se agend hit eft [7]
ætfo, geteme to cynges sele gif he mæge, ⁊ þoneᵍ æt
gebrenge þe him sealde.
   5.1. Gif he þæt ne mæge, læte án ⁊ fo se agend to.

---

a This line extends into the left margin.
b g is lower case; there is no point after preceding *tohyre*.
c The line break occurs after *gono*, but this is almost surely to be divided *gonoh age*; Whitelock, *English Historical Documents*, 394, points out that the copyist 'may have been influenced by the verb *onhagian* which can mean "to afford."'
d This word extends into the right margin.
e Manuscript reads *ge̲felle*. I follow Liebermann in emending this to *ge̲selle*. Cf. §6.
f This line extends into the left margin.
g Changed from *þa̲ne* by scribe.

3. If a freeman steals a person, if he[a] afterwards comes as an informer,[b] let him announce it in the presence [of the thief]. Let him [the man accused] clear himself if he is able; let each man [so charged] have a number of free oathmen and one with [him] in the oath from the dwelling to which he belongs.
   3.1. If he is not able to do that [oath-swearing], let him pay to the extent he owns enough.
4. If a freeman should die with a living wife and child, it is right that it, that child, should be under the protection of the mother, and one should give for him one among his father's kin who willingly gives surety to maintain his property, until he should be 10 years old.
5. If a person steals property from another person, and the owner afterwards takes possession of it, let him [the accused] vouch[c] in the king's hall, if he is able, and bring him who sold it to him.
   5.1 If he is not able [to do] that, let him relinquish [it], and the owner take possession.

---

a It is not clear whether 'he' refers to the stolen person, presumably a slave, or to his owner. See Commentary under 'Oath supporters.'

b *Stermelda* only occurs here, and the first element is obscure, so it is difficult to interpret precisely, although the second element, *melda*, clearly means 'informer.' Bosworth emends the compound to *stelmelda*, 'informer about the theft,' which gives a satisfactory meaning in context, but postulates that this careful scribe would have committed the unusual error of copying l for r. If we play on the e/æ variation found so frequently in Hloþhere & Eadric (see 'Some notes on the language') we might get *stærmelda*, 'informer about [this] history'; I am uncomfortable with this suggestion, however, as the use of *stær-* generally implies a history grander in scope than the personal realm. It seems likely that the general meaning is 'open accuser,' as Liebermann, *Gesetze*, 3:29 suggests; pending a more conclusive analysis of the first element, I have chosen to translate only the second.

c Whitelock, *English Historical Documents*, uses the term 'vouch to warranty,' which seems redundant. 'Vouch' is defined in *Black's Law Dictionary* as 'to call upon witness to give warrantee of title, to substantiate with evidence.' Here it stands for the process of bringing the person from whom you purchased property or goods as a witness that the sale was legitimate. See discussion in Sir Frederick Pollock and Frederic Maitland, *The History of English Law Before the Time of Edward I* (London: Cambridge University Press, 1968), 58–60.

6. Gif man oþerne sace tihte, ⁊ he þane mannan[a] mote an medle [8]
oþþe an þinge, symble se man þam oðrum byrigean[b] geselle
⁊ þam riht awyrce[c] þe to hiom cantwara deman gescrifen.
 6.1. Gif he ðonne byrigan forwærne, XII scillingas agylde [9]
 þam cyninge, ⁊ sio se[o][d] sacy swa open swa hio ær
 wes.
 6.2. Gif man oþerne /4v/ tihte, siþþan he him byrigan [10]
 gesealdne hæbbe, ⁊ ðonne ymb III niht, gesecæn hiom
 sæmend, buton þam ufor leofre sio þe þa tihtlan age.
 Siþþan sio sace gesemed sio, an seofan nihtum se man
 þam oþrum riht gedo, gecwime an feo oððe an aþe,
 swa hwæder swa him leofre sio.
 6.3. Gif he þonne þæt nylle,[e] gelde þonne C buton aðe, siþþan
 ane neaht ofer þæt gesem[eþ] hie.[f]
7. Gif man mannan an oþres flette manswara hateþ oððe hine [11]
mid bismærwordum scandlice grete, scilling agelde þam þe
þæt flet age, ⁊ VI sciłł þam þe he þæt word togecwæde, ⁊
cyninge XII sciłł forgelde.

---

a *mannan* is written above an insertion mark, and extends over *mote*.
b **ea** on erasure.
c **y** on erasure.
d I follow Liebermann in emending *se* to *seo*.
e Changed from **i** to **y** by scribe.
f This passage is grammatically corrupt as it stands: see note b to translation.

6. If a person brings a charge against another in a matter, and he should meet that person in the assembly or in the public meeting,[a] the person [charged] is always to give surety to the other and carry out that right [= judgment] which the judges of the Kentish people may appoint for them.
  6.1. If he then refuses surety, let him pay 12 shillings to the king, and the matter shall be as open as it was before.
  6.2. If a person brings a charge against another, after he has given him surety, and then within 3 nights, let them seek out for themselves an arbitrator, unless later be preferable to him who brings the charge; after the matter shall be arbitrated, in seven nights the person [charged] should do right to the other; let him satisfy [him] with property or with oath, whichever is preferable to him.
  6.3. If he will not do that, let him then pay 100 without oath, after one night following their coming to arbitration.[b]
7. If a person in another's house calls a person a perjurer or accosts him shamefully with mocking words, let him pay a shilling to him who owns that house, and 6 shillings to him to whom he spoke that utterance, and let him pay 12 shillings to the king.

---

a It is not clear what the distinction is between the *meðel* and the *þing*. See discussion under 'The process of bringing a charge' in Commentary.

b The final two words of this passage, *gesem hie*, are corrupt in the transmission. Liebermann suggests taking *gesem* as a noun, 'arbitration,' and emending *hie*, 'them' to the verb *bie*, 'should be,' giving a reading of 'after the arbitration is wont to be.' But *beon* usually has consuetudinal connotations; a preferable emendation would be to *sie*, 'should be,' which is the verb used with *gesemed*, 'arbitrated,' in the immediately preceding clause. Another question is raised by the fact that the noun *gesem*, although a perfectly possible word, does not occur elsewhere in the corpus; otherwise we find only forms of the verb *geseman*, 'to come to arbitration' (per *Microfiche Concordance to Old English* [Delaware, 1980]). We could also emend the phrase to *gesemeþ hie*, 'they should come to arbitration'; this presupposes that the ending was inadvertently omitted in copying but allows the pronoun to stand unchanged. I have followed this choice in my translation, as the text of Hloþhere & Eadric often uses abbreviations. Postulating an inadvertent omission of an extension stroke that indicated the standard third plural ending seems to me less of a stretch than the miswriting of an **s** or **b** for an **h**, none of which are confusingly close in shape. It must be stated in fairness that nowhere else are endings indicated by an extension stroke in this copy. But this does not rule out the possibility that they existed in the exemplar and were elsewhere expanded. It is also possible that the scribe simply overlooked the ending written out in his exemplar. Although the precise parsing is unclear, the meaning is fairly straightforward.

8. Gif man oþrum steop asette ðær mæn drincen buton scylde, [12]
an eald riht scH agelde þam þe *þæt* flet age, ⁊ VI scH þam þe
man þone steap aset, ⁊ cynge XII scH.
9. Gif man wæpn abregde þær mæn drincen ⁊ ðær man nan [13]
yfel ne deþ, scilling þa[m]^a þe *þæt* flet age, ⁊ cyninge XII
scH.
    9.1. Gif *þæt* flet geblodgad wyrþe, forgylde þem mæn his [14]
mundbyrd ⁊ cyninge L sciH.
10. Gif man cuman feormæþ III niht an his agenum hame, [15]
cepeman oþþe oðerne þe sio ofer mearce cumin, ⁊ hine
þon*ne* his mete fede, ⁊ he þon*ne* ænignum mæn yfel gedo,
se man /5r/ þane oðerne æt rihte gebrenge oþþe riht
forewyrce.
11. ^bGif cantwara ænig in lundenwic feoh gebycge, hæbbe [16]
him þonne twegen oððe ðreo unfacne ceorlas to gewitnesse
oþþe cyninges wicgerefan.
    11.1. Gif hit man eft æt þam mæn in cænt ætfó, þonne [16.1]
tæme he to wic to cyngæs sele to þam mæn ðe him
sealde, gif he þane wite ⁊ æt þam teame gebrengen
mæge.
    11.2. Gif he *þæt* ne mæge, gekyþe ðanne in wiofode [16.2]
mid his gewitena anum oþþe mid cyninges
wicgerefan *þæt* he *þæt* feoh undeornunga his cuþan
ceape in wic gebohte, ⁊ him man þanne his weorð
agefe.
    11.3. Gif he þanne *þæt* ne mæge gecyþan mid rihtre [16.3]
canne, læte þanne án, ⁊ se agend^c tofó.

---

a Manuscript reads *þan*.
b This line extends into the left margin.
c n added above insertion mark; no space.

The Laws of Hloþhere & Eadric

8. If a person takes a cup from another where men are drinking without [the man from whom the cup was taken being at] fault, according to established right let him give a shilling to him who owns that house, and 6 shillings to him from whom the cup was taken, and 12 shillings to the king.
9. If a person should draw a weapon where men are drinking and no harm is done there, a shilling to him who owns that house, and 12 shillings to the king.
   9.1. If that house becomes bloodied, let him pay the man [the price for violation of] his protection and 50 shillings to the king.
10. If a person provides for a visitor for 3 nights in his own home, a merchant or other who has come across the border, and [the host] there feeds him [the guest] his food, and he [the guest] then does harm to any person, that man [the host] should bring the other to justice or do [what is required by] justice for him.
11. If any of the people of Kent buys property in London, let him then have two or three unblemished freemen to witness or the king's town-reeve.[a]
    11.1. If a person afterwards claims possession of it from that man in Kent,[b] then let him [the person who bought the goods] vouch in the king's hall in that town that man who sold it to him, if he knows him and is able to bring him to that vouching.[c]
    11.2. If he is unable to do that, let him declare then at the altar with one of his witnesses or with the king's town-reeve that he bought that property without secrecy by his public purchase in the town; and [the] one [who sold it to him] should then give him back the price of it.[d]
    11.3. If he cannot then declare that by lawful cognizance, let him then relinquish [it], and the owner take possession.

---

a Although *wicgerefan*, 'town-reeve,' is the word from which we later get the ending for 'sheriff,' the reeve at this time is more akin to the bailiff of an estate.
b In other words, a previous owner or his representative has tracked the purchaser down in Kent to claim that the sale was not legitimate.
c See note c to §5 above.
d Grammatically it is ambiguous as to whether *his* refers to the owner or the object, but the verb *agifan*, 'restore,' implies that the *weorþ*, 'price,' must be the purchase price rather than a new fine assessed for the damage to the owner's honour. If *his* is taken to mean 'the owner's,' the translation would read 'give him back his [purchase]-price.' As the next clause discusses the stolen property, it seems more logical to similarly relate *his* in this clause to the purloined goods. The result would be the same under either reading.

134   The Beginnings of English Law

Commentary

Interestingly for a kingdom so recently converted, there are no clauses in the laws of Hloþhere & Eadric dealing with the church, which we might expect to be the subject of new legislation. The position of the king in the payment of fines is given greater prominence than in the earlier laws of Æthelberht: several fines are payable to what in this day we might term the public coffer. The principal difference, however, between the laws of Æthelberht and those of Hloþhere & Eadric is that whereas the former almost never concern themselves with procedure, the latter often take this as their focus.

Rubric and prologue

> These are the decrees which Hloþhere and Eadric, kings of the Kentish people, set.

The laws of Hloþhere & Eadric are preceded by a rubric similar to that which precedes the laws of Æthelberht. Both function as headings in the *Textus Roffensis* collection, but are not part of the body of text itself. The rubric, written in red ink, begins directly after the last word of Æthelberht's text (see 3^v in Diplomatic Transcription, Appendix 1). It is followed by a line break and then a prologue, typical of later Anglo-Saxon laws.

> Hloþhære ⁊ Eadric, Cantwara cyningas, ecton þa æ þa ðe heora aldoras ær geworhton ðyssum domum, þe hyr efter sægeþ.
>
> *Hloþhere and Eadric, kings of the people of Kent, added to the laws that their ancestors made before with these decrees, which are stated hereafter.*

There is an interesting juxtaposition here between the terms *æ* and *domum*; the difference between the two reflects their etymological origins. The former comes from Proto-Indo-European **ei-**, 'go,' and represents ongoing legal tradition. The latter comes from Proto-Indo-European **dhē-**, 'set, place'; frequently translated 'judgment' or 'decree,' it here refers to law set by these two kings to augment or elaborate on the pre-existent or 'long-going' *æ*.[40] The statement that the two kings 'added to the laws, which their ancestors made' might imply that the text represents new legislation, but it could also simply mean that they added established stipulations to the corpus of written law.

In fact, both meanings seem to apply. On the one hand, as discussed in chapter 2, the first two clauses seem to be filling gaps left by the laws laid out in Æthelberht.[41] On the other hand, §11, dealing with a buyer from Kent ensuring the legality of a transaction in the distant town of London, is clearly recent (as London had only regained its prominence as a centre of commerce in the preceding century), which could account for its position at the end of the text.

The use of the plural *æ*, 'laws,' might refer simply to the collection of laws set down in writing under Æthelberht. It might also be used to argue that the prologue refers to other laws that have not come down to us. Certainly orally transmitted laws must have augmented the rather selective compilation recorded during Æthelberht's reign. And, as discussed earlier, there may even have been other written laws. Bede discusses laws of Eorconberht, which may represent a written text lost to us; given the vagaries of transmission of early medieval texts, it is also not out of the question that other kings committed laws to writing for which no reference survived.[42]

Fines

The only clause in Æthelberht to internally lay out the financial recompense for injury both to the injured party and to the king is §8, which states:

> *If the king summons his people to him and a person does any harm to them there, 2[-fold] restitution and 50 shillings to the king.*

Although it is to be inferred that the king as head of government also receives payment for other offences (for example, in §12, the payment to the king of 50 shillings for killing a freeman, over and above the 100 shillings *wergild* due to the kin stipulated in §24), Æthelberht's laws separate these payments by rank in the delineated societal ordering. Hloþhere & Eadric's laws, in contrast, arrange the payment schedule according to the offence rather than the rank of the offended party.

7. *If a person in another's house calls a person a perjurer or accosts him shamefully with mocking words, let him pay a shilling to him who owns that house, and 6 shillings to him to whom he spoke that utterance, and let him pay 12 shillings to the king.*
8. *If a person takes a cup from another where men are drinking without [the man from whom the cup was taken being at] fault, according to established*

136   The Beginnings of English Law

> *right let him give a shilling to him who owns that house, and 6 shillings to him from whom the cup was taken, and 12 shillings to the king.*
>
> 9. *If a person should draw a weapon where men are drinking and no harm is done there, a shilling to him who owns the house, and 12 shillings to the king.*
>
>   9.1. *If that house becomes bloodied, let him pay the man [the price for violation of] his protection and 50 shillings to the king.*

Clauses 7–9.1 all deal with disturbances of the peace, in increasing degrees of seriousness. They internally establish fines due not only to the offended party, but also to the owner of the property where the offence took place, as a violation of his protection, and to the king as the keeper of public safety. The payment due to the insulted party in §§7 and 8 is 6 shillings, equal to the fine for violating the *mund*, 'protection,' of a freeman stipulated in Æbt §20; it is assessed for the loss of reputation – the violation of personal protection – brought about by the insult(ing action). Such a fine is not unprecedented. Recall that in Æthelberht's personal injury laws, more apparent wounds are fined at a higher rate than those which are less visible: the greater the visibility, the greater the damage to honour (see discussion under 'Personal injury' in chapter 2). It is interesting, however, that full payment is due to the owner of the establishment only in §9.1, when blood is drawn. An insult to an individual is equivalent to a violation of his protection, but while insulting a person or even offering threats in a man's house may offend, it does not constitute a full transgression of the owner's protection unless physical injury is inflicted.

Hloþhere & Eadric §7 begins the consideration of disturbance of the peace by addressing the issue of verbal insult offered under a third party's roof. It extends the principle of payment for damage to honour from personal injury to an instance in which there has been no physical harm: the offence consists rather of mockery or accusation of perjury. The injured party receives the payment due for violation of his *mund*, double this sum is paid to the king as a fine for the disorder, and the owner of the establishment receives a shilling for the trouble caused in his house.

Clause 8 depicts a more physical form of insult: a goblet is seized from another drinker without provocation.[43] Anglo-Saxon poetry abounds in images of boasting at drink in the meadhall: one of the most poignant is found in a speech by Ælfwine as the Anglo-Saxon troops face almost certain defeat at the battle of Maldon: *Gemunan þa mæla þe we oft æt meodo spræcon, þonne we on bence beot ahofon, hæleð on healle, ymbe heard gewinn; nu mæg cunnian hwa cene sy*,[44] 'Think of the times that we often spoke at mead, when we warriors in the hall raised a boast on the bench about fierce combat; now he who is brave may come to know it.' If one imagines that it is in a similar situation that the goblet is seized – and this is certainly only one of many possible scenarios – the man who snatches the cup from the drinker's hand is in a sense committing both of the violations described in §7. By challenging the vow the drinker is making, he not only mocks the drinker but implicitly accuses him of false swearing. It is, of course, also possible that the provocation occurs under less epic circumstances: a man drinking peacefully has his cup seized from him for no apparent cause. Under whatever circumstances the goblet is taken, the fine for this offence is the same assigned to mockery or accusation of perjury in §7: a shilling to the host, the *mund* to the offended party, and twice that to the king.

Clauses 9 and 9.1 move beyond insult to the threat or use of force. It is interesting that these clauses do not stipulate a payment to the person wronged. In §9, the threat may not be addressed to any particular individual: a man has drawn a sword where men are drinking and thus in a state of some inebriation, an inherently dangerous situation. (This ruling probably encompasses any gathering at a meal.) It also seems possible that the clause describing the payment to the person against whom the sword was drawn was overlooked by the scribe, although, as a rule, speculating about what may have been omitted is a dangerous practice. A third, and in my opinion most likely, option is that §9 augments §§7 and 8. That is, it seems unlikely that a sword would be drawn without prior provocation. A similar situation is portrayed in the laws of the West-Saxon king Ine §6.5:[45]

> If, however, two men quarrel over their cups and one endures it patiently, the other [who has recourse to violence] shall pay a fine of 30 shillings.

Following the sequence described in Hloþhere & Eadric, if the threatened party has already been insulted by the sword-wielder, the latter must pay an additional fine for physical intimidation. If the sword is drawn in response to an insult (threatening force rather than letting the legal ruling provide reparation), both parties in the dispute are assessed. Under any of the interpretations offered above, §9 describes assault, whether the threat is against an individual or against the group as a whole. The subsequent (possible) battery is discussed in §9.1. Only in this last instance is the full *mund* due to the owner of the house (12 shillings for a nobleman and 6 for a freeman, if we take the earlier rulings in Æbt §§18 and 20, respectively, to remain valid a century later). The perpetrator must in addition pay the king 50 shillings, which, according to Æbt §14, is the fine levied for violating the king's protection. There is no stipulation of the amount payable to the one who was actually bloodied; this reckoning is, however, subsumed under the existing personal injury laws laid out in Æbt §§33–71 (which seem to have remained valid, as they are to a great degree repeated in Alfred §§44–64).

Legal responsibilities in hospitality

> 10. *If a person provides for a visitor for 3 nights in his own home, a merchant or other who has come across the border, and [the host] there feeds him [the guest] his food, and he [the guest] then does harm to any person, that man [the host] should bring the other to justice or do [what is required by] justice for him.*

It is a host's responsibility to see that those staying under his roof by his invitation obey the law. The verb *feormæþ*, 'provides,' is taken from the noun *feorm*, which typically refers to the food render provided to the king (see discussion under 'King' in Commentary to chapter 2) but could also refer to a similar liability towards lower ranks.[46] It generally implies an obligation, which seems to point to reciprocal trade relations across borders, in which those travelling on business might house each other in their own homes. Note that the only type of guest specifically mentioned is a merchant; this, along with H & E §11, provides evidence of a healthy trading economy.[47] The guest coming 'over the border' may be an Anglo-Saxon from a different region of England, but Welshmen and foreigners from across the sea are not necessarily excluded.

Although the visitor is subject in his native land to the law of his own province or kingdom, he is here being required to obey the law of the territory in which he temporarily resides. If he violates that law in any way, his host must see that he is brought to justice. A householder who fails in this regard is himself liable for the reparation for the offence.

The three-night term eliminates from consideration shorter gatherings such as those described in §§7, 8, and 9. Although a host is responsible for the behaviour of guests whom he is supporting for an extended period, he is protected against liability for dinner guests becoming unruly under his roof.

The process of bringing a charge

6. *If a person brings a charge against another in a matter, and he should meet that person in the assembly or in the public meeting, the person [charged] is always to give surety to the other and carry out that right [= judgment] which the judges of the Kentish people may appoint for them.*
   6.1. *If he then refuses surety, let him pay 12 shillings to the king, and the matter shall be as open as it was before.*
   6.2. *If a person brings a charge against another, after he has given him surety, and then within 3 nights, let them seek out for themselves an arbitrator, unless later be preferable to him who brings the charge; after the matter shall be arbitrated, in seven nights the person [charged] should do right to the other; let him satisfy [him] with property or with oath, whichever is preferable to him.*
   6.3. *If he will not do that, let him then pay 100 without oath, after one night following their coming to arbitration.*

Clauses 6–6.3 clearly lay out the process of bringing a charge against another, although the exact nature of the place(s) in which the charge is brought is unclear. Clause 6 uses both the terms *meðel* and *þing*, which seems to imply a distinction between the two, although it is not clear what the distinction might be. Henry Adams points out that the Franks use *meðel* while *þing* is employed elsewhere in Germanic: the two terms could, in fact, simply be dialectal variants.[48] E.G. Stanley similarly claims that they are 'perhaps of two kinds, but probably ... of one kind to be described by either or both of two synonyms.'[49] But it is then unclear why both are used in this ruling. Liebermann translates the first as *Versammlung, Gericht*, 'gathering, court,' and the second as *Gerihtstätte*, 'place of judgment.' The one is thus the assembly itself and the other the place where the assembly is held.[50] If Lieberman is correct, the use of both terms in this paragraph would seem redundant: why bring a charge in a place of judgment where there is no one present to judge your case?

The Proto-Indo-European root forms are not particularly helpful. *meðel* comes from **mōd-*, 'meet, come together,' and over time takes on – unsurprisingly – the meaning of 'conversation' as well as 'meeting.' It is from this root that we get every *Beowulf* student's favourite (because most often-repeated) verb, *mathelode*, 'spoke.' In the Salic laws, *mallberg* probably means 'the hill on which the assembly takes place,' although this may have been reinterpreted by the Latin redactor as 'the language of the *mallberg*.' Pokorny derives *þing* from Proto-Indo-

European *ten-(k)-, 'stretch out.' It seems a circuitous route of semantic change to reach the meaning of 'court; legal affair,' but this route is not unique to Germanic, as we find it also in Middle Irish *techtae*, 'legal, prescribed.'[51]

The *Beowulf* poet may provide a clue in his use of the two words. Beowulf, when he plans *ana gehēgan ðing wið þyrse*, 'alone to achieve the *þing* against the giant,' seems by *þing* to mean something akin to a public, legal confrontation. But both the confrontational and legal implications are lacking when, at Beowulf's departure, Hroþgar mourns that *hīe seoððan no gesēon mōston, modige on meþle*, 'they might not again see each other, brave in the assembly.'[52] Perhaps a similar distinction may be present in H & E §6: the *meðel* is a public gathering assembled for a variety of reasons, which may, but need not, include legal hearings, while the *þing* concentrates more specifically on matters of law.

The process itself is as follows:

A. The accused gives surety – that is, an oath or promise to abide by the law – to abide by the judgment of the arbitrator, or else becomes subject to a fine of 12 shillings; this fine does *not* prevent the matter from going to arbitration. (Liebermann takes the phrase 'the matter shall be as open as it was before' to mean that the accuser can continue to bring the charge until the surety is proffered, presumably with a 12-shilling fine incurred each time surety is denied.[53] Another possible interpretation is that the payment of a fine rather than the offering of surety does not prejudice the case going into arbitration.)

B. Within three days (or later, if the accuser so desires) accuser and accused seek out a mutually acceptable arbitrator.

C. Within seven nights following the arbitration, the accused must either satisfy the accuser by payment or swear upon oath that he is innocent. He has one day to declare his intention to exculpate himself. (See under 'Exculpation' in Commentary to chapter 4). If he refuses to do this, or to acknowledge the arbitration against him (in other words, if he denies the validity of the arbitration), he is subject to a fine of 100 shillings – the price of a freeman's *wergild* – and gives up his right to swear his innocence at a later time.[54]

Clauses 6–6.3 augment the knowledge of early Anglo-Saxon arbitration process that we glimpsed in the tersely phrased Æbt §65.1, which states for a man wounded in the thigh: '[i]f he becomes lame, then friends/kinsmen must arbitrate.' Liebermann distinguishes between an arbitrator and a judge, claiming that the former lacks the official legal position of the latter. It seems reasonable to assume that there was a difference between the force of arbitration by friends and/or family (*-seman*) and a ruling by a figure who bears the authority of the Kentish people (*-deman*).

However, we cannot assume that the laws of Hloþhere & Eadric necessarily present us with a view of legal process as it would have existed at the time of Æthelberht, as they postdate the earlier text (which is notably silent as to process) by almost a century. And even the fuller picture provided by H & E §§6 and 7 gives us only a partial description of legal practice. For example, if the charge is bogus, and thus adjudged by the arbitrator(s), does the falsely accused man have any recompense? The two clauses immediately following stipulate recompense for a man (presumably falsely) accused of perjury and for a man who has (unjustly) had a cup seized from him: it might well be that the same fine would be paid to a man falsely accused and brought to arbitration.

The giving of surety is another element of process not demonstrated in Æthelberht. In addition to the example given above, surety must be offered by the kin of a deceased man to maintain the property of his son until the child shall have reached the age of ten years. (See §4, and the discussion under 'Women and children (widows)' in Commentary to chapter 2.)

The regulation of commerce

A different type of oath-swearing can be seen in the act of vouching (to warranty), which occurs in cases dealing with property.

5. *If a person steals property from another person, and the owner afterwards takes possession of it, let him [the accused] vouch in the king's hall if he is able, and bring him who sold it to him.*
    5.1. *If he is not able [to do] that, let him relinquish [it], and the owner take possession.*
11. *If any of the people of Kent buys property in London, let him then have two or three unblemished freemen to witness or the king's town-reeve.*
    11.1. *If a person afterwards claims possession of it from that man in Kent, then let him [the person who bought the goods] vouch in the king's hall in that town that man who sold it to him, if he knows him and is able to bring him to that vouching.*

142   The Beginnings of English Law

> 11.2. *If he is unable to do that, let him declare then at the altar with one of his witnesses or with the king's town-reeve that he bought that property without secrecy by his public purchase in the town; and [the] one [who sold it to him] should then give him back the price of it.*
>
> 11.3. *If he cannot then declare that by lawful cognizance, let him then relinquish [it], and the owner take possession.*

'Vouch' is the legal term used in property cases for bringing evidence for lawful ownership (in these instances, for property acquired through purchase).[55] Clause 5 delineates the process to be followed in the case of accusation of theft. If the accused person is unable to swear in the king's hall that he obtained the goods in legal sale and to produce the seller, the property is assumed to be stolen and is returned to the previous owner. Clause 11 presents a variation more specific in its localization, namely, *Lundenwic*: even in the seventh century, London seems to have been full of sharpers!

The suffix -*wic* was generally applied to places of trade near a waterway, and archaeological evidence shows that, in fact, the London of the early Saxon period did not lie within the old Roman walls but was centred on the Strand.[56] Bede ii.3, in discussing the consecration of Mellitus and Justus by Augustine in 604, says of the city that it lies 'on the banks of that river [Thames] and is an emporium for many nations who come to it by land and sea.'[57] It is unclear whether he is describing the London of 604 or that of his own time, more than a century later.[58] The latter may be more likely, as archaeological records for the end of the seventh-century show that while London was growing as a commercial centre, the same does not seem to have been true of the city in the time of Æthelberht (who focused his attention on Rochester and Canterbury).[59] It is around 670–80 that the Anglo-Saxons (and the Frisians) began to mint silver *sceattas* in place of gold coins; the former were more useful for commerce.[60] At least forty eighth-century *sceattas* have been discovered in London, implying that trade involving coinage was active in or after that period.[61]

The term -*wic* is important for reasons other than geography. The *wics* were the places at which toll was paid to a representative of the king.[62] Although London was part of the kingdom of the East Saxons, this territory was subject off and on to the overlordship of Kent during the seventh century. The designation in Kentish law of the city as *Lundonwic* and of an official as *cyninges wicgerefan*, 'the king's *wic*-reeve' (the second element comes down to us in sheriff, 'the reeve of a shire') imply that at this time the kings of Kent had some authority over at least a section of this important market city. Note that §11.1 specifically states that there is a king's hall in London. Recall also that a gold coin bearing the name of Æthelberht's son Eadbald was minted there.[63] The function of the king's reeve, then, was to serve as the representative of the law of the Kentish kings – at least in purchase transactions – and likely as well to collect the tolls owed to them. Large numbers of wine bottles imported from Gaul are found in some male graves both at Sarre and Dover, which seem to have been the major ports of entry for imported goods. Sonia Hawkes postulates that these graves are those of the king's custom's officers, and that the presence of the wine bottles shows that they were 'getting their "cut."'[64] Her suggestion implies an attempt at royal regulation of trade (although doubtless private transactions continued to take place).[65] It is perhaps not coincidental that while in the general procedure for bringing a charge discussed in §6 the litigants are free to choose their own arbitrator, for matters dealing specifically with commerce the judgment must be made by a representative of the king.

What did this commerce consist of? The 'emporium' of London, located at the centre of the old Roman road system of southern Britain, was, among other things, the centre of the Mercian slave trade;[66] Bede iv.22 recounts the story of a thegn named Imma who was sold to a Frisian in *Lundoniam*.[67] Thus human chattel may not be excluded from the definition of 'property' referred to here, but the usual trade referred to was likely the sale/purchase of cattle. Throughout the British Isles, theft of cattle was common in this period. Two early Irish sagas, *The Cattle Raid of Cooley* and *The Cattle Raid of Froech*, describe such events. The legal sale of cattle took place in urban centres under the watchful eye of royal officials,[68] hence the designation here of London as the place of purchase. The archaeological evidence accords well with this, as shown by studies of the late mid-Saxon material from the Treasury, Whitehall: 'The overall ratio of meat bones by weight from the site showed that cattle were far and away the most important source of meat consumed, with sheep and pigs an equal second ... The majority of cattle were mature, and could therefore have been driven to London. The ratio of humerus and femur fragments to mandibles shows that only about one half of the cattle slaughtered on the site were eaten there.'[69]

The sequence of clauses in H & E §§11–11.3 establishes the procedure by which a Kentishman could protect himself against being taken for a sucker, or ensure his ability subsequently to bring a claim of legality in a doubtful transaction. The purchase must be witnessed either by freemen who can stand witness to the legality of the transaction or by the king's reeve as representative of public order. If a third party afterwards claims the goods were stolen, the purchaser must swear before a representative of the king that he obtained the property in legal sale and produce the person who sold it. If he is unable to do so, the setting for the proceeding then moves to the altar. (In W §7, manumission similarly takes place before the altar, although in the parallel Frankish law the setting specified is in the presence of the king, and in Lombard law, at the crossroads.)[70] At the altar, the purchaser must swear, supported either by one of his witnesses (see discussion in 'Oath supporters' below) or by the Kentish king's reeve, that the false transaction was unintentional on his part. He must then return the goods, and the seller must restore to him his purchase price. The difficulty here is that unless the defendant brought in under duress the man who conned him, the seller has probably long since absconded with the money, or he would originally have appeared in court to validate the purchase. But at least the Kentish man's reputation stands unblemished, and he does have a legal right to restitution if he can locate the seller. If he is unable to swear to his belief in the legality of the transaction, the goods revert to the real owner and the purchaser has no right to recompense.

Note that the Kentish man in London to buy cattle may well be lodged at the house of a fellow merchant, as described in §10.

Oath supporters

Oath supporters appear for the first time in the Kentish laws in the text of Hloþhere & Eadric. These are men who will stand up in court and vouch for a man bringing an oath (generally of innocence) in a legal matter. Their word is presumably considered to be good since they themselves would fear the wrath of God or the reprisal of justice should they support a false oath.[71]

If a servant who has killed a man escapes over the border, his master must bring an oath supporter to stand by him in his swearing that he was unable to seize the killer (§§1 and 2), presumably to prove that the servant's master did not order the killing. As seen above (§11), a man swearing his innocence of fraud in a contested transaction must provide oath helpers at his swearing that he had no knowledge the goods may have been stolen. A similar provision addresses the theft of a man.

3. *If a freeman steals a person, if he afterwards comes as an informer, let him announce it in the presence [of the thief]. Let him [the man accused] clear himself if he is able; let each man [so charged] have a number of free oathmen and one with [him] in the oath from the dwelling to which he belongs.*
3.1. *If he is not able to do that [oath-swearing], let him pay to the extent he owns enough.*

In §§3–3.1 the disputed property is human and able to speak for himself. The man accused of theft must swear to his innocence, supported by a number of free oath supporters, at least one of whom must be from the accused man's township. There is no stipulation that the oath-swearers must be of the kin-group; recall that in Æbt §65.1 the term used for those who arbitrate for a lamed man is *freond*, which can mean either 'friends' or 'kinsmen.' The number of oath supporters is not stated (possibly because it is fixed) but there must be at least three.[72] W §16.2 requires a freeman to exculpate himself by swearing as one of four. Closer in content is §39.2 from the Salic laws of ?481–507,[73] whose textual similarity – despite the two-century difference in date of compilation – is close enough that it seems likely to have served as a pattern or to have come from a common model: 'If a foreign slave is stolen and taken across the sea, and there is found by his master, and in the public *mallus* (=*meðel*) names the one by whom he was carried away, he must call there three witnesses. Likewise when the slave himself has been called back across the sea, nevertheless in another *mallus* he must name [the robber] again, and at the same time three suitable witnesses must be gathered ...'[74] T.J. Rivers and Katherine Fisher Drew both assume that it is the master and not the slave who appears at the *mallus*,[75] but this is not at all clear in the grammatically ambiguous Latin.[76] In any case, the Frankish passage implies the existence of an exchange of legal liability across the Channel at a very early date (as it is difficult to imagine what else is meant by 'across the sea' in the Frankish text).[77]

Liebermann translates and interprets Hloþhere & Eadric slightly differently, assuming that each of the oath supporters must be from the village to which the accused man belongs,[78] but that only one of the oath-swearers is actually required to stand with the defendant in the oath, as in §11 discussed above. The clause is, in fact, grammatically ambiguous. I know of no outside evidence that would give preference to either reading.

If the defendant is unable to swear that he is guiltless, he pays the fine to the extent to which he is able. The penalty is similar to that specified in Æbt §15, in which the king takes a three-fold repayment for theft, or all the person's possessions if the perpetrator cannot afford to pay the fine in full. Liebermann postulates that if the accused man is unable to pay the full amount, he must submit himself to servitude,[79] thus, presumably, taking on the status of servant or slave. This seems reasonable: the seventh-century Penitentials of Theodore tell us that 'a person of fourteen [years] can make himself a slave.'[80]

The laws dealing with inheritance have already been discussed under the Commentary to 'Women and children' in chapter 2. As the text lacks an epilogue, there is no way of telling whether it is complete as it stands.

4

The Laws of Wihtred

Historical background

Following the death of Eadric in 686, Kent entered a four-year period of turmoil, during which, according to Bede iv.26, 'various usurpers or foreign kings plundered the kingdom.'[1] The *Anglo-Saxon Chronicle* tells us that in 686 'Cædwalla [of Wessex] and Mul, his brother, laid waste Kent and the Isle of Wight.'[2] Mul seems to have taken over as king of the Kentish territories. It was a short reign, however, for the *Chronicle* entry for 687 declares that 'Mul was burned in Kent and twelve other men with him, and that year Cædwalla again laid waste Kent.'[3] (Mul's killing was later expiated, as the entry for 694 says that 'the people of Kent made terms with Ine, and paid him thirty thousand [pence] because they had burnt Mul.')[4] A charter in St Augustine's implies that Swæfheard, son of King Sebbi of the East Saxons, was ruling in 688.[5] Three charters issued around the year 690 indicate that the rule was shared by Kentish Oswine, who seems to have come into power in 689. After 690 Oswine disappears from the record, to be replaced in the charter evidence of 692 by Eadric's younger brother Wihtred.

For a while Wihtred and the Saxon Swæfheard claimed an apparently shared sovereignty in Kent.[6] The *Chronicle* implies that their joint rule lasted until 694; according to the entry for that year, 'Wihtred succeeded to the kingdom of the people of Kent, and held it for 33 years.'[7] This reckoning is contradicted, however, by the *Chronicle*'s later entry of 725, which states that 'in this year, Wihtred, king of the people of Kent, died on 23 April. He had ruled 34 years.'[8] The 725 entry would imply that Wihtred's rule began in 690 or 691; evidence from the indiction cycle would point towards a date late in 690 (see Commentary under 'Rubric and prologue').[9] The confusion appears to stem from the question of whether it is joint or sole rule whose inception is being noted. In any event, Wihtred issued a charter in July of 694 that contains no reference to a co-ruler, so it would seem that he was ruling alone by that date. (Swæfheard may have died young, as he is not listed by Bede among the sons who succeeded his father Sebbi.)[10] Again reckoning on the basis of the indiction, it seems that Wihtred probably promulgated his laws in September of 695. Bede, characteristic in his admiration for this most Christian king, simplifies the narrative by telling us only that Wihtred reunited the kingdom of Kent and 'established himself on the throne and freed the nation from foreign invasion by his devotion and zeal.'[11]

At Wihtred's death the kingdom was divided among his three sons, Æthelberht, Eadberht, and Alric, and quickly succumbed to the ascendancy of the kings of Mercia. As Bede concludes his *Ecclesiastical History* in 731, he provides in v.23 a list of the bishoprics in the southern kingdoms; 'all these kingdoms,' he says, 'and the other southern kingdoms which reach right up to the Humber, together with their various kings, are subject to Æthelbald, king of Mercia.'[12] And in a charter of 736[13] Æthelbald is named 'by the gift of God king not only of the Mercians but also of all provinces which are called by the general name "South English."' In the witness list he is styled 'king of Britain,' and in a note on the reverse side, 'king of the South English.'[14] It is a Mercian king rather than any of the successors of Æthelberht who assumed the overlordship of the southern territories. Kent would never again stand as an independent kingdom.

Some notes on the language

The language of the laws of Wihtred demonstrates more archaic retention than that of the laws of Hloþhere & Eadric but more modernization than found in the laws of Æthelberht.

Archaisms

Wihtred shares many of the archaisms present in Æthelberht, namely:

1. The representation of the dental fricative as **th** in *æltheodige* for *ælðeodige*, 'foreign' (§3.1), and as **d** in *gehwæder* for *gehwæðer*, 'each of the two' (§4.1).

2. The archaic genitive singular in -æs#, retained in *ciriclicæs gemanan*, 'of churchly company' (§3.2); *cyngæs*, 'of the king' (§4), and *sylfæs*, 'of himself' (§14). Similarly, retention of an archaic æ in an unstressed syllable in the dative singular ending of *þegnunæ*, 'from service' (§5).
3. Retention of the archaic diphthong -eu- in *þeuw(ne)*, 'slave' (§§10, 19, 23) and *leud*, 'person' (§21).
4. Retention of -e# in *ænde*, 'and' (§7) (see discussion under 'Manumission' in Commentary).

Modernizations

As in the laws of Hloþhere & Eadric, there are several instances of vowel replacement in Wihtred, indicating that at the time at least of the most recent copy, the distinction between vowels in unstressed syllables (which would have been maintained at the time of the original recording of the text) was beginning to blur.

The use of e in place of Classical Old English a occurs in *þare* for the genitive plural demonstrative *þara*, 'their' (§3), and *gemacene* for the genitive plural *gemacena*, 'of equals' (§§15, 16.1). Further difficulty with the older forms is shown by the use of *æhtan* for the genitive plural *æhtena*, 'possessions' (§§9, 9.1). The use of a in place of e can be seen in *gesamnad* for the past participle *gesamned*, 'gathered' (Prologue), and *bycgan* for the plural subjunctive *bycgen*, 'they should perform' (§15).

In a stressed syllable, we find a in place of æ in *habbe* for *hæbbe*, 'he should have' (§6) and in *rade* (§8.1) versus *ræde* (§11.1), if we accept that the latter two both mean 'by counsel' (see discussion in Commentary under 'Transgressing the laws of the church').

Dialect features

As in the laws of Hloþhere & Eadric, both the dative singular and nominative plural of *man* regularly appear as *mæn*, which is more usually *men*; a similar apparent partial umlaut is found in *læng* for *leng*, 'longer' (§6). These may, however, simply be instances of the typically Kentish practice by which e is lowered to æ before a nasal,[15] of which we have several other examples: *ærnæmda*, 'afore-mentioned' (Prologue); *clænsie*, 'should clear' (§§14, 15, 16, 18 – cf. *clensie*, §§17, 19); and *fræmde*, 'stranger' (§28). The æ found in *ænde*, 'and' (§7) may well be an archaic retention of the partial umlaut, as the form is found elsewhere in Kentish as *end*.[16] Alternation between æ and e occurs also in *unlægne* (§12) versus *unlegnæ* (§16), 'uncontrovertible.' Once a appears for o in the accusative third person singular masculine demonstrative *ðane* for *ðone* (§8.2; see parallels in Hloþhere & Eadric). And a also appears once for ea; we get both the forms *halsfang* (§9) and *healsfang* (§11) for the term describing payment in exchange for imprisonment.

The third person singular subjunctive 'let it/him be' appears both as *sio* (§§5, 8.2) and *sie* (§§7 [2x], 9, 16.1, 18); see the parallel in Hloþhere & Eadric. Similarly, we find the form *sion* for the third person plural subjunctive present *sien*, 'let them be,' and *hio* for the nominative plural first person pronoun *hie*, 'they' (contiguously in §9). Clause 21 uses *heom* for *hiom*, which itself is a dialect form of the dative third person plural pronoun *him* (see discussion under 'Some notes on the language' in chapter 3).

And again as in Hloþhere & Eadric, we find spelling of y for e in stressed syllables *hyr*, 'here,' and *cwyþ*, 'says' (Prologue) and in *wyrgelde*, 'wergild' (§20). I believe Brunner is correct in extending this substitution to the non-stressed ending of *folcy*, 'with the people,' although Sievers and Liebermann both assume the y represents an old instrumental in i (*folci*) rather than an orthographic variant of the normal dative (*folce*).[17]

EDITION AND TRANSLATION

ðis synd Wihtredes domas Cantwara cyninges.[a]

Ðam mildestan cyninge Cantwara Wihtrede, rixigendum þe fiftan wintra his rices, þy niguðan gebanne, sextan dæge Rugernes, in þære stowe þy hatte Berghamstyde, ðær wæs gesamnad eadigra ge[þ]eahtendlic[b] ymcyme: Ðær wæs Birhtwald Bretone heahbiscop, ⁊ se ærnæmda cyning; eac þan Hrofesceastre bisceop, se ilca Gybmund wæs haten, andward wæs; ⁊ cwæð ælc had ciricean ðære mægðe anmodlice mid þy hersuman folcy. Þær ða eadigan fundon mid /5v/ ealra gemedum ðas domas ⁊ Cantwara rihtum þeawum æcton, swa hit hyr efter segeþ ⁊ cwyþ:

1. Ciricean freolsdom(e) gafola;[c] [1]
    1.1. ⁊ man for cyning gebidde ⁊ hine buton neadhæse [1.1]
    heora willum weorþigen[d]
2. Ciricean mundbyrd sie L scłł, swa cinges. [2]

---

a This superscript, written in red ink, immediately follows the final word in the laws of Hloþhere & Eadric. There is a line break following the rubric.
b Emendation following Liebermann and Bosworth: manuscript reads *geheahtendlic*.
c Manuscript spacing is *Cirice anfreols dome gafola*. See note e to translation.
d Manuscript has erasure between e and n: *weorþige_n*.

These are the decrees of Wihtred, king of the Kentish people.

To the most gracious king of the Kentish people, Wihtred, ruling in the fifth winter of his reign,[a] in the ninth indiction,[b] sixth day of Rugern,[c] in that place which is called Berghamstead,[d] there was gathered a consiliary assembly of great men.

There was Brihtwald, archbishop of Britain, and the afore-mentioned king; likewise the bishop of Rochester, which same was called Gebmund, was present; and each order of the church of that people spoke with a single mind with the loyal populace.

There the great men devised, with the consent of all, these decrees, and added to the just customs of the Kentish people, as it hereafter says and declares:

1. Freedom of the church from taxation [is to be];[e]
    1.1 and one should pray for the king, and do him honour of their own will without compulsion.
2. [Violation of the] protection of the church shall be 50 shillings, as the king's.

---

a Germanic peoples (not surprisingly, given the climate) counted years in winters.
b The term 'indiction' dates back to imperial Rome, when tax assessment was calculated in fifteen-year cycles with the internal years reckoned as *indictio primo, secundo*, etc. Probably 695: see Commentary under 'Rubric and prologue' for further discussion.
c *Rugern* means 'rye-harvest': this was probably in September.
d Perhaps Bearsted, near Maidstone.
e This clause is grammatically somewhat problematic, although the import is clear. The spacing of the manuscript makes no sense (see note c to the Old English text); as most previous editors, I have chosen *Ciricean*. This could be genitive (as translated above) or dative, the latter giving a reading of 'To the church is to be freedom from taxation' (literally 'of tributes'). Note, however, that the next clause begins with a genitival *ciricean*, which has governed my choice. The difficulty is that *freolsdome* is in the dative case; both of the proposed readings presuppose an emendation to *freolsdom*. If one were to edit the phrase *Cirice an freolsdome gafola*, 'One church [is to be] with freedom from taxation,' no emendation would be necessary, but the translation is nonsensical in the absence of competing church religions. (Even more unlikely is the supposition that the clause might refer to a single specific church.) It is also on the threshold of ungrammaticality to have the numeral following the noun. See discussion in Liebermann, *Gesetze*, 3:26.

3. Unrihthæmde mæn to rihtum life mid synna hreowe tofon [3]
oþþe of ciricean ge[m]a[n]anª ascadene sien.
   3.1. Ældeodige mæn, gif hio hiora hæmed rihtan nyllað, [4]
of lande mid hiora æhtum ⁊ mid synnum gewiten.
   3.2. Swæse mæn in leodum ciriclicæs gemanan [4.1]
ungestrodyne þoligen.
4. Gif ðæs geweorþe gesiþcundne mannan ofer þis gemot, [5]
þæt he unrihthæmed genime ofer cyngæs bebod ⁊ biscopes
⁊ boca dom, se þæt gebete his dryhtneᵇ C scⱧ an ald reht. [5.1]
   4.1. Gif hit ceorlisc man sie, gebete L scⱧ. [5.1]
   4.2. ⁊ gehwæder þæt hæmed mid hreowe forlæte.
5. Gif priost læfe unrihthæmed, oþþe fulwih[t]eᶜ untrumes [6]
forsitte, oþþe to þon druncen sie þæt he ne mæge, sio he
stille his þegnungæ oþ biscopes dom.
6. Gif bescoren man steorleas gange him an gestliðnesse, [7]
gefe him man ænes, ⁊ þæt ne geweorðe, buton he leafnesse
habbe, þæt hine man læng feormige.

---

a Emendation following Liebermann: manuscript reads *genaman*. See parallel in §3.2.
b **ne** on erasure.
c Emendation following Liebermann: manuscript reads *fulwihðe*.

3. Men in an unlawful union shall take up a just life with repentance of sins, or be separated from the community of the church.
    3.1. Foreign men, if they will not set their union to right, must depart from the land with their possessions and with [their] sins.
    3.2. Our own men among the people [i.e., native] shall suffer loss of the community of the church without forfeiture of goods.
4. If after this assembly [something] of this [nature] befalls to a *gesiþ-*born[a] man, that he should take up an unlawful union against the king's command and the bishop's and the decrees of the books,[b] he makes restitution for that to his lord with 100 shillings according to established right.[c]
    4.1. If it is one of freeman's rank, let him make 50 shillings restitution.
    4.2. And let each of them relinquish the union with repentance.
5. If a priest allows an unlawful union, or neglects the baptism of a sick person, or is so drunk that he is not able [to perform his duties], let him be inactive in his service pending the bishop's decree.
6. If a tonsured man[d] not under [any ecclesiastical/monastic] rule seeks out hospitality for himself, one should give it to him once; and it should not happen that he be supported for a longer time, unless he should have permission.

---

a According to Whitelock, *English Historical Documents*, 396: 'This is the only occurrence in Kentish law of a term common in the West-Saxon code of Ine, contemporary with Wihtred. It seems to refer to the same class which the earlier Kentish laws called *eorlcund*. The word *gesith* means "companion" and is applied in poetry and elsewhere to the members of a king's *comitatus*. But it is clear from the term *gesith-cund* "born a *gesith*" that it has come to denote the member of a class.'

b Liebermann, *Gesetze*, 3:27 says this includes compilations of canon (church) law as well as the Bible.

c Liebermann, *Gesetze*, 3:27 points out that this statute, with its reference to the bishop and (religious) books, could not be very ancient, and suggests translating *ald*, 'old, ancient,' along the lines of 'established.' This seems likely, as in any event the 'ancient' payments to the king for disturbance of public peace as laid out in Æthelberht §§8, 11, 12, and 14 was 50 rather than 100 shillings.

d That is, a man with his head shaved in the tonsure of a cleric.

7. Gif man his mæn an wiofode freols gefe, se sie folcfry; [8]
   freolsgefa age his erfe ænde /6r/ wergild ⁊ munde þare
   hina,[a] sie ofer mearce ðær he wille.
8. Gif esne of(er)[b] dryhtnes hæse þeowweorc wyrce an sunnan [9]
   æfen efter hire setlgange oþ monan æfenes setlgang, LXXX
   scll se dryhten[c] gebete.
   8.1. Gif esne deþ his rade þæs dæges, VI se wið dryhten [10]
        gebete oþþe sine hyd.
   8.2. Gif friman þonne an ðane forbodenan timan, sio he [11]
        healsfange scyldig, ⁊ se man se þæt arasie, he age healf
        þæt wite ⁊ ðæt weorc.
9. Gif ceorl buton wifes wisdome deoflum gelde, he sie [12]
   ealra his æhtan scyldig ⁊ healsfange.
   9.1. Gif butwu deoflum geldaþ, sion hio healsfange
        scyldigo ⁊ ealra æhtan.

---

a Changed from þina.
b Liebermann, correctly in my opinion, suggests emending this to of; he postulates that the cross-bar of the f may have been mistaken for an extension stroke representing -er.
c This clause is grammatically corrupt; manuscript reads se dryhtne. See discussion under 'Transgressing the laws of the church' in Commentary.

7. If a person sets his man free at the altar, he shall have the rights of a free man of the people; the freedomgiver owns his inheritance and *wergild* and protection of the kin, let him [the newly freed man] be over the border wherever he wishes.[a]
8. If a servant according to[b] his lord's order does slave-work after sunset on the eve of Sunday until sunset on the eve of Monday,[c] let the lord pay 80 shillings [?*sceattas*].[d]
   8.1. If a servant performs [work] on his own counsel on that day, let him pay 6 towards his lord or his hide.[e]
   8.2. If, however, a freeman [works] in that forbidden time, let him be liable for *healsfang*,[f] and the man who detects that, he shall own half that fine and/or that work.[g]
9. If a freeman[h] without his wife's knowledge makes offering to devils, he shall be liable for all his possessions or[i] *healsfang*.[j]
   9.1. If both make offering to devils, they are [both] liable for *healsfang*[j] or all possessions.

---

a Strong parallels with clauses found in Frankish, Lombard, and Old Norse law indicate that §7 may contain oral-formulaic remnants from an earlier Germanic source. See discussion under 'Manumission' in Commentary.

b See note b to the Old English text. I have translated as if the text read *of*, 'according to,' rather than *ofer*, 'against,' as the meaning of this clause is in opposition to the following clause. See discussion under 'Transgressing the laws of the church' in Commentary.

c That is, work is forbidden from Saturday's sunset to Sunday's sunset.

d This clause is grammatically corrupt; translation follows Liebermann's emendations, with a possible change of *shillings* to *sceattas* to correct for the unreasonably stiff fine. See discussion under 'Transgressing the laws of the church' in Commentary.

e Contra Whitelock, *English Historical Documents*, 397, who translates this 'If a servant rides on his own business on that day, he is to pay six [shillings] to his lord, or be flogged.' See discussion under 'Transgressing the laws of the church' in Commentary.

f This probably means 'fine in lieu of imprisonment,' and likely represents 20 per cent of the *wergild*, that is, 20 shillings for a freeman. (See discussion under 'Transgressing the laws of the church' in Commentary).

g ⁊ can represent 'and' or 'or'; in the next two clauses it is almost certainly adversative. See note i to §9.

h *ceorl* can also mean 'husband.'

i Here and in the next clause, Whitelock takes ⁊ as 'or.' Although the meaning of 'and' is more common, ⁊ appears elsewhere with adversative meaning in the Kentish laws. See e.g., Æbt §§15, 30, and 80, and compare the previous clause. If the possessions were forfeit anyway, one would have nothing with which to pay *healsfang*.

j See note f to §8.2.

10. Gif þeuw deoflum geldaþ, VI scll gebete oþþe his hyd. [13]
11. Gif mon his heowum in fæsten flæsc gefe, frigne ge [14]
þeowne halsfange alyse.
    11.1. Gif þeow ete his sylfes ræde, VI scll oþþe his hyd. [15]
12. Biscopes word ꞇ cyninges sie unlægne buton aþe. [16]
13. Mynstres aldor hine cænne in preostes canne. [17]
14. Preost hine clænsie sylfæs soþe in his halgum hrægle [18]
ætforan wiofode, ðus cweþende: *Veritatem dico in xro non mentior.*
    14.1. Swylce diacon hine clænsie.
15. Cliroc feowra sum hine clænsie his heafodgemacene, ꞇ [19]
ane his hand on wiofode; oþre ætstanden aþ abycgan.
16. Gest hine clænsie sylfes aþe on wiofode;[a] swylce cyninges [20]
ðe[gn][b]
    16.1 Ceorlisc man hine feowra sum his heafodgemacene [21]
on weofode;
    16.2 ꞇ ðissa ealra að sie unlegnæ
Ðanne is cirican /6v/ canne riht. [21.1]
17. Gif man biscopes esne tihte oþþe cyninges, cænne hine an [22]
gerefan hand oþþe hine gerefa clensie, oþþe selle to
swinganne.

---

a Manuscript here has a symbol similar to ✤ with a long descender extending into the right margin as an insertion mark; it is repeated before the words *swylce ... weofode* which, inadvertently omitted, are written below the text at the bottom of the page.
b Manuscript reads *ðeng*.

10. If a slave makes offering to devils, let him pay 6 shillings or his hide.
11. If a person gives his household meat in a fast, let him redeem both free and slave with *healsfang*.[a]
    11.1. If a slave eats of his own accord, 6 shillings or his hide.
12. A bishop's word and the king's shall be incontrovertible without oath.
13. The head of a minster should exculpate himself as per a priest's exculpation.[b]
14. A priest should clear himself with his own truth in his holy vestments before the altar, thus saying: *Ueritatem dico in Christo, non mentior*.[c]
    14.1. Similarly should a deacon clear himself.
15. A cleric[d] should clear himself as one of four of his equals, and his hand alone on the altar; the others should stand by to validate the oath.
16. A stranger should clear himself with his own oath at the altar;
    16.1. similarly the king's thegn.
    16.2. A man of freeman rank as one of four of his equals at the altar; and let the oath of all these be incontrovertible.
(This,)[e] then is the church's right of exculpation.
17. If a person should bring a charge against a bishop's servant or the king's, let him clear himself in the presence of the reeve: either let the reeve clear him, or give him to be flogged.

---

a See note f to §8.2, and discussion of this clause under 'Transgressing the laws of the church' in Commentary.
b This could also mean *with a priest's cognizance*.
c *I speak truth in Christ, I do not lie.*
d Probably includes the positions of doorkeeper, psalmist, reader, exorcist, acolyte, and subdeacon; see discussion under 'Church and public assembly' in Commentary to chapter 2.
e As this statement seems to sum up the foregoing rather than introduce the following clauses, I have inserted the demonstrative in the translation for clarity.

18. Gif man gedes^a þeuwne esne in heora gemange^b tihte, his [23]
dryhten hine his ane aþe geclænsie, gif he huslgenga sie.
    18.1 Gif he huslgenga nis, hæbbe him in aþe oðirne
æwdan godne,^c oþþe gelde, oþþe selle to swinganne.
19. Gif folcesmannes esne tihte ciricanmannes esne, oþþe [24]
ciricanmannes esne tihte folcesmannes esne, his dryhten
hine ane his aþe geclensige.
20. Gif man leud ofslea an þeofðe, licge buton wyrgelde. [25]

---

a *Sic* in manuscript. See note a to translation.
b Point added to separate words inadvertently run together.
c n added above insertion mark.

18. If a person should bring a charge against an unfree servant of a fellowship(?)[a] in their midst, let his lord clear him by his oath alone, if he [the lord] is a communicant.[b]
    18.1. If he is not a communicant, he should have for himself in the oath another good oath-helper, or he should pay recompense, or he should give [his servant] to be flogged.
19. If a layman's servant brings a charge against a churchman's servant, or a churchman's servant brings a charge against a layman's servant, his lord should clear him by his oath alone.
20. If a person kills a man in the act of theft, let him lie without *wergild*.

---

a The difficulty in this clause is that *gedes* is not a known Old English word. Liebermann emends it to *gædes*, which is not out of the question, as the variation between e and æ in this text has already been discussed above in 'Some notes on the language.' See also Liebermann, *Gesetze*, 3:29. Technically the word requires no emendation, as under this interpretation the variant vowels simply represent dialectal alternatives. The problem is that *gæd* itself only occurs once in the corpus, in the poetical *Solomon and Saturn* 451–2: *Nolde gæd geador in godes rice eadiges engles and ðæs ofermodan*, 'There would not be fellowship together in God's kingdom of the blessed angel and the arrogant.' See Elliot Dobbie, ed., *The Anglo-Saxon Minor Poems* (New York: Columbia University Press, 1942), 47. To assume that a corrupt reading is a dialectal variant of a *hapax* is a dangerous practice. Even if this possibility were demonstrable, where a word occurs only once we have no opportunity to determine shades of meaning, or often any precise meaning at all. In support of Liebermann's reading is the fact that the interpretation of 'fellowship' as a collective provides an explanation for *heora*, 'their,' which otherwise lacks an antecedent.

The term might be emended to *Godes*, 'of God,' presumably standing for 'of a house of God'; the difference in meaning between this and fellowship is not substantial, if, in fact, fellowship is the appropriate translation for *gæd*. This emendation has two serious drawbacks, however. First, it seems inconceivable that a medieval scribe would miscopy the name of the Lord. And the literal meaning, 'an unfree servant of God,' leaves the third person plural possessive pronoun *heora* stranded.

Like Attenborough and Whitelock, I follow Liebermann's analysis in the absence of any more convincing explanation; Attenborough remarks gloomily, 'I do not feel any confidence in the suggestion.' See F.L. Attenborough, *The Laws of the Earliest English Kings* (Cambridge: Cambridge University Press, 1922), 182.

b Communicant may differentiate a cleric from a layman; perhaps, however, the owner is simply a communicant of a different fellowship. See discussion of this clause under 'Transgressing the laws of the church' in Commentary.

21. Gif man frigne man æt hæbbendre handa gefo, þanne [26]
wealde se cyning ðreora anes: oððe hine man cwelle,
oþþe ofer sæ selle, oþþe[a] hine his wergilde alese.
   21.1. Se þe hine gefo ⁊ gegange, healfne hine age. Gif [26.1]
   hine man cwelle, geselle[b] heom man LXX scll.
22. Gif þeuw stele ⁊ hi[ne] man[c] alese: LXX scll, swa hweder [27]
swa cyning wille.
   22.1. Gif hine man acwelle, þam agende hi[ne] man
   healfne agelde.
23. Gif feorran[-]cumen man oþþe fræmde buton wege gange, [28]
⁊ he þonne nawðer ne hryme ne he horn ne blawe, for ðeof
he bið to profianne, oþþe to sleanne oþþe to alysenne.

---

a þ added above insertion mark.
b *selle* added in right margin.
c Both here and in §22.1, *himan* is run together, eliminating the ending on the pronoun. Liebermann, *Gesetze*, 3:30, restores both of these as the accusative *hine*, and suggests that perhaps originally there was a - nasal extension mark over the *hi* which the copyist overlooked. We might also emend the last phrase *þam agende him man healfne agelde*, 'one should pay the owner half for him,' which grammatically is far preferable. But see the parallel (without the awkward intrusion) in §21; the double accusative construction, however, works better with *age* than with *agelde*.

21. If a person seizes a free man having [the goods in] hand, then the king rules one of three things: either one should kill him, or sell [him] across the sea, or release him in return for his *wergild*.
    21.1. He who seizes and delivers him [the thief], owns him half;[a] if he [the thief] is killed, let them be paid 70 shillings.[b]
22. If a slave steals and a person redeems him: 70 shillings, whichever the king wants.[c]
    22.1. If he [the slave] is put to death, one should pay the owner[d] half his [the slave's] value.
23. If a man [who is] come from afar or a stranger should go off the track, and he then neither calls out nor does he blow a horn, he is to be regarded as a thief, either to be killed or to be redeemed.

---

a Presumably half the value of the stolen goods. From Æbt §15, we know that the original owner was recompensed three-fold. Conceivably half of the total fine goes to the captor. It is possible that this might either mean half the thief's possessions or half his labour as an *esne*, although in the latter case one might expect the time period to be stipulated.

b 'His capturers, who would otherwise lose by the king's choice of the death-penalty. But if *heom* is a mistake for the singular *him*, it could mean "for him" and the situation envisaged might be if the capturer took the law into his own hands, killed the thief, and thus robbed the king of his choice. He would have to compensate for it.' See Whitelock, *English Historical Documents*, 398.

c That is, fine or death. See under 'Theft' in Commentary.

d It is not clear what 'the owner' refers to here. It seems unlikely that it is the owner of the slave (who should have overseen his property better). Liebermann and Attenborough both assume that it is the man who currently holds the slave in his power. But I think it most likely that the payment goes to the man whose property was stolen.

164   The Beginnings of English Law

Commentary

Rubric and prologue

> *These are the decrees of Wihtred, king of the Kentish people.*

Like the previous Kentish laws, the laws of Wihtred are preceded by a rubric in red ink. This follows immediately on the last word in the laws of Hloþhere & Eadric (see 5recto in Diplomatic Transcription, Appendix One). There is then a line break before the beginning of the prologue proper.

> *To the most gracious king of the Kentish people, Wihtred, ruling in the fifth winter of his reign, in the ninth indiction, sixth day of Rugern, in that place which is called Berghamstead, there was gathered a consiliary assembly of great men.*
>
> *There was Brihtwald, archbishop of Britain, and the afore-mentioned king; likewise the bishop of Rochester, which same was called Gebmund, was present; and each order of the church of that people spoke with a single mind with the loyal populace.*
>
> *There the great men devised, with the consent of all, these decrees, and added to the just customs of the Kentish people, as it hereafter says and declares:*

From the prologue on, Wihtred's laws demonstrate a focus on church matters which is not present in those of his predecessors.[18] Æthelberht's laws lack a prologue in the text as we have it (although there may have been one in the original composition) and Hloþhere & Eadric's laws mention only the two kings themselves. Wihtred's prologue, however, lists first among the 'deliberative assembly of great men' Brihtwald, archbishop of Britain. This title shows that the see of Canterbury still subscribed to Pope Gregory I's plan that Augustine should have authority over all churches in Britain; the archbishopric of York was not permanently established until after Wihtred's death.[19] Also present was Gebmund, bishop of Rochester, as well as lower ranks of churchmen. Both bishops of Kent – the archbishop of Canterbury and the bishop of Rochester – are present, giving this gathering much of the appearance of a church council,[20] and further emphasizing the distinction between the territories of East and West Kent.

The ecclesiastic group was augmented by secular advisers, as was often the case in formal synods. Bede ii.5 tells us that Æthelberht established his laws with the advice of his counsellors.[21] Wihtred too assembled the 'great men' of the kingdom, who included (and perhaps comprised the totality of) his *gesiþas* – those of the rank known in earlier laws as *eorl*.[22] This would be the group of counsellors referred to in later Old English writings as the *witan*.

The prologue sets the date of the assembly on the sixth day of *Rugern* – probably 'rye-harvest'[23] – in the fifth winter of Wihtred's reign, in the ninth indiction. The indiction was a cycle of fifteen years, based on the old Roman system of assessing taxes in a fifteen-year rotation. The system of reckoning was inaugurated in 312, so that date would be the *indictio primo*, 'first year of the indiction,' for the first cycle; 313 would be the second year of the first indiction, 314 the third year, and so forth. The cycle we are concerned with here is the twenty-fifth, which would have begun in 687 (*indictio primo*), and the ninth year would thus be 695. The actual day from which the indiction would be calculated varied. The two most common were 1 September (according to the Greek system from Constantinople) and 24 September (according to the Roman system). As the Roman system seems to have been introduced into England by Bede, who postdates Wihtred, we must employ the Greek. In any event, six days after 24 September would be past the rye harvest. Reckoning according to the Greek indiction would set the date at 6 September 695.[24] The *Anglo-Saxon Chronicle* entry of 725 relates that 'In this year, Wihtred, king of the people of Kent, died on 23 April. He had ruled 34 years.'[25] Bede more specifically tells us that the reign was thirty-four and a half years, which would put the beginning of the reign at a late date in 690 and the fifth year of his reign (in which the deliberative assembly was held) at 695. This reckoning tallies with the date established by that of the indiction.

Withred's text concentrates on matters ecclesiastical rather than civil, and it is primarily legislation dealing with the church that his lawmakers added 'to the just customs of the Kentish people.' (This last phrase reflects the fact that in the early periods a ruler held power over people rather than territory, as demonstrated by the grammatical use of the genitive plural *Cantwara*, 'of the people of Kent.') Several parallels to these laws can be found in the 'Penitentials of Theodore,' a set of ecclesiastical rulings attributed to Theodore of Tarsus, archbishop of Canterbury 668–90; as Wihtred's laws were compiled around 695, these penitentials may well have been known to his compiler, and even served in some instances as a model.[26]

Liebermann asserts that the laws of Wihtred are the first of the English laws to use literary citation.[27] First, the prologue strongly echoes that of Hloþhere & Eadric. Second, §8 is so similar in content to §§3–3.2 of the slightly earlier West-Saxon laws of Ine, although it employs a very different phraseology, that Liebermann assumes both to have been drawn from Latin canons drafted by an English synod (see further discussion under 'Theft' below). Third, §14 contains the Latin oath formulation to be spoken by the priest. Fourth, §23 is almost identical in language to a clause in the laws of Ine; the similarity might reflect a lost common source (written or oral), or the clause in Wihtred may be a deliberate borrowing from existing written laws of Ine. Finally, it is possible that the laws in Wihtred prohibiting the worship of idols are based on a lost text of Eorcenberht's laws (see 'Historical background' in chapter 3).

The existence of the prologue implies that the beginning of the text is complete as it stands; in the absence of an epilogue, it is impossible to say whether this is also true of the ending.

The clauses are grouped according to their subject matter: rights of the church, unlawful matrimony, abuse by ecclesiastics, manumission, transgressing the laws of the church, exculpation, and theft.

Rights of the church

1. *Freedom of the church from taxation [is to be];*
   1.1 *and one should pray for the king, and do him honour of their own will without compulsion.*
2. *[Violation of the] protection of the church shall be 50 shillings, as the king's.*

The first clause in Wihtred unites the causes of church and state: while the church is not required to pay into the public coffer, the members of the church are exhorted to pray for the king 'without compulsion.' In exchange for the king's consideration, the church offers him its own.[28]

This clause is echoed in a charter of 699, in which Wihtred freed the Kentish minsters from public tribute, but then ordered 'that they shall show to me and to my successors such honour and obedience as they showed to the kings, my predecessors, under whom they were preserved in justice and liberty.'[29] Honouring the king refers to the duties owed to the sovereign as head of state. A (probably reliable) account of a synod held at Clofeshoh in 792 records Offa of Mercia's grant of immunity to the Kentish churches 'from secular services, from payments to the king and to lesser persons, from the obligation of feeding the king [the *fedesl* of Æbt §12], the men called *fæstincmenn* and the keepers of the king's hounds, horses and hawks, also from any burden on their woods, fields and meadows, and from all work at royal vills.'[30] (Whether or not the common burdens of military service, bridge work, and road work could still be demanded from the church when required *contra paganos*, 'against pagans,' as stated in the earliest authentic Kentish charters, is unclear.)[31]

The church is given the same protection as the king; the 50-shilling fine for theft from the church is the same stipulated as the king's protection in Æthelberht. (And again, one is struck by the discrepancy between the twelvefold restitution for theft from the church and the ninefold fine for theft from the king as laid out in the initial clauses in Æthelberht!)

Unlawful matrimony

> 3. *Men in an unlawful union shall take up a just life with repentance of sins, or be separated from the community of the church.*
>   3.1. *Foreign men, if they will not set their union to right, must depart from the land with their possessions and with [their] sins;*
>   3.2. *Our own men among the people [i.e., native] shall suffer loss of the community of the church without forfeiture of goods.*
> 4. *If after this assembly [something] of this [nature] befalls to a gesiþ-born man, that he should take up an unlawful union against the king's command and the bishop's and the decrees of the books, he makes restitution for that to his lord with 100 shillings according to established right.*
>   4.1. *If it is one of freeman's rank, let him make 50 shillings restitution.*
>   4.2. *And let each of them relinquish the union with repentance.*

As we know from §§9 and 10, pagan practices still lurked at the edges of Christianity, and there still surely remained unions not sanctified by the sacrament of marriage. Clause 3 of Wihtred may refer to Clause X laid out by the Synod of Hertford, convened by Theodore of Tarsus, archbishop of Canterbury, in 672:[32]

> On marriage. That nothing be allowed but lawful wedlock. Let none be guilty of incest, and let none leave his own wife except for fornication, as the holy gospel teaches.[33]

The 'Penitentials of Theodore' discuss an extensive further array of illicit unions for which penance must be done: sodomy, homosexuality, incest, defiling a woman who has committed to holy orders, and marrying within the prohibited degrees of consanguinity.[34] Further, they stipulate that a man who has taken a second or third wife (sequentially, not polygamously) must do penance, although they do not require him to give up his new wife.[35] Wihtred may not have been so understanding. According to W §3, a man living in a prohibited relationship must give up the union 'with repentance.' If he refuses to do so, then he is excommunicated. Excommunication would certainly place his immortal soul in danger; the extent to which he would also be cast out from society at large is unclear. Note that he is allowed to retain his possessions (as opposed to the regulation for those newly entering unlawful marriage established in §4). Foreigners, however, are not only cast out from society, but banished from the land if they persist in their unlawful union. Kent, as the easternmost territory of the British Isles, was often the first landfall for foreign traders, whose behaviour away from home might match that of many modern sailors in ports abroad.[36]

For those entering into an unlawful union, the amount of restitution to be paid is high. For a *gesiþ*-born man (the noble known in the earlier laws as *eorl*), the fine is 100 shillings, a third of his *wergild*; the fine is even stiffer for a freeman, who must pay 50 shillings, half his 100-shilling *wergild*. But the fine for violating an *eorl*'s protection is double that for a similar offence committed against a freeman, and the fine for concubinage is similarly twice as high for an *eorl* as for a freeman. To whom this fine should be paid is not specified; we might expect it to go to the king, as an instance of payment for disturbance of the public peace, but perhaps a man with immediate allegiance to a lord other than the king owed the payment to his overlord.

Abuses by ecclesiastics

5. *If a priest allows an unlawful union, or neglects the baptism of a sick person, or is so drunk that he is not able [to perform his duties], let him be inactive in his service pending the bishop's decree.*
6. *If a tonsured man not under [any ecclesiastical/monastic] rule seeks out hospitality for himself, one should give it to him once; and it should not happen that he be supported for a longer time, unless he should have permission.*

Clause 5 is clearly transparent: a priest neglecting his duties is suspended until the bishop has ruled on his penance. The roughly contemporary 'Penitentials of Theodore' begin with rulings against clerics who succumb to the vice of drunkenness, and also contain strictures against priests who refuse penance to the dying.[37]

Following Stubbs, Liebermann takes §6 to refer to a man 'in neglect of rule,' and assumes the clause to deal with monks or clerics fleeing the monastery.[38] This clause would then absolve the householder from the normal responsibility for hospitality in the case of a fraudulent cleric: the friar in Chaucer's 'Summoner's Tale' certainly has a long pedigree! Similar strictures were laid down by Theodore of Tarsus in 672 at the Synod of Hertford, as reported in Bede iv.8:

> Chapter V. That no clergy shall leave their own bishop nor wander about at will; nor shall one be received anywhere without letters commendatory from his own bishop. If he has once been received and is unwilling to return when summoned, both the receiver and the received shall suffer excommunication.[39]

Wihtred §§5 and 6 provide the first instances in English legal writing of royal law regulating the behaviour of clerics.

Manumission

7. *If a person sets his man free at the altar, he shall have the rights of a free man of the people; the freedomgiver owns his inheritance and wergild and protection of the kin, let him [the newly freed man] be over the border wherever he wishes.*

Clause 7 delineates the procedure for freeing a slave. The ritual takes place at the altar although in the Continental Germanic parallels the setting is before the king. The change of locale in the laws of the deeply Christian Wihtred is hardly surprising. The older Germanic practice has largely been replaced by the Roman *manumissio in ecclesia*, which immediately transforms the former slave into a free man,[40] in contrast to the four generations required in the laws of Æthelberht to achieve fully free status.[41]

Some relics of the older ritual remain, however. The freedom-giver continues to own the inheritance, *wergild*, and protection of the freedman's kin. The form *ænde* is a hapax, and appears to be archaic from the partially umlauted *æ* (as the later, typically Kentish form is *end*) and in particular from the final vowel, which appears nowhere else in the corpus of Old English. By expanding the second ⁊ to match the disyllabic *ænde* of the first conjunction and changing from the third to the first person possessive pronoun (as it would have been in a spoken declaration) we get the collocation *erfe ænde wergild ænde munde mine hine,* 'inheritance and *wergild* and protection of my kin,' which probably represents an ancient oath formulation, echoing the words actually spoken in the manumission ceremony. The existence of such an oral formula could long predate the written text in which it is included, accounting for the preservation of the archaic form *ænde*.[42]

The phrase 'owns his inheritance' probably means one or both of two things. First, the previous owner is responsible for protecting the claims to inheritance, *wergild*, and protection of the new freeman, who may well not have any free kinsmen to help guarantee these rights. Second, should the newly freed man die without naming his beneficiaries, his inheritance reverts to the previous owner. If he has been killed, the *wergild* would also be paid to that owner; if anyone stands under the freedman's protection, that protection is similarly taken up by the owner.

As members of defeated neighbouring peoples were often enslaved, the clause about a freed slave going 'over the border' – that is, leaving Kent – is unsurprising. It may also suggest that the freed slave might move outside the specific area of jurisdiction in which his previous master lived, but still reside within the boundaries ruled by the Kentish king.[43]

Transgressing the laws of the church

8. If a servant according to his lord's order does slave-work after sunset on the eve of Sunday until sunset on the eve of Monday, let the lord pay 80 shillings [?sceattas].
   8.1. If a servant performs [work] on his own counsel on that day, let him pay 6 towards his lord or his hide.
   8.2. If, however, a freeman [works] in that forbidden time, let him be liable for healsfang, and the man who detects that, he shall own half that fine and/or that work.
9. If a freeman without his wife's knowledge makes offering to devils, he shall be liable for all his possessions or healsfang.
   9.1. If both make offering to devils, they are [both] liable for healsfang or all possessions.
10. If a slave makes offering to devils, let him pay 6 shillings or his hide.
11. If a person gives his household meat in a fast, let him redeem both free and slave with healsfang.
    11.1. If a slave eats of his own accord, 6 shillings or his hide.

The next group of clauses addresses transgression of churchly life. Two of the offences are fined by *healsfang*. Although the component morphemes of this term (*heals*, 'neck,' and *fang*, 'capture') are clear, the precise definition of the compound is not as certain. It stands in opposition to the reversed compound *freols*, 'freedom' from *freo hals*, 'free neck,' but seems here to represent a payment in lieu of captivity rather than captivity itself. (Thorpe defines it as 'the sum every man sentenced to the pillory would have had to pay to save him from that punishment had it been in use,'[44] but it seems nonsensical to define a term in reference to a practice that did not exist.) As to the amount involved, Whitelock says that *healsfang* represented 'a proportion of the wergild which went to the nearest relatives of the slain man. When the wergild was 1200 shillings it was 120 shillings, and it may be that this ratio applies to other wergilds.'[45] Attenborough indicates that 'the Norse *halsfang* ("embrace") suggests the possibility that this payment denoted the re-establishment of peace between the families involved in the vendetta,' and, following Schmid, links it to the payment made at the grave in Æbt §24.1.[46] Although I am unconvinced of a subtextual meaning of 'embrace' in the Anglo-Saxon laws, Schmid's connection otherwise seems reasonable. This would then imply that the *healsfang* in Kent was 20 per cent of the *wergild*, rather than the 10 per cent of Whitelock's analysis. By the time of Wihtred, the meaning must have been extended more generally to 'fine to avoid imprisonment,' as there is no question of a *wergild* payment to injured kin in this clause.

One of the offences for which *healsfang* is assessed is making offerings to devils (i.e., idols). If a husband sacrifices without his wife's knowledge – if, that is, he continues to indulge in pagan practice while she is Christian – it is his *healsfang* alone which must be rendered. Thus a wife is not liable for criminal activity engaged in by her husband if she is not complicit;[47] a husband-and-wife team, however, must each pay their own *healsfang* (another indication that a woman could control her own finances). If they do not have sufficient resources to pay the *healsfang* in full, all their possessions are confiscated. The confiscation may well have the effect of reducing their status to that of servant or *esne* (unless perhaps the kinship group supports them?). We know from §48 of the laws of Ine (which refers to 'a newly enslaved penal slave')[48] that the position of slave (and presumably *esne*) was not necessarily determined by birth, but could be entered into in later life. Recall, as well, that the 'Penitentials of Theodore' tell us a person could make himself a slave at the age of fourteen.[49]

A person is also liable for *healsfang* if he gives his household meat in time of fast: the law stipulates that both slave and freeman are to be redeemed with *healsfang*. Liebermann says that the fine here must be the householder's *healsfang*, as a slave, having no *wergild*, can have no percentage of it that would represent his *healsfang*.[50] However, given that §22 shows that a slave can be redeemed from hanging by payment of a fine, it seems possible that a similar amount would be payable to/for a slave in this instance. Liebermann assumes that *healsfang* must be paid for each individual so fed.[51] The fine could be crippling if the household were of any size; it thus seems more likely that the *healsfang* is that of the householder. It then becomes unclear, however, whether the payment is split between the meat-fed parties or, more probably, goes as a fine to the public coffer.

Failing to observe a cessation of labour on the Sabbath (from Saturday sunset to Sunday sunset) also attracts a fine. If a freeman works of his own accord, he must pay his *healsfang*. A servant who breaks the Sabbath by performing work on his own account must pay 6 shillings: this fine is payable to his lord. If a slave either makes offering to idols or eats meat in a fast, he is similarly liable for 6 shillings. This fine too is probably to be rendered to his master, parallel to the similar financial liability of a servant. Notable here is the possibility that both servants and slaves could own property. If either servant or slave is unable to scrape the necessary sum together, he pays with a flogging.

The grammar of §8 is corrupt. The problems lie in the underlined phrases: *Gif esne <u>ofer dryhtnes hæse</u> þeow weorc wyrce ... LXXX scíł <u>se dryhtne</u> gebete*. First, the preposition *ofer* generally means 'beyond' or 'against'; if this clause is taken as being in opposition to the following clause, then *ofer* should be emended to *of*, 'according to,' or 'from.' The phrase *se dryhtne*, with nominative article but dative noun, must be amended to the nominative *se dryhten* (the agent of the action) to achieve the translation given previously: *If a servant <u>according to his lord's order</u> does slave-work ... let <u>the lord</u> pay 80 shillings*.[52] Attenborough suggests emending shillings here to *sceattas* ('possibly due to [the scribe's having misunderstood] the abbreviation *sc.*' in an earlier copy). The suggestion seems plausible for two reasons. First, the penalty if assessed in shillings seems disproportionate to the offence, when one considers that the owner's *wergild* itself was 100 shillings if he was a freeman; 80 per cent of a person's *wergild* seems a very stiff fine. Second, in the parallel §§3 and 3.2 in the laws of Ine, a man's responsibility for working on the Sabbath of his own accord is far greater than his master's liability for ordering a slave to do such work.[53] Eighty *sceattas* would be four shillings, which is roughly equivalent to the assessment demanded in Ine §3.2.

Clause 8.1 tells us that in contradiction to working for his lord, a servant who works on the Sabbath on his own accord must pay 6 shillings. Whitelock presents a different translation of the phrase *deþ his rade*, which I have rendered 'performs [work] on his own counsel.' In fact, *rade* can mean 'ride,' and Whitelock translates the clause 'If a servant rides on his own business ...'[54] Against this I would argue that the noun *rade* does not appear elsewhere with (any form of) the verb *dōn*, 'to do.' More convincing is Liebermann's interpretation of *rade* as an alternative form of *rǣde*, 'counsel.'[55] The confusion of a and æ in this text also occurs in the substitution of *habbe* for *hæbbe*, 'he should have' (§6). Further, §11.1 begins *Gif þeow ete his sylfes rǣde*, which unambiguously means 'If a slave eats according to his own counsel ...' And the ruling in §11 taken with that of §11.1 provides a direct parallel to the difference in responsibility between a slave who is forced to an action and one who undertakes it on his own accord. Finally, we find comparable clauses in Ine, as translated by Whitelock:

§3. If a slave works on Sunday at his master's command [*hǣse*], he is to be free, and the master is to pay 30 shillings as a fine.
§3.1 If, however, the slave works without his knowledge [*gewitnesse*], he is to be flogged.[56]

Once again, there is no mention of riding: the issue is clearly that the slave is breaking the Sabbath rest in the first case with and in the second without his master's cognizance.

Finally, the person who turns in someone who transgresses by working on the Sabbath receives a reward. The grammar of the clause and the ambiguity of expansion for the character ⁊ as 'and' or 'or'[57] allows for several options in interpreting what that reward is. As we see in the English translation 'half the fine and/or the work': it could be half the fine *and all* the work which the transgressor has performed, or half the fine *and half* the work, or half the fine *or all* the work or half the fine *or half* the work. The alliteration of *wite*, 'fine,' and *weorc*, 'work,' inclines me to take the conjunction as 'and,' and the *healf*, 'half,' as governing the alliterative pair; namely, the reward consists of half the fine *and* half the work. This is the only instance in the Kentish laws of moneys being paid, not as a recompense for injury, but as a reward for turning informant, although it parallels the half-fine given to a person who captures a thief red-handed described in §21.1.

The strictures addressed in these clauses all find correspondences in the 'Penitentials of Theodore,' which prohibit working on the Lord's day, despising a fast appointed in the church, and worshipping of idols. The last includes sacrificing to demons, performing incantations, and a woman putting her daughter 'upon a roof or into an oven for the cure of a fever'![58]

Exculpation

12. *A bishop's word and the king's shall be incontrovertible without oath.*
13. *The head of a minster should exculpate himself as per a priest's exculpation.*
14. *A priest should clear himself with his own truth in his holy vestments before the altar, thus saying: Veritatem dico in Christo, non mentior.*
    14.1. *Similarly should a deacon clear himself.*
15. *A cleric should clear himself as one of four of his equals, and his hand alone on the altar; the others should stand by to validate the oath.*
16. *A stranger should clear himself with his own oath at the altar;*
    16.1. *similarly the king's thegn.*
    16.2. *A man of freeman rank as one of four of his equals at the altar; and let the oath of all these be incontrovertible.*

The next group of clauses deals with purification: the declaration of innocence in the case of accusation of wrongdoing. It is interesting to note that none of the clauses in question is paralleled in the 'Penitentials of Theodore': although the rite of exculpation takes place at the altar, it is regulated by royal rather than ecclesiastical decree.

First, both the bishop's and the king's word stands alone, with no necessity to bring it to oath. The precedence of the ecclesiastic position here is probably formulaic rather than hierarchical: compare the modern phrase 'church and state' (rather than the reverse), and see the parallel in §17. Priest and deacon must both swear oaths – are thus subject to royal law – but they have the privilege of standing alone at the oath-swearing. To solemnize the ritual, they are required to wear their holy vestments. Clause 13 is grammatically ambiguous in Old English as well as Modern English: either the head of a religious house gives his oath *in the same way* as a priest (that is, alone-standing), or he must have a priest to witness (i.e., his position makes him answerable to a higher standard of proof). The first interpretation seems more likely. A minster could have been headed by a priest or an abbot, but although this leader of a religious community may have had considerable economic and political power, he would not have had the standing of a bishop. Only a bishop could induct someone into the priesthood, for example, or endow another with episcopal status. The head of the minster would have had no more ecclesiastical status than a priest; §13 apparently similarly equates him to a priest in terms of his legal standing.[59]

Two types of laymen require no witnesses at exculpation, although for very different reasons. The king's thegn – a nobleman in service to the king[60] – can stand alone by virtue of his position; a stranger, because he is an outsider within the community, could not be expected to have kin or friends to stand with him in the oath. H.R. Loyn draws a connection between the two by postulating that the thegn is 'a servant sent on royal business to a locality not his own.' Coupling the thegn with the stranger would therefore 'be clearly understandable.'[61] This seems to me, however, to limit the application of the term 'king's thegn' rather severely; I assume rather that it refers to the king's servant whether at home or abroad.

Both cleric (i.e., a clergyman of lower standing than a deacon) and freeman require three equals with them in the oath-swearing; notably, his witnesses are not necessarily from his kin group. The accused lays his hand on the altar, with the others there to bear witness (and vouch for the truth of the oath?).

(This,) then is the church's right of exculpation.

Without the demonstrative, which I have added in the translation, this phrase is a rather puzzling interpolation. The three preceding clauses all stipulate that the exculpation take place at the altar, which one might consider the church's right. In the three following clauses, by contrast, the place for the act of exculpation is not fixed, although in §17 a reeve must be present. More likely the phrase serves to sum up the preceding clauses, and I have thus expanded the translation. Note that the three following clauses involve those of unfree status, while the preceding ones concerned freemen.

17. *If a person should bring a charge against a bishop's servant or the king's, let him clear himself in the presence of the reeve: either let the reeve clear him, or give him to be flogged.*
18. *If a person should bring a charge against an unfree servant of a fellowship(?) in their midst, let his lord clear him by his oath alone, if he [the lord] is a communicant.*

18.1. *If he is not a communicant, he should have for himself in the oath another good oath-helper, or he should pay recompense, or he should give [his servant] to be flogged.*

19. *If a layman's servant brings a charge against a churchman's servant, or a churchman's servant brings a charge against a layman's servant, his lord should clear him by his oath alone.*

A servant who has been accused must rely for purification on a higher authority. Bishop's and king's servants both may be exculpated by the respective reeve – the bailiff of the estate or area to which the servant belongs.[62] If this is not possible (because the servant is, in fact, guilty), then the servant is flogged. The distinction between §17 and the two following is that only a king or bishop is permitted to have a reeve stand in for him and represent his authority.

Clause 18 is corrupt in transmission (see notes to translation), but probably considers the case of a servant accused in a clerical community. Presumably the accuser is of higher status than the servant, as the situation of one servant accusing another is addressed in the following clauses. Here, the servant's lord must exculpate his servant if the servant is innocent. If the servant's lord is a communicant in the churchly community, his oath stands alone. Any monk would naturally be a communicant; however, communion was not offered to the laity on a regular basis; maybe the distinction being made is between a member of the clergy and a layman. (The head of the monastery would certainly be responsible for the labourers belonging to the community, and some lower-ranking members of the fellowship may also have retained servants.) Or perhaps this phrase simply means that the servant's lord is a communicant in another fellowship. It is also possible, however, that it refers to someone who is deliberately excluded from the Eucharist. The 'Penitentials of Theodore' contain an entire chapter, 'Those Who Are Deceived by Heresy,'[63] on those who would naturally not be communicants in the Roman Church. They would, however, presumably still be subject to the laws of the state. This category also includes those who are only temporarily separated from the communion: §XII.4 states that '[p]enitents according to the canons ought not to communicate before the conclusion of the penance; we, however, out of pity give permission after a year or six months.' That is, one who has been assigned penance for any of the many reasons stipulated in Theodore's 'Penitentials' would not be a communicant for the period of his or her penance, which could last as long as twelve years.

For whatever reason, if the servant's lord is not a communicant, he must bring an oath-helper to the swearing. This requirement parallels §15.1 in the contemporary laws of Ine (given here in Whitelock's translation):

§15. *He who is accused of [taking part in] the raid of any army is to redeem himself with his wergild or clear himself by [an oath in the amount of] his wergild.*
§15.1. *With communicants, the oath shall be only half as much.*[64]

It is interesting that the primary stipulation assumes that the wrongdoer is *not* a communicant, so this cannot have been be a remarkably unusual state. Unfortunately the scanty remaining materials from this period do not offer any further elucidation of the precise meaning of the clause.

In the case of lay versus clerical accusations (or the reverse) by one servant against another, the master need not have an oath-helper in order to exculpate his servant. Where a freeman needs three oath-helpers in order to exculpate *himself*, the lowlier status of the servants involved in the dispute seems to abrogate the need for witnesses. We might assume that if the servant is guilty, his lord can choose between paying recompense or giving the servant to flogging.

Theft

20. *If a person kills a man in the act of theft, let him lie without wergild.*
21. *If a person seizes a free man having [the goods in] hand, then the king rules one of three things: either one should kill him, or sell [him] across the sea, or release him in return for his wergild.*
    21.1. *He who seizes and delivers him [the thief], owns him half; if he [the thief] is killed, let them be paid 70 shillings.*
22. *If a slave steals and a person redeems him: 70 shillings, whichever the king wants.*
    22.1. *If he [the slave] is put to death, one should pay the owner [of the stolen property] half his [the slave's] value.*

The final clauses in the laws of Wihtred deal with theft, actual or anticipated. Clause 20 is the only one in the Kentish laws which implies the right to self-defence: someone who kills a man in the act of robbery need not pay recompense. Clause 21 demonstrates that if a thief is caught red-handed, the choice of punishment falls to the king: he may have the thief put to death, sell him into exile (as a slave), or let him (or his kin) buy his life with his *wergild*. (In this clause we see an uncharacteristic use of rhyme in oððe man him cwelle, oððe ofer sæ selle; the clauses are also rhythmically parallel. This usage might be taken as another example of the literary character of Wihtred's compilation, as discussed earlier.)

The man who captures the thief receives half the fine should the thief choose to ransom himself. Should he be put to death, the reward is fixed at 70 shillings. Whitelock sees ambiguity in the last phrase *Gif hine man cwelle, geselle heom man LXX scH*, 'if he [the thief] is killed, let them be paid 70 shillings.' She gives preference to an interpretation of *heom* as a plural referring to 'his capturers, who would otherwise lose by the king's choice of the death-penalty.'[65] This implies, however, that the earlier 'owns him half' does not refer simply to his *wergild*, which would net the captors a mere 50 shillings: they would surely become the strongest advocates for the death penalty in every instance, as they would then reap an extra 20 shillings! Recall that Æbt §15 sets the recompense for theft at threefold the value of the goods – perhaps both fines are payable, in which case the captor(s) receive(s) 50 shillings plus one and a half times the worth of the purloined property. Whitelock gives as an alternative the possibility that *'heom* is a mistake for the singular *him*, [in which case] it could mean "for him" and the situation envisaged might be if the capturer took the law into his own hands, killed the thief, and thus robbed the king of his choice, he would have to compensate for it.'[66] This reading seems more baroque than usual for these laws, and I consider more likely Whitelock's own preferred interpretation.

In the instance of a slave caught red-handed, the king can have him put to death or allow his master to redeem him for 70 shillings (= 70 per cent of the *wergild* for a free man). If the king orders execution, the 'owner' – presumably the man from whom the property was stolen – is entitled to 'half.' 'Half' likely means half the value of the slave, as it would be a gross injustice for the robbed man to receive only half the value of his stolen goods. Extrapolating from above, the payment would be 35 shillings, or half the amount paid in the event that a free man who committed robbery is put to death. Certainly the owner of the slave does not receive compensation, as he allowed a man under his control opportunity to commit the crime – the early medieval equivalent of the leash law. Attenborough, following Liebermann, assumes that 'the owner' refers to the man who currently has the slave in his power:[67] that is, a reward for the capture. Under this interpretation, the stolen goods must be redeemed for a fine similar to that stipulated in Æbt §15. This hypothesis, however, relies on a somewhat unusual interpretation of *agende*, 'owner.' In any event, as Liebermann points out, the captor is likely in most instances to be identical to the man from whom goods were robbed.

Being sold across the water is hardly a punishment for someone who is enslaved already, and who may well have originally come from the continent, won as a prize in battle or perhaps even sold across the sea for slavery in a geographic reversal of §21.[68] Clause 11 of the laws of Ine regulates against selling one's own countryman, free or unfree, across the sea. And XII22 in the 'Penitentials of Theodore' describe the rights of a man whose enemy has carried off his wife, comparing the situation to that of 'slaves from over sea.'[69] (Anglo-Saxon slaves had the same origins as those in early Ireland: they were prisoners taken in battle, foreigners captured in marauding slave expeditions, or relegated to slavery due to the non-payment of debt or fine.)[70] Thus the third option for a freeman – deportation – is not available for a slave.[71]

In the last clause in Wihtred we find a legal precept that seems common in primitive societies.

> 23. *If a man [who is] come from afar or a stranger should go off the track, and he then neither calls out nor does he blow a horn, he is to be regarded as a thief, either to be killed or to be redeemed.*

Any foreigner straying from the public way without giving notification of his presence thus may be assumed to be up to no good! The wording of this phrase almost exactly mirrors §20 of the slightly earlier West Saxon laws of Ine (688x94).

> Gif feorcund mon oððe fremde buton wege geond wudu gonge ond ne hrieme ne horn blawe, for ðeof he bið to profianne: oððe to sleanne oððe to áliesanne.[72]
>
> *If a man who is come from afar or a stranger should go outside the track towards the woods and neither calls out nor blows a horn, he is to be regarded as a thief, either to be killed or to be redeemed.*

Liebermann assumes that Wihtred borrowed directly from Ine,[73] although it is also possible that the two clauses stem from a common original. Certainly the concept of a stranger's loudly announcing his friendly intentions is quasi-universal, transcending both place and time. For example, Albert Cook points out 'a curious parallel in an account of travel in Africa by Sir Harry H. Johnston, in the *Youth's Companion* for October 29, 1903 ... "You are seldom received with active hostility by savage Africans if you announce your approach with a great deal of noise or a firing of guns or shouting. It is the silent and stealthy coming which precipitates hostile acts on their part."'[74] And once again I owe thanks to Patrick Wormald, in this case for reminding me that this custom also held true in the American Wild West.

Conclusion

The face of the law has changed substantially from the days of Æthelberht. Whereas the first Anglo-Saxon laws, most of them inherited to some extent from their Germanic past, deal primarily with simple offence and restitution, the written laws of Wihtred legislate primarily within and about the new religion of Christianity. Bede ii.5 tells us that Æthelberht established his laws with the advice of his counsellors, the Anglo-Saxon *witan* who are descendents of the Germanic group responsible for advising the king. Wihtred's prologue gives specific prominence to the Christian bishops of Canterbury and Rochester over the other 'great men' who had gathered in his 'consiliary assembly.' And yet, Wihtred's world remained in many respects much the same as it had been in the time of his great-great grandfather: Christian practices were not yet as deeply ingrained as Wihtred surely wished them to be. Some of his subjects continued to ignore the Christian injunction against eating meat or working on the Sabbath. Despite the influence of the sacrament, irregular marriage practices persisted: Wihtred had to legislate against unions such as Æthelberht's son Eadbald took up with his stepmother. Finally, some holdouts still made offerings to devils, or the old pagan gods. Although law is notoriously conservative, in these early days of recording legal statutes, the world might not, in fact, have been changing as fast as the written law.

Appendix I: Diplomatic Transcription

The diplomatic transcription is provided for those wanting to refer to manuscript readings of the text. An excellent facsimile of the *Textus Roffensis* appears as Volume VII in the series *Early English Manuscripts in Facsimile*, prefaced by a very helpful codicological introduction by Peter Sawyer. The three texts reproduced here constitute the first six pages of this manuscript (verso and recto). The facsimile is well-produced, and the hand easily readable with a little practice, even by those unfamiliar with early insular paleography. The diplomatic transcription in the present volume is intended to serve as a road map to the facsimile to assist those unused to reading medieval manuscript, and as a field reference for those who do not have immediate access to the reproduction. It also reveals what the text under discussion looks like in its original form. Of particular interest to linguists is the system of word division and the clustering of phrases, which may provide prosodic clues for syntactic analysis. Readers encountering medieval manuscript convention for the first time may be surprised at the apparently random division within individual words at line breaks.

Editorial conventions

I have reproduced to the best of my ability the spacing of the manuscript; variations in the shapes of letters have been omitted for the sake of clarity. The þ and ð (with its capital Ð) both represent the sounds represented by modern English 'th'; þ represents *þæt*. Although ƿ is used throughout to the *Textus Roffensis* to represent 'w,' I have chosen the modern English equivalent for easier reading.

The character . represents a point in the manuscript; this is used when modern English might choose a comma, semicolon, colon, or period. It is also employed when modern English would use no punctuation at all, for instance, to set off numerals.

† refers the reader to a note in my editions of the texts.

1 recto

Þis syndon þa domas þe æðelbirht cyning
asette on aGustinus dæge.†

G†ODES FEOH. ꝫCI   1

        ricean.XII.gylde.Biscopes feoh.
        XI.gylde.Preostes feoh.IX.gylde.
        Diacones feoh.VI.gylde.Clero
        ces feoh.III.gylde Ciric friþ.   5
II.gylde.M † friþ.II.gylde.Gif cyning his
leode tohim gehateþ ꝫheom mon þær yfel gedo.
II.bóte.ꝫcyninge.L.scillinga.Gif cyning æt
mannes ham drincæþ.ꝫðær man lyswæs hwæt
gedo.twi bote gebete. Gif frigman cyninge   10
stele.IX.gylde for gylde .Gif incyninges tu
ne man mannan of slea.L.scill gebete.Gif man
frigne mannan of sleahþ.cyninge.L.scill.to
drihtin beage.Gif cyninges ambiht smið oþþe
laadrinc mannan of slehð[ ]umanleod† gelde   15
forgelde.Cyninges mundbyrd.L.scillinga.Gif
frigman freum stelþ.III.gebete.ꝫcyning age þ
wite ꝫealle þa æhtan.Gif man wið cyninges mæg
denman geligeþ.L.scillinga gebete.Gif hio grin
dende þeowa sio.XXV.scillinga gebete.Sio þridde   20
XII.scillingas.Cyninges fedesl.XX.scillinga
forgelde.Gif on eorles   tune man mannan

1 verso

          of slæhþ.XII.scᚻ gebete.Gif wið eorles
birele man geligeþ.XII.scᚻ gebete.Ceorles mund
byrd.VI.scillingas.Gif wið ceorles birelan man
ge ligeþ.VI.scillingū gebete.Aet þære oþere ðeo
wan^t.L.scætta. Aet þare þriddan.XXX.scætta.Gif   5
man inmannes tún ærest ge irneþ.VI.scillingū
gebete. Se þe æfter irneþ.III.scillingas. Siððange
hwylc scilling. Gif man mannan wæpnum bebyreþ
ðær ceas weorð.⁊man nænig yfel ne gedeþ.VI.scillin
gum gebete.Gif weg reaf sy^t gedón.VI.scillingum   10
gebete.Gif man þone man of slæhð.XX.scillingū
gebete.Gif man mannan of slæhð.medume leod
geld.C.scillinga gebete.Gif man mannan of slæhð
æt openum græfe.XX.scillinga forgelde.⁊in.XL.
nihta ealne leo_d forgelde.Gif bana of lande   15
ge witeþ.ða magas healfne leod forgelden.Gif man
frigne man geb   þ^t.XX.scᚻ gebete.Gif man
ceorlæs hlaf ætan of slæhð.VI.scillingum gebete.
Gif læt of slæhð þone selestan.LXXX.^{scᚻt} for gelde.
Gif þane oþerne of slæhð.LX.scillingum forgelde.   20
Ðane þriddan.XL.scilling̃.forgelden.Gif friman
edor brecþe gedeþ.VI.scillingum gebete.Gif man
inne feoh genimeþ.seman.III.gelde gebete.Gif
fri man edor gegangeð.IIII.scillingum gebete.

2 recto

Gif man mannan of slea agene scætte.⁊unfacne feo
ge hwilce gelde.Gif fri man wið fries mannes wif
geligeþ.his wer gelde abicge.⁊oðer wif his agenū
scætte begete.⁊ðæm oðrum æt þam gebrenge.
Gif man riht ham scyld þurh stinð.mid weorðe for
gelde.Gif feax fang geweorð.L.sceatta tobote.
Gif banes blice weorðeþ.III.scillingum gebete.Gif
banes bite weorð.IIII.scillingum gebete.Gif sio
uterre hion gebrocen weorðeþ.X.scillingum ge
bete.Gif butu sien.XX.scillingum gebete.Gif
eaxle gelæmed weorþeð.XXX.scill gebete.Gif
oþer eare nawiht[†] gehereð.XXV.scill gebete.
Gif eare of weorð[†] aslagen.XII.scill gebete.Gif
eare þirel weorðeþ.III.scill gebete.Gif eare
sceard weorðeþ.VI.scill gebete.Gif eage of we
orð.L.scilling[u-†] gebete.Gif muð oþþe eage woh
weorðeþ.XII.scill gebete.Gif nasu ðyrel weorð
VIIII.scillingum gebete.Gif hit sio an hleore
III.scill gebete.Gif butu ðyrele sien.VI.scill
gebete.Gif nasu ælcor sceard weorð gehwylc.
VI.scill gebete.Gif ðirel weorþ.VI.scill gebete.
Se þe cinban for slæhð.mid.XX.scillingum for
gelde.Æt þam feower toðum fyrestum æt
ge hwylcum.VI.scillingas.Se toþ se þanne

2 verso

    bi standeþ.IIII.sciⱠⱠ. Se þe ðonne bi ðam standeþ.
    III.sciⱠⱠ. And[†] þoñ siþþan gehwylc scilling.Gif
    spræc awyrd weorþ.XII.scillingas.Gif widoba
    ne gebroced weorðeþ.VI.sciⱠⱠ gebete.Seþe earm
    þurh stinð.VI.scillingum gebete.Gif earm 5
    forbrocen weorð.VI.sciⱠⱠ gebete.Gif þuman of
    aslæhð.XX.sciⱠⱠ.Gif ðuman nægl of weorðeþ.
    III.sciⱠⱠ gebete.Gif man scyte finger of aslæhð.
    VIIII.sciⱠⱠ gebete.Gif man middel finger of aslæhð.
    IIII.sciⱠⱠ gebete.Gif man goldfinger of aslæhð. 10
    VI.sciⱠⱠ gebete.Gif man þone lytlan[†] finger of
    aslæhð.XI.sciⱠⱠ gebete.Æt þam neglum ge
    hwylcum.scilling.Æt þam lærestan wlitewam
    me.III.scillingas.And[†] æt þam maran.VI.sciⱠⱠ.
Gif man oþerne mid fyste in naso slæhð.III.sciⱠⱠ. 15
Gif dynt sie.scilling.Gif he heahre handa dyn
    tes onfehð.sciⱠⱠ forgelde.Gif dynt sweart sie
    buton wædum.XXX.scætta gebete.Gif hit sie
    binnan wædum.ge hwylc.XX.scætta gebete.
Gif hrif wund weorðeþ.XII.sciⱠⱠ gebete.Gif he 20
    þurh ðirel weorðeþ.XX.sciⱠⱠ gebete.Gif man
    gegemed weorðeþ.XXX.sciⱠⱠ gebete.Gif man
    cear wund sie.XXX.sciⱠⱠ gebete.Gif man ge
    kyndelice lim awyrdeþ.þrym leud geldum hine

3 recto

man for gelde.Gif he þurh stinð.VI.scill gebete.
Gif man inbestinð.VI.scill gebete.Gif þeoh gebro
cen weorðeþ.XII.scillingum gebete.Gif he healt
weorð.þær motan freond seman.Gif rib forbro
cen weorð.III.scill gebete.Gif man þeoh ðurh stingþ   5
stice gehwilce.VI.scillingas.Gyfe⁺ofer ynce scilling.
æt twam yncum twegen.ofer þry.III.scll.Gif
wælt wund weorðeþ.III.scillingas gebete.Gif fot
of weorðeþ.L.scillingum forgelden.Gif seo mi
cle⁺ ta of weorðeþ.X.scll forgelden.Æt þam o   10
ðrum taum gehwilcum healf gelde.eal swa æt þam
fingrum ys cwiden.Gif þare mycclan taan nægl
of weorþeð.XXX.scætta tobote.Æt þam oþrum
gehwilcum.X.scættas gebete.Gif fri wif locbore
les wæs hwæt ge deþ.XXX.scll gebete.Mægþ   15
bot.sy⁺ swa friges mannes.Mund þare betstan
widuwan eorlcundre.L.scillinga gebete.Ðare
oþre.XX.scll.ðare þriddan.XII.scll-. Þare
feorðan.VI.scll.Gif man widuwan unagne ge
nimeþ.II. seo mund sy⁺.Gif man⁺ mægþ   20
gebigeð⁺ ceapi geceapod sy⁺.gif hit unfacne is.
gif hit þonne facne is.ef þær æt ham gebren
ge ꝥhim man his scæt agefe.Gif hio cwic bearn
ge byreþ healfne scæt age.gif ceorl ær swylteþ.

3 verso

Gif mid bearnum bugan wille.healfne scæt age.Gif ceorl
agan wile swa an bearn.Gif hio bearn negebyreþ fæ
dering magas fioh agan.⁊morgen gyfe.Gif man
mægþman⁺ nede genimeþ.ðam agende.L.scillinga.⁊
eft æt þam agende.sinne willan æt gebicge.Gif hio   5
oþrum mæn insceat bewyddod sy.XX.scillinga ge
bete.Gif gæn gang⁺geweorðeþ.XXXV.sciɫɫ.⁊cyninge
XV.scillingas.Gif man mid esnes cwynan geligeþ
be cwicum ceorle.II.gebete.Gif esne $^{oþerne⁺}$ of slea unsyn
ningne.ealne weorðe forgelde.Gif esnes eage ⁊foot   10
of weorðeþ aslagen.ealne weorðe hine forgelde.
Gif man mannes esne gebindeþ.VI.sciɫɫ gebete.Ðeo
wæs weg reaf se.III.scillingas.Gif þeow⁺ steleþ.
II.gelde gebete. *Þis syndon þa domas ðe hloþhæ*   15
*re ⁊eadric cantwara cyningas asetto*N.⁺
hloþhære. ⁊eadric cantwara cyning,$^{as⁺}$ecton þa
æ.þa ðe heora aldoras ær ge worhtoN.⁺
ðyssum domum þe hyr efter sægeþ.Gif man
nes esne eorlcundne mannan ofslæhð. þane ðe
sio þreom hundum sciɫɫ gylde.seagend þone   20
banan agefe.⁊do þær þrio manwyrð to.Gif
se bane oþ̇ byrste feorþe manwyrð he togedo.
⁊hine gecænne mid godum æwdum⁺.þ he þane
banan begeten ne mihte.Gif mannes esne

4 recto

frigne mannan of slæhð, þane þesie.hund scillin
ga gelde. seagend þone banan agefe.⁊oþer man
wyrð þær tó.Gif bana oþ byrste.twam man wyr
þum hine man forgelde.⁊hine gecænne mid go
dum æwdum.þ he þane banan begeten ne mihte.   5
Gif frigman mannan for stele.gif he eft cuma.
ster melda secge an andweardne.gecænne hine
gif he mæge.hæbbe þare freora rim æwda man
na.⁊ ænne mid inaþe.æghwilc man æt þam tune
þe he tohyre gif he þ nemæge gelde swa he gono   10
háge⁺. Gif ceorl acwyle belibbendum wife ⁊bearne.
riht is þ hit þ bearn medder folgige.⁊ himman
an his fædering magum wilsumne berigean ge
felle his feoh tohealdenne.oþ þ he.X.wintrasie.
Gif man oþrum mæn feoh for stele.⁊seagend hit   15
eft æt fo. geteme to cynges sele gif he mæge .
⁊þane⁺ æt gebrenge þe him sealde.gif he þ ne
mæge.læte án.⁊fo se agend to.Gif man oþerne
sace tihte.⁊he þane, mannan⁺mote anmedle oþþe an þin
ge.symble seman þam oðrum byrigean⁺.gesel   20
le ⁊ þam riht awyrce⁺ þeto hiom cantwara de
man gescrifen. Gif he ðonne byrigan for wær
ne.XII.scillingas agylde þam cyninge.⁊sio se
sacy swa open swa hio ær wes. Gif man oþerne

4 verso

tihte siþþan he him byrigan gesealdne hæbbe.
˥ðonne ymb.III.niht gesecæn hiom sæmend bu
ton þam.ufor leofre sio þeþa tihtlan age.Siþ
þan sio sace gesemed sio anseofan nihtum se
man þam oþrum riht gedo.ge cwime anfeo 5
oððe anaþe. swa hwæder swa him leofre sio.
gif he þonne ꝥ nylle⁺ gelde þoñ.c.buton aðe.
siþþan ane neaht ofer ꝥ. gesem hie.Gif man
mannan an oþres flette manswara hateþ.oððe
hine mid bismær wordum scandlice grete.scil 10
ling agelde þam þe ꝥ flet age.˥ VI. sciłł. þam þe
he ꝥ word to gecwæde. ˥cyninge.XII.sct for
gelde.Gif man oþrum steop asette.ðær mæn
drincen buton scylde.an ealdriht.scłł agelde
þam þe ꝥ flet age. ˥ VI.scłł þam þeman þone 13
steap aset. ˥cynge.XII.scłł.Gif man wæpn
abregde þær mæn drincen. ˥ðær man nan
yfel nedeþ.scilling.þan þeꝥ flet age. ˥cynin
ge. XII.scłł.Gif ꝥ flet geblodgad wy_Rþe.for
gylde þem mæn his mundbyrd. ˥cyninge . L. 20
sciłł. Gif man cuman feormæþ.III.niht an
his agenum hame.cepe man oþþe oðerne þe
sio ofer mearce cuman ˥hine þoñ his mete
fede. ˥he þoñ ænigum mæn yfel gedo se man

5 recto

    þane oðerne æt rihte gebrenge oþþe riht fore wyrce.
Gif cant wara ænig inlundenwic feoh gebycge.hæbbe
    him þonne twegen oððe ðreo unfacne ceorlas to
    gewitnesse.oþþe cyninges wic gerefan. gif hit man
    eft æt þam mæn incænt ætfó þonne tæme he   5
    to wic to cyngæs sele to þam mæn ðe him sealde.gif
    he þane wite ꝥæt þam teame ge brengen mæge.gif
    he þ ne mæge.gekyþe ðanne inwiofode mid his
    gewitena anum oþþe mid cyninges wic gerefan.
    þ he þ feoh undeornunga his cuþanceape inwic   10
    gebohte.ꝛhim man þanne his weorð agefe.gif he
    þanne þ ne mæge gecyþan mid rihtre canne.læte
    þanne.án. ꝛse age^{n}d† tofó. Ðis synd Wihtrædes
    domas Cantwara cyninges.†
Ð†am mildestan cyninge cantwara.wihtræde   15
    rixigendum þe fiftan wintra his rices.
    þy.niguðan gebanne.sextan dæge rugernes.in
    þære stowe þy hatte bergham styde.ðær wæs
    gesamnad eadigra geheahtendlic ymcyme.ðær
    wæs birhtwald bretone heahbiscop.ꝛse ærnæm   20
    da cyning.eacþan hrofesceastre bisceop se ilca
    gybmund wæs haten.and ward wæs ꝛ cwæð.ælc
    had ciricean ðære mægðe anmodlice mid þy
    hersuman folcy. Þæʀ ða eadigan fundon mid

5 verso

ealra gemedum ðas domas. ꜩcantwara rihtum
þeawum æcton swahit hyr efter segeþ ꜩcwyþ.
Cirice anfreols dome gafola ꜩman for cyning ge
  bidde.ꜩhine buton neadhæse heora willum weor
  þige‿n†.Ciricean mundbyrd sie.L.scH swa cin   5
  ges.Vnriht hæmde mæn to rihtum life mid syn
  na hreowe to fon. oþþe of ciricean genaman.asca
  dene sieN.Æltheodige mæn gif hio hiora hæmed
  rihtan nyllað.of lande mid hiora æhtum ꜩmid
  synnum gewiten.swæse mæn inleodum ciriclicæs   10
  gemanan ungestrodyne þoligen.Gif ðæs geweor
  þe gesiþcundne mannan ofer þis gemot þ he un
  riht hæmed genime ofer cyngæs bebod ꜩbiscopes
  ꜩboca dom.se þæt gebete his dryhtne†.c.scH.an
  ald reht.Gif hit ceorlisc mansie.gebete.L.scH.   15
  ꜩgehwæder þ hæmed mid hreowe forlæte.Gif
  priost læfe unriht hæmed.oþþe fulwihðe.untru
  mes forsitte.oþþe toþon druncen sie.þ he nemæ
  ge.sio he stille his þegnungæ oþ biscopes dom.
Gif bescoren man steor leas. gange him angest   20
  liðnesse gefe him man ænes ꜩþ nege weorðe bu
  ton he leafnesse habbe þæt hine man læng feor
  mige.Gif man his mæn an wiofode freols gefe.
  se sie folc fry.freols gefa age his erfe ænde

6 recto

wergeld.ꝫmunde þare hina[†]. sie ofer mearce ðær he
wille. Gif esne ofer dryhtnes hæse þeow weorc wyr
ce ansunnan æfen efter hire setl gange oþ monan
æfenes setl gang.LXXX.scɫɫ se dryhtne[†] gebete.Gif
esne deþ his rade þæs dæges.vi.se wið dryhten gebe 5
te oþþe sine hyd. Gif friman þonne anðane for
bodenan timan sio he heals fange scyldig.ꝫse man
se þ ara sie he age healf þ wite ꝫðæt weorc.Gif ceorl
buton wifes wisdome deoflum gelde. he sie ealrahis
æhtan scyldig.ꝫheals fange.gif butwu deoflum 10
geldaþ.sion hio heals fange.scyldigo ꝫealra æhtan.
Gif þeuw deoflum geldaþ.vi.scɫɫ gebete.oþþe his hyd.
Gif mon his heowum infæsten flæsc gefe.frigne ge
þeowne halsfange alyse.Gif þeow ete his sylfes
ræde.vi.scɫɫ oþþe his hyd. Biscopes word ꝫcynin 15
ges sie unlægne buton aþe. Mynstres aldor
hine cænne inpreostes canne. preost hine clæn
sie sylfæs soþe inhis halgum hrægle æt foran
wiofode ðus cweþende.Veritatem dico inxro non
mentior.swylce diacon hine clænsie.Cliroc 20
feowra sum hine clænsie his heafod gemacene
ꝫane his hand on wiofode oþre æt standen aþ
abycgan.Gest hine clænsie sylfes aþe on wiofode ✤
ꝫðissa ealra að sie unlegnæ Ðanne is cirican

✤   swylce cyninges ðeng . Ceorlisc man hine feowra
    sum his heafod gemacene on weofode .

6 verso

  canne riht. gif man biscopes esne tihte oþþe cy
ninges cænne hine an gerefan hand oþþe hine
gerefa clensie oþþe selle to swinganne.Gif man
gedes þeuwne esne inheora gemange.tihte his
dryhten hine his ane aþe geclænsie gif he husl   5
gengasie. gif he husl genga nis hæbbe him inaþe
oðirne æwdan god,ⁿeᵗ.oþþe gelde.oþþe selle toswin
ganne. Gif folces mannes esne tihte cirican man
nes esne.oþþe cirican mannes esne tihte folces
mannes esne.his dryhten hine ane his aþe ge   10
clensige. Gif man leud ofslea anþeofðe.licge
buton wyrgelde. Gif man frigne man æt hæb
bendre handa gefo þanne wealde se cyning ðreo
ra anes.oððe hine man cwelle.oþþe ofer sæ selle.
oþ,Þeᵗ hine his wer gelde alese.Se þe hine gefo ⁊ge   15
gange. healfne hine age.gif hine man cwelle.ge selleᵗ
heom man.LXX.scH. Gif þeuw stele ⁊himan
alese.LXX scH swa hweder swa cyning wille.gif
hine man acwelle þam agende himan healfne
agelde.Gif feorran cumen man oþþe fræmde   20
buton wege gange.⁊he þonne nawðer ne hryme.
ne he horn neblawe.for ðeof he bið toprofi
anne oþþe to sleanne. oþþe to alysenne.

Appendix II: Comparison of Restitution According to Amount in Æthelberht

Personal Injury	Other
10 sceattas (=½ shilling)	
striking off each toenail except big toenail	
20 sceattas or 1 shilling	
additional payment for causing a bruise covered by clothing	breaking into a freeman's dwelling as 3rd man or following
knocking out a back tooth	
striking off a fingernail	
striking a blow with raised hand	
causing an inch-wide wound in thigh	
additional fee for causing a bruise when striking	
30 sceattas (=1 ½ shillings)	
striking off big toenail	lying with 3rd rank of freeman's female slaves
additional payment for causing a bruise visible outside clothing	
2 shillings	
causing a 2-inch-wide wound in thigh	
striking off middle toe	
50 sceattas (=2 ½ shillings)	
seizing of hair	lying with 2nd rank of freeman's female slaves
3 shillings	
causing exposure of a bone	breaking into a freeman's dwelling as 2nd man
piercing an ear	
piercing the cheek (2x for 2)	highway robbery by a slave
knocking out the tooth two down from foremost four	
striking off a thumbnail	

Appendix II

(continued)

Personal Injury	Other
causing slight disfigurement of the countenance	
striking another in the nose with the fist	
breaking a rib	
causing a 3-inch-wide wound in thigh	
causing a 'welt-wound'	
striking off the 4th toe	

4 shillings

Personal Injury	Other
cutting into a bone	passing over a fence into an enclosure (with intention to rob or do injury)
knocking out the tooth beside the foremost four	
striking off a middle finger	
striking another in the nose with the fist and causing a bruise	

4 ½ shillings

Personal Injury	Other
striking off the 2nd toe	

5 ½ shillings

Personal Injury	Other
striking off the little toe	

6 shillings

Personal Injury	Other
notching an ear	violating a freeman's protection
piercing both cheeks	lying with a freeman's cupbearer
for each gash on a nose	the first of a gang to break into a freeman's dwelling
piercing ?unknown body part (?throat)	
knocking out foremost four teeth (each)	providing weapons where no harm occurs
breaking a collarbone	killing a freeman's loaf-eater
stabbing through an arm	breaking into an enclosure (fence-breaking)
breaking an arm	
striking off a ringfinger	violating protection of 4th rank of widow
causing greater disfigurement of the countenance	binding a servant
stabbing through the penis (?or scrotum)	
stabbing into the penis (?or scrotum)	
stabbing through a thigh	

9 shillings

Personal Injury	Other
piercing the nose	
striking off a forefinger	

10 shillings

Personal Injury	Other
breaking the outer ?skin of the skull	
striking off a big toe	

11 shillings

Personal Injury	Other
striking off a little finger	

Comparison of Restitution According to Amount in Æthelberht

(continued)

Personal Injury	Other
	12 shillings
striking off an ear	lying with 3rd rank of king's female slaves
knocking mouth or eye crooked	killing someone in a nobleman's dwelling
damaging speech	lying with a nobleman's (female) cupbearer
causing a stomach wound	
breaking a thigh	providing weapons for highway robbery
	violating protection of 3rd rank of widow
	15 shillings
	payment to king for taking a maiden by force, but returning her (?still a virgin)
	20 shillings
?fracturing the skull	payment in lieu of feeding of the king
breaking a jawbone	fine in addition to *wergild* for killing man during highway robbery
striking off a thumb	
piercing through the stomach	binding a freeman
	violating protection of 2nd rank of widow
	payment to man for abducting his betrothed
	25 shillings
causing either ear to hear nothing	lying with a 'grinding' female slave of king
	30 shillings
laming a shoulder	a housekeeper doing something 'seriously dishonest'
payment for a cure [=doctor's fee]	
grievously wounding a person	
	35 shillings
	to owner of a maiden's protection for taking her by force but returning her (?still a virgin)
	40 shillings
	killing 3rd rank of freedman
	50 shillings
striking off an eye	to king for harm at king's assembly
striking off a foot	to king for killing someone in king's dwelling
	to king for killing a freeman
	violating the king's protection
	lying with the first rank of king's female slaves
	violating protection of first rank of widow
	taking a maiden by force and keeping her
	60 shillings
	killing 2nd rank of freedman

Appendix II

(continued)

Personal Injury	Other
	80 shillings
	killing 1st rank of freedman
	100 shillings
	medium wergild (freeman or woman)
	killing king's offical [?,] smith or ?guide
	3 wergilds
causing serious damage to penis (?or scrotum)	

Appendix III: Comparison of Restitution According to Status in Æthelberht

	King	Nobleman	Freeman	Freedman Servant	Woman
Harm at assembly	2-fold + 50 shillings				
Harm at host's house	2-fold				
Theft	9-fold		3-fold		
Killing in dwelling	50 shillings	12 shillings			
Lord-price for killing freeman	50 shillings				
Lord-price for killing members of retinue	100 shillings				
Violating protection	50 shillings		6 shillings		For 4 ranks of widows: 50:20:12:6 shillings [a]
Lying with 1st rank of female slave	50 shillings	12 shillings	6 shillings		
2nd rank	25 shillings		50 sceattas		
3rd rank	12 shillings		30 sceattas		

a This amount doubles if the widow is under someone else's protection. (See discussion under 'Women and Children' in Commentary to chapter 2).

Appendix III

(continued)

	King	Nobleman	Freeman	Freedman Servant	Woman
Defaulting responsibility for feeding of king	12 shillings				
Wergild		300 shillings	100 shillings according to H & E §1	For 3 ranks of freedmen: 80:60:40 shillings	100 shillings
Binding			20 shillings	6 shillings for servant	
Killing loaf-eater			2 shillings		
Abduction					50 shillings

Appendix IV: Payment to the King for Disturbance of the Peace

Payments for disturbance of the public peace are often stipulated as payments to the king (who is responsible for maintaining the common weal); in some cases it is not clear to whom the fine is due. I have chosen to be inclusive rather than exclusive. Most payments to the king are included, with the exception of the specific fine of 50 shillings for violation of the king's protection, which seems more a personal than public offence. All such fines included in the Kentish laws, followed by the clauses in which they appear, are reproduced below.

	6 shillings	
Æthelberht	for providing another with weapons where no harm results	(§23)
	12 shillings	
Æthelberht	for providing weapons where highway robbery results	(§23.1)
Hloþhere & Eadric	for refusing to give surety when accused of a charge	(§6.1)
	for falsely accusing a man of a charge	(§7)
	for taking a cup from a man in another's dwelling	(§8)
	for drawing a weapon against a man but doing no harm	(§9)
	15 shillings	
Æthelberht	for taking a maiden by force, but returning her[?still a virgin]	(§77.2)
	20 shillings	
Æthelberht	for defaulting the responsibility for feeding the king	(§17)
	for killing a person during highway robbery, fine in addition to *wergild* [this fine may be the part of the *wergild* the weapon-provider must pay]	(§23.2)

202 Appendix IV

(continued)

	50 shillings	
Æthelberht	for harm done at king's assembly	(§8)
	for killing someone in king's dwelling	(§11)
	for killing a freeman	(§12)
Hloþhere & Eadric	for drawing a weapon against a man where blood is shed	(§9)
	80 shillings	
Wihtred	paid by the lord of a servant for ordering him to do work on the Sabbath [if the interpretation is that the fine is payable by the lord to the public coffer]	(§8)
	100 shillings	
Æthelberht	for killing king's official [?,] smith or ?guide/herald	(§13)
Wihtred	for taking up an unlawful (sexual) union [payment 'to his lord'; this is only relevant if this is interpreted as 'to the king']	(§4.1)
	healsfang or all possessions	
Wihtred	payable by a freeman for sacrificing to pagan idols	(§9)
	payable by a freeman's wife if she also sacrifices to pagan idols	(§9.1)
	a fine 2-fold the otherwise-stipulated payment	
Æthelberht	for violation of assembly peace	(§7)

Notes

Chapter One: Background

1. A very helpful bibliography of scholarship on the history of Anglo-Saxon England can be found in Simon Keynes, *Anglo-Saxon History: A Select Bibliography*, Subsidia 13 (3rd ed. 1998). The most recent version can be found on the internet at http://www.wmich.edu/medieval/rawl/keynes1
2. In preface to manuscripts D, E, and F. Dorothy Whitelock, ed., *English Historical Documents, Volume I: c.500–1042* (London: Eyre & Spottiswoode, 1955; repr. 1979), 148.
3. The traditional theory is that the Celtic dialects were brought by tribes migrating west from their Indo-European homeland; see J.P. Mallory, *In Search of the Indo-Europeans: Language, Archaeology and Myth* (New York: Thames and Hudson, 1989), esp. 222–65. This assumption has recently been questioned by Colin Renfrew, *Archaeology and Language: The Puzzle of Indo-European Origins* (London: J. Cope, 1986), esp. 211–49.
4. See Katherine Forsyth, *Language in Pictland: The Case Against Non-Indo-European Pictish*, Studia Hameliana, 2 (Utrecht: Keltische Draak, 1997) for recent discussion of this question.
5. See James Campbell, 'The End of Roman Britain,' in James Campbell, Eric John, and Patrick Wormald, eds., *The Anglo-Saxons* (Oxford: Phaidon, 1982), 10.
6. Bertram Colgrave and R.A.B. Mynors, eds., *Bede's Ecclesiastical History of the English People* (Oxford: Clarendon, 1969), 43. For Bede citations, see also Charles Plummer, *Venerabilis Baedae: Historiam Ecclesiasticam Gentis Anglorum; Historiam Abbatum; Epistolam ad Ecgberctum una cum Historia Abbatum Auctore Anonymo*, 2 vols. (Oxford: Clarendon, 1846). Colgrave and Mynors base their edition on the Moore manuscript, while

Plummer follows Lenigrad. Plummer does not provide a translation, but his introduction and notes are very useful.
7 See Campbell, 'The End of Roman Britain,' 16.
8 See David Dumville, 'Sub-Roman Britain: History and Legend,' *History*, N.S. 62 (1977): 173–92, reprinted in Dumville, *Histories and Pseudo-Histories of the Insular Middle Ages* (Aldershot: Variorum, 1990); Barbara Yorke, *Kings and Kingdoms of Early Anglo-Saxon England* (London: Seaby, 1990), 1–4.
9 See discussion in Nicholas Higham, *Rome, Britain and the Anglo-Saxons: The Archaeology of Change* (London: Seaby, 1992), 69–108, 156–7, and 224. My summary of the takeover of lowland Britain by the Germans owes much to Higham's analysis, with its skilful blend of historical and archaeological evidence. See also Patrick Sims-Williams, 'The Settlement of England in Bede and the *Chronicle*,' *Anglo-Saxon England* 12 (1983): 1–42.
10 Colgrave and Mynors, *Bede's Ecclesiastical History*, 47. For Gildas, see Michael Winterbottom, ed. and trans., *Gildas: The Ruin of Britain and Other Works* (London and Chichester: Phillimore, 1978), 23–4, 95.
11 Canto 31. See, e.g., Robert Pinsky, trans. *The Inferno of Dante: A New Verse Translation* (New York: Farrar, Straus, and Giroux, 1994), 330–1.
12 See Higham, *Rome, Britain and the Anglo-Saxons*, 164; J.M. Wallace-Hadrill, *Early Germanic Kingship in England and on the Continent* (Oxford: Clarendon, 1971), 21.
13 Winterbottom, trans. *Gildas*, 26.
14 Giorgio Ausenda, 'Current Issues and Future Directions in the Study of the Early Anglo-Saxon Period,' in John Hines, ed., *Anglo-Saxon England from the Migration Period to the Eighth Century: An Ethnographic Perspective* (Woodbridge: Boydell, 1997), 419.
15 Della Hooke, 'The Anglo-Saxons in England in the Seventh and Eighth Centuries: Location in Space,' in Hines, ed., *The Anglo-Saxons*, 67, claims that 'as yet, it is impossible to judge the numbers of Anglo-Saxons involved in either the early migrations or in subsequent waves. It seems that extensive areas of the North Sea littoral were deserted in this period, never to be reoccupied, and many of these migrants must have added to the numbers hoping to carve out a new life in Britain. The Anglo-Saxon burial evidence has been taken by some to indicate that the numbers have, in the past, been grossly exaggerated. But it is hardly likely that more than a minority of burials have been discovered ... Neither is it known what proportion of the settlers were buried in cemeteries.' Contra this, see Higham, *Rome, Britain and the Anglo-Saxons*, 168–88.

16 See Higham, *Rome, Britain and the Anglo-Saxons*, 223; Ian Wood, 'Before and After the Migration to Britain,' in Hines, ed., *The Anglo-Saxons*, 46; Yorke, *Kings and Kingdoms*, 8.
17 Higham, *Rome, Britain and the Anglo-Saxons*, 228.
18 Colgrave and Mynors, *Bede's Ecclesiastical History*, 51 and fn 1, 50. An excellent discussion can be found in Ian Wood, 'Before and After the Migration,' 41–6, and subsequent debate. See also Walter Pohl, 'Ethnic Names and Identities in the British Isles: A Comparative Perspective,' in Hines, ed., *The Anglo-Saxons*, 14.
19 Bede i.26 mentions the old Roman church of St Martin's near Canterbury, for one, and, as Nicholas Brooks points out, this memory that the building was a place of Christian worship gives us an indication of ongoing practice. 'For on the one hand, in Canterbury, as in other Romano-British towns, there were innumerable buildings standing in derelict condition and available for the Christian missionaries; on the other the pagan Anglo-Saxon ruling class is not likely to have known or to have been concerned that a particular structure had been a church.' See Nicholas Brooks,*The Early History of the Church of Canterbury: Christ Church from 597 to 1066* (Leicester: Leicester University Press, 1984), 17. The dedication of this church to Saint Martin may well be attributed to the Frankish princess, Bertha; her mother Ingoberg was committed to the cult of the saint, and both this church and the chapel of the early royal necropolis were named after the Frankish saint. See Ian Wood, 'Augustine and Gaul,' in Richard Gameson, ed., *St. Augustine and the Conversion of England* (Stroud: Sutton, 1999), 72. Canterbury also contains 'possible vestiges of a cult of a martyr Sixtus,' according to Richard Gameson, 'Context and Achievement,' in *St. Augustine and the Conversion of England*, 5.
20 Tim Tatton-Brown, 'Canterbury and the Early Medieval Towns of Kent,' in Peter Leach, ed., *Archaeology in Kent to AD 1500* (London: Council for British Archaeology, 1982), 79–83.
21 Nicholas Brooks, 'The Creation and Early Structure of the Kingdom of Kent,' in Steven Bassett, ed., *The Origins of Anglo-Saxon Kingdoms* (London and New York: Leicester University Press, 1989), 67.
22 Sonia Chadwick Hawkes, 'Anglo-Saxon Kent c. 425–725,' in Leach, ed., *Archaeology in Kent to AD 1500*, 64–78; Yorke, *Kings and Kingdoms*, 13, 27, 70; Brooks, 'Creation and Structure,' 68.
23 For a list of the dual kings, see Yorke, *Kings and Kingdoms*, 33. Further discussion of joint rule can be found in Brooks, 'Creation and Structure,' 68, and Barbara A.E. Yorke, 'Joint Kingship in Kent c. 560 to 785,' *Archaeologia Cantiana* 99 (1983): 1–19.

24 Here an early royal double monastery was founded for Æthelburh, the daughter of Æthelberht of Kent and the widow of Edwin of Northumbria.
25 See Hawkes, 'Anglo-Saxon Kent,' 75; also Brooks 'Creation and Structure,' 69–74.
26 K.P. Witney, *The Jutish Forest: A Study of the Weald of Kent from 450 to 1380 AD* (London: Athelone Press, 1976), 22.
27 Hawkes, 'Anglo-Saxon Kent,' 72–3.
28 Ibid., 72.
29 Sir Thomas Wyatt, *The Complete Poems*, ed. R.A. Rebholz (Harmondsworth: Penguin, 1978). Wyatt adapts the proverb in the first of his 'Epistolary Satires' (CXLIX, p. 189). See also note to l. 100, p. 445.
30 G.O. Sayles, *The Medieval Foundations of England* (London: Methuen, 1948), 22.
31 Colgrave and Mynors, *Bede's Ecclesiastical History*, 51.
32 Wallace-Hadrill, *Early Germanic Kingship*, 22.
33 Whitelock, *English Historical Documents*, 154; see discussion in Hawkes, 'Anglo-Saxon Kent,' 70.
34 Hawkes, 'Anglo-Saxon Kent,' 72.
35 Colgrave and Mynors, *Bede's Ecclesiastical History*, 151. See discussion in Barbara A.E. Yorke, 'The Reception of Christianity at the Anglo-Saxon Royal Courts,' in Gameson, ed., *St. Augustine and the Conversion of England*, 153–6. Other sources provide different genealogies: the later *Historia Brittonum* and the Anglian chronicles list Octa as Hengist's son and Oisc – with a variant name – as his grandson (see Yorke, *Kings and Kingdoms*, 26).
36 Brooks, 'Creation and Structure,' 55–74, contains a very thorough analysis of the question of Æthelberht's dates. This has been expanded on by Ian Wood, 'The Mission of Augustine of Canterbury to the English,' *Speculum* 69 (1994): 1–17. This discussion owes much to these two sources. See also D.P. Kirby, *The Earliest English Kings* (London and Boston: Unwin Hyman, 1991), 30–47 and 114–41.
37 See Colgrave and Mynors, *Bede's Ecclesiastical History*, 149. Bede ii.5 actually states that when Æthelberht died in 616, it was 'the twenty-first year after Augustine and his companions *had been sent* to preach to the English nation' (my emphasis). It is also possible that this refers to the departure of the mission from Rome in 595.
38 Regardless of the actual year of death, Brooks, 'Creation and Structure,' 66, does not accept Wheeler's argument 'that Bede here is contrasting Æthelberht's *life* on earth with his everlasting *life* in heaven, and is therefore telling us that Æthelberht was 56 years old when he died'; he

postulates, rather, that Bede is comparing the temporal rule on earth with God's eternal rule in heaven. C.R. Cheney, *A Handbook of Dates for Students of English History*, rev. Michael Jones (Cambridge: Cambridge University Press, 2000), 22, cites only the possibility of 616.

39 Brooks, 'Creation and Structure,' 66.
40 Wood, 'The Mission of Augustine,' 11.
41 Lewis Thorpe, trans., *Gregory of Tours: The History of the Franks* (Harmondsworth: Penguin, 1974), 219. For Gregory, see also O.M. Dalton, ed. and trans., *The History of the Franks by Gregory of Tours*, 2 vols. (Oxford: Clarendon, 1927), with a fine introduction in Volume One. The critical edition is Bruno Krusch and William Levison, eds., *Monumenta Germaniae Historica: Scriptores Rerum Merovingicarum, Vol, I, Part I. Gregorii Episcopi Turonensis: Libri Historiarum X* (Hannover: Hahn, 1951).
42 Kirby, *Earliest English Kings*, 34, says that this may even be taken to indicate that Æthelberht's father Eormenric was not yet on the throne.
43 See Wood, 'Augustine and Gaul,' 71; Gameson, 'Context and Achievement,' 16; Brooks, 'Creation and Structure,' 66–7.
44 Whitelock, *English Historical Documents*, 157.
45 Per Wood, 'The Mission of Augustine.'
46 Thorpe, trans. *Gregory of Tours*, 513.
47 Whitelock, *English Historical Documents*, 158.
48 Colgrave and Mynors, *Bede's Ecclesiastical History*, 73.
49 Bede never actually uses the term *imperator*, but does tell us that Æthelberht was the third who *imperauit*, 'ruled over all.' See Colgrave and Mynors, *Bede's Ecclesiastical History*, 148–9; also discussion in N.J. Higham, *An English Empire: Bede and the Early Anglo-Saxon Kings* (Manchester and New York: Manchester University Press, 1995), 47–63.
50 Contra Colgrave and Mynors, *Bede's Ecclesiastical History*, 144, fn 1, who narrow the date to 604x5. See Brooks, *Early History of the Church of Canterbury*, 332 and E.B. Fryde et al., eds., *Handbook of British Chronology* 3rd ed. (London: Office of the Royal Historical Society, 1986), 213.
51 Colgrave and Mynors, *Bede's Ecclesiastical History*, 133–5.
52 David A.E. Pelteret, 'Slavery in Anglo-Saxon England,' in J. Douglas Woods and David A.E. Pelteret, eds., in *The Anglo-Saxons: Synthesis and Achievement* (Waterloo: Wilfrid Laurier University Press, 1985), 120.
53 Henry Mayr-Harting, *The Coming of Christianity to Anglo-Saxon England*, 3rd ed. (London: B.T. Batsford, 1991), 59. Chapter 3 of this book contains an invaluable discussion of Pope Gregory and the evangelizing mission. See also R.A. Markus, 'Augustine and Gregory the Great,' in Gameson, ed., *St. Augustine and the Conversion of England*, 41–9.

208   Notes to pages 11–15

54   Mayr-Harting, *The Coming of Christianity*, 60–1.
55   Gameson, 'Context and Achievement,' 7; Wood, 'Augustine and Gaul,' 69, 80.
56   See Gameson, 'Context and Achievement,' 10–4; Stéphane Lebecq, 'The Question of Logistics,' in Gameson, ed., *St. Augustine and the Conversion of England*, 60–2.
57   Mayr-Harting, *The Coming of Christianity*, 61, citing Margaret Deansley, *Augustine of Canterbury* (London: Nelson, 1964).
58   Wallace-Hadrill, *Early Germanic Kingship*, 29.
59   Colgrave and Mynors, *Bede's Ecclesiastical History*, 69.
60   Ibid., 75.
61   A coin ornament, bearing the name of *Levardus*, was found in St Martin's graveyard in the nineteenth century; Philip Grierson, *The Coins of Medieval Europe* (London: Seaby, 1991), 18, points out that this 'has some claim to be regarded as the earliest monument of English Christianity.'
62   Colgrave and Mynors, *Bede's Ecclesiastical History*, 74–5, fn 2; see also Ausenda, 'Current Issues and Future Directions,' 445.
63   Gameson, 'Context and Achievement,' 18.
64   Tatton-Brown, 'Canterbury and the Early Medieval Towns of Kent,' 81–2.
65   Brooks, *Early History of the Church of Canterbury*, 8.
66   Mayr-Harting, *The Coming of Christianity*, 63.
67   Higham, *Rome, Britain and the Anglo-Saxons*, 231.
68   See discussion in Henry G. Richardson and George O. Sayles, *Law and Legislation from Æthelberht to Magna Carta* (Edinburgh: Edinburgh University Press, 1966).
69   Kenneth Jackson, *Language and History in Early Britain* (Edinburgh: Edinburgh University Press, 1953), 73.
70   See Anthony Harvey, 'Some Significant Points of Early Insular Celtic Orthography,' in Donnchadh O'Corrain, Liam Breatnach, and Kim McCone, eds., *Sages, Saints and Storytellers: Celtic Studies in Honour of Professor James Carney* (Maynooth: An Sagart, 1989), 55–66, and Jane Stevenson, 'The Beginnings of Literacy in Ireland,' *Proceedings of the Royal Irish Academy* 89C/6 (1989): 127–65.
71   Specifically, the writing of long vowels as doubled. See Thomas Charles-Edwards and Patrick Wormald, 'Addenda' to J.M. Wallace-Hadrill, *Bede's Ecclesiastical History of the English People* (Oxford: Clarendon, 1988), 218–19 for British and Lisi Oliver, *Language of the Early English Laws* (Ann Arbor: University Microfilms International, 1995), 53–9 for Irish. The representation of the dental fricative as <d>

similarly echoes Old Irish practice; this is not restricted to Æthelberht, but occurs sporadically throughout the Kentish laws, although not elsewhere in the *Textus Roffensis*. See Lisi Oliver, 'Irish Influence on Orthographic Practice in Early Kent,' *Nowele* 33 (1998): 93–113.
72 See R.I. Page, *An Introduction to English Runes* (London: Methuen, 1973), 21–34, 163–5, 169–70, 182–6.
73 See Wallace-Hadrill, *Early Germanic Kingship*, 26.
74 Richardson and Sayles, *Law and Legislation*, 1–12 and 157–69.
75 Colgrave and Mynors, *Bede's Ecclesiastical History*, 151.
76 See later discussion in chapter 1, 'Chronological layering.'
77 An even later addition is the introductory sentence with its reference to Augustine, which is written in different ink. (See Commentary to 'Rubric and prologue,' chapter 2, for dating.) This rubric matches in ink and style similar chapter headings to Hloþhere & Eadric and to Wihtred, but for the latter two laws a prologue proper follows. All three rubrics belong to the compilation, and do not actually constitute part of the individual texts.
78 Sir Frederick Pollock and Frederic Maitland, *The History of English Law Before the Time of Edward I* (London: Cambridge University Press, 1968), 12.
79 Wallace-Hadrill, *Early Germanic Kingship*, 40–4.
80 A.W.B. Simpson, 'The Laws of Ethelberht,' in Morris Arnold et al. eds., *On the Laws and Customs of England* (Chapel Hill: University of North Carolina Press, 1981), 14–15.
81 Warren Winfred Lehman, 'The First English Law,' *Journal of Legal History* 6(1) (1985): 1–32.
82 At times Lehman certainly goes too far in his attributions to Æthelberht. For example, he twice praises the detailed listing in the personal injury section of the laws, which we can postulate on both syntactic grounds and the evidence of comparative Germanic law to be an inheritance rather than an innovation of Æthelberht. See discussion under 'Chronological layering' later in this chapter, and Oliver, 'Dative of Quantity,' *Language of the Early English Laws*, 223–9.
83 See Grierson, *Coins of Medieval Europe*, 18; also Wallace-Hadrill, *Early Germanic Kingship*, 26. The famous medallion with the name *Levardus Eps* ('Liudhard Bishop,' who had come over as Bertha's chaplain) is meant to function as an ornament rather than a coin (see Grierson, *Coins of Medieval Europe*.)
84 Patrick Wormald, '*Lex Scripta* and *Verbum Regis*: Legislation and Germanic Kingship, from Euric to Cnut,' in P.H. Sawyer and I.N. Wood, eds., *Early Medieval Kingship* (Leeds: The Editors, 1977), 105–38.

210 Notes to pages 17–20

85 Patrizia Lendinara, 'The Kentish Laws,' in Hines, ed., *The Anglo-Saxons*, 219–20. Considering the vocabulary question, she suggests that some of the *hapax legomena* were loan-translations of Latin terms; since she does not present any Latin models, there appears to be no evidence to support this speculation.
86 Colgrave and Mynors, *Bede's Ecclesiastical History*, 149.
87 See Ian Wood et al., *Discussion* to David N. Dumville, 'The Terminology of Overkingship in Early Anglo-Saxon England,' in Hines, ed., *The Anglo-Saxons*, 371.
88 Wood, 'Before and After the Migration,' 50.
89 Thomas Charles-Edwards in discussion appended to Ian Wood, 'Before and After the Migration,' 59.
90 Brooks, 'Creation and Structure,' 59.
91 Wormald, '*Lex Scripta* and *Verbum Regis*,' 137.
92 Patrick Wormald, '*Exempla Romanorum*: The Earliest English Legislation in Context,' in Alvar Ellegård and Gunilla Åkerström-Hougen, eds., *Rome and the North* (Jonsered, Sweden: Paul Astroms forlag, 1996). Wormald also discusses this in *The Making of English Law: King Alfred to the Twelfth Century, Volume One: Legislation and its Limits* (Oxford: Blackwell, 1999), 93–101.
93 I owe these observations to discussions with Patrick Wormald.
94 Wallace-Hadrill, *Early Germanic Kingship*, 37, 44.
95 Wormald, *The Making of English Law*, 95.
96 Wallace-Hadrill, *Early Germanic Kingship*, 46.
97 Throughout this section I rely heavily on the excellent introduction by Peter Sawyer to *Early English Manuscripts in Facsimile, Vol. VII: Textus Roffensis, Part I* (Copenhagen: Rosenkilde and Bagger, 1957). In places I have augmented Sawyer's discussion with material drawn from Felix Liebermann's prefatory remarks to *Die Gesetze der Angelsachsen*, vol. 1 (Halle: M. Niemeyer, 1897–1916), xxvi–xxviii. Whenever I have quoted either of these scholars directly, this is noted. To have acknowledged their contributions in full would result in more citations than text, and I refer the reader to these two excellent studies for elaboration. The manuscript is #373 in N.R. Ker, ed., *Catalogue of Manuscripts Containing Anglo-Saxon* (Oxford: Clarendon, 1957), 443–7.
98 Mary P. Richards, *Texts and Their Traditions in the Medieval Library of Rochester Cathedral Priory* (Philadelphia: American Philosophical Society, 1988), x.
99 Sawyer, *Textus Roffensis*, 11.
100 These are Trinity College, Cambridge, MS. O. 4. 7; Cambridge University Library, MS. Ff. 4. 32; Eton College, MS. 90; British Museum, MSS. Royal 3 B xii; 5 C i; 6 A iv; 6 C iv; 8 D xvi; 12 C I, table of contents and

prologue on first 2 leaves; 15 a xxii, fos. 110–117; Lambeth Palace, MS. 76; Bodleian Library, MS Bodley 134. Listed in Sawyer, *Textus Roffensis*, 13. See also Ker, *Catalogue*, 447.

101 Liebermann reads this as an open *a*; however, as discussed in 'Chronological layering' below, the dative *scillingum* rather than the genitive *scillinga* would be expected here. I read this rather as a *u* with an extension stroke. Nowhere else does the scribe use an open *a*, and Liebermann's reading does not account for the horizontal stroke appended to the character. Note, however, that Richard Emms, 'The Scribe of the Paris Psalter,' *Anglo-Saxon England* 28 (1999): 179–83 at 180, discusses 'the open-topped letter **a** as a feature of some late 10th-century manuscripts produced at St. Augustine's Abbey, Canterbury.'

102 It is not uncommon for a copyist to start by carefully preserving archaism but gradually become less careful: see, for example, Onofrio Carruba, 'Die Chronologie der heth. Texte und die heth. Geschichte,' *Zeitschrift der Deutschen Morgenländische Gesellschaft*, Supplementa I (1969): 226–49 for a parallel in Hittite.

103 Liebermann, *Gesetze*, 1:xxvii.

104 Ibid., 1:xxvii; Sawyer, *Textus Roffensis*, 18; N.R. Ker, *English Manuscripts in the Century after the Norman Conquest* (Oxford: Clarendon, 1960), 30–1.

105 Richards, *Texts and Their Traditions*, 44.

106 Cited in Sawyer, *Textus Roffensis*, 20.

107 The history of editions of the laws is contained in 'Previous Editions and Translations' beginning on p. 251.

108 By the time of Sir Edward Dering's transcription in 1632–3, only *m- - - -frith* was legible.

109 Samuel Pegge, *An Historical Account of that Venerable Monument of Antiquity the* TEXTUS ROFFENSIS, (London: Society of Antiquaries, 1727), 6.

110 venerandum hoc antiquitatis monumentum per integrum biennium desideratum surreptore tandem detecto, sed restitutionem strenue negante, Decreto Supremæ Curiæ quam cancellariam vocant; non exiguis hujus Ecclesiæ sumptibus recuperavit [et] reddi pristinis Dominis curavit Gualterus Balcanqual hujus Ecclesiæ Decanus. Anno post Natum incarnatum 1633. I am grateful to Ben Fortson for the translation.

111 Pegge, *Historical Account*, 10.

112 Thoresby as cited by Pegge, *Historical Account*, 23. An excellent biographical sketch of Elizabeth Elstob, including a full list of her publications, can be found in Kathryn Sunderland, 'Elizabeth Elstob,' in Helen Damico and Joseph B. Zavadil, eds., *Medieval Scholarship: Biographical Studies in the Formation of a Discipline* (New York and London: Garland, 1998), 2:59–74. See also Elizabeth Elstob, *The Rudiments of Grammar for the English-Saxon Tongue, First Given in English:*

212 Notes to pages 24–8

With an Apology for the Study of Northern Antiquities. Being Very Useful Towards the Understanding Our Ancient English Poets, and Other Writers (London: Bowyer, 1715).
113 Pegge, *Historical Account*, 22.
114 Ibid., 29.
115 The cartulary was produced as vol. 11 in 1962, also edited by Peter Sawyer.
116 Colgrave and Mynors, *Bede's Ecclesiastical History*, 151.
117 Whitelock, *English Historical Documents*, 408–9.
118 This is an abbreviated discussion of these archaisms, which I examine in detail in Oliver, *Language of the Early English Laws*.
119 Alistair Campbell, *Old English Grammar* (Oxford: Clarendon, 1959), 8–9.
120 Citations from the laws give paragraph number according to the editions in this volume (see editions themselves for correlation to previous numeration), followed by folio and line number on which the citation can be found in the *Textus Roffensis*. The facsimile of this manuscript is vol. 7, Sawyer, ed., *Early English Manuscripts in Facsimile*.
121 For general discussion of doubling to indicate vowel length, see Campbell, *Old English Grammar*, 12–13.
122 Per the transcription made by Tate in 1589; -*æthl* is no longer legible, except for what appears to be the upper hook of the **h**.
123 In Anglo-Norman times, <th> returns as an option. It is unlikely that these instances stem from the time of the compilation, however, as the <th> representation does not appear elsewhere in the manuscript.
124 See Oliver, 'Irish Influence in Early Kent,' for discussion on the chronology of these representations.
125 It is interesting that the only attestation of <th> in Æthelberht's laws is in the word *mæthlfriþ* 'assembly peace' (§1.6, 1ʳ6) in the section dealing with restitution to the church. To judge by syntax and lexicon, this portion of the laws may well be a later accretion. This use of the digraph, secondary for an early Kentish scriptorium, may perhaps be adduced as further evidence that this first section of the laws represent an addition to the original text, and one specifically influenced by Latin orthographic practice.
126 This spelling variant of <e> for <y> is typically Kentish, as discussed below. The translation of this word is taken from Christine Fell, 'A "friwif locbore" Revisited,' *Anglo-Saxon England* 13 (1984): 157–66.
127 Peter Sawyer, *Anglo-Saxon Charters: An Annotated List and Bibliography* (London: Royal Historical Society, 1968), 75.
128 Eduard Sievers, 'Altnordisches im *Beowulf*?' *Beiträge zur Geschichte der deutschen Sprache und Literatur* 12 (1887): 168–200.

129 See discussion in Oliver, *Language of the Early English Laws*, 87–93.
130 Sievers, 'Altnordisches im *Beowulf*?' 168–200.
131 Karl Brunner, *Altenglische Grammatik* (Tübingen: Niemeyer, 1965), 195 fn 2.
132 Æbt §10 also uses the spelling *forgylde*.
133 Although the Old English conjunction is usually *ond* or *and*, we find an umlauted *end* which appears primarily in early texts, and one occurrence of *ænd* in the Épinal glossary, whose original exemplar dates to the turn of the eighth century. See J.D. Pfeifer, 'Early Anglo-Saxon Glossaries and the School of Canterbury,' *Anglo-Saxon England* 16 (1987): 17–44.
134 See discussion of this clause under 'Manumission' in Commentary to chapter 4, and also Lisi Oliver, 'Towards Freeing a Slave in Germanic Law,' in Jasanoff, Melchert, and Oliver, eds., *Mír Curad* (Innsbruck: Institut für Sprachwissenschaft der Jniversität Innsbruck, 1998), 549–60.
135 Per Tate's copy; see note 122.
136 See discussion under 'Personal injury' in Commentary to chapter 2.
137 See discussion of these varying interpretations under 'Women and children' in Commentary to chapter 2.
138 See discussion under 'Women and children' in Commentary to chapter 2.
139 See also Patrizia Lendinara, 'The Kentish Laws,' in Hines, ed., *The Anglo-Saxons*, 211–44. I do not find her hypothesis that some of these may be calques on Latin terms convincing in the absence of any actual models.
140 See 'Freedman' for discussion of *læt* and 'Personal injury' for *hion* and *wælt*.
141 See Brunner, *Altenglische Grammatik*, 149.
142 See Oliver, *Language of the Early English Laws*, 135–51.
143 Although it may be tempting at first glance to view this as a Verner's law variant, that would be prevented by the root-accentuation of the superlative form in Indo-European. See Karl Brugmann and Berthold Delbrück, *Grundriss der vergleichende Grammatik der Indogermanischen Sprachen*, vol. II¹ *Vergleichende Laut-, Stammbildungs- und Flexionslehre der Indogermanischen Sprachen* (Strassburg: Karl J. Trubner, 1906), 392. For the Old Frisian forms see Rolf Bremmer and Patrick Stiles, 'An Old Frisian Primer' (unpublished), 29.
144 For spirant dissimilation in Gothic, see Rudolf Thurneysen, 'Spirantenwechsel im Gotischen,' *Indogermanische Forschungen* 8 (1897): 208–14. The argument presented follows Antoine Meillet, 'Notes sur quelque faits de morphologie,' *Mémoires de la Société de Linguistique de Paris* (1900): 111–21.

145 In Oliver, *Language of the Early English Laws*, 170–243, I analyse these examples in depth, and also discuss other syntactic/stylistic features which, due to their questionable archaism, are omitted here, such as pro-drop and copular constructions.

146 R.M. Liuzza, *The Old English Version of the Gospels: Volume 1: Text and Translation* (New York and Oxford: Oxford University Press, 1994), 195.

147 See Calvert Watkins, 'Preliminaries to a Historical and Comparative Analysis of the Syntax of the Old Irish Verb,' *Celtica* 6 (1963): 1–49.

148 See Paul J. Hopper, *The Syntax of the Simple Sentence in Proto-Germanic* (The Hague: Mouton, 1975), 52–6; Brugmann and Delbrück, *Grundriss*, vol. 5, *Vergleichende Syntax* (Strassburg: Karl J. Trubner, 1900), 80–3; Calvert Watkins, 'The Syntax of the Early Irish Verb,' 1–47, and 'Towards Proto-Indoeuropean Syntax: Problems and Pseudo-Problems,' in S. Steever et al., eds., *Papers from the Parasession on Diachronic Syntax* (Chicago: Chicago Linguistic Society, 1976), 305–26.

149 By my reckoning, the breakdown in the apodoses are as follows:
Verb-final
H & E §§1; 1.1; 2 (2x); 4; 6; 6.2; 7; 10; 11.2.
W §§1.1 (2x); 3; 3.1; 3.2; 8; 8.1; 11; 14.1; 17; 18; 19; 21 (3x); 21.1; 22.
Verb-initial
H & E §§1; 3 (3x); 3.1; 5; 5.1 (2x); 6.1; 6.2; 6.3; 9.1; 11; 11.1; 11.2; 11.3.
W §§5; 6; 8.2; 9.1; 17 (2x); 20; 21; 21.1.
Verb-second (Although it may be possible to assign at least some of these examples to the category of verb-final, if one invokes heavy NP displacement.)
H & E §§1.1; 2.1; 5; 6; 6.1; 7; 8.
W §§2; 7 (2x); 8.2; 9; 10; 12; 16.2.
Clauses which do not on the surface represent any of these patterns
W §§4; 13; 14; 15; 23.

150 In §42, *scilling* has a superscript u with a following nasal suspension, which Liebermann in my opinion misreads as an open a (although there is no explanation then for the suspension mark). This instance is counted here among the datives (cf. note 101).

151 For example, the laws of Rothari (see Ausenda's chart in *Discussion* to Lendinara, 'The Kentish Laws,' 235 and her comments at 234–6), and the laws of the Salian Franks (see Karl Eckhardt, *Die Gesetze des Merowingerreiches 481–714, I: Pactus Legis Salicae, Recensiones Merovingicae* [Göttingen: Musterschmidt, 1955] 63–7).

152 Wormald, 'Exempla Romanorum,' 19, 21. See also under 'Servants' in Commentary to chapter 2.

153 See Oliver, *Language of the Early English Laws*, 234–44, for full discussion.

154 Sir Henry Spelman, 'Of the Ancient Government of England,' in *The English Works of Henry Spelman* (London: D. Brown, 1723), 2:102.
155 Wormald, '*Exempla Romanorum*,' 25.
156 See, for example, Sally Falk Moore, *Law as Process: An Anthropological Approach* (London and Boston: Routledge and Kegan Paul, 1978).
157 There are isolated Germanic words and phrases incorporated into the Latin text, most notably in the Lombard and Merovingian laws. These are generally remnants of Germanic designations of rank, or oath formulations. But the Latin texts which surround these oral-formulaic fragments represent a literate rather than pre-literate structure.
158 Kirsten Hastrup, *Culture and History in Medieval Iceland: An Anthropological Analysis of Structure and Change* (Oxford: Clarendon, 1985), 122–4; Yrjö Blomstedt Hafström, Torfinn Tobiasson, and Magnús Már Lárusson, 'lagman,' in Johannes Brønsted et al., eds., *Kulturhistorisk Leksikon for Nordisk Middelalder* (Copenhagen: Rosenkilde and Bagger, 1965), 10:150–63; Magnús Már Lárusson, 'lǫgsǫgumaðr,' in Brønsted et al., *Kulturhistorisk Leksikon*, 11:137.
159 D.H. Green, *Language and History in the Early Germanic World* (Cambridge and New York: Cambridge University Press, 1998), 33.
160 Lilian H. Jeffery and Anna Morpurgo-Davies, 'ΠΟΙΝΙΚΑΣΤΑΣ and ΠΟΙΝΙΚΑΖΕΝ: BM 1969. 4–2. 1, A New Archaic Inscription from Crete,' *Kadmos* 9 (1970): 150; Calvert Watkins, *How to Kill a Dragon: Aspects of Indo-European Poetics* (New York: Oxford University Press, 1995), 69.
161 See Dorothy Whitelock, *The Beginnings of English Society* (Harmondsworth: Penguin, 1952), 135; Wallace-Hadrill, *Early Germanic Kingship*, 40. Citations from *The Gifts of Men* are ll. 40–1 and ll. 72–3 in George Philip Krapp and Eliot van Kirk Dobbie, eds., *The Exeter Book* (New York: Columbia University Press, 1936), 138–9.
162 Wormald, '*Exempla Romanorum*,' 15–28.
163 Rosamund McKitterick, *The Carolingians and the Written Word* (Cambridge and New York: Cambridge University Press, 1989), 23.
164 See discussion in Wormald, *The Making of English Law*, 101.
165 Mary J. Carruthers, *The Book of Memory: A Study of Memory in Medieval Culture* (Cambridge and New York: Cambridge University Press, 1990), 71.
166 Richard Corliss, 'Jackie Can!' *Time*, 13 February, 1995: 82.
167 See citations in following editions respectively: Eckhardt, *Die Gesetze des Merowingerreiches*, 62–7; Jan Wybren Buma and Wilhelm Ebel, *Das Brokmer Recht* (Göttingen: Vanderhoeck and Ruprecht, 1965), 102–9; Johannes Friedrich, *Die Hethitischen Gesetze* (Leiden: E.J. Brill, 1971), 16–21; Chilperic Edwards, *The Hammurabi Code* (London: Watts, 1904), 61–3.

216 Notes to pages 38–46

168 Unabashedly taken from Dan Donoghue, personal communication.
169 Paradoxically, alliteration becomes a more common stylistic device in later Anglo-Saxon laws. See Dorothy Bethurum, 'Stylistic Features of the Old English Laws,' *Modern Language Review* 27 (1932): 263–79. But Bethurum (279) credits this to an ongoing ancient custom: 'In certain specific phrases of the Old English laws and in a tendency to alliteration wherever the subject matter was archaic or of emotional importance, we still have traces of the vanishing tradition.'
170 Ibid., 266.
171 For this and the following reference, CIH refers to D.A. Binchy, ed., *Corpus Iuris Hibernici* (Dublin: Institiuid Ard-Lenin Bhaile Atha Cliath, 1978), 2192ff. The 'False Judgements of Caratnia' is edited and translated by Rudolf Thurneysen, 'Gúbretha Caratniad,' *Zeitschrift für celtische Philologie* 15 (1924/5): 302–70; for this gloss see 361–2. For readers unfamiliar with Old Irish law, an excellent introduction is provided in Fergus Kelly, *A Guide to Early Irish Law* (Dublin: Dublin Institute for Advanced Studies, 1988). A useful list of text editions and translations can be found in Thomas Charles-Edwards, *The Early Mediaeval Gaelic Lawyer* (Cambridge: Cambridge University Press, 1999), 63–6.
172 See Thomas Charles-Edwards, *Early Irish and Welsh Kinship* (Oxford: Clarendon, 1993), 6.
173 See discussion in ibid., 3–17.
174 Wormald, 'Exempla Romanorum,' 18.
175 McKitterick, *The Carolingians*, 23.
176 Spelman, *English Works*, 1:7.
177 Liebermann, *Gesetze*, 3:2.
178 D.A. Binchy, 'Bretha Déin Chécht,' *Ériu* 20 (1966): 1–48.
179 G. Hickes and H. Wanley, *Linguarum Vett. Septentrionalium Thesaurus Grammatico-Criticus et Archaeologicus* (1703–5; repr. Menston: Scolar, 1970), 1:89–92.
180 I have followed the latter in the translation here. See discussion in note a to §1 in the translation.
181 See Oliver, *Language of the Early English Laws*, 214–19.
182 See Wallace-Hadrill, *Early Germanic Kingship*, 41.
183 Colgrave and Mynors, *Bede's Ecclesiastical History*, 259.
184 Wallace-Hadrill, *Early Germanic Kingship*, 85–6.
185 Eoin MacNeill, 'Ancient Irish Law: The Law of Status or Franchise,' *Proceedings of the Royal Irish Academy* C 36 (1923): 306. For dating see D.A. Binchy, ed., *Críth Gablach* (Dublin: Dublin Institute for Advanced Studies, 1979), xiii–xv.
186 Wormald, *The Making of English Law*, 97.

187 See discussion in William A. Chaney, *The Cult of Kingship in Anglo-Saxon England* (Manchester: Manchester University Press, 1970), 225–6.
188 Doubt has been raised concerning the authenticity of this letter, but Rob Meens, 'A Background to Augustine's Mission to Anglo-Saxon England,' *Anglo-Saxon England* 23 (1994): 5–17 at 6–8, argues persuasively that it is genuine.
189 Colgrave and Mynors, *Bede's Ecclesiastical History*, 83.
190 John T. MacNeill and Helena M. Gamer, *Medieval Handbooks of Penance* (New York: Columbia University Press, 1990), 198.
191 Wallace-Hadrill, *Early Germanic Kingship*, 40.
192 Colgrave and Mynors, *Bede's Ecclesiastical History*, 151.
193 A much later parallel for beginning with laws of the church occurs in the ninth-century laws of Alfred, in which the first portion consciously reiterates Mosaic law.
194 Dafydd Jenkins, *The Law of Hywel Dda: Law Texts from Medieval Wales* (Dyfed: Gomer, 1990), 41.
195 I would like to thank Dan Donoghue for bringing this to my attention.
196 As noted in the edition, this could also mean 'kinsmen.'
197 Patrick Wormald, 'Inter cetera bona – genti suae: Law-Making and Peace-Keeping in the Earliest English Kingdoms,' *Settimane dello studio del Centro italiano di studi sull'alto medioevo* 42 (1995): 974. Elsewhere Wormald states that 'Franz Beyerle showed how Lex Salica was made up partly of Weistum, descriptive, systematic, comprehensive and concerned with criminal law, and partly of Satzung, prescriptive, ad hoc, specific and often procedural in character.' See Wormald, '*Lex Scripta* and *Verbum Regis*,' 112.

Chapter Two: The Laws of Æthelberht

1 There is no distinction made between voiced and voiceless consonants in the use of these graphemes.
2 Note that the scribe similarly twice corrects *mon* to *man* (§76, 77).
3 See Lisi Oliver, 'Towards Freeing a Slave in Common Germanic Law,' in J. Jasanoff, H. Craig Melchert, and Lisi Oliver, eds., *Mír Curad: Studies in Honor of Calvert Watkins* (Innsbruck: Institut für Sprachwissenschaft der Universität Insbruck, 1998), 549–50.
4 'Classical Old English' refers to the West Saxon employed at the time of Alfred (r. 871–899) that has come to be regarded as a grammatical norm. See Alistair Campbell, *Old English Grammar* (Oxford: Clarendon, 1959), 8–9.

218   Notes to pages 82–4

5 This section draws heavily on Philip Grierson, 'La Fonction Sociale de la Monnaie en Angleterre aux VIIe–VIIIe Siècles,' in *Dark Age Numismatics, Selected Studies* (London: Variorum Reprints, 1979), 9; also Philip Grierson and Mark Blackburn, *Medieval European Coinage I: The Early Middle Ages* (Cambridge and New York: Cambridge University Press, 1986), 155–89; Alan Vince, 'The Economic Basis of Ango-Saxon London,' Richard Hodges and Brian Hobley, eds., in *The Rebirth of Towns in the West, AD 700–1050* (London: Council for British Archaeology, 1988), 83–92.
6 See Grierson, 'La Fonction Sociale de la Monnaie,' 345.
7 Nineteenth-century numismaticists gave the name *sceatt* to the earliest Anglo-Saxon silver coins. This term is anachronistic, however, as silver coins would not be used for at least three quarters of a century after the time of Æthelberht's laws. See Grierson, 'La Fonction Sociale de la Monnaie,' 346, 352.
8 Grierson, 'La Fonction Sociale de la Monnaie,' 345; also H. Munro Chadwick, *Studies on Anglo-Saxon Institutions* (Cambridge: Cambridge University Press, 1905; repr. New York, 1963), 18.
9 Kemp Malone, ed., *Widsith* (Copenhagen: Rosenkilde and Bagger, 1962), 25. Example is given in Grierson, 'La Fonction Sociale de la Monnaie,' 346.
10 Chadwick, *Studies on Anglo-Saxon Institutions*, 61.
11 D.P. Kirby, *The Making of Early England* (London: Batsford, 1967), 270.
12 Grierson and Blackburn, *Medieval European Coinage*, 158, 160–1.
13 Stéphane Lebecq. 'The Question of Logistics,' Richard Gameson, ed., in *St. Augustine and the Conversion of England* (Stroud: Sutton, 1999), 55.
14 Grierson and Blackburn, *Medieval European Coinage*, 161–2. See Vince, 'The Economic Basis of Ango-Saxon London,' 86.
15 Philip Grierson, *The Coins of Medieval Europe* (London: Seaby, 1991), 36.
16 Felix Liebermann, *Die Gesetze der Angelsachsen* (Halle: M. Niemeyer, 1897–1916), 3:2; Bertram Colgrave and R.A.B. Mynors, eds., *Bede's Ecclesiastical History of the English People* (Oxford: Clarendon, 1969), 151.
17 J.M. Wallace-Hadrill, *Early Germanic Kingship in England and on the Continent* (Oxford: Clarendon, 1971), 39.
18 Arthur West Haddan and William Stubbs, *Councils and Ecclesiastical Documents Relating to Great Britain and Ireland* (Oxford: Clarendon, 1881), 3:368.
19 Liebermann, *Gesetze*, 3:4.
20 See entry under *clerici* in Domino Du Cange, ed., *Glossarium Mediæ et Infimæ Latinitatis* (1678; repr. Paris: Librairie de Sciences et des Arts, 1937), 2:367–8; *Thesaurus Linguae Latinae* (Leipzig: Tübner: 1906–12), 3:1339–40;

also Michael Lapidge, 'clergy,' in Michael Lapidge et al., eds., *The Blackwell Encyclopedia of Anglo-Saxon England* (Malden, Mass. and Oxford: Blackwell, 1999), 106–7.
21 Richard Gameson, 'Context and Achievement,' in Gameson, ed., *St. Augustine and the Conversion of England*, 26.
22 See discussion in chapter 1 under 'Chronological layering.'
23 See discussion of this term under 'The process of bringing a charge' in Commentary to chapter 3.
24 Dafydd Jenkins, *The Law of Hwyel Dda: Law Texts from Medieval Wales* (Dyfed: Gomer, 1990), 41.
25 For a discussion of extended meanings of *mund*, see E.G. Stanley, 'Some Words for the *Dictionary of Old English*,' *Subsidia* 26 (1998): 33–56 at 39–47.
26 Nicholas Brooks, 'Arms, Status and Warfare in Late-Saxon England,' in David Hill, ed., *Ethelred the Unready: Papers from the Millenary Conference* (Oxford: British Archaeological Reports, 1978), 86.
27 Lisi Oliver, '*Cyninges fedesl*: The Feeding of the King in Æthelberht ch. 12,' *Anglo-Saxon England* 27 (1998): 31–40. See also Thomas Charles-Edwards, 'Early Medieval Kingships in the British Isles,' in Steven Basset, ed., *The Origins of Anglo-Saxon Kingdoms* (London and New York: Leicester University Press, 1989), 30–1.
28 By the time of the Domesday Book, this becomes known as the 'farm of one night,' which certainly sets its own time period. But 12 oxen seems like a lot for a single night; note that H & E §10 describe a host who *feormþ*, 'provides for,' a person for three nights.
29 Renato Gendre, 'Le leggi di Æthelberht: "*iuxta exempla Romanoru*" e "*iuxta consuetudines Germanorum*,"' in Loredana Lazzari, ed., *Testi giuridici germanici* (Potenza: Il Salice, 1992), 7–21.
30 Thomas Charles-Edwards, *Early Irish and Welsh Kinship* (Oxford: Clarendon, 1993), 376–7.
31 Dorothy Whitelock, ed., *English Historical Documents, Volume I: c. 500–1042* (London: Eyre & Spottiswoode, 1955; repr. 1979), 391.
32 Whitelock, *English Historical Documents*, 402.
33 Earlier interpreters took *medume* to mean 'half.' See Liebermann, *Gesetze*, 3:6. Perhaps the payment to the king is only 50 shillings. This would, however, make no distinction between the killing of the king's man and the killing of *any* man, unless one were to interpret the 50 shillings as still another additional fine. And this reading makes no sense in the context of §24, the purpose of which is to set the *wergild* for a freeman.
34 Karl von Amira, *Grundriss des Germanischen Rechts* (Strassburg: K.J. Trubner, 1913), 131.

35 David A.E. Pelteret, 'Slavery in Anglo-Saxon England,' in J. Douglas Woods and David A.E. Pelteret, eds., *The Anglo-Saxons, Synthesis and Achievement* (Waterloo: Wilfrid Laurier University Press, 1985), 123.
36 I owe this observation to one of the anonymous readers of the manuscript.
37 Line 369; Fr. Klaeber, *Beowulf and the Fight at Finnsburg* 3rd ed. (Boston and New York: D.C. Heath, 1950), 14.
38 H.R. Loyn, 'Gesiths and Thegns in Anglo-Saxon England from the Seventh to the Tenth Century,' *English Historical Review* 70 (1955): 529–40. Contra this, see Liebermann, *Gesetze*, 3:7 and Chadwick, *Studies on Anglo-Saxon Institutions*, 111, who argue for the position of *eorl* as dependent on noble birth.
39 See 'Comparison of Restitution in Æthelberht According to Status' in Appendix 3.
40 Liebermann, *Gesetze*, 2:313.
41 See, for example, David A.E. Pelteret, *Slavery in Early Mediaeval England* (Woodbridge and Rochester: Boydell, 1995), 294–5; also Georg Baesecke, 'Die deutschen Worte der germanischen Gesetze,' *Beiträge zur Geschichte der Deutschen Sprache und Literatur* 59 (1935): 1–101. I am grateful to Jay Jasanoff for discussing this problem with me.
42 Charlton T. Lewis and Charles Short, *A Latin Dictionary* (Oxford: Clarendon, 1879, repr. 1962).
43 Thomas Wright and Richard Paul Walker, *Anglo-Saxon and Old English Vocabularies* (London: Trubner, 1884), 1:30, 53, 111, 432.
44 Heinrich Brunner, *Deutsche Rechtsgeschichte* (Leipzig: Duncker and Humblot, 1887–92), 147.
45 Seebohm's oft-cited parallel in the *leysingi* of Norse law, of which there were also three classes 'gradually growing by successive steps towards a higher grade of freedom,' is slightly off-beam, as he conflates the positions of the *frialsgiafi* (newly made freedman), the *leysingi* (freedman after making 'freedom-ale') and the *leysinga-son* (highest rank of *leysingi*, whose great-grandfather was a *leysingi*). Although all three of these ranks appear in Norse law, I have found nowhere where they are mentioned in the same clause: generally the middle is paired with the first or third. Furthermore, it is only after four generations (*not* three) that a *frialsgiafi* kin becomes a *leysingi* kin, and after a further four that *leysingi* kin becomes fully free. The *frialsgiafi* can circumvent any part of the first generational span by making 'freedom-ale' (i.e., he invites his previous owner to a banquet, serves a legally determined amount of ale, and offers his former master money). But in any case, the shortest span from *frialsgiafi* to freeman must be

five generations, and the longest nine, so this does not provide as clear a parallel to the Kentish situation as the examples closer to home. This also renders less likely Pelteret's postulation 'that the *lætas* represent a Germanic system of manumission introduced into Britain by the Jutes, but that it is a system that was not observed by invaders from other tribal groupings.' See Pelteret, *Slavery in Early Medieval England*, 295. See Fredric Seebohm, *Tribal Custom in Anglo-Saxon Law* (London: Longsman, Green, 1902), 484; also Konrad Maurer, *Altnorwegisches Staatsrecht und Gerichtswesen* (Leipzig: Gesellschaft der Wissenschaften in Kristiana, 1907), 103–21; Arne Bøe and Magnús Már Lárusson, 'leysingi,' in Johannes Brønsted, et al., eds., *Kulturhistorisk Leksikon for Nordisk Middelalder* (Copenhagen: Rosenkilde and Bagger, 1965), 10:521–6; Kirsten Hastrup, *Culture and History in Medieval Iceland: An Anthropological Analysis of Structure and Change* (Oxford: Clarendon, 1985), 108–9.
46 Alexander C. Murray, *Germanic Kinship Structure: Studies in Law and Society in Antiquity and the Early Middle Ages* (Toronto: Pontifical Institute of Mediaeval Studies, 1983), 158–9.
47 Charles-Edwards, *Early Irish and Welsh Kinship*, 405.
48 Ibid. For Welsh, see 403–4. For Old Irish, see 330, 364, 406.
49 Pelteret, *Slavery in Early Mediaeval England*, 295–6.
50 See, e.g., Stenton, *Anglo-Saxon England*, 315 and references therein.
51 Whitelock, *English Historical Documents*, 402.
52 Liebermann, *Gesetze*, 3:73. Ine §24.2 states that 'a Welshman, if he has five hides, is a man of a six-hundred wergild' (Whitelock, *English Historical Documents*, 401) – not coincidentally five times the 120-shilling *wergild* stipulated in §32 for a one-hide Welshman.
53 Stenton, *Anglo-Saxon England*, 300.
54 See also A.R. Bridbury, 'Seventh-Century England in Bede and the Early Laws,' in A.R. Bridbury, ed., *The English Economy from Bede to the Reformation* (Woodbridge: Boydell, 1992), 70 and 72, where he surmises that the *esne* mentioned in Wihtred §8 is equivalent to the earlier *læt* (but this seems unlikely, given the fact that the term *esne* already appears in Æthelberht and continues to be used in Hloþhere & Eadric as well).
55 The late seventh-century 'Penitentials of Theodore' indicate that a man may make himself a slave through theft or fornication, and that he may do so once he has attained the age of fourteen years. See John T. MacNeill and Helena M. Gamer, *Medieval Handbooks of Penance* (1938; New York: Columbia University Press, 1990), 209, 211.
56 Liebermann, *Gesetze*, 3:9.

57 Gustav Neckel, 'Under Eoderas,' *Beiträge zur Geschichte der Deutschen Sprache und Literatur* 41 (1916): 163–70.
58 See Mary P. Richards, 'The *Dictionary of Old English* and Old English Legal Terminology,' *The Dictionary of Old English: Retrospects and Prospects. Subsidia* 26 (1998): 59.
59 Neckel, 'Under Eoderas,' 167–8.
60 Liebermann, *Gesetze*, 3:9.
61 Ibid., 3:8.
62 The forty-day period occurs elsewhere in both Anglo-Saxon and Continental laws; see Liebermann, *Gesetze*, 2:417.
63 Reinhold Schmid, *Die Gesetze der Angelsachsen* (Leipzig: F.A. Brockhaus, 1858), 4; Liebermann, *Gesetze*, 3:8.
64 See Patrick Wormald, '*Inter cetera bona – genti suae*: Law-Making and Peace-Keeping in the Earliest English Kingdoms,' *Settimane dello Studio del Centro Italiano di Studi Sull'Alto Medioevo* 42 (1995): 973–4.
65 Wallace-Hadrill, *Early Germanic Kingship*, 42.
66 See also Dorothy Whitelock, *The Beginnings of English Society* (Harmondsworth: Penguin, 1952), 39ff.
67 Liebermann, *Gesetze*, 3:10 and 'Ags. *rihthamscyld*: echtes Hoftor,' *Archiv fur das Studium der neueren Sprachen und Literaturen* 115 (1905): 389–91.
68 F.L. Attenborough, ed., *The Laws of the Earliest English Kings* (Cambridge: Cambridge University Press, 1922), 177.
69 Jacob Grimm, *Review* of 'Ancient Laws and Institutes of England [ed. Benjamin Thorpe].' Repr. in *Kleinere Schriften* (Hildesheim: Olms, 1991), 5:318.
70 This possibility was first brought to my attention by Dan Donoghue. See discussion of the terms *hæmen/hæmed* in Loredana Lazzari, 'Il Codice di Wihtræd: incidenza di canoni ecclesiastici sulle leggi secolari,' in Loredana Lazzari, ed., *Testi giuridici germanici* (Potenza: Il Salice, 1992), 31–8. Lazzari does not connect these terms with *rihthæmscyld*.
71 MacNeill and Gamer, *Medieval Handbooks of Penance*, 208–9.
72 I am indebted to my colleagues Dominique Homberger and John Lynn for advice on this section.
73 Liebermann, *Gesetze*, 3:11.
74 Ibid., 3:13.
75 See discussion in chapter 1 under 'Chronological layering.'
76 I am indebted to my colleague John Lynn for this observation.
77 Fergus Kelly, *A Guide to Early Irish Law* (Dublin: Dublin Institute for Advanced Studies, 1988), 19 and 133.

78 There is little difference between the stretch between the thumb and little finger and the thumb and middle finger, so this is clearly a visual rather than a utilitarian distinction.
79 Liebermann, *Gesetze*, 3:11.
80 Per search through *utere* and *innere* in Richard L. Venezky and Antonette de Paolo Healey, *A Microfiche Concordance to Old English* (Newark: University of Delaware, 1980).
81 Liebermann, *Gesetze*, 3:10.
82 Felix Liebermann, 'Kentische *hionne*: Hirnhaut,' *Archiv für das Studium der neueren Sprachen und Literaturen* 115 (1905): 177–8.
83 Ibid.
84 Karl Eckhardt, *Die Gesetze des Merowingerreiches 481–714, I: Pactus Legis Salicae, Recensiones Merovingicae* (Göttingen: Musterschmidt, 1955), 62–5.
85 See, for example, Thorpe, *Ancient Laws*, 7; Schmid, *Gesetze*, 7. Liebermann translates the phrase '*Wenn [jener] im Bauch verwundet wird ...*', 'If [that person] is wounded in the stomach ...' but prints the form as *hrifwund*, citing as justification the Alamann parallel. (See Liebermann, *Gesetze*, 1:6 and 3:12.)
86 Ferdinand Holthausen, *Altfriesisches Wörterbuch* (Heidelberg: C. Winter, 1925), 123.
87 Jacob Grimm, *Geschichte der Deutschen Sprache* (Leipzig: S. Herzel, 1868), 666.
88 I am indebted to an anonymous reader of the manuscript for this suggestion.
89 See Eckhardt, *Die Gesetze des Merowingerreiches*, 64–5.
90 A.N. Toller, in the *Supplement* to Bosworth's *Anglo-Saxon Dictionary*, suggests a possible emendation to *scearwund* 'wounded in the groin.' Since this term appears nowhere else in the corpus, and, furthermore, the word as it stands is easily interpreted, I find this suggestion unsatisfactory.
91 Calvert Watkins, 'Sick-Maintenance in Indo-European,' *Ériu* 27 (1976): 21–5. Also in Lisi Oliver, ed., *Selected Writings of Calvert Watkins* (Innsbruck: Institut für Sprachwissenschaft der Universtät Innsbruck, 1994), 560–4.
92 See Lisi Oliver, 'The Language of the Early English Laws' (PhD dissertation, Harvard University, 1995), 123–35.
93 See D.A. Binchy, 'Bretha Crólige,' *Ériu* 12 (1934): 1–2 and related text; further, Kelly, *Guide to Early English Law*, 133 and Thomas Charles-Edwards, *The Early Mediaeval Gaelic Lawyer* (Cambridge: Cambridge University Press, 1999), 28–36.
94 Klaeber, *Beowulf and the Fight at Finnsburg*, 58.

95 E.G. Stanley, 'Did Beowulf Commit *feaxfang* Against Grendel's Mother?' *Notes and Queries* 221 (1976): 339–40. For *Judith* see Elliot Dobbie, ed., *Beowulf and Judith* (New York: Columbia University Press, 1953), 102.
96 George Krapp and Elliot Dobbie, eds., *The Exeter Book* (New York: Columbia University Press, 1936), 159.
97 See Anne L. Klinck, 'Anglo-Saxon Women and the Law,' *Journal of Medieval History* 8 (1982): 107–21. For citation from *Maxims* II see Elliot Dobbie, ed., *The Anglo-Saxon Minor Poems* (New York: Columbia University Press, 1942), 56–7.
98 See Christine Fell, *Women in Anglo-Saxon England and the Impact of 1066* (Bloomington: Indiana University Press, 1984); Mary P. Richards and J. Stanfield, 'Concepts of Anglo-Saxon Women in Law,' in Helen Damico and Alexandra Hennesey Olsen, eds., *New Readings on Women in Anglo-Saxon Literature* (Bloomington: Indiana University Press, 1990), 89–99; also Whitelock, *The Beginnings of English Society*, 151.
99 Fell, *Women in Anglo-Saxon England*, 56–7.
100 Kelly, *Guide to Early Irish Law*, 72 states that these have 'apparently the same meaning.' But Rudolf Thurneysen, 'Gúbretha Caratniad,' *Zeitschrift für celtische Philologie* 15 (1924/5): 302–70 at 356–62 points out that the attestation of *tindscra* in §44 – the first we have in a legal text and perhaps our earliest attestation altogether – seems to be distinguished from the *coibche* discussed in Gloss 3 to this clause.
101 Grimm, *Review* of Thorpe, *Ancient Laws and Institutes*, 319.
102 Fell, *Women in Anglo-Saxon England*, 57.
103 I am indebted to Stephanie Jamison for the Sanskrit parallel; see also Liebermann, *Gesetze*, 3:15.
104 Jenkins, ed., *Hywel Dda*, 49.
105 Stephanie Jamison, 'Penelope and the Pigs: Indic Perspectives on the *Odyssey*,' *Classical Antiquity* 18(2) (1999) 227–72.
106 See Dorothy Bethurum, 'Stylistic Features of the Old English Laws,' *Modern Language Review* 27 (1932): 263–79.
107 Christine Fell, 'An Appendix to Carole Hough's Article: A "Reappraisal of Æthelberht 84,"' *Nottingham Medieval Studies* 37 (1993): 8.
108 Liebermann, *Gesetze*, 3:16.
109 Carole A. Hough, 'A Reappraisal of Æthelberht 84,' *Nottingham Medieval Studies* 37 (1993): 1–6.
110 See Liebermann, *Gesetze*, 3:16.
111 Ludwig Rudolf von Salis, *Leges Burgundionum* (Hannover: Hahnsche Buchhandlung, 1973), 51; for dating see ibid., 5–11.
112 T.J. Rivers believes that this must be the man's *wergild*, as the woman's is addressed by paying the bride-price for the new wife. But this does not deal with the damage to the first wife's honour. See Theodore John Rivers,

'Adultery in Early Anglo-Saxon Society: Aethelberht 31 in Comparison with Continental Germanic Law,' *Anglo-Saxon England* 20 (1991): 19–26.
113 See Liebermann, *Gesetze*, 3:9.
114 Ibid., 2:263.
115 F.L. Attenborough, ed., *The Laws of the Earliest English Kings* (Cambridge: Cambridge University Press), 177.
116 See, for example, Liebermann, *Gesetze*, 3:13; Attenborough, *The Laws of the Earliest English Kings*, 178; Whitelock, *English Historical Documents*, 393.
117 Giorgio Ausenda, *Discussion* to Patrizia Lendinara, 'The Kentish Laws,' in J. Hines ed., *The Anglo-Saxons from the Migration Period to the Eighth Century: An Ethnographic Perspective* (Woodbridge: Boydell, 1997), 233–4. Note that both his examples come from Langobardic rather than Anglo-Saxon evidence.
118 Fell, *Women in Anglo-Saxon England*, 60.
119 Christine Fell, 'A "friwif locbore" Revisited,' *Anglo-Saxon England* 13 (1984): 157–66 at 161, citing Sonia Chadwick Hawkes, 'The Dating and Social Significance of the Burials in the Polhill Cemetary,' in Brian Philip, ed., *Excavations in West Kent 1960–1970* (Dover: Kent Archaeological Rescue Unit [for] the West Kent Border Archaelogical Group, 1973), 195.
120 Henrietta Leyser, *Medieval Women: A Social History of Women in England, 450–1500* (London: Weidenfeld and Nicolson, 1995), 14.
121 For example, Hartman von Aue's Gregorius saves a widowed queen from a knight who has been laying siege to marry her and gain her kingdom, and as a reward is himself given her hand in marriage. Unfortunately she turns out to be his mother.
122 See Fell, *Women in Anglo-Saxon England*, 61.
123 See Whitelock, *English Historical Documents*, 403.
124 Carole A. Hough, 'The Early Kentish "divorce laws": A Reconsideration of Æthelberht, chs. 79 and 80,' *Anglo-Saxon England* 23 (1994): 19–34.
125 Whitelock, *English Historical Documents*, 393.
126 Ibid., 393.
127 See K.P. Witney, *The Jutish Forest: A Study of the Weald of Kent from 450 to 1380 AD* (London: Athelone Press, 1976), 22.
128 Liebermann, *Gesetze*, 3:19.
129 Ibid., 3:2.

Chapter Three: the Laws of Hloþhere & Eadric

1 D.P. Kirby, *The Making of Early England* (London: Batsford, 1967), 41.
2 Bertram Colgrave and R.A.B. Mynors, eds., *Bede's Ecclesiastical History of the English People* (Oxford: Clarendon, 1969), 191 and 190, fn 2.

3 The last outburst of paganism in the kingdom of the East Saxons was as late as 663x4, following an eruption of plague. See Barbara A.E. Yorke, 'The Reception of Christianity at the Anglo-Saxon Royal Courts,' in Richard Gameson, ed., *St. Augustine and the Conversion of England* (Stroud: Sutton, 1999), 162.
4 See the discussion 'Women and children' in Commentary to chapter 2. Also Yorke, 'The Reception of Christianity,' 165.
5 Colgrave and Mynors, *Bede's Ecclesiastical History*, 153. For St Peter's discussion of fornication, see I Corinthians 5.1; for the image of a dog returning to his own vomit, see Proverbs 26.11.
6 Ibid., 155.
7 See D.P. Kirby, *The Earliest English Kings* (London and Boston: Unwin Hyman, 1991), 38.
8 See Nicholas Brooks, 'The Creation and Early Structure of the Kingdom of Kent,' in Steven Bassett, ed., *The Origins of Anglo-Saxon Kingdoms* (London and New York: Leicester University Press, 1989), 64.
9 This seems to be the probable explanation of this name. It was not uncommon for bynames to be added to the proper name, such as the well-known Æthelred Unræd, often mistranslated as 'Ethelred the Unready' rather than the accurate 'Ethelred the Uncounselled.' In this case, the byname seems to have functioned alone as a nickname. See Gillian Fellows-Jensen, 'Bynames,' in Michael Lapidge et al., eds., *The Blackwell Encyclopedia of Anglo-Saxon England* (Malden, Mass. and Oxford: Blackwell, 1999), 76–8.
10 The initial conversion of the Northumbrians was also short-lived, however. Upon Edwin's death, the bishop Paulinus, who had converted the king and members of his council, was driven out by the heathen Penda, and returned to Kent to end his days as bishop of Rochester. Tate similarly ended her days in the royal double monastery founded for her at Lyminge, Kent.
11 The actual rulership in Kent was often shared with a joint or 'junior' king. I present here the main line of succession. For detailed discussion, see Barbara A.E. Yorke, 'Joint Kingship in Kent c. 560 to 785,' *Archaeologia Cantiana* 99 (1983): 1–19.
12 Colgrave and Mynors, *Bede's Ecclesiastical History*, 237.
13 J.M. Wallace-Hadrill, *Early Germanic Kingship in England and on the Continent* (Oxford: Clarendon, 1971), 28.
14 Colgrave and Mynors, *Bede's Ecclesiastical History*, 237.
15 Felix Liebermann, *Die Gesetze der Angelsachsen* (Halle: M. Niemeyer, 1897–1916), 3:17.
16 See Kirby, *Making of Early England*, 157; also Barbara A.E. Yorke, *Kings and Kingdoms of Anglo-Saxon England* (London: Seaby, 1990), 34–5. The

story is preserved in the 'Legend of St. Mildreth,' the hagiographical biography of the murdered men's niece.
17 Dorothy Whitelock, ed., *English Historical Documents, Volume I: c. 500–1042* (London: Eyre & Spottiswoode, 1955. repr. 1979), 167.
18 See Yorke, 'Joint Kingship in Kent,' 1–19; also Yorke, *Kings and Kingdoms*, 32–4.
19 For charters, see W. de Gray Birch, ed., *Cartularium Saxonicum* (London: Whiting, 1885–99), #45 and Peter Sawyer, *Anglo-Saxon Charters: An Annotated List and Bibliography* (London: Royal Historical Society, 1968), #8. For discussion, see K.P. Witney, *The Kingdom of Kent: A History from c. A.D. 450 to 825* (London: Phillimore, 1982), 149.
20 S.E. Kelly, ed., *Charters of St. Augustine's Abbey Canterbury and Minster-in-Thanet* (Oxford and New York: Oxford University Press, 1995), 196.
21 See Kirby, *Earliest English Kings*, 118.
22 Liebermann, *Gesetze*, 3:17.
23 See C.R. Cheney, *A Handbook of Dates for Students of English History*, rev. Michael Jones (Cambridge: Cambridge University Press, 2000), 22–3. They allow only the possibility that Æthelberht died in 616 and that Eadbald's reign began in that year.
24 See discussion under 'Oral transmission' in chapter 1.
25 Eduard Sievers, 'Altnordisches in Beowulf?' *Beiträge zur Geschichte der deutschen Sprache und Literatur* 12 (1887): 174.
26 See discussion in chapter 1 under 'Archaic traces in the language.'
27 See note in chapter 1 under 'Archaic traces in the language.'
28 Karl Brunner, *Altenglische Grammatik* (Tübingen: Niemeyer, 1965), 262.
29 Alistair Campbell, *Old English Grammar* (Oxford: Clarendon, 1959), 75.
30 Brunner, *Altenglische Grammatik*, 262; Campbell, *Old English Grammar*, 290.
31 Campbell, *Old English Grammar*, 349.
32 Brunner, *Altenglische Grammatik*, 353.
33 Campbell, *Old English Grammar*, 290–1.
34 Kenneth Sisam, *Studies in the History of Old English Literature* (Oxford: Clarendon, 1953), 207.
35 Ibid., 94.
36 Brunner, *Altenglische Grammatik*, 259; Campbell, *Old English Grammar*, 289.
37 Campbell, *Old English Grammar*, 122.
38 See Brunner, *Altenglische Grammatik*, 22.
39 Spelling variations between i and y, such as *ðissum* vs. *ðyssum*, 'with these' (Prologue) or *simble* vs. *symble*, 'always' are common throughout Old English, and thus not of interest here.

228 Notes to pages 134-40

40 For roots see Julius Pokorny, *Indogermanisches Etymologisches Wörterbuch* (Bern: Francke, 1989), 2:293-6; 235-8. The issue of terminology for 'law' is briefly addressed by Patrick Wormald, 'Inter cetera bona – genti suae: Law-Making and Peace-Keeping in the Earliest English Kingdoms,' *Settimane dello studio del Centro italiano di studi sull'alto medioevo* 42 (1995): 963.

41 See Commentary under 'Servants,' chapter 2.

42 An interesting exercise in detection of a 'lost' legal collection can be found in Patrick Wormald, 'In Search of King Offa's "Law Code,"' in I. Wood and N. Lund, eds., *People and Places in Northern Europe, 500-1600: Studies Presented to P.H. Sawyer* (Woodbridge: Boydell Press, 1991), 25-45.

43 One is reminded of the terms *ealuscerwen* 'pouring out of ale' [*Beowulf* 769] and *meoduscewen* 'pouring out of mead' [*Andreas* 1526], which Klaeber translates metaphorically as 'distress, terror.' See Fr. Klaeber, ed., *Beowulf and the Fight at Finnsburg*, 3rd ed., (Boston and New York: D.C. Heath, 1950), 320-1. See also the discussion on the meaning of 'drinking' in Commentary under 'King' in chapter 2.

44 Elliot Dobbie, ed., *The Anglo-Saxon Minor Poems* (New York: Columbia University Press, 1942), 13.

45 F.L. Attenborough, ed., *The Laws of the Earliest English Kings* (Cambridge: Cambridge University Press), 39.

46 See Rosamund Faith, 'feorm,' in Michael Lapidge et al., eds., *The Blackwell Encyclopedia of Anglo-Saxon England* (Malden, Mass. and Oxford: Blackwell, 1999), 181-2; also Pauline A. Stafford, 'The "Farm of One Night" and the Organization of King Edward's Estates in Domesday,' *Economic History Review* 2nd series 33 (4) (1980): 491-502.

47 A.R. Bridbury, 'Seventh-Century England in Bede and the Early Laws,' in A.R. Bridbury, ed., *The English Economy from Bede to the Reformation* (Woodbridge: Boydell, 1992), 71.

48 Henry Adams, 'The Anglo-Saxon Courts of Law,' in Henry Adams, ed., *Essays in Anglo-Saxon Law* (Boston: Little, Brown, 1876), 6.

49 E.G. Stanley, 'Two Old English Poetic Phrases Insufficiently Understood for Literary Criticism: *þing gehegen* and *seonoþ gehegen*,' in Daniel G. Calder, ed., *Old English Poetry: Essays in Style* (Berkeley: University of California Press, 1979), 83.

50 Liebermann, *Gesetze*, 2:138, 222.

51 Pokorny, *Indogermanisches Etymologisches Wörterbuch*, 746 and 1065-7. See also Friedrich Kluge and Elmer Seebold, *Etymologisches Wörterbuch der deutschen Sprache* 22nd ed. (Berlin: de Gruyter, 1989), 144-5.

52 Klaeber, *Beowulf and the Fight at Finnsburg*, ll:435-6 and ll:1875-6.

53 Liebermann, *Gesetze*, 3:21.
54 See Whitelock, *English Historical Documents*, 395.
55 See Henry Campbell Black, et al., *Black's Law Dictionary* (St Paul: West, 1990), 1577.
56 For discussion of the archaeology of early London, see Alan Vince, *Saxon London: An Archaeological Investigation* (London: Seaby, 1990), 4–26; Alan Vince, 'The Economic Basis of Ango-Saxon London,' in Richard Hodges and Brian Hobley, eds., *The Rebirth of Towns in the West, AD 700–1050* (London: Council for British Archaeology, 1988), 83–92; Alan Vince, 'The *Aldwych*: Mid-Saxon London Discovered?' *Current Archeology* 93 (1984): 310–12; Brian Hobley, '*Lundenwic* and *Lundenburh*: Two Cities Rediscovered,' in Hodges and Hobley, eds., *The Rebirth of Towns in the West, AD 700–1050*, 69–82; M. Biddle, 'London on the Strand,' *Popular Archeology* (July 1984): 23–7; Tim Tatton-Brown, 'The Topography of Anglo-Saxon London,' *Antiquity* 60 (1986): 22–5; Tim Tatton-Brown, 'Canterbury and the Early Medieval Towns of Kent,' in Peter Leach, ed., *Archaeology in Kent to AD 1500* (London: Council for British Archaeology, 1982), 79–81; Robert Cowie and Robert Whytehead, '*Lundenwic*: The Archeological Evidence for Middle Saxon London,' *Antiquity* 241 (1989): 700–18; Christopher Scull, 'Urban Centers in Pre-Viking England?' in John Hines, ed., *The Anglo-Saxons from the Migration Period to the Eighth Century: An Ethnographic Perspective* (Woodbridge: Boydell, 1997), 269–310. Giorgio Ausenda, 'Current Issues and Future Directions in the Study of the Early Anglo-Saxon Period,' in Hines, ed., *The Anglo-Saxons*, 439, points out that this abandonment of Roman urban centers is unsurprising, given the fact that the Germanic peoples were unfamiliar with stonework, and thus masonry repair would be a dangerous occupation.
57 Colgrave and Mynors, eds., *Bede's Ecclesiastical History*, 143.
58 See Vince, *Saxon London*, 104.
59 Patrick Wormald, *The Making of English Law: King Alfred to the Twelfth Century, Volume One: Legislation and its Limits* (Oxford: Blackwell, 1999), 103.
60 See Stéphane Lebecq, 'The Question of Logistics,' in Richard Gameson, ed., *St. Augustine and the Conversion of England* (Stroud: Sutton, 1999), 56–9 and esp. 59.
61 Peter Sawyer, 'Early Fairs and Markets in England and Scandanavia,' in R.L. Anderson and A.J. Latham, eds., *The Market in History* (London and Dover, NH: Croom Helm, 1986), 67.
62 Ibid., 62.

230   Notes to pages 143–6

63 Philip Grierson and Mark Blackburn, *Medieval European Coinage I: The Early Middle Ages* (Cambridge and New York: Cambridge University Press, 1986), 161–2.
64 Sonia Chadwick Hawkes, 'Anglo-Saxon Kent c. 425–725,' in Leach, *Archaeology in Kent*, 64–78.
65 See A.R. Bridbury, 'Markets and Freedom in the Middle Ages,' in Anderson and Latham, eds., *The Market in History*, 108.
66 Liebermann, *Gesetze*, 3:22.
67 Colgrave and Mynors, eds., *Bede's Ecclesiastical History*, 404–5.
68 See Kirby, *Making of Early England*, 180.
69 Vince, *Saxon London*, 94; see also Cowie and Whitehead, 'Lundenwic,' 713–14.
70 Lisi Oliver, 'Towards Freeing a Slave in Germanic Law,' in Jay Jasanoff, H. Craig Melchert, and Lisi Oliver, eds., *Mír Curad: Studies in Honor of Calvert Watkins* (Innsbruck: Institut für Sprachwissenschaft der Universität Innsbruck, 1999), 549–60.
71 Dirk Korte, *Untersuchungen zu Inhalt, Stil und Technik angelsächsicher Gesetze und Rechtsbücher des 6. bis 12. Jahrhunderts* (Meisenheim am Glan: A. Hain, 1974), 146.
72 Liebermann, *Gesetze*, 3:19.
73 For dating, see Ian Wood, *The Merovingian Kingdoms 450–751* (London and New York: Longman, 1994), 108–12.
74 The Latin reads as follows: 'Si quis servus alienus fuerit plagiatus et ipse trans mare ductus fuerit et ibidem a domino suo fuerit inventus et, ad quo ipse in patria <sua> plagiatus est, in mallo publico nominaverit, tres ibidem testes debet colligere. Iterum cum servus ipse detrans mare fuerit revocatus, in alterum vero mallum debet <iterum> nominare, ibidem simul tres testes debent collegi <(i)done(o)s>.' The Latin text is to be found in Karl Eckhardt, *Die Gesetze des Merowingerreiches 481–714, I: Pactus Legis Salicae, Recensiones Merovingicae* (Göttingen: Musterschmidt, 1955), 114; translation is my own.
75 Theodore John Rivers, trans., *Laws of the Salian and Ripuarian Franks* (New York: AMS Press, 1986), 82; Katherine Fisher Drew, trans., *The Laws of the Salian Franks* (Philadelphia: University of Pennsylvania Press, 1991).
76 See note 74, above.
77 Ian Wood, 'Before and After the Migration to Britain,' in Hines, ed., *The Anglo-Saxons*, 47.
78 Liebermann, *Gesetze*, 1:10.
79 Ibid., 2:708.
80 John T. MacNeill and Helena M. Gamer, *Medieval Handbooks of Penance* (New York: Columbia University Press, 1938, repr. 1990), 211.

Chapter Four: The Laws of Wihtred

1 Bertram Colgrave and R.A.B. Mynors, eds., *Bede's Ecclesiastical History of the English People* (Oxford: Clarendon, 1969), 431. Thomas Charles-Edwards, 'Anglo-Saxon Kinship Revisited,' in John Hines, ed., *The Anglo-Saxons from the Migration Period to the Eighth Century: An Ethnographic Perspective* (Woodbridge: Boydell, 1997), 190 suggests that 'an "outside king," *rex externus*, would be external to the entire royal kindred ... but the dubiousness of the *rex dubius* was presumably his untrustworthy pedigree.'
2 Dorothy Whitelock, ed., *English Historical Documents, Volume I: c.500–1042* (London: Eyre & Spottiswoode, 1955; repr. 1979), 168.
3 Ibid., 168.
4 Ibid., 169.
5 An excellent discussion of the charter evidence for the succession of the kings of Kent can be found in S.E. Kelly, ed., *Charters of St. Augustine's Abbey Canterbury and Minster-in-Thanet* (Oxford and New York: Oxford University Press, 1995), 195–9.
6 This may have represented a division between East Kent and West Kent; see Barbara A.E. Yorke, 'Joint Kingship in Kent c. 560 to 785,' *Archaeologia Cantiana* 99 (1983): 1–19; also Nicholas Brooks, 'The Creation and Early Structure of the Kingdom of Kent,' in Steven Bassett, ed., *The Origins of Anglo-Saxon Kingdoms* (London and New York: Leicester University Press, 1989), 68.
7 Whitelock, *English Historical Documents*, 169.
8 Ibid., 172.
9 Ibid., 396; Kelly, *Charters of St. Augustine's Abbey*, 198.
10 Kelly, *Charters of St. Augustine's Abbey*, 197.
11 Colgrave and Mynors, eds., *Bede's Ecclesiastical History*, 431.
12 Ibid., 559.
13 Peter Sawyer, *Anglo-Saxon Charters: An Annotated List and Bibliography* (London: Royal Historical Society, 1968), #89.
14 Whitelock, *English Historical Documents*, 493–4.
15 Karl Brunner, *Altenglische Grammatik* (Tübingen: Neimeyer, 1965), 40.
16 See Lisi Oliver, 'Towards Freeing a Slave in Common Germanic Law,' in J. Jasanoff, H. Craig Melchert, and Lisi Oliver, eds., *Mír Curad: Studies in Honor of Calvert Watkins* (Innsbruck: Insitut für Sprachwissenschaft der Universität Innsbruck, 1998), 549–50.
17 Brunner, *Altenglische Grammatik*, 195; Eduard Sievers, 'Altnordisches im Beowulf?' *Beiträge zur Geschichte der deutschen Sprache und Literatur* 12

(1887): 184; Felix Liebermann, *Die Gesetze der Angelsachsen* (Halle: M. Niemeyer, 1897–1916) 3:1.

18 But what else would one expect from a king who implemented 'at least three of the Ten Commandments as matters of royal law?' per Patrick Wormald, *The Making of English Law: King Alfred to the Twelfth Century, Volume One: Legislation and its Limits* (Oxford: Blackwell, 1999), 103.

19 Sir Frank Stenton, *Anglo-Saxon England*, 3rd ed. (Oxford: Clarendon, 1971), 108.

20 This is not listed in Catherine Cubitt, *Anglo-Saxon Church Councils c. 650–c. 850* (London and New York: Leicester University Press, 1995), 258–9. But see earlier discussion in same (1–75) for similarities in format and structure.

21 Colgrave and Mynors, eds., *Bede's Ecclesiastical History*, 151.

22 See H. Munro Chadwick, *Studies on Anglo-Saxon Institutions* (Cambridge: Cambridge University Press, 1905; repr. New York, 1963), 111.

23 Whitelock, *English Historical Documents*, 396.

24 See ibid., 396; Lieberman, *Gesetze*, 3:24; C.R. Cheney, *A Handbook of Dates for Students of English History* (Cambridge: Cambridge University Press, 2000), 2–4; Charles Arnold-Baker, *The Companion to British History* (Tunbridge Wells: Longcross, 1996), 691.

25 Whitelock, *English Historical Documents*, 172.

26 The authorship of these penitentials is a matter of some question: see discussion in John T. MacNeill and Helena M. Gamer, *Medieval Handbooks of Penance* (New York: Columbia University Press, 1938; repr. 1990), 179–82; also F.W.H. Wasserschleben, *Die Bussordnungen der abendländischen Kirche* (Graz: Akademische Druck, 1958), 13–37.

27 Liebermann, *Gesetze*, 3:24. But see discussion in chapter 3 under 'Oath supporters' for a close parallel between Salic law and the laws of Hloþhere & Eadric, which may also represent literate borrowing.

28 Dirk Korte, *Untersuchungen zu Inhalt, Stil und Technik angelsächsicher Gesetze und Rechtsbücher des 6. bis 12. Jahrhunderts* (Meisenheim am Glan: A. Hain, 1974), 78.

29 Translation from Nicholas Brooks, *The Early History of the Church of Canterbury: Christ Church from 597 to 1066* (Leicester: Leicester University Press, 1984), 183 of Birch #99, Sawyer #20. Not all scholars accept the authenticity of this document. See citations in Sawyer, *Anglo-Saxon Charters*, 76, but Nicholas Brooks argues for it in 'The Development of Military Obligations in Eight- and Ninth-Century England,' in Peter Clemeos and Kathleen Hughes, eds., *England before the Conquest: Studies in Primary Sources Presented to Dorothy Whitelock* (Cambridge: Cambridge University Press, 1971).

Notes to pages 167–72   233

30 Brooks, 'The Development of Military Obligations,' 79.
31 Ibid.
32 See discussion of dating problems in Cubitt, *Anglo-Saxon Church Councils*, 249.
33 Colgrave and Mynors, eds., *Bede's Ecclesiastical History*, 353. See discussion in Loredana Lazzari, 'Il Codice di Wihtræd: incidenza di canoni ecclesiastici sulle leggi secolari,' in Loredana Lazzari, ed., *Testi giuridici germanici* (Potenza: Il Salice, 1992), 31–2.
34 See MacNeill and Gamer, *Medieval Handbooks of Penance*, 184–213; Wasserschleben, *Bussordnungen*, 184–219.
35 MacNeill and Gamer, *Medieval Handbooks of Penance*, 195–8; Wasserschleben, *Bussordnungen*, 197–200.
36 See Liebermann, *Gesetze*, 3:26.
37 See MacNeill and Gamer, *Medieval Handbooks of Penance*, 184 and 191–2; Wasserschleben, *Bussordnungen*, 184 and 192–3.
38 Liebermann, *Gesetze*, 3:27.
39 Colgrave and Mynors, eds., *Bede's Ecclesiastical History*, 351.
40 See David A.E. Pelteret, *Slavery in Early Mediaeval England* (Woodbridge and Rochester: Boydell, 1995), 296.
41 See discussion under 'Freedman' in Commentary to chapter 2.
42 See Oliver, 'Towards Freeing a Slave.'
43 See Liebermann, *Gesetze*, 3:27.
44 Benjamin Thorpe, ed., *Ancient Laws and Institutes of England* (London: Commissioners of the Public Records, 1840), Glossary.
45 Whitelock, *English Historical Documents*, 397. See also A.J. Robertson, trans., *The Laws of the Kings of England from Edmund to Henry I* (Cambridge: Cambridge University Press, 1925), 297–8 for other examples.
46 F.L. Attenborough, ed., *The Laws of the Earliest English Kings* (Cambridge: Cambridge University Press), 181. Schmid is cited in Chadwick, *Studies on Anglo-Saxon Institutions*, 129.
47 Christine Fell, *Women in Anglo-Saxon England and the Impact of 1066* (Bloomington: Indiana University Press, 1984), 59.
48 Whitelock, *English Historical Documents*, 404.
49 MacNeill and Gamer, *Medieval Handbooks of Penance*, 211; Wasserschleben, *Bussordnungen*, 217.
50 Liebermann, *Gesetze*, 3:28.
51 Ibid., 3:29.
52 In the first edition (1955) of *English Historical Documents*, Whitelock interpreted the clause otherwise, using the more common meaning of *ofer* and amending *se dryhtne* to the dative *þam dryhtne* (indirect object), giving a reading of 'If a servant, against his lord's command, do servile

234 Notes to pages 173-80

work ... he is to pay 80 sceattas to his lord.' This interpretation also forced Whitelock to change the shillings to sceattas, as it is highly unlikely that an *esne* would be fined at the rate of 80 shillings (which is, after all, almost the *wergild* of a freeman). She amended this reading in the second edition (1979).

53 Attenborough, *Laws of the Earliest English Kings*, 181.
54 Whitelock, *English Historical Documents*, 397.
55 Liebermann, *Gesetze*, 3:28.
56 Whitelock, *English Historical Documents*, 399.
57 See parallels in Æthelberht §§15, 23, 30, 80.
58 See MacNeill and Gamer, *Medieval Handbooks of Penance*, 194 and 198; Wasserschleben, *Bussordnungen*, 195 and 200-1.
59 I am indebted to an anonymous reader of this manuscript for this observation.
60 See Chadwick, *Studies on Anglo-Saxon Institutions*, 84; Liebermann, *Gesetze*, 2:680.
61 H.R. Loyn, 'Gesiths and Thegns in Anglo-Saxon England from the Seventh to the Tenth Century,' *English Historical Review* 70 (1955): 540-1.
62 For the position of reeve, see Liebermann, *Gesetze*, 2:718-23.
63 Book I, Chap. V: *De his qui per heresim decipiuntur*; translation from MacNeill and Gamer, *Medieval Handbooks of Penance*, 188; see also Wasserschleben, *Bussordnungen*, 188-90.
64 Whitelock, *English Historical Documents*, 400; see Liebermann, *Gesetze*, 1:96.
65 Whitelock, *English Historical Documents*, 398.
66 Ibid., 398.
67 See Liebermann, *Gesetze*, 3:30; Attenborough, *Laws of the Earliest English Kings*, 182.
68 See Liebermann, *Gesetze*, 3:30.
69 MacNeil and Gamer, *Medieval Handbooks of Penance*, 210; Wasserschleben, *Bussordnungen*, 215-6.
70 See Fergus Kelly, *A Guide to Early Irish Law* (Dublin: Dublin Institute for Advanced Studies, 1988), 95.
71 Liebermann, *Gesetze*, 3:30.
72 Ibid., 1:98.
73 Ibid., 3:30.
74 Albert S. Cook, 'Laws of Wihtred, No. 28,' *Modern Language Notes* 20 (1905): 30.

Glossary

The focus of this glossary is on the content words in the texts of the Kentish laws. It thus does not include grammatical words such as auxiliary or copular verbs, pronouns, or prepositions. Nor does it include numbers in noun or adjective forms. A concordance of proper names follows.

The glosses generally provide the stem meaning; this is occasionally augmented when the context or grammatical form is unique or important to understanding the gloss. Emendations and questionable readings, as they are discussed at length in the appropriate sections of the text, are tacitly assumed.

The prefix *ge-* is ignored in the alphabetization. æ follows a; þ and ð follow t.
Æbt = Æthelberht; H & E = Hloþhere & Eadric; W = Wihtred
Numbers refer to clauses; Rub = Rubric; Pro = Prologue

abregde 'draw' H & E 9
abycgan 'validate' W 15; *abicge* 'buy (him) off' Æbt 31
acwyle 'die' H & E 4; *acwelle* 'put to death' W 22.1
age 'obtain' Æbt 15; Æbt 76.2; Æbt 76.3; *agan* 'own' Æbt 76.5; H & E 3.1; H & E 7; H & E 8; H & E 6.2; W 7; W 8.2; W 21.1; 'bring (a charge)' H & E 9
   agan 'take (a husband)' Æbt 76.4
agefe 'give (up/back)' Æbt 76.1; H & E 1; H & E 2; H & E 11.2
agelde 'pay' H & E 7; 8; W 22.1; *agylde* H & E 6.1 (See also *forgelde*)
agene '(one's) own' Æbt 30; *agenum* Æbt 31; H & E 10
agend 'owner' H & E 1; H & E 2; H & E 5; H & E 5.1; H & E 11.3
   agende Æbt 77 (2x); W 22.1
agylde See *agelde*
ald See *eald*
aldor 'head (of a minster)' W 13; *aldoras* 'ancestors' H & E Pro

Glossary

alyse 'redeem' W 11; *alese* W 21; W 22; [to] *alysenne* W 23
ambiht(?-smið) 'official(?-smith)' Æbt 13
andward 'present' W Pro; *andweardne* H & E 3
án-læte 'relinquish' H & E 5.1; H & E 11.3
anmodlice 'with a single mind' W Pro
anum 'one' H & E 11.2; *anes* W 21; *ane* W 15
  ænes 'once' W 6
  ane 'sole' W 18; W 19
arasie 'detect' W 8.2
ascadene 'separated' W 3
asette 'set' Æbt Rub; H & E 8; *asetton* H & E Rub
  aset 'take away' H & E 8;
aslagen See *of-aslagen*
aþ 'oath' W 15; *að* W 16; *aþe* H & E 3; H & E 6.2; W 12; W 16 ; W 18; W 18.1; W 19; *aðe* H & E 6.3
awyrce 'carry out' H & E 6
awyrd 'damaged' Æbt 49
  awyrdeþ 'damage' Æbt 64
æ 'laws' H & E Pro
æcton 'added' W Pro
æfen 'eve' W 8; *æfenes* W 8
æhtan 'possessions' Æbt 15; W 9; W 9.1; *æhtum* W 3.1
ælc 'each' W Pro
ælcor 'otherwise' Æbt 45
æltheodige 'foreign' W 3.1
ær 'before' H & E Pro; H & E 6.1; 'first (of two)' Æbt 76.2
ærnæmda 'afore-mentioned' W Pro
ætfo 'take/claim possession of' H & E 5; H & E 11.1
ætgebicge 'buy' Æbt 77 (See also *bycgan*)
ætstanden 'stand by' W 15
æwdamanna 'oathmen' H & E 3
æwdan 'oath' W 18.1
  æwdum 'oath-helpers' H & E 1.1; H & E 2.1

bana 'killer' Æbt 24.2; H & E 2.1; *bane*; H & E 1.1; *banan* H & E 1; H & E 1.1; H & E 2; H & E 2.1
banes 'bone' Æbt 34
gebanne 'indiction' W Pro
bearn 'child' Æbt 76.2; Æbt 76.4; Æbt 76.5; H & E 4
  bearne H & E 4
  bearnum Æbt 76.3
bebod 'command' W 4

bebyreþ 'provide' Æbt 23
begete 'obtain' Æbt 31; *begeten* 'seize' H & E 1.1; H & E 2.1
berigean See *byrigean*
bescoren 'tonsured' W 6
gebete 'pay (restitution)' Æbt 9, Æbt 11; Æbt 15; Æbt 16; Æbt 16.1; Æbt 18; Æbt 19; Æbt 21; Æbt 22; Æbt 23; Æbt 23.1; Æbt 23.2; Æbt 24; Æbt 24; Æbt 25; Æbt 28; Æbt 28.1; Æbt 29; Æbt 34; Æbt 35; Æbt 36; Æbt 36.1; Æbt 37; Æbt 38; Æbt 39; Æbt 40; Æbt 41; Æbt 42; Æbt 43; Æbt 44; Æbt 44.1; Æbt 44.2 Æbt 45; Æbt 46; Æbt 50; Æbt 51; Æbt 52; Æbt 54; Æbt 55; Æbt 56; Æbt 57; Æbt 58; Æbt 61.3; Æbt 61.4; Æbt 62; Æbt 62.1; Æbt 63; Æbt 63.1; Æbt 64.1; Æbt 64.2; Æbt 65; Æbt66; Æbt 68; Æbt 71.1; Æbt 72; Æbt 74; Æbt 77.1; Æbt 78; Æbt 81; Æbt 83; W 4; W 4.1; W 8; W 8.1; W 10 (See also *bote*)
betstan 'foremost' Æbt 74
bewyddod 'betrothed' Æbt 77.1
gebidde 'pray for' W 1.1
gebigeð 'buy' Æbt 76; *gebycge* H & E 11
   gebohte H & E 11.2
gebindeþ 'bind' Æbt 25; Æbt 81
birele 'cupbearer' Æbt 19; *birelan* Æbt 21
bisceop 'bishop' W Pro; *biscopes* Æbt 2; W 4; W 5; W 12; W 17
bismærwordum 'mocking words' H & E 7
bite 'cutting' Æbt 35
blawe 'blow' W 23
blice 'exposure' Æbt 34
geblodgad 'bloodied' H & E 9.1
boca 'book' W 4
bote 'restitution' Æbt 8; Æbt 33; Æbt 71
   twibote 'a 2-fold restitution'
   (See also *gebete*)
gebrenge 'bring' Æbt 31; Æbt 76.1; H & E 5; H & E 10; *gebrengen* H & E 11.1
gebrocen 'broken' Æbt 36; Æbt 50; Æbt 65
bugan 'dwell' Æbt 76.3
butu 'both' Æbt 36.1; Æbt 44.2; *butwu* W 9.1
gebycge See *gebigeð*
gebyreþ 'bear (a child)' Æbt 76.2; Æbt 76.5
byrigean 'surety' H & E 6; *byrigan* H & E 6.1; H & E 6.2; *berigean* H & E 4

canne 'cognizance' H & E 11.3; 'exculpation' W 13; W interpolation following 16.2
cænne 'exculpate/clear (oneself from accusation)' W 13; W 17; *gecænne* H & E 1.1; H & E 2.1; H & E 3

238 Glossary

ceape 'purchase/price' H & E 11.2; *ceapi* Æbt 76
  geceapod 'having made a valid bargain/purchase' Æbt 76
cearwund 'grievously wounded' Æbt 63.1
ceas 'strife' Æbt 23
ceorl 'man, husband' Æbt 76.2; Æbt 76.4; H & E 4; W 9; *ceorle* Æbt 78
  '(free)man' *ceorles* Æbt 20, Æbt 21; *ceorlæs* Æbt 26; *ceorlas* H & E 11
ceorlisc 'of freeman rank' W 4.1; W 16.1
cepeman 'merchant' H & E 10
cinban 'jawbone' Æbt 47
ciricanmannes 'churchman' W 19 (2x)
ciricean 'church' Æbt 1; W Pro; W 1; W 2; W 3; *cirican* W interpolation following 16.2
ciricfriþ 'church peace' Æbt 6
ciriclicæs 'of the church' W 3.2
clænsie 'clear (oneself from accusation)' W 14; W 14.1; W 15; W 16; *clensie* W 17.
  geclænsie W 18; *geclensige* W 19
cliroc 'cleric' W 15; *cleroces* Æbt 5
cuma '(let him) come' H & E 3
  cuman '(one who has) come' H & E 10; *cumin* 'has come' H & E 10;
  cumen 'having come' W 23
cuþan 'public' H & E 11.2
cwæð 'say' W Pro; *cwyþ* W Pro;
  cwiden Æbt 70.1
  cweþende W 14
cwelle 'kill' W 21; W 21.1 (See also *acwyle*)
cwic 'living/alive' Æbt 76.2; *cwicum* Æbt 78
cwiden See *cwæð*
gecwime 'let him satisfy' H & E 6.2
cwynan 'wife' Æbt 78
cyning 'king' Æbt Rub; Æbt 8; Æbt 9 ; Æbt 15; W Pro; W 1; W 21; W 22
  cyninge Æbt 8, Æbt 10, Æbt 12; Æbt 77.2; H & E 6.1; H & E 7; H & E 9; H & E 9.1; W Pro; *cynge* H & E 8
  cyninges Æbt 11, Æbt 13, Æbt 14, Æbt 16, Æbt 17; H & E 11; H & E 11.2; W Rub; W 12; W 16; W 17; *cynges* H & E 5; *cyngæs* H & E 11.1; W 4; *cinges* W 2
  cyningas H & E Pro
gecyþan See *gekyþe*

dæge 'day/time' Æbt Rub; W Pro; *dæges* W 8.1
deman 'judges' H & E 6
deoflum 'idols' W 9; W 9.1; W 10

diacon 'deacon' W 14.1; *diacones* Æbt 4
gedo 'do/perform' Æbt 8; Æbt 9; H & E 1
 gedon Æbt 23.1
 deþ H & E 9; W 8.1
 gedeþ Æbt 23; Æbt 28; Æbt 72
dom 'judgment/decree' W 4; W 5
 domas Æbt Rub; H & E Rub; W Rub; W Pro
 domum H & E Pro
drihtinbeage 'lord-payment' Æbt 12
drincæþ 'drink' Æbt 9
 drincen H & E 8; H & E 9
 druncen W 5
dryhten 'lord' W 8; W 8.1; W 18; W 19
 dryhtnes W 8
 dryhtne W 4
dynt 'blow' Æbt 61.1; Æbt 61.3
 dyntes Æbt 61.2
eadigan 'great men' W Pro; *eadigra* W Pro
eage 'eye' Æbt 42; Æbt 43; Æbt 80
eald 'ancient/established' H & E 8; *ald* W 4
ealne 'all' Æbt 24.1; Æbt 79; Æbt 80
 ealra W Pro; W 9; W 9.1; W 16.2
ealswa 'likewise/already discussed' Æbt 70.1
eare 'ear' Æbt 38; Æbt 39; Æbt 40; Æbt 41
earm 'arm' Æbt 51; Æbt 52
eaxle 'shoulder' Æbt 37
ecton 'add to' H & E Pro
edor 'hedge/enclosure' Æbt 29
edorbrecþe 'breaking into a hedge/enclosure' Æbt 28
eft 'after/afterwards' Æbt 76.1; Æbt 77; H & E 3; H & E 5; H & E 11.1
 efter H & E Pro; W Pro; W 8
eorlcundre 'of noble rank/birth' Æbt 74; *eorlcundne* H & E 1
eorles 'nobleman' Æbt 18, Æbt 19
erfe 'inheritance' W 7
esne 'servant (labourer)' Æbt 79; Æbt 81; H & E 1; H & E 2; W 8; W 8.1; W 17; W 18; W 19 (4x)
 esnes Æbt 78; Æbt 80
ete 'eat' W 11.1

facne 'deceptive' Æbt 76.1
fæderingmagas 'father's kin' Æbt 76.5; *fæderingmagum* H & E 4

240 Glossary

fæsten 'fast (from food)' W 11
feaxfang 'seizing of hair' Æbt 33
fede 'feed' H & E 10
fedesl 'feeding' Æbt 17
feoh 'property' Æbt 1; Æbt 2; Æbt 3; Æbt 4; Æbt 5; Æbt 28.1; H & E 4; H & E 5; H & E 11; H & E 11.2; *feo* Æbt 30; H & E 6.2; *fioh* Æbt 76.5
feormæþ 'provide for/support' H & E 10; *feormige* W 6
feorran 'from afar' W 23
finger 'finger' Æbt 58;
    fingrum Æbt 70.1
    (See also *scytefinger, middelfinger, goldfinger*)
flæsc 'meat' W 11
flet 'house' H & E 7; H & E 8; H & E 9; H & E 9.1; *flette* H & E 7
fo 'take possession' H & E 5.1
    gefo 'seize' W 21; W 21.1
folcesmannes 'layman' W 19 (2x)
folcfry 'having the rights of a free man of the people' W 7
folcy 'populace' W Pro
folgige 'follow' H & E 4
forbodenan 'forbidden' W 8.2
forbrocen 'broken' Æbt 52; Æbt 66 (See also *gebrocen*)
forewyrce 'do what is required' H & E 10
forgelde 'pay' Æbt 13, Æbt 17; Æbt 24.1 (2x), Æbt 27, Æbt 27.1, Æbt 32, Æbt 47, Æbt 61.2; Æbt 64; Æbt 79; Æbt 80; H & E 2.1; H & E 7; *forgylde* Æbt 10; H & E 9.1; *forgelden* Æbt 24.2; Æbt 27.2; Æbt 69; Æbt 70
forlæte 'relinquish' W 4.2
forsitte 'neglect' W 5
forslæhð 'break' Æbt 47
forstele 'steal' H & E 3; H & E 5
forwærne 'refuse' H & E 6.1
fot 'foot' Æbt 69; *foot* Æbt 80
fræmde 'stranger' W 23
freols 'free' W 7
freolsdom(e) 'freedom' W 1
freolsgefa 'freedom-giver' W 7
freond 'friend, kinsman' Æbt 65.1
freora 'free' H & E 3
frigman 'freeman' Æbt 10; Æbt 15; H & E 3; *friman* Æbt 28; Æbt 31; W 8.2
    fries mannes Æbt 31; *friges mannes* Æbt 73
    frigne mannan Æbt 12; H & E 2; *frigne man* Æbt 25; W 21; *frigne (man)* W 11
    freum Æbt 15

-friþ 'peace' Æbt 6; Æbt 7
friwif 'free woman' Æbt 72
fulwihte 'baptism' W 5
fundon 'devise' W Pro
fyrestum 'first' Æbt 48
fyste 'fist' Æbt 61

gafola 'tribute' W 1
gange 'go' W 23; *gange him* 'seek out' W 6
  gegangeð 'enter' Æbt 29; *gegange* 'deliver' W 21.1
gængang 'return' Æbt 77.2
gedes '?community' W 18
gefe 'give' W 6; W 7; W 11
gegemed 'cured' Æbt 63
gekyndelice 'genital' Æbt 64
gekyþe 'declare' H & E 11.2; *gecyþan* 11.3
gelde 'let him pay' Æbt 28.1; Æbt 30; Æbt 70.1; H & E 2; H & E 3.1; H & E 6.3;
  W 9; W 18.1; *gylde* H & E 1
  geldaþ W 9.1; W 10
gelde 'compensation' Æbt 75; Æbt 83; *gylde* Æbt 1; Æbt 2; Æbt 3; Æbt 4; Æbt
  5; Æbt 6; Æbt 7; Æbt 10
  (See also *forgelde*)
gest 'stranger' W 16
gestliðnesse 'hospitality' W 6
Godes 'God's' Æbt 1
godne 'good' W 18.1
goldfinger 'ring-finger' Æbt 57
gonoh 'enough' H & E 3.1
græfe 'grave' Æbt 24.1
grete 'accost' H & E 7
grindende 'grinding' Æbt 16.1
gylde See *gelde*

had 'order (of rank)' W Pro
halgum 'holy' W 14
ham 'home' Æbt 9; Æbt 76.1; *hame* H & E 10
hand 'hand' W 15; W 17; *handa* Æbt 61.2; W 21
hateþ 'call' H & E 7; *hatte* W Pro; *haten* W Pro
  gehateþ 'summon' Æbt 8
hæbbendre 'having in hand' W 21
hæmed '(marital) union' W 3.1; W 4.2 (See also *unrihthæmed*)

hæse 'order' W 8
heafodgemacene 'equal (in rank)' W 15; W 16.2
heahbiscop 'archbishop' W Pro
heahre 'raised' Æbt 61.2
healdenne 'maintain' H & E 4
healf 'half' Æbt 70.1; W 8.2
    healfne Æbt 24.2; Æbt 76.2; Æbt 76.3; W 21.1; W 22.1
healsfange 'payment in lieu of imprisonment' W 8.2; W 9; W 9.1; *halsfange* W 11
healt 'lame' Æbt 65.1
heowum See *hina*
gehereð 'hear' Æbt 38
hersuman 'obedient' W Pro
hina 'kin/household' W 7
    heowum W 11
hion 'skull' Æbt 36
hlafætan 'loaf-eater/dependent' Æbt 26
hleore 'cheek' Æbt 44.1
horn 'horn' W 23
hrægle 'vestment' W 14
hreowe 'repentence' W 3; W 4.2
hrif 'abdomen' Æbt 62
hryme 'call out' W 23
huslgenga 'communicant' W 18; W 18.1
hyd 'hide/skin' W 8.1; W 10; W 11.1

inbestinð 'stab into' Æbt 64.2
geirneþ 'break in' Æbt 22
    irneþ Æbt 22.1

laadrincmannan '?guide/herald' Æbt 13
lande 'land' Æbt 24.2; W 3.1
læfe 'allow' W 5
gelæmed 'lamed' Æbt 37
læng 'longer' W 6
lærestan 'least' Æbt 60
læt 'freedman' Æbt 27
læte See *an-læte*
leafnesse 'permission' W 6
leode 'people' Æbt 8; *leodum* W 3.2
    leud 'person' W 20

leod 'person(-price)' Æbt 24.1; Æbt 24.2
leodgeld 'person-price' Æbt 24
  leodgelde Æbt 13
  leudgeldum Æbt 64
leofre 'preferable' H & E 6.2 (2x)
libbendum 'living' H & E 4
life 'life' W 3
geligeþ 'lie (with)' Æbt 16, Æbt 19, Æbt 21; Æbt 31; Æbt 78; *licge* 'lie' W 20
lim 'limb/member' Æbt 64
locbore 'in charge of locks/bearing locks' Æbt 72
lyswæs 'an act of dishonesty' Æbt 9; *leswæs* Æbt 72
lytlan 'little' Æbt 58

magas 'kinsmen' Æbt 24.2
gemanan 'community' W 3; W 3.2
gemange 'midst' W 18
manswara 'perjurer' H & E 7
manwyrð 'man-worth' H & E 1; H & E 1.1; H & E 2
  manwyrþum H & E 2.1
maran 'greater' Æbt 60.1
mægdenman 'maiden' Æbt 16 (See also *mægþ, mægþbot*)
mægþ 'maiden' Æbt 76
  mægþman Æbt 77
mægþbot 'compensation for a maiden' Æbt 73
mægðe 'people/race' W Pro
mæthlfriþ 'assembly peace' Æbt 7 (See also *medle*)
mearce 'border' H & E 10; W 7
medder 'mother' H & E 4
medle 'assembly' H & E 6 (See also *mæthlfriþ*)
gemedum 'consent' W Pro
meduman 'ordinary' Æbt 13, *medume* Æbt 24
mete 'food' H & E 10
micle 'big' Æbt 70
  mycclan Æbt 71
middelfinger 'middle finger' Æbt 56
mildestan 'most gracious' W Pro
monan 'Monday' W 8
morgengyfe 'morning-gift' Æbt 76.5
gemot 'assembly' W 4
mote 'meet' H & E 6
mund 'protection' Æbt 74; Æbt 75; *munde* W 7 (See also *mundbyrd*)

244   Glossary

mundbyrd 'protection' Æbt 14, Æbt 20; H & E 9.1; W 2 (See also *mund*)
muð 'mouth' Æbt 43
mynstres 'minster' W 13

nasu 'nose' Æbt 44; Æbt 45; *naso* Æbt 61
nawiht 'nothing' Æbt 38
nægl 'nail' Æbt 54; Æbt 71; *neglum* Æbt 59
neadhæse 'compulsion' W 1
nede 'force' Æbt 77
niht 'night' H & E 6.2; H & E 10; *neaht* H & E 6.3; *nihta* Æbt 24.1; *nihtum* H & E 6.2
genimeþ 'take' Æbt 28.1; Æbt 75; Æbt 77; *genime* W 4

of '(struck) off' Æbt 42; Æbt 54; Æbt 69; Æbt 70; Æbt 71 (See also following entries)
ofslea 'stike off' Æbt 11, Æbt 30; Æbt 79; W 20; *of-sleaþ* Æbt 12; *ofslehð* Æbt 13; *ofslæhþ* Æbt 18; *ofslæhð* Æbt 23.2, Æbt 24, Æbt 24.1; Æbt 26; H & E 1; H & E 2
    of-aslæhð Æbt 53; Æbt 55; Æbt 56; Æbt 57; Æbt 58
    of ... aslagen Æbt 39; Æbt 80
onfehð 'receive (a blow)' Æbt 61.2
open 'open' H & E 6.1; *openum* Æbt 24.1
oþbyrste 'escape' H & E 1.1; H & E 2.1
oþer 'second/other' Æbt 38; H & E 2
    oþerne Æbt 61; Æbt 79; H & E 6; H & E 6.2; *oðerne* H & E 10 (2x); *oðirne* W 18.1
    oþres H & E 7
    oðrum Æbt 70.1; H & E 6; *oþrum* Æbt 71.1; Æbt 77.1; H & E 5; H & E 6.2
    oþre Æbt 74.1; W 15

preost 'priest' W 14; *priost* W 5; *preostes* Æbt 3; W 13
profianne 'regard' W 23

rade 'counsel' W 8.1; *ræde* 'accord' W 11.1
gerefa 'reeve' W 17; *gerefan* W 17
reht See *riht*
rib 'rib' Æbt 66
rices 'reign' W Pro
riht 'right/lawful' H & E 4
    rihtre H & E 11.3
    rihtum W Pro; W 3

riht 'law/justice' H & E 6; H & E 6.2; H & E 8; H & E 10; W interpolation following 16.2
  reht W 4
  rihte H & E 10
rihtan 'set to right' W 3.1
rihthamscyld '?' Æbt 32
rim 'number' H & E 3
rixigendum 'ruling' W Pro
rugernes '?time of rye harvest' W Pro

sace '(legal) matter' H & E 6; H & E 6.2; *sacy* H & E 6.1
gesamnad 'gathered' W Pro
sæ 'sea' W 21
sægeþ See *segeþ*
sæmend 'arbitrator' H & E 6.2 (See also *seman*)
scandlice 'shamefully' H & E 7
scæt 'money/goods' Æbt 76.1; Æbt 76.2; Æbt 76.3; *sceat* Æbt 77.1
  scætte Æbt 30; Æbt 31
sceard 'gashed' Æbt 41; Æbt 45
sceatta 'sceatta/unit of money' Æbt 21.1; Æbt 21.2; Æbt 33; Æbt 61.3; Æbt 61.4
scilling- 'shilling/unit of money' Æbt 8; Æbt 11; Æbt 12; Æbt 14; Æbt 16; Æbt 16.1; Æbt 16.2; Æbt 17; Æbt 18; Æbt 19; Æbt 20; Æbt 21; Æbt 22; Æbt 22.1; Æbt 22.2; Æbt 23; Æbt 23.1; Æbt 23.2; Æbt 24; Æbt 24.1; Æbt 25; Æbt 26; Æbt 27; Æbt27.1; Æbt 27.2; Æbt 28; Æbt 29; Æbt 34; Æbt 35; Æbt 36; Æbt 36.1; Æbt 37; Æbt 38; Æbt 39; Æbt 40; Æbt 41; Æbt 42; Æbt 43; Æbt 44; Æbt 44.1; Æbt 44.2; Æbt 45; Æbt 46; Æbt 47; Æbt 48; Æbt 48.1; Æbt 48.2; Æbt 48.3; Æbt 49; Æbt 50; Æbt 51; Æbt 52; Æbt 53; Æbt 54; Æbt 55; Æbt 56; Æbt 57; Æbt 58; Æbt 59; Æbt 60; Æbt 60.1; Æbt 61; Æbt 61.1; Æbt 61.2; Æbt 62; Æbt 63; Æbt 63.1; Æbt 64.1; Æbt 64.2; Æbt 65; Æbt 66; Æbt 67; Æbt 67.1; Æbt 67.3; Æbt 68; Æbt 69; Æbt 70; Æbt 71; Æbt 72; Æbt 74; Æbt 74.1; Æbt 74.2; Æbt 74.3; Æbt 77.1; Æbt 77.2; Æbt 81; Æbt 82; H & E 1; H & E 2; H & E 6.1; H & E 7 (3x); H & E 8 (3x) ; H & E 9; H & E 9.1; W 2; W 4; W 4.1; W 8; W 21.1; W 22
gescrifen 'appoint' H & E 6
scylde 'fault' H & E 8
scyldig 'liable' W 8.2; W 9; *scyldigo* W 9.1
scytefinger 'forefinger' Æbt 55
sealde See *selle*
gesecæn 'seek out' H & E 6.2
segeþ 'say' W Pro; *sægeþ* H & E pro; *secge (an)* H & E 3
sele 'hall' H & E 5; H & E 11.1

selestan 'of the first rank' Æbt 27
selle 'give' W 17; W 18.1; *geselle* H & E 4; H & E 6; W 21.1
   gesealdne H & E 6.2
   selle 'sell' W 21
   sealde H & E 5; H & E 11.1
seman 'arbitrate' Æbt 65.1
   gesem[eþ] H & E 6.3
   gesemed H & E 6.2 (See also *sæmend*)
setlgang 'sunset' W 8; *setlgange* W 8
gesiþcundne '*gesiþ*-born/noble' W 4
sleanne 'kill' W 23; *slæhð* Æbt 61
(-)*smið* 'smith' Æbt 13
soþe 'truth' W 14
spræc 'speech' Æbt 49
(*bi-*)*standeþ* 'stands beside' Æbt 48.1; Æbt 48.2
stele 'steal' Æbt 10; W 22; *stelþ* Æbt 15; *steleþ* Æbt 83
steop 'cup/goblet' H & E 8; *steap* H & E 8
steorleas 'not under ecclesiastic/monsastic rule' W 6
stermelda '?informer' H & E 3
stice 'thrust (with a weapon)' Æbt 67
stille 'inactive' W 5
stowe 'place' W Pro
sunnan 'Sunday' W 8
swæse 'own' W 3.2
sweart 'black' Æbt 61.3
swinganne 'hang (by the neck)' W 17; W 18.1
swylteþ 'die' Æbt 76.2
sylfes 'own/self' W 11.1; W 16; *sylfæs* W 14
symble 'always' H & E 6
synna 'sins' W 3; *synnum* W 3.1

ta 'toe' Æbt 70
   taan Æbt 71
   taum Æbt 70.1
tæme 'vouch' H & E 11.1; *geteme* H & E 5
   teame 'vouching' H & E 11.1
tihte 'bring a charge' H & E 6; H & E 6.2; W 17; W 18; W 19 (2x)
   tihtlan 'a charge' H & E 6.2
timan 'time' W 8.2
tofo 'take possession' H & E 11.3; *tofon* 'take up' W 3
togecwæde 'speak to' H & E 7

tohyre 'belong' H & E 3
toþ 'tooth' Æbt 48.1
   toðum Æbt 48
tune 'dwelling' Æbt 11, Æbt 18, H & E 3
   tun Æbt 22

geþeahtendlic 'consilary' W Pro
þeawum 'custom' W Pro
ðegn 'thegn' W 16
þegnungæ 'service' W 5
ðeof 'thief' W 23
þeofðe 'theft' W 20
þeoh 'thigh' Æbt 65; Æbt 67
þeow 'slave' Æbt 83; W 11.1; *þeuw* W 10; W 22
   þeowne W 11; *þeuwne* W 18
   þeowa Æbt 16; *ðeowan* Æbt 21.1; *Ðeowæs* Æbt 82
þeowweorc 'slave-work' W 8
þinge 'public meeting' H & E 6
þirel 'pierced' Æbt 40; *ðyrel* Æbt 44; *ðyrele* Æbt 44.2; *ðirel* Æbt 46
   (See also *þurhðirel*)
þoligen 'suffer' W 3.2
þuman 'thumb' Æbt 53; *ðuman* Æbt 54
þurhstinð 'stab through' Æbt 32; Æbt 51; Æbt 64.1; *ðurhstingþ* Æbt 67
þurhðirel 'pierced through' Æbt 62.1 (See also *þirel*)

ufor 'later' H & E 6.2
unagne 'not one's own' Æbt 75
undeornunga 'without secrecy' H & E 11.2
unfacne 'undeceptive/unblemished' Æbt 30; Æbt 76; H & E 11
ungestrodyne 'without loss of goods' W 3.2
unlægne 'incontrovertible' W 12; *unlegnæ* W 16.2
unrihthæmed 'unlawful union' W 4; W 5; *unrihthæmde* W 3 (See also *hæmed*)
unsynningne 'guiltless' Æbt 79
untrumes 'sick person' W 5
uterre 'outer' Æbt 36

wædum 'clothing' Æbt 61.3; Æbt 61.4
wælt[-]wund 'welt-wound' Æbt 68
wæpn 'weapon' H & E 9; *wæpnum* Æbt 23
wealde 'give a ruling' W 21
wege 'track' W 23

248 Glossary

wegreaf 'highway robbery' Æbt 23.1; Æbt 82
weofode See *wiofode*
weorc 'work' W 8.2
weorð 'worth' H & E 11.2; *weorðe* Æbt 32; Æbt 79; Æbt 80
weorþigen 'do honour' W 1.1
wergild 'man-price' W 7; *wergilde* Æbt 31; W 21; *wyrgelde* W 20
wic 'town' H & E 11.1; 11.2
wicgerefan 'town reeve' H & E 11; H & E 11.2
widobane 'collarbone' Æbt 50
widuwan 'widow' Æbt 74; Æbt 75
wif 'wife' Æbt 31 (2x)
   wife H & E 4
   wifes W 9
willan 'consent' Æbt 77; *willum* 'free will' W 1.1
   wille 'he wishes' W 7
wilsumne 'willingly' H & E 4
wintra 'winters (=years)' H & E 4; W Pro
wiofode 'altar' H & E 11.2; W 7; W 14; W 15; W 16; *weofode* W 16.1
wisdome 'knowledge' W 9
wite 'fine' Æbt 15; W 8.2
wite 'know' H & E 11.1
gewitena 'witnesses' H & E 11.2
   [to] gewitnesse 'to witness' H & E 11
gewiteþ 'depart' Æbt 24.2; *gewiten* W 3.1
wlitewamme 'disfigurement of the appearance' Æbt 60
woh 'damaged' Æbt 43
word 'word' H & E 7; W 12
geworhton 'made' H & E Pro
wund 'wound/wounded' Æbt 62; 63; [-] Æbt 68
wyrce 'does/performs' W 8

yfel 'harm' Æbt 8; Æbt 23; H & E 9; H & E 10
ymcyme 'assembly' W Pro
ynce 'inch' Æbt 67.1
   yncum Æbt 67.2
ys 'already' Æbt 70.1

Concordance of proper names

AGustinus Æbt Pro
Æðelbirht Æbt Pro
Berghamstyde W Pro
Birhtwald W Pro
Bretone W Pro
Cantwara H & E Rub; H & E Pro; H & E 6; H & E 11; W Rub; W Pro (2x)
Cænt H & E 11.1
Eadric H & E Rub; H & E Pro
Gybmund W Pro
Hloþhære H & E Rub; H & E Pro
Hrofesceastre W Pro
Lundenwic H & E 11
Monan W 8
Rugernes W Pro
Sunan W 8
Wihtredes W Rub; *Wihtrede* W Pro

Previous Editions and Translations of the Kentish Laws[a]

1589 Francis Tate made a transcript of the *Textus Roffensis*, British Museum ms. Cotton Julius CII. This is the earliest surviving transcription, and the source Liebermann relies on for his restoration of *mæthlfrith* on 1ʳ6.

1640 Johann de Laet of Antwerp published a translation into Latin of the laws of Æthelberht and of Hloþhere & Eadric, based on a copy of the manuscript sent to him by Sir Henry Spelman. There are no extant copies of this publication, but Hickes (1703–5), Harris (1719), and Wilkins (1721) all claim to reproduce it. The (minor) differences in their versions must be attributed to editorial changes, although lacking the original, we cannot now determine which editor was responsible for any specific change.

1664 Sir Henry Spelman, *Ecclesiarum Orbis Brittanici* (London).
In this revision of his work of 1639, Sir Henry Spelman published in Latin translation those of Æthelberht's laws dealing with the church, as well as the first two pertaining to the king (127–8). Spelman gives as his reason for not printing the remaining laws of Æthelberht the fact that they are irrelevant to his topic of canon law, as there is *alioquin vero nihil ad rem Ecclesiæ* 'otherwise, however, nothing pertinent to the Church.'

---

a For the pre-Liebermann material, see the very helpful discussion in Felix Liebermann, 'Bearbeitung der Gesetze,' *Die Gesetze der Angelsachsen* (Halle, 1897–1916), vol. 1, xlv–liii. For setting these editions in the context of legal scholarship, see Patrick Wormald, *The Making of English Law: King Alfred to the Twelfth Century* (Oxford: Blackwell, 1999), 1–28.

252   Previous editions and translations

1703–5   George Hickes and H. Wanley, *Linguarum Vett. Septentrionalium Thesaurus Grammatico-Criticus et Archaelogicus* (Oxford), 2 vols.
This contains an edition and a Latin translation of Æthelberht's and Hloþhere & Eadric's laws based on de Laet's edition of 1640 (vol. 2, pt. 2: 88–93).

1719   John Harris, *The History of Kent* (London).
Contains Latin versions of the laws of Æthelberht, Hloþhere & Eadric and Wihtred (401–10); also relies heavily on de Laet's edition of 1640.

1720   Thomas Hearne, *Textus Roffensis* (Oxford).
Hearne printed an edition of the *Textus Roffensis* based on a transcription made by Edward Dering in the 1630s; the sections not contained in his exemplar are thus missing here. Liebermann, criticizing the choice of this exemplar, states that 'sonst zeigt auch dieses Buch seinen Mangel an Kritik und Auswahl (elsewhere also this book shows its deficiency in critical ability and choice).' (Kentish laws at 1–11.)

1721   David Wilkins, *Leges Anglo-Saxonicae Ecclesiasticae & Civilis* (London).
Wilkins (actually a Prussian named Wilke, who dedicated his book to George I, similarly a German immigrant)[a] also purported to reproduce de Laet's Latin versions of Æthelberht, Hloþhere & Eadric, and Wihtred (1–12), although there are some minor differences between his version and that of Hickes (lacking the original, we cannot tell where these differences come from). This is the first edition of the Anglo-Saxon laws to draw comparisons to other early Germanic laws.

1832   Reinhold Schmid, *Die Gesetze der Angelsachsen* (Leipzig).
Professor Schmid of the University of Bern published an edition with German translation of the laws of the Anglo-Saxons (Kentish laws at 1–13). Working from the texts and variants produced by his predecessors (as he was unable himself to travel to consult the manuscripts),[b] he regularized the text, which removed all but some syntactic archaisms, and restored *monkesfrith* for the partially legible *m- - - -frith* (although this would have required a compression of the missing letters). A thorough examination of this edition would be more appropriate for a

---

a Wormald, *The Making of English Law*, 22.
b Ibid.

history of methods of nineteenth-century scholarship than for a philological analysis of the texts it contains. Still, Schmid's text could well be considered the first modern edition of these laws.

1839, 1847 Editions published by H.F. Massemann and F.W. Ebeling, respectively. Both, according to Liebermann, are based on 'veralteten Drucken' (outdated editions).

1840 Benjamin Thorpe published *Ancient Laws and Institutions of England; comprising Laws enacted under the Anglo-Saxon Kings from Aethelbirht to Cnut, with an English Translation of the Saxon ... also, Monumenta Ecclesiastica Anglicana from the Seventh to the Tenth Century* (London), comprising editions and English translations based on work he had taken over from Richard Price upon the latter's death. Liebermann criticizes many of the changes Thorpe made to Price's original work, but considers the textual work to be better than the legal analysis. Nonetheless, Thorpe's edition is the first to include a concordance; it also contains some of the major penitentials, which are useful for comparative purposes. His text was published in both a one-volume edition (Kentish laws at 3–19) and a two-volume edition (Kentish laws at 1:2–43).
Reviewed by:
Jacob Grimm. 'Ancient Laws and Institutes of England,' *Göttingische Gelehrte Anzeigen* 36/37 (1841): 345–62.

1845 Garabed Artin Davoud-Oghlou, under the section entitled 'Anglo-Saxons,' in *Histoire de la législation des anciens Germains* (Berlin) 2:271–743, translated into French most of the clauses of the early Kentish laws. He organized his discussion of the corpus of Anglo-Saxon law by topic; for example, *Classes privilégiés, Esclaves, Attentats aux moeurs*. His interpretations are outdated, and sometimes his analysis is wrong, as when he assigns the Northumbrian Cefi's words about the benefits of conversion to a Kentish locale!

1849 Louis Klipstein published *Analecta Anglo-Saxonica: Selections in Prose and Verse from the Anglo-Saxon Literature, with an Introductory Ethnological Essay, and Notes, Critical and Explanatory* (New York; new ed., 1871), 2 vols., 'with the object of promoting the study of Anglo-Saxon among American youth,' as he states in his preface. Here he reproduces (preceding other later laws) Thorpe's edition of Æthelberht and Hloþhere & Eadric (in first ed., vol. 1:268–75; notes 417–24). The notes – unsurprisingly not extensive in an anthology of this nature – are his own; although some of his observations are odd and all are dated, they still make interesting reading. There is no translation or glossary.

1850 L. Ettmüller included, in a variorum of Old English texts entitled *Engla & Seaxona: Scôpas & Bôceras* (Quedlinburgh and Leipzig), parts of several law texts, including selections from Æthelberht (portions of the personal injury laws and the laws dealing with women, at 54–5) and Hloþhere & Eadric (the section dealing with damage to or within another person's home, at 55).

1858 Revision of Schmid, 1832.
Schmid draws upon the work of Thorpe (unpublished at the time of his first edition), and adds a valuable legal commentary (Kentish laws at 2–19).

1880 Albert Cook, ed., *Extracts from the Anglo-Saxon Laws* (New York).
Cook published selections from several law texts for his class in English Constitutional History; there is no translation. This edition includes six clauses from Æthelberht, three from Hloþhere & Eadric, and four from Wihtred (1–2).

1881 Arthur West Haddan and William Stubbs, *Councils and Ecclesiastical Documents Relating to Great Britain and Ireland* (Oxford), Vol. III.
Contains a reprint of Thorpe's editions of the 'Laws of Ethelberht' (42–50) and 'The Ecclesiastical Laws of Wihtred' (233–7).

1889 John M. Stearns, *The Germs and Developments of the Laws of England* (New York and Albany).
Stearns published the Modern English translation by Thorpe of the Kentish laws, with no Old English original (27–42). Although he does not take credit for the translation, neither does he mention Thorpe by name.

1897–1916 Felix Liebermann, *Die Gesetze der Angelsachsen* (Halle).
Commissioned by the Savigny-Stiftung, Felix Liebermann brought out an edition of *Die Gesetze der Angelsachsen* in 6 fascicles, now bound in three volumes. The first volume, published in 1897, presents the texts with translations into German of all the early English laws up to the time of Edward the Confessor (compiled 1130x5 per Liebermann). The second, published in 1906, contains a glossary to this body of texts; definitions in the glossary often serve as short essays on aspects of

Anglo-Saxon law. The third volume, published in 1916, consists of notes to the individual texts. (The texts of the Kentish laws are in 1:1–14; commentary in 3:1–30). Liebermann carefully preserved the orthography of the original, normalizing only in the domain of word division, punctuation, and expansion of abbreviations.

Liebermann's edition is justly referred to by Peter Sawyer as 'monumental.' With his careful philological, historical, and paleographic research, Liebermann set a standard not only for students of Anglo-Saxon law, but for medieval scholars in general. His analyses tend to regard the Anglo-Saxon period as a legal unity: little attention is paid to internal development over the course of more than five centuries of legislation. Nevertheless, all work on early English law since his time, including this volume, has relied heavily on Liebermann's edition.
Reviewed by:

F.W. Maitland. 'The Laws of the Anglo-Saxons,' *Quarterly Review* 200 (1904): 139–57.

H.W.C. Davis. 'The Anglo-Saxon Laws,' *English Historical Review* 28 (1913): 417.

1922 F.L. Attenborough, *The Laws of the Earliest English Kings* (Cambridge).
Attenborough included editions and translations of the Kentish laws (2–30; notes 175–182) in his collection of *The Laws of the Earliest English Kings*: selections up to VI Æthelstan (ca. 930–940 per Liebermann). This is principally an English version of Liebermann's translations, perhaps necessitated by the fact that much of Liebermann's work was published during the tumultuous period surrounding the First World War and was thus not generally available to non-German scholars.

1955, revised 1979 Dorothy Whitelock, *English Historical Documents Volume I: c. 500–1042* (London).
This includes English translations of all three Kentish law texts, omitting the personal injury section from the laws of Æthelberht. Whitelock's notes, although not extensive, are very useful. In some – albeit not many – instances Whitelock has changed her interpretation of the reading of the laws from the first edition (Kentish laws 357–64) to the second (Kentish laws 391–8).

1957 Peter Sawyer, ed., *Early English Manuscripts in Facsimile, Vol. VII: Textus Roffensis, Part I* (Copenhagen).
This nicely produced facsimile of the *Textus Roffensis* is prefaced by an excellent codicological introduction by Peter Sawyer. The Kentish laws

are on 1 recto to 6 verso (see Diplomatic transcription in Appendix One).

1958 Karl Eckhardt, *Leges Anglo-Saxonum 601–925*. In *Germanenrechte: Texte und Übersetzungen, Neue Folge, Vol. IV* (Weimar).
This volume contains German translations of the Kentish laws (17–55), as well as those of Alfred/Ine and Edward. Eckhardt provides a simplistic version of Liebermann's translation, ignoring any issues of uncertainty or ambiguity; there is no accompanying commentary. This edition is useless for any serious scholarly purposes – atypical of most of Eckhardt's work.

1995 Bill Griffiths, *An Introduction to Early English Law* (Hockwold cum Wilton).
In a volume which also contains the laws of Alfred, Edmund, and Æthelred, Griffiths publishes a translation of the laws of Æthelberht (31–42). The footnotes citing previous editors/translators are helpful, but some of Griffith's interpretations seem odd, and in §§14 and 61 he misreads .XX. as 12.

Bibliography

This bibliography contains works published prior to 1999 which are primarily concerned with the early history of Kent, the Kentish laws or the Textus Roffensis: it aims at reasonable completeness. Included as well are works referred to in the text, which may not be directly concerned with the Kentish laws.

Adams, Henry, ed. *Essays in Anglo-Saxon Law*. Boston: Little, Brown, 1876.
– 'The Anglo-Saxon Courts of Law.' In Adams, *Essays in Anglo-Saxon Law*, 1–55.
Anderson, R.L., and A.J. Latham, eds. *The Market in History*. London and Dover: Croom Helm, 1986.
Angenendt, A. 'The Conversion of the Anglo-Saxons Considered Against the Background of the Early Medieval Mission.' *Angli e Sassoni al di qua e al di la Mare*. Settimane de studio del Centro italiano di studi sull'alto medioevo, 32(2) (1986): 747–81.
Arnold, Morris S., Thomas A. Green, Sally A. Scully, and Stephen D. White, eds. *On the Laws and Customs of England: Essays in Honor of Samuel E. Thorne*. Studies in Legal History. Chapel Hill: University of North Carolina Press, 1981.
Arnold-Baker, Charles. *The Companion to British History*. Tunbridge Wells: Longcross, 1996.
Attenborough, F.L., ed. *The Laws of the Earliest English Kings*. Cambridge: Cambridge University Press, 1922.
Ausenda, Giorgio. 'Current Issues and Future Directions in the Study of the Early Anglo-Saxon Period.' In Hines, ed., *The Anglo-Saxons*, 411–50.
Baesecke, Georg. 'Die deutschen Worte der germanischen Gesetze.' *Beiträge zur Geschichte der Deutschen Sprache und Literatur* 59 (1935): 1–101.

Bammesberger, Alfred, and Alfred Wollmann, eds. *Britain 400–600: Language and History*. Anglistische Forschungen, 205. Heidelberg: C. Winter, 1990.

Bassett, Steven, ed. *The Origins of Anglo-Saxon Kingdoms*. Studies in the Early History of Britain. London and New York: Leicester University Press, 1989.

Bazell, C.E. 'Caseforms in -i in the Oldest English Texts.' *Modern Language Notes* 55(2) (1940): 136–9.

Bethurum, Dorothy. 'Stylistic Features of the Old English Laws.' *Modern Language Review* 27 (1932): 263–279.

Beyerle, Franz. *Das Entwicklungsproblem im germanischen Rechtsgang. I. Sühne, Rache und Preisgabe in ihrer Beziehung zum Strafprozess der Volksrechte*. Deutschrechtliche Beiträge. Heidelberg: C. Winter, 1915.

Biddle, M. 'London on the Strand.' *Popular Archeology* (July 1984): 23–7.

Binchy, D.A. 'Bretha Crólige.' *Ériu* 12 (1934): 1–77.

– 'Bretha Déin Chécht.' *Ériu* 20 (1966): 1–66.

– ed. *Corpus Iuris Hibernici*. Dublin: Institiuid Ard-Leinn Bhaile Atha Cliath, 1978.

– ed. *Críth Gablach*. Dublin: Dublin Institute for Advanced Studies, 1941; repr. 1979.

Birch, W. de Gray, ed. *Cartularium Saxonicum*. London: Whiting, 1885–93.

Black, Henry Campbell, et al. *Black's Law Dictionary*. St Paul: West, 1990.

Bøe, Arne, and Magnús Már Lárusson, 'leysingi.' In Brønsted et al., eds., *Kulturhistorisk Leksikon*, 10:521–6.

Bosworth, Joseph. *An Anglo-Saxon Dictionary*. Oxford: Clarendon, 1898.

Brechter, Heinrich Suso. *Die Quellen zur angelsachsenmission Gregors den Grossen: Eine historiographische Studie*. Beiträge zur Geschichte des alten Mönchtums und des Benediktinerordens, Heft 22. Münster: Aschendorff, 1941.

Bremmer, Rolf, and Patrick Stiles. 'An Old Frisian Primer.' Unpublished.

Bridbury, A.R. 'Markets and Freedom in the Middle Ages.' In Anderson and Latham, eds., *The Market in History*, 79–120.

– 'Seventh-Century England in Bede and the Early Laws.' In Bridbury, ed., *English Economy*, 56–85.

– ed. *The English Economy from Bede to the Reformation*. Woodbridge: Boydell, 1992.

Brønsted, Johannes, et al., eds. *Kulturhistorisk Leksikon for Nordisk Middelalder* vols. 10–11. Copenhagen: Rosenkilde and Bagger, 1965–6.

Brooks, Nicholas. 'Arms, Status and Warfare in Late-Saxon England.' In Hill, ed., *Ethelred the Unready*, 86.

– 'The Creation and Early Structure of the Kingdom of Kent.' In Bassett, ed., *The Origins of Anglo-Saxon Kingdoms*, 55–74.

– 'The Development of Military Obligations in Eighth- and Ninth-Century England.' In Clemoes and Hughes, eds., *England Before the Conquest*, 69–85.

– *The Early History of the Church of Canterbury: Christ Church from 597 to 1066.* Studies in the Early History of Britain. Leicester: Leicester University Press, 1984.
Brugmann, Karl, and Berthold Delbrück. *Grundriss der vergleichende Grammatik der indogermanischen Sprachen,* vol. II^i *Vergleichende Laut-, Stammbildungs- und Flexionslehre der indogermanischen Sprachen.* Strassburg: Karl J. Trubner, 1906.
– vol. 5. *Vergleichende Syntax.* Strassburg: Karl J. Trubner, 1900.
Brunner, Heinrich. *Deutsche Rechtsgeschichte.* Systematisches Handbuch der deutschen Rechtswissenschaft. Leipzig: Duncker and Humblot, 1887–92.
Brunner, Karl. *Altenglische Grammatik.* Sammlung kurzer Grammatiken germanischer Dialekte, Hauptreihe Nr. 3. Tübingen: Niemeyer, 1965.
Bruns, Carl Georg. *Fontes Iuris Romani Antiqui.* Tübingen: Mohr, 1909.
Buckstaff, G. 'Married Women's Property in Anglo-Saxon and Anglo-Norman Law and the Origin of the Common Law Dower.' *Annals of the American Academy of Political and Social Sciences* 4 (1893–4): 233–64.
Bullough, D.A. 'Anglo-Saxon Institutions and Early English Society.' *Annali della fondazione italiana per la storia amministrativa* 2 (1965): 647–59.
Buma, Jan Wybren, and Wilhelm Ebel. *Das Brokmer Recht.* Altfriesische Rechtsquellen, Bd. 2. Göttingen: Vandenhoeck and Ruprecht, 1965.
Calder, Daniel G., ed. *Old English Poetry: Essays on Style.* Contributions of the UCLA Center for Medieval and Renaissance Studies, 10. Berkeley: University of California Press, 1979.
Campbell, Alistair. *Old English Grammar.* Oxford: Clarendon, 1959.
Campbell, James. 'The End of Roman Britain.' In Campbell, John, and Wormald, eds., *The Anglo-Saxons.*
– 'The First Century of Christianity in England.' *Ampleforth Journal* 76 (1971): 12–29. Repr. *Essays in Anglo-Saxon History.* London: Ronceverte, 1986. 49–68.
– 'Observations on the Conversion of England.' *Ampleforth Journal* 78 (1972): 12–26. Repr. *Essays in Anglo-Saxon History.* History Series Hambledon Press. London: Ronceverte, 1986. 69–84.
Campbell, James, Eric John, and Patrick Wormald, eds. *The Anglo-Saxons.* Oxford: Phaidon, 1982.
Carruba, Onofrio. 'Die Chronologie der heth. Texte und die heth. Geschichte.' *Zeitschrift der deutschen Morgenländische Gesellschaft* Supplementa I (1969): 226–49.
Carruthers, Mary J. *The Book of Memory: A Study of Memory in Medieval Culture.* Cambridge Studies in Medieval Literature, 10. Cambridge and New York: Cambridge University Press, 1990.
Chadwick, H. Munro. *Studies on Anglo-Saxon Institutions.* Cambridge: Cambridge University Press, 1905. Repr. New York 1963.

Chaney, William A. *The Cult of Kingship in Anglo-Saxon England*. Manchester: Manchester University Press, 1970.

Charles-Edwards, Thomas. 'Anglo-Saxon Kinship Revisited.' In Hines, ed., *The Anglo-Saxons*, 171–210.

– 'The Distinction Between Land and Moveable Wealth in Anglo-Saxon England.' In Sawyer, ed., *Medieval Settlement*, 180–7.

– *Early Irish and Welsh Kinship*. Oxford: Clarendon, 1993.

– *The Early Mediaeval Gaelic Lawyer*. Quiggin Pamphlets on the Sources of Mediaeval Gaelic History, 4. Cambridge: Cambridge University Press, 1999.

– 'Early Medieval Kingships in the British Isles.' In Bassett, ed., *The Origins of Anglo-Saxon Kingdoms*, 28–39.

– and Patrick Wormald. 'Addenda' to J.M. Wallace-Hadrill, *Bede's Ecclesiastical History of the English People*. Oxford Medieval Texts. Oxford: Clarendon, 1988.

Cheney, C.R. *A Handbook of Dates for Students of English History*. Rev. Michael Jones. Royal Historical Society Guides and Handbooks, 4. Cambridge: Cambridge University Press, 2000

Christiansen, E. Review of Witney, *The Kingdom of Kent. A History from c. A.D. 450 to 825*. *English Historical Review* 100 (1985): 860–2.

Clemoes, Peter, and Kathleen Hughes, eds. *England Before the Conquest: Studies in Primary Sources Presented to Dorothy Whitelock*. Cambridge: University Press, 1971.

Colgrave, Bertram, and R.A.B. Mynors, eds. *Bede's Ecclesiastical History of the English People*. Oxford Medieval Texts. Oxford: Clarendon, 1969.

Colman, Rebecca V. 'The Abduction of Women in Barbaric Law.' *Florilegium* 5 (1983): 62–75.

– '*Hamsocn*: Its Meaning and Significance in Early English Law.' *American Journal of Legal History* 25 (1981): 95–110.

Cook, Albert S., ed. *Extracts from the Anglo-Saxon Laws*. New York: H. Holt, 1880.

– 'Laws of Wihtred, No. 28.' *Modern Language Notes* 20 (1905): 30.

Corliss, Richard. 'Jackie Can!' *Time*, 13 February 1995, 82–3.

Cowie, Robert, and Robert Whytehead. '*Lundenwic*: The Archeological Evidence for Middle Saxon London.' *Antiquity* 241 (1989): 700–18.

Cubitt, Catherine. *Anglo-Saxon Church Councils c. 650–c. 850*. Studies in the Early History of Britain. London and New York: Leicester University Press, 1995.

Dalton, O.M., ed. and trans. *The History of the Franks by Gregory of Tours*. 2 vols. Oxford: Clarendon, 1927.

Damico, Helen, and Alexandra Hennessey Olsen, eds. *New Readings on Women in Old English Literature*. Bloomington: Indiana University Press, 1990.
Damico, Hellen, and Joseph B. Zavadil, eds. *Medieval Scholarship: Biographical Studies in the Formation of a Discipline*, 2 vols. Garland Reference Library of the Humanities. New York and London: Garland, 1998.
Dammery, Richard. 'Editing the Anglo-Saxon Laws: Felix Liebermann and Beyond.' In Scragg and Szarmach, eds., *The Editing of Old English*, 251–61.
Davis, H.W.C. 'The Anglo-Saxon Laws.' *English Historical Review* 28 (1913): 417.
Davoud-Oghlou, Garabed Artin. *Histoire de la legislation des anciens Germains*. 2 vols. Berlin: G. Reimer, 1845.
Deansley, Margaret. *Augustine of Canterbury*. Leaders of Religion. London: Nelson, 1964.
Dobbie, Elliot, ed. *The Anglo-Saxon Minor Poems*. The Anglo-Saxon Poetic Records, A Collective Edition, VI. New York: Columbia University Press, 1942.
– ed. *Beowulf and Judith*. The Anglo-Saxon Poetic Records: A Collective Edition. New York: Columbia University Press, 1953.
Dölling, Hildegard. *Haus und Hof in westgermanischen Volksrechten*. Veröffentlichungen der Altertumskommission im Provinzialinstitut für Westfalische Landes- und Volkskunde, Bd. 2. Münster: Aschendorff, 1958.
Drew, Katherine Fischer. 'Another Look at the Origins of the Middle Ages: A Reassessment of the Role of the Germanic Kingdoms.' *Speculum* 62 (1987): 803–12.
– trans. *The Laws of the Salian Franks*. Middle Ages Series. Philadelphia: University of Pennsylvania Press, 1991.
Drewett, Peter, David Rudling, and Mark Gardiner. *The South East to AD 1000*. Regional History of England. London and New York: Longman, 1988.
Du Cange, Domino, ed. *Glossarium Mediæ et Infimæ Latinitatas*. Paris: Librairie de Sciences et des Arts. 1678; repr. 1937.
Dumville, David N. *Histories and Pseudo-Histories of the Insular Middle Ages*. Collected Studies, cs316. Aldershot: Variorum, 1990.
– 'Sub-Roman Britain: History and Legend.' *History*, N.S. 62 (1977) 173–92; repr. in Dumville, *Histories and Pseudo-Histories*, Essay #1.
– 'The Terminology of Overkingship in Early Anglo-Saxon England.' In Hines, ed., *The Anglo-Saxons*, 345–73.
Eckhardt, Karl. *Die Gesetze des Merowingerreiches 481–714, I: Pactus Legis Salicae, Recensiones Merovingicae*. Germanenrechte, Bd. 1. Göttingen: Musterschmidt, 1955.

– *Leges Anglo-Saxonum 601–925*. Germanenrechte. Neue Folge. Westgermanisches Recht, Bd. 4. Göttingen: Musterschmid, 1958.
Edwards, Chilperic. *The Hammurabi Code*. London: Watts, 1904.
Ellegård, Alvar and Åkerström-Hougen, eds. *Rome and the North. Studies in Mediterranean Archaeology and Literature*, 135. Jonsered, Sweden: Paul Astroms Forlag, 1996.
Elstob, Elizabeth. *The Rudiments of Grammar for the English-Saxon Tongue, First Given in English: With an Apology for the Study of Northern Antiquities. Being Very Useful Towards the Understanding Our Ancient English Poets, and Other Writers*. London: Bowyer. Repr. as *The Rudiments of Grammar for the English-Saxon Tongue, 1715*. English Linguistics, 1500–1800; A Collection of Facsimile Reprints, 57. Menston, Yorkshire: Scolar, 1968.
Emms, Richard. 'The Scribe of the Paris Psalter.' *Anglo-Saxon England* 28 (1999): 179–83.
Ettmüller, Ludwig. *Engla and Seaxna: Scôpas & Bôceras*. Bibliothek der gesammten deutschen National-Literatur. Quedlinburgh and Leipzig: G. Bassii, 1850.
Everitt, Alan. *Continuity and Colonization: The Evolution of Kentish Settlement*. Communities, Context and Cultures. Leicester: Leicester University Press, 1986.
Faith, Rosamund. 'feorm.' In Lapidge et al., eds., *Blackwell Encyclopedia of Anglo-Saxon England*, 181–2.
Falk Moore, Sally. *Law as Process: An Anthropological Approach*. London and Boston: Routledge and Kegan Paul, 1978.
Fanning, Steven. 'Bede, *Imperium* and the Bretwaldas.' *Speculum* 6 (1991): 1–27.
Fell, Christine. 'An Appendix to Carole Hough's Article "A Reappraisal of Æthelberht 84."' *Nottingham Medieval Studies* 37 (1993): 7–8.
– 'A "friwif locbore" Revisited.' *Anglo-Saxon England* 13 (1984): 157–66.
– *Women in Anglo-Saxon England and the Impact of 1066*. Bloomington: Indiana University Press, 1984.
Fellows-Jensen, Gillian. 'Bynames.' In Lapidge et al., eds., *Blackwell Encyclopedia of Anglo-Saxon England*, 76–8.
Finberg, H.P.R., ed. *The Agrarian History of England and Wales: A.D. 43–1042*. London: Cambridge University Press, 1972.
Förster, Max. 'Zur i-epenthese im Alt-Englischen.' *Anglia* 59 (1935): 287–98.
Forsyth, Katherine. *Language in Pictland: The Case Against Non-Indo-European Pictish*. Studia Hameliana, 2. Utrecht: Keltische Draak, 1997.
Frantzen, Allen J., and Douglas Moffat, eds. *The Work of Work: Servitude, Slavery, and Labor in Medieval England*. Glasgow: Cruithne, 1994.

Friedrich, Johannes. *Die Hethitischen Gesetze*. Documenta et monumenta Orientis antiqui, 7. Leiden: E.J. Brill, 1959.
Fryde, E.B., et al., eds. *Handbook of British Chronology*, 3rd ed. Guides and Handbooks / Royal Historical Society, 2. London: Office of the Royal Historical Society, 1986.
Gameson, Richard. 'Context and Achievement.' In Gameson, ed., *St. Augustine and the Conversion of England*, 1-40.
- ed. *St. Augustine and the Conversion of England*. Stroud: Sutton, 1999.
Gendre, Renato. 'Le leggi di Æthelberht: *"iuxta exempla Romanoru"* e *"iuxta consuetudines Germanorum."*' In Lazzari, ed., *Testi guiridici*, 7-21.
Genzmer, Felix. *Rache, Wergeld und Klage im alt-germanischen Rechtsleben*. Tübingen: J.C.B. Mohr, 1941.
Girsch, Elizabeth Stevens. 'Metaphorical Usage, Sexual Exploitation, and Divergence in the Old English Terminology for Male and Female Slaves.' In Frantzen and Moffatt, eds., *The Work of Work*, 30-54.
Glare, P.G.W., ed. *Oxford Latin Dictionary*. Oxford: Clarendon, 1982.
Görnemann, Willy. *Zur Sprache des Textus Roffensis: Inaugural-Dissertation*. Berlin, 1901.
Green, D.H. *Language and History in the Early Germanic World*. Cambridge and New York: Cambridge University Press, 1998.
Green, Michael A. *St. Augustine of Canterbury*. London: Janus, 1997.
Grierson, Philip. *The Coins of Medieval Europe*. London: Seaby, 1991.
- 'La Fonction Sociale de la Monnaie en Angleterre aux VIIe-VIIIe Siècles.' In *Dark Age Numismatics, Selected Studies*, vol. 9. London: Variorum Reprints, 1979.
- and Mark Blackburn. *Medieval European Coinage I: The Early Middle Ages*. Cambridge and New York: Cambridge University Press, 1986.
Griffiths, Bill. *An Introduction to Early English Law*. Norfolk: Anglo-Saxon Books, 1995.
Grimm, Jacob. *Deutsche Rechtsalterthümer*. Göttingen: Dieterich, 1828; repr. Darmstadt: Wissenschaftliche Buchgesellschaft, 1983.
- *Geschichte der deutschen Sprache*. Leipzig: S. Herzel, 1868.
- '*Review* of Ancient Laws and Institutes of England [ed. Benjamin Thorpe].' *Göttingische gelehrte Anzeigen* 36/37 (1841): 345-62. Repr. *Kleinere Schriften*. Hildesheim: Olms, 1991, 312-23.
Haddan, Arthur West, and William Stubbs. *Councils and Ecclesiastical Documents Relating to Great Britain and Ireland*. Vol. 3. Oxford: Clarendon, 1881.
Hafström, Yrjö Blomstedt, Torfinn Tobiasson, and Magnús Már Lárusson. 'lagman.' In Brønsted et al., eds., *Kulturhistorisk Leksikon*, 10:150-63.
Harris, John. *The History of Kent. In Five Parts*. London: D. Midwinter, 1719.

Harvey, Anthony. 'Some Significant Points of Early Insular Celtic Orthography.' In O'Corrain, et al., eds., *Sages, Saints and Story Tellers*, 56–66.

Hastrup, Kirsten. *Culture and History in Medieval Iceland: An Anthropological Analysis of Structure and Change*. Oxford: Clarendon, 1985.

Hausner, Margrit. 'Entgegnung auf Th. J. Rivers: Widows' Rights in Anglo-Saxon Law.' *Zeitschrift fur Anglistik und Amerikanistik* 33 (1985): 161–3.

Hawkes, Sonia Chadwick. 'Anglo-Saxon Kent c. 425–725.' In Leach, ed., *Archaeology in Kent*, 64–78.

– 'The Dating and Social Significance of the Burials in the Polhill Cemetery.' In Philip, ed., *Excavations in West Kent*, 186–201.

Hayashi, Hiroshi. 'Felix Liebermann and Recent Studies of Anglo-Saxon Laws (I).' *Gakushuin Review of Law and Politics* 16 (1981): 165–84.

– 'The Laws of Anglo-Saxon Kings, Offa et al.: A Memorandum on the Study of Express Legislative Development in the Anglo-Saxon Period (2).' *Gakushuin Review of Law and Politics* 19 (1984): 125–51.

– 'The Lost Laws of Some Anglo-Saxon Kings: A Memorandum on the Study of Express Legislative Development in the Anglo-Saxon Period (7).' *Gakushuin Review of Law and Politics* 24 (1989): 179–231.

– 'The Lost Laws of Some Anglo-Saxon Kings. Part II. Some Observations on the Nature of Anglo-Saxon Laws (1).' *Gakushuin Review of Law and Politics* 25 (1990): 147–215.

Healey, Antonette diPaolo, et al. *The Dictionary of Old English*. Toronto: Pontifical Institute of Mediaeval Studies, 1986.

Hearne, Thomas. *Textus Roffensis*. Oxford: Theatro Sheldoniano, 1720.

Hickes, George, and H. Wanley. *Linguarum Vett. Septentrionalium Thesaurus Grammatico-Criticus et Archaeologicus* 2 vols., 1703–5. Repr. Menston: Scolar, 1970.

Higham, Nicholas. *An English Empire: Bede and the Early Anglo-Saxon Kings*. Manchester and New York: Manchester University Press, 1995.

– *Rome, Britain and the Anglo-Saxons: The Archaeology of Change*. London: Seaby, 1992.

Hill, David, ed. *Ethelred the Unready: Papers from the Millenary Conference*. B.A.R. British Series, 59. Oxford: British Archaeological Reports, 1978.

Hines, John, ed. *The Anglo-Saxons from the Migration Period to the Eighth Century: An Ethnographic Perspective*. Studies in Historical Archaeoethnology, 2. Woodbridge: Boydell, 1997.

Hobley, Brian. '*Lundenwic* and *Lundenburh*: Two Cities Rediscovered.' In Hodges and Hobley, eds., *The Rebirth of Towns*, 69–82.

Hodges, Richard, and Brian Hobley, eds. *The Rebirth of Towns in the West, AD 700–1050*. CBA Research Report, 68. London: Council for British Archaeology, 1988.

Holthausen, Ferdinand. *Altenglisches Etymologisches Wörterbuch*. Heidelberg: Carl Winter, 1925.
- *Altfriesisches Wörterbuch*. Germanische Bibliothek. 1. Abt., Sammlung germanischer Elementar -und Handbucher. 4. Reihe: Wörterbucher. 5. Bd. Heidelberg: C. Winter, 1925.
Hooke, Della. 'The Anglo-Saxons in England in the Seventh and Eighth Centuries: Location in Space.' In Hines, ed., *The Anglo-Saxons*, 65–84.
Hopper, Paul J. *The Syntax of the Simple Sentence in Proto-Germanic*. Janua linguarum: Series practica, 143. The Hague: Mouton, 1975.
Hough, Carole A. 'The Early Kentish "Divorce Laws": A Reconsideration of Æthelberht, chs. 79 and 80.' *Anglo-Saxon England* 23 (1994): 19–34.
- 'A Reappraisal of Æthelberht 84.' *Nottingham Medieval Studies* 37 (1993): 1–6.
Jackson, Kenneth. *Language and History in Early Britain*. Edinburgh University Publications, Language and Literature. Edinburgh: Edinburgh University Press, 1953.
Jamison, Stephanie. 'Draupadī on the Walls of Troy: *Iliad* 3 from an Indic Perspective.' *Classical Antiquity* 13(1) (1984): 5–16.
- 'Penelope and the Pigs: Indic Perspectives on the *Odyssey*.' *Classical Antiquity* 18(2) (1999): 227–72.
Jasanoff, Jay, H. Craig Melchert, and Lisi Oliver, eds. *Mír Curad. Studies in Honor of Calvert Watkins*. Innsbrucker Beiträge zur Sprachwissenschaft, Bd. 9. Innsbruck: Institut für Sprachwissenschaft der Universität Innsbruck, 1998.
Jeffery, Lilian H., and Anna Morpurgo-Davies. 'ΠΟΙΝΙΚΑΣΤΑΣ and ΠΟΙΝΙΚΑΖΕΝ: BM 1969. 4-2. 1, A New Archaic Inscription from Crete.' *Kadmos* 9 (1970): 118–54.
Jenkins, Dafydd. *The Law of Hywel Dda: Law Texts from Medieval Wales*. Dyfed: Gomer, 1990.
- 'The Medieval Welsh Idea of Law.' *Tijdschrift voor rechtsgeschiedenis* 49 (1981): 323–48.
Jolliffe, John Edward Austin. *The Constitutional History of Medieval England*. London: A. & C. Black, 1961.
Kanner, Barbara, ed. *The Women of England: From Anglo-Saxon Times to the Present*. Hamden, Conn.: Archon Books, 1979.
Kelly, Fergus. *A Guide to Early Irish Law*. Early Irish Law Series, 3. Dublin: Dublin Institute for Advanced Studies, 1988.
Kelly, S.E., ed. *Charters of St. Augustine's Abbey Canterbury and Minster-in-Thanet*. Anglo-Saxon Charters, 4. Oxford and New York: Oxford University Press, 1995.
Kempf, Johann Georg, et al., eds. *Thesaurus Linguae Latinae*. Leipzig: Tübner, 1906–12.

Ker, N.R., ed. *Catalogue of Manuscripts Containing Anglo-Saxon.* Oxford: Clarendon, 1957.
– *English Manuscripts in the Century after the Norman Conquest.* The Lyell Lectures, 1952–3. Oxford: Clarendon, 1960.
Keynes, Simon. *Anglo-Saxon History: A Select Bibliography*, Subsidia 13. 3rd ed. Most recent version available at http://www.wmich.edu/medieval/rawl/keynes1.
Kiralfy, Albert. 'Law and Right in English Legal History.' *Journal of Legal History* 6(1) (1985): 49–61.
Kirby, D.P. 'Bede and Northumbrian Chronology.' *English Historical Review* 78 (1963): 514–27.
– *The Earliest English Kings.* London and Boston: Unwin Hyman, 1991.
– *The Making of Early England.* London: Batsford, 1967.
Klaeber, Fr. *Beowulf and the Fight at Finnsburg.* 3rd ed. Boston and New York: D.C. Heath, 1950.
Klinck, Anne L. 'Anglo-Saxon Women and the Law.' *Journal of Medieval History* 8 (1982): 107–21.
Klipstein, Louis. *Analecta Anglo-Saxonica: Selections in Prose and Verse from the Anglo-Saxon Literature.* 2 vols. New York: G.P. Putnam, 1856.
Kluge, Friedrich. *Hildebrandslied, Ludwigslied und Merseburger Zaubersprüche.* Deutschkundliche Bücherei. Leipzig: Quelle & Meyer, 1919.
Kluge, Friedrich, and Elmer Seebold. *Etymologisches Wörterbuch der deutschen Sprache.* 22nd ed. Berlin: de Gruyter, 1989.
Korte, Dirk. *Untersuchungen zu Inhalt, Stil und Technik angelsächsischer Gesetze und Rechtsbücher des 6. bis 12. Jahrhunderts.* Archiv für vergleichende Kulturwissenschaft, Bd. 10. Meisenheim am Glan: A. Hain, 1974.
Krapp, George, and Elliot Dobbie, eds. *The Exeter Book.* New York: Columbia University Press, 1936.
Krusch, Bruno, and William Levison, eds. *Monumenta Germaniae Historica: Scriptores Rerum Merovingicarum, Vol. I, Part I. Gregorii Episcopi Turonensis: Libri Historiarum X.* Hannover: Hahn, 1951.
Lancaster, L. 'Kinship in Anglo-Saxon Society–I.' *British Journal of Sociology* 9 (1958): 230–50.
– 'Kinship in Anglo-Saxon Society–II.' *British Journal of Sociology* 9 (1958): 359–77.
Lapidge, Michael, et al., eds. *The Blackwell Encyclopedia of Anglo-Saxon England.* Oxford and Malden, Mass.: Blackwell, 1999.
– 'clergy.' In Lapidge et al., eds. *The Blackwell Encyclopedia of Anglo-Saxon England*, 106–7.
Lárusson, Magnús Már. 'lǫgsǫgumaðr.' In Brønsted et al., eds., *Kulturhistorisk Leksikon*, 11:137.

Latham, R.E., et al., eds. *Dictionary of Medieval Latin from British Sources*. London: Oxford University Press, 1975.
Lazzari, Loredana. 'Il Codice di Wihtræd: incidenza di canoni ecclesiastici sulle leggi secolari.' In Lazzari, ed., *Terti giuridici*, 23–42.
– ed. *Testi giuridici germanici*. Atti e memorie / Universita degli studi della Basilicata-Potenza, 11. Potenza: Il Salice, 1992.
Leach, Peter E., ed. *Archaeology in Kent to AD 1500: In Memory of Stuart Eborall Rigold*. Research Report / Council for British Archaeology, 48. London: Council for British Archaeology, 1982.
Lebecq, Stéphane. 'The Question of Logistics.' In Gameson, ed., *St. Augustine and the Conversion of England*, 50–67.
Lehman, Warren Winfred. 'The First English Law.' *Journal of Legal History* 6(1) (1985): 1–32.
Lendinara, Patrizia. 'The Kentish Laws.' In Hines, ed., *The Anglo-Saxons*, 211–44.
Lewis, Charlton T., and Charles Short. *A Latin Dictionary*. Oxford: Clarendon, 1879; repr. 1962.
Leyser, Henrietta. *Medieval Women: A Social History of Women in England 450–1500*. London: Weidenfeld and Nicolson, 1995.
Liebermann, Felix. *Die Gesetze der Angelsachsen*. Halle: M. Niemeyer, 1897–1916.
– 'Ags. *rihthamscyld*: echtes Hoftor.' *Archiv für das Studium der neueren Sprachen und Literaturen* 115 (1905): 389–91.
– 'Kentish *hionne*: Hirnhaut.' *Archiv für das Studium der neueren Sprachen und Literaturen* 115 (1905) 177–8.
– 'Zu Wihtraeds Gesetz.' *Archiv für das Studium der neueren Sprachen und Literaturen* 146 (1923): 242.
Liuzza, R.M., ed. *The Old English Version of the Gospels, Volume 1: Text and Translation*. Early English Text Society, OS 304, 314. New York and Oxford: Oxford University Press, 1994.
Loyn, H.R. 'Gesiths and Thegns in Anglo-Saxon England from the Seventh to the Tenth Century.' *English Historical Review* 70 (1955): 529–49.
– *The Governance of Anglo-Saxon England 500–1087*. London: E. Arnold, 1984.
– 'Kinship in Anglo-Saxon England.' *Anglo-Saxon England* 3 (1974): 197–210.
MacCormack, G. 'Inheritance and Wergild in Early Germanic Law – I.' *Irish Jurist* n.s. 8 (1973): 143–63.
MacNeill, Eoin. 'Ancient Irish Law: The Law of Status or Franchise.' *Proceedings of the Royal Irish Academy* 36 (1923): 306.
MacNeill, John T., and Helena M. Gamer. *Medieval Handbooks of Penance*. Records of Western Civilization, Sources and Studies, 29. 1938; New York: Columbia University Press, 1990.

Maitland, F.W. 'History of English Law.' *Selected Historical Essays of F.W. Maitland*, ed. Helen M. Cam. Cambridge: Cambridge University Press, 5 (1957): 97-121.
- 'The Laws of the Anglo-Saxons.' *Quarterly Review* 200 (1904): 139-57.
Mallory, J.P. *In Search of the Indo-Europeans: Language, Archaeology and Myth.* New York: Thames and Hudson, 1989.
Malone, Kemp, ed. *Widsith*. Anglistica, 13. Methuen's Old English Library. London: Methuen, 1936; repr. Copenhagen: Rosenkilde and Bagger, 1962.
Markus, R.A. 'Augustine and Gregory the Great.' In Gameson, ed., *St. Augustine and the Conversion of England*, 41-9.
Matthew, Donald, et al., eds. *Stenton's 'Anglo-Saxon England' Fifty Years On.* Reading Historical Studies I. Reading: University of Reading, 1994.
Maurer, Konrad. *Altnorwegisches Staatsrecht und Gerichtswesen*. Leipzig: Gesellschaft der Wissenschaften in Kristiana, 1907.
Mayr-Harting, Henry. *The Coming of Christianity to Anglo-Saxon England*. 3rd ed. London: B.T. Batsford, 1991.
- 'Two Conversions to Christianity: The Bulgarians and the Anglo-Saxons.' In Matthew et al., eds., *Stenton's 'Anglo-Saxon England' Fifty Years On*, 1-30.
McKitterick, Rosamund. *The Carolingians and the Written Word*. Cambridge and New York: Cambridge University Press, 1989.
McLeod, Neil. 'Parallel and Paradox: Compensation in the Legal Systems of Celtic Ireland and Anglo-Saxon England.' *Studia Celtica* 16-17 (1981): 25-72.
Meens, Rob. 'A Background to Augustine's Mission to Anglo-Saxon England.' *Anglo-Saxon England* 23 (1994): 5-17.
Meillet, Antoine. 'Notes sur quelque faits de morphologie.' *Mémoires de la Société de Linguistique de Paris* (1900): 111-21.
Meyer, Marc A. 'Land Charters and the Legal Position of Anglo-Saxon Women.' In Kanner, ed., *The Women of England*, 57-82.
Meyvaert, Paul. 'Bede's Text of the *Libellus Responsionum* of Gregory the Great to Augustine of Canterbury.' In Clemoes and Jughes, eds., *England Before the Conquest*, 15-34.
- *Benedict, Gregory, Bede and Others*. London: Variorum Reprints, 1977.
Mezger, F. 'Did the Institution of Marriage by Purchase Exist in Old Germanic Law?' *Speculum* 18 (1943): 369-71.
Mirams, Michael David. *Ethelbert's Kingdom – The Story of the Jutish and Saxon Kings of Kent*. Rochester: North Kent Books, 1981.
Morris, John. *Arthurian Sources II: Annals and Charters*. Arthurian Period Sources, 1-6. Chichester: Phillimore, 1995.
Murray, Alexander C. *Germanic Kinship Structure. Studies in Law and Society in Antiquity and the Early Middle Ages*. Studies and Texts 65. Toronto: Pontifical Institute of Mediaeval Studies, 1983.

Myres, J.N.L. *The English Settlements*. The Oxford History of England, 1B. Oxford: Clarendon, 1986.

Neckel, Gustav. 'Under Eoderas.' *Beiträge zur Geschichte der Deutschen Sprache und Literatur* 41.163–170, 1916.

O'Corrain, Donnchadh, Liam Breatnach, and Kim McCone, eds. *Sages, Saints and Storytellers: Celtic Studies in Honour of Professor James Carney*. Maynooth Monographs, 2. Maynooth: An Sagart, 1989.

Oliver, Lisi. '*Cyninges fedesl*: The Feeding of the King in Æthelberht ch.12,' *Anglo-Saxon England* 27 (1998): 31–40.

– 'Irish Influence on Orthographic Practice in Early Kent.' *Nowele* 33 (1998): 93–113.

– The Language of the Early English Laws. PhD dissertation, Harvard University, 1995.

– ed. *Selected Writings / Calvert Watkins*. Innsbrucker Beiträge zur Sprachwissenschaft, Bd. 80. Innsbruck: Institut für Sprachwissenschaft der Universität Innsbruck, 1994.

– 'Towards Freeing a Slave in Germanic Law.' In Jasanoff, Melchert, and Oliver, eds., *Mír Curad*, 549–60.

– 'Who was Æthelberht's Laet?' In Linda Hall, ed., *Transformation of Law in Late Antiquity*. Cambridge: Academic Press, 2002.

Ortenberg, Veronica. '*Angli aut angeli*: les Anglo-Saxons ont-ils "sauvé" la papauté au VIIe siècle?' *Revue Mabillon* n.s. 6 (1995): 5–32.

Page, R.I. *An Introduction to English Runes*. London: Methuen, 1973.

Pegge, Samuel. '*An Historical Account of that Venerable Monument of Antiquity the* TEXTUS ROFFENSIS.' London: Society of Antiquaries, 1767.

Pelteret, David A.E. 'Slavery in Anglo-Saxon England.' In Woods and Pelteret, eds., *The Anglo-Saxons*, 117–33.

– *Slavery in Early Mediaeval England*. Studies in Anglo-Saxon History, 7. Woodbridge and Rochester: Boydell, 1995.

Pfeifer, J.D. 'Early Anglo-Saxon Glossaries and the School of Canterbury.' *Anglo-Saxon England* 16 (1987): 17–44.

Philip, Brian, ed. *Excavations in West Kent, 1960–1970*. Research Report in the Kent Series, 2. Dover: Kent Archaeological Rescue Unit [for] the West Kent Border Archaeological Group, 1973.

Pinsky, Robert, trans. *The Inferno of Dante: A New Verse Translation*. New York: Farrar, Straus and Giroux, 1994.

Plummer, Charles. *Venerabilis Baedae: Historiam Ecclesiasticam Gentis Anglorum; Historiam Abbatum; Epistolam ad Ecgberctum una cum Historia Abbatum Auctore Anonymo*. 2 vols. Oxford: Clarendon, 1846.

Pohl, Walter. 'Ethnic Names and Identities in the British Isles: A Comparative Perspective.' In Hines, ed., *The Anglo-Saxons*, 7–31.

Pokorny, Julius. *Indogermanisches Etymologisches Wörterbuch.* Bern: Francke, 1989.
Pollock, Sir Frederick, and Frederic Maitland. *The History of English Law Before the Time of Edward I.* London: Cambridge University Press, 1968.
Post, Gaines. Review of Wallace-Hadrill *Early Germanic Kingship in England and on the Continent. American Journal of Legal History* 16 (1981): 283–8.
Radcliffe-Brown, A.R. *African Systems of Kinship and Marriage.* London and New York: Oxford University Press, 1950.
Renfrew, Colin. *Archaeology and Language: The Puzzle of Indo-European Origins.* London: J. Cape, 1986.
Richards, Mary P. 'The *Dictionary of Old English* and Old English Legal Terminology.' *The Dictionary of Old English: Retrospects and Prospects. Subsidia* 26 (1998): 57–62.
– 'Elements of a Written Standard in the Old English Laws.' In Trahern, ed., *Standardizing English,* 1–22.
– 'The Manuscript Contexts of the Old English Laws: Tradition and Innovation.' In Szarmach, ed., *Studies in Older English Prose,* 171–92.
– *Texts and Their Traditions in the Medieval Library of Rochester Cathedral Priory.* Transactions of the American Philosophical Society, 78/3. Philadelphia: American Philosophical Society, 1988.
– and J. Stanfield. 'Concepts of Anglo-Saxon Women in Law.' In Damico and Olsen, eds., *New Readings on Women,* 89–99.
Richardson, Henry G., and George O. Sayles. *Law and Legislation from Æthelberht to Magna Carta.* Edinburgh University Publications; History, Philosophy and Economics, 20. Edinburgh: Edinburgh University Press, 1966.
Review: Michael M. Sheehan. *Catholic History Review* 56 (1971): 715–17.
Richter, Michael. *The Formation of the Medieval West: Studies in the Oral Culture of the Barbarians.* New York: St Martin's, 1994.
Rivers, Theodore John. 'Adultery in Early Anglo-Saxon Society: Aethelberht 31 in Comparison with Continental Germanic Law.' *Anglo-Saxon England* 20 (1991): 19–26.
– trans. *Laws of the Salian and Ripuarian Franks.* AMS studies in the Middle Ages, 8. New York: AMS Press, 1986.
– 'A Reevaluation of Aethelberht 3.' *Zeitschrift der Savigny-Stiftung für Rechtsgeschichte, germanistische Abteilung* 93 (1976): 315–18.
– 'Widow's Rights in Anglo-Saxon Law.' *American Journal of Legal History* 19 (1975): 208–15.
Robertson, A.J., trans. *The Laws of the Kings of England from Edmund to Henry I.* Cambridge: Cambridge University Press, 1925.

Rubin, Stanley. 'The *Bot*, or Composition in Anglo-Saxon Law: A Reassessment.' *Journal of Legal History* 17 (1995): 144–54.
Sawyer, Peter. *Anglo-Saxon Charters, An Annotated List and Bibliography.* Royal Historical Society Guides and Handbooks, 8. London: Royal Historical Society, 1968.
- 'Early Fairs and Markets in England and Scandanavia.' In Anderson and Latham, eds., *The Market in History*, 59–76.
- 'Kings and Merchants.' In Sawyer and Woods, eds., *Early Medieval Kingship*, 139–58.
- *Medieval Settlement: Continuity and Change.* London: Edward Arnold, 1976.
- ed. *Early English Manuscripts in Facsimile VII: Textus Roffensis, Part I.* Copenhagen: Rosenkilde and Bagger, 1957.
- ed. *Early English Manuscripts in Facsimile XI: Textus Roffensis, Part II.* Copenhagen: Rosenkilde and Bagger, 1962.
Sawyer, Peter, and I.N. Woods, eds. *Early Medieval Kingship.* Leeds: The Editors, 1977.
Sayles, G.O. *The Medieval Foundations of England.* London: Methuen, 1948.
Schmid, Reinhold. *Die Gesetze der Angelsachsen.* 2nd ed. Leipzig: F.A. Brockhaus, 1858.
Schwyter, J.R. *Old English Legal Language.* North-Western European Language Evolution. Supplement, 15. Odense: Odense University Press, 1996.
Scragg, D.G. and Paul E. Szarmach, eds. *The Editing of Old English: Papers from the 1990 Manchester Conference.* Cambridge and Rochester: D.S. Brewer, 1994.
Scull, Christopher. 'Urban Centers in Pre-Viking England?' In Hines, ed., *The Anglo-Saxons*, 269–310.
Seebohm, Frederic. *Tribal Custom in Anglo-Saxon Law.* London: Longmans, Green, 1902.
Seebold, Elmar. 'Was ist jütish? Was ist kentish?' In Bammesberger and Wollmann, eds., *Britain 400–600*, 335–52.
Sheehan, Michael M. Review of Richardson and Sayles, *Law and Legislation from Æthelberht to Magna Carta.* 971. *Catholic History Review* 56 (1971): 715–17.
Shirley-Price, Leo, trans. *Bede: Ecclesiastical History of the English People.* Harmondsworth: Penguin, 1990.
Siems, H. 'Zu Problemen der Bewertung frühmitterlalterlicher Rechtstexte.' *Zeitschrift der Savigny-Stiftung für Rechtsgeschichte, germanistische Abteilung* 56 (1989): 201–303.
Sievers, Eduard. 'Altnordisches im *Beowulf*?' *Beiträge zur Geschichte der deutschen Sprache und Literatur* 12 (1887): 168–200.
Simpson, A.W.B. 'The Laws of Ethelbert.' In Arnold et al., eds., *On the Laws and Customs of England*, 3–17.

Sims-Williams, Patrick. 'The Settlement of England in Bede and the *Chronicle*.' *Anglo-Saxon England* 12 (1983): 1–42.
Sisam, Kenneth. *Studies in the History of Old English Literature*. Oxford: Clarendon, 1953.
Spelman, Sir Henry. *Ecclesiarum Orbis Brittanici*. London: Apud Aliciam Warren, 1664.
– 'Of the Ancient Government of England.' *The English Works of Sir Henry Spelman*. London: D. Browne, 1723.
Stafford, Pauline A. 'The "Farm of One Night" and the Organization of King Edward's Estates in Domesday.' *Economic History Review*, 2nd Series 33(4) (1980): 491–502.
Stanley, E.G. 'Did Beowulf Commit *feaxfeng* Against Grendel's Mother?' *Notes and Queries* 221 (1976): 339–40.
– 'Some Words for the *Dictionary of Old English*.' *The Dictionary of Old English: Retrospects and Prospects. Subsidia* 26 (1998): 33–56.
– 'Two Old English Poetic Phrases Insufficiently Understood for Literary Criticism: *þing gehegen* and *seonoþ gehegen*.' In Calder, ed., *Old English Poetry*, 67–90.
Stearns, John M. *The Germs and Developments of the Laws of England*. New York: Banks, 1889.
Steever, Sanford B., Carol A. Walker, and Salikoko S. Mufwene, eds. *Papers from the Parasession on Diachronic Syntax, April 22, 1976*. Chicago: Chicago Linguistic Society, 1976.
Stenton, Sir Frank. *Anglo-Saxon England*. 3rd ed. Oxford: Clarendon, 1971; repr. Oxford and New York: Oxford University Press, 1989.
Stevenson, Jane. 'The Beginnings of Literacy in Ireland.' *Proceedings of the Royal Irish Academy* 89C/6 (1989): 127–65.
Sunderland, Kathryn. 'Elizabeth Elstob.' In Damico and Zavadil, eds., *Medieval Scholarship*, 2:59–74.
Szarmach, Paul E., ed. *Studies in Earlier Old English Prose: Sixteen Original Contributions*. Albany: State University of New York Press, 1986.
Tate, Francis. Transcript of *Textus Roffensis*: British Museum ms. Cotton Julius CII, 1589.
Tatton-Brown, T. 'Canterbury and the Early Medieval Towns of Kent.' In Leach, ed., *Archaeology in Kent*, 79–83.
– 'The Topography of Anglo-Saxon London.' *Antiquity* 60 (1986): 21–8.
Thacker, A. 'Some Terms for Noblemen in Anglo-Saxon England, ca. 650–900.' *Anglo-Saxon Studies in Archeology and History* 2 (1981): 201–36.
Thesaurus Linguae Latinae. Leipzig: Tübner, 1906–12. 3:1339–40.
Thorpe, Benjamin, ed. *Ancient Laws and Institutes of England; Comprising Laws enacted under the Anglo-Saxon Kings from Aethelbirht to Cnut, with an English Translation of the Saxon ... also, Monumenta Ecclesiastica Anglicana*

from the Seventh to the Tenth Century. London: Commissioners of the Public Records, 1840.

Thorpe, Lewis, trans. *Gregory of Tours: The History of the Franks*. Harmondsworth: Penguin, 1974.

Thurneysen, Rudolf. 'Gúbretha Caratniad.' *Zeitschrift für celtische Philologie* 15 (1924/5): 302–70.

– 'Spirantenwechsel im Gotischen.' *Indogermanische Forschungen* 8 (1897): 208–14.

Toller, T. Northcote. *An Anglo-Saxon Dictionary Based on the Manuscript Collections of the Late Joseph Bosworth: Supplement*. Oxford: Clarendon, 1921.

Trahern, J.B., ed. *Standardizing English: Essays in the History of Language Change. In Honor of John Hurt Fisher*. Knoxville: University of Tennessee Press, 1989.

Turville-Petre, J.E. 'Hengist and Horsa.' *Saga Book of the Viking Society* 14 (1957): 273–90.

Venezky, Richard L., and Antonette de Paolo Healey. *A Microfiche Concordance to Old English*. Publications of the Dictionary of Old English, 1. Newark: University of Delaware, 1980.

Vince, Alan. 'The *Aldwych*: Mid-Saxon London Discovered?' *Current Archeology* 93 (1984): 310–2.

– 'The Economic Basis of Anglo-Saxon London.' In Hodges and Hobley, eds., *The Rebirth of Towns*, 83–92.

– *Saxon London: An Archaeological Investigation*. London: Seaby, 1990.

Vinogradoff, Sir Paul. *The Growth of the Manor*. London: S. Sonnenschein, 1904; repr. New York: A.M. Kelley, 1968.

von Amira, Karl. *Grundriss des Germanischen Rechts*. Grundriss der germanischen Philologie 5. Strassburg: K.J. Trubner, 1913.

von Salis, Ludwig Rudolf. *Leges Burgundionum*. Monumenta Germaniae Historica: Leges Nationum Germanicarum vol. 2, pt 1. Hannover: Hahnsche Buchhandlung, 1973.

Wallace-Hadrill, J.M. *Bede's Ecclesiastical History of the English People*. Oxford Medieval Texts. Oxford: Clarendon, 1988.

– *Early Germanic Kingship in England and on the Continent*. The Ford Lectures, 1970. Oxford: Clarendon, 1971.
Review: Gaines Post. *American Journal of Legal History* 16 (1981): 283–8.

– *The Long-Haired Kings, and Other Studies in Frankish History*. London: Methuen 1962; repr. Medieval Academy Reprints for Teaching, 11. Toronto and Buffalo: University of Toronto Press, 1982.

Wasserschleben, F.W.H. *Die Bussordnungen der abendländischen Kirche*. Graz: Akademische Druck, 1958.

Watkins, Calvert. *How to Kill a Dragon: Aspects of Indo-European Poetics*. New York: Oxford University Press, 1995.

- 'Preliminaries to a Historical and Comparative Analysis of the Syntax of the Old Irish Verb.' *Celtica* 6 (1963): 1–49. Also in Oliver, ed., *Selected Writings*, 1:3–51.
- 'Sick Maintenance in Indo-European.' *Ériu* 27 (1976): 21–5. Also in Oliver, ed., *Selected Writings*, 2:560–4.
- 'Towards Proto-Indoeuropean Syntax: Problems and Pseudo-Problems.' In Steever et al., eds., *Papers ... on Diachronic Syntax*, 305–26. Also in Oliver, ed., *Selected Writings*, 1.242–63.

Whitelock, Dorothy. *The Beginnings of English Society*. The Pelican History of England, 2. Harmondsworth: Penguin, 1952.
- ed. *English Historical Documents, Volume I: c. 500–1042*. London: Eyre & Spottiswoode, 1955; repr. 1979.

Wilda, Wilhelm E. *Geschichte des deutschen Strafrechts I*. Halle: C.A. Schwetschke, 1842.

Wilkins, David. *Leges Anglo-Saxonicae Ecclesiasticae & Civilis*. London: G. Bowyer, 1721.

Winterbottom, Michael, ed. and trans. *Gildas: The Ruin of Britain and Other Works*. Arthurian Period Sources, 7. London: Phillimore, 1978.

Witney, K.P. *The Jutish Forest: A Study of the Weald of Kent from 450 to 1380 AD*. London: Athelone Press, 1976.
- *The Kingdom of Kent. A History from c. A.D. 450 to 825*. London: Phillimore, 1982.
Review: E. Christiansen. *English Historical Review* 100 (1985): 860–2.

Wood, Ian. 'Augustine and Gaul.' In Gameson, ed., *St. Augustine and the Conversion of England*, 68–82.
- 'Before and After the Migration to Britain.' In Hines, ed., *The Anglo-Saxons*, 41–64.
- *The Merovingian Kingdoms, 450–751*. London and New York: Longman, 1994.
- 'The Mission of Augustine of Canterbury to the English.' *Speculum* 69 (1994): 1–17.

Wood, Ian, and N. Lund, eds. *People and Places in Northern Europe, 500–1600: Studies Presented to P. H. Sawyer*. Woodbridge: Boydell Press, 1991.

Woods, J. Douglas, and David A.E. Pelteret, eds. *The Anglo-Saxons: Synthesis and Achievement*. Waterloo: Wilfrid Laurier University Press, 1985.

Wormald, Patrick. 'Bede, the Bretwaldas and the Origins of the *Gens Anglorum*.' In Wormald, ed., *Ideal and Reality*, 99–129.
- '*Exempla Romanorum*: The Earliest English Legislation in Context.' In Ellegård Åkerström-Hougen, eds., *Rome and the North*, 15–28.
- 'In Search of King Offa's "Law Code."' In Wood and Lund, eds., *People and Places in Northern Europe*, 24–45. Also in Wormald, *Legal Culture*, 201–24.

- *'Inter cetera bona – genti suae*: Law-Making and Peace-Keeping in the Earliest English Kingdoms.' *Settimane dello studio del Centro italiano di studi sull'alto medioevo* 42 (1995): 963–93. Also in Wormald 1999, *Legal Culture*, 179–200.
- *'Laga Eadwardi*: The *Textus Roffensis* and its Context.' *Anglo-Norman Studies* 17 (1995): 243–66. Also in Wormald, *Legal Culture*, 115–38.
- *Legal Culture in the Early Medieval West: Law as Text, Image and Experience.* London and Rio Grande: Hambledon, 1999.
- *'Lex Scripta* and *Verbum Regis*: Legislation and Germanic Kingship, from Euric to Cnut.' In Sawyer and Woods, eds., *Early Medieval Kingship*, 105–38. Also in Wormald, *Legal Culture*, 1–44.
- *The Making of English Law: King Alfred to the Twelfth Century, Volume One: Legislation and its Limits.* Oxford: Blackwell, 1999.
- ed. *Ideal and Reality in Frankish and Anglo-Saxon Society*. Oxford: B. Blackwell, 1983.

Wright, Thomas, and Richard Paul Walker. *Anglo-Saxon and Old English Vocabularies*. London: Trubner, 1884.

Wyatt, Sir Thomas. *The Complete Poems*. Ed. R.A. Rebholz. Harmondsworth: Penguin, 1978.

Young, Ernest. 'The Anglo-Saxon Family Law.' In Adams, ed., *Essays in Anglo-Saxon Law*, 121–83.

Yorke, Barbara A.E. 'Joint Kingship in Kent c. 560 to 785.' *Archaeologia Cantiana* 99 (1983): 1–19.
- *Kings and Kingdoms of Early Anglo-Saxon England*. London: Seaby, 1990.
- 'The Reception of Christianity at the Anglo-Saxon Royal Courts.' In Gameson, ed., *St. Augustine and the Conversion of England*, 152–73.

Index

The character æ is indexed under ae. þ and ð are indexed under th. St is indexed as if it were expanded to Saint. For references to peoples, look under territory. For example, West Saxon is a sub-entry under Wessex. For references to language, look under main language entry. For example, Old English, Middle English, and Modern English are all sub-entries under English. All glossed terms are in Old English, unless otherwise designated by one of the abbreviations shown below.

F = Frankish
L = Latin
MG = Modern German
OF = Old Frisian
OHG = Old High German

OI = Old Irish
ON = Old Norse
OS = Old Saxon
OSw = Old Swedish
OW = Old Welsh

Scholars are indexed only as their analyses are discussed in the body of the text, footnotes, or endnotes.

abbot, 174–5
abdomen, 54, 75, 103
abduction, 108–9. *See also* adultery
accusation: of murder, 97; of perjury, 136–7; of servile status, 91; of theft, 129, 142, 145–6; of wrongdoing, 139–41, 174–7
acwyle, 'die,' 123, 128
Adams, Henry, 139
adultery, 98–9, 110, 111

adversative use of 'and,' 55, 65n.d, 67n.e, 69n.d, 81n.a, 157n.g, 173
æ, 'law,' 126, 134–5
Ælfric, 91
Ælle, 11, 17–18
æltheodige, 'foreign,' 26, 148
ænd, 'and,' 213n.133
aende, 'and,' 27, 28–9, 55, 149, 156, 169–70
ærnæmda, 'aforementioned,' 149, 152

278   Index

Aet, 'at, for,' 27, 66
Æthelbald of Mercia, 8
Æthelberht of Kent:
- biographical information, 8–14, 23, 117, 120, 206nn.37–8, 207nn.42, 49, 227n.23; conversion, 9–14, 119; genealogy, 14, 18–19
- laws: content, 51–116; — compared with other Kentish laws, 134–6, 138, 140–6, 148, 155n.c, 157n.i, 163n.a, 164, 166, 167, 169, 171, 178–9, 180, 221n.54; dating, 34–51; editorial practice, 52–7; linguistic analysis, 21, 22, 25–34, 120–3, 209n.71; setting, 14–20, 209n.82
- marriage to Bertha, 8–9, 118
Æthelberht, son of Wihtred of Kent, 148
Æthelburh, daughter of Æthelberht, 119
Æthelred II of England, 112, 226n.9
Æthelstan, 22
Aetius, 4
æwda(mann), 'oath-helper,' 29, 126, 127n.b
Aidan, bishop of Northumbria, 46
Albinus, abbot of St Augustine's, Canterbury, 18
Alfred of Wessex, 11, 26, 95, 102, 138; language, 31–2, 217n.4; laws, 25, 38–9, 46, 95, 102, 138, 217n.193
alliteration, 39–41, 48–9, 108, 173, 216n.168
Alric, son of Wihtred, 148
altar, 92, 117, 133, 142, 144, 157, 159, 169, 174, 175
ambiht smið, 'official (–) smith,' 48, 54, 64–5, 87
Angles, 5, 10, 11
Anglia, 5
Anglian Chronicles, 206n.35

Anglo-Norman (scriptorial practice), 212n.123
Anglo-Saxon: conversion, 10; kingdoms, 5, 6–7, 13; kings and kingship, 8, 17–18, 19, 46; language, 15, 20, 69n.f, 104; laws, 5, 15, 20, 23, 34, 36, 40–1, 83, 101, 105, 114, 134, 171, 180, 216n.169, 222n.62 (*see also* English: Old English: laws); literacy, 14; medical knowledge, 99–102; monetary system, 82–3, 86, 142, 218n.7; ranks of people, 87, 138, 142, 180; Saxon (used for Anglo-Saxon), 24, 44; settlement, 5–7, 93; studies, 23; territories, 5, 11–12, 14, 18, 35, 41, 51, 69n.f; wills, 107, 114; women, marriage and divorce, 106, 110, 114; written sources, 11, 25, 27, 136
Anglo-Saxon Chronicle, 3, 7, 9, 10, 23, 119, 147, 165
angylde, '(with) single compensation,' 61n.a
ar, 'herald, messenger,' 87, 88
arbitration, 49, 99, 131, 139–41, 143
archaeology, 4–5, 7, 110–11, 142–3, 229n.56
Archaionomia, 24
archaism, linguistic, 14, 22, 25–31, 33–4, 36, 42–4, 51, 55–6, 66n.b, 108, 120–2, 148–9, 169–70, 211n.101, 214n.145, 216n.169
archbishop of Britain, 46, 153, 164
archbishop of Canterbury, 23, 83, 164. *See also* Augustine, Saint; Laurence; Mellitus; Theodore of Tarsus
Arian heresy, 12
arm (= body part), 37, 39, 73, 99–100
Ash/Gilton, 15
Ashdown Forest, 6
Áss, 7

assassination, 89
assault, 94, 96, 137. *See also* threat
assembly, 26, 29, 33, 35–6, 44–5, 48–9, 53, 61n.a, 83–5, 121, 131, 139–40, 153, 155, 159, 164–5, 167, 180
assembly-peace, 86. *See also* assembly; gathering; *mæthl*; *mæthlfrith*; *meðle*
Atilla, 4
Attenborough, F.L., 79n.c, 98, 100, 161n.a, 163n.d
Augustine, Saint, archbishop of Canterbury, 8, 10, 12–18, 46–8, 60–1, 63n.a, 83–4, 118, 120, 142, 147, 164, 206n.37, 209n.77

Babylon, 19
Balcanqual, Walter, dean of Rochester Cathedral, 24
bana, 'killer,' 42, 50, 66, 122, 126
bane, 'killer,' 122, 126
banquet, 86, 220n.45
baptism, 13–14, 118, 155, 168
Baron Ochs, 107
battery, 137
beaga bryttan, 'distributer of rings,' 86
Bearsted, 153n.d
bebyreþ, 'provide,' 29, 66
Bede, 3–13, 15, 17–18, 23, 25, 27, 35, 46, 48, 51, 83, 117–19, 135, 142–3, 147–8, 164–5, 169, 180, 206nn.37, 38, 207n.49. See also *Ecclesiastical History of the English People*
begeten, 'obtain,' 122, 126
beon, 'be,' 31–2, 131n.b
Beorhtwald, abbot, 119
Beowulf, 7, 86, 88, 95, 105, 139–40; Beowulf, 86, 87, 95
Berghamstead, 153, 164
Bertha, wife of Æthelberht of Kent, 8–10, 13–15, 118

Betherum, Dorothy, 39, 216n.169
betrothal, 79, 108–9
Beyerle, Franz, 50, 217n.197
Bible, 12, 19, 155n.b
binding, 67, 81, 89–90, 94, 114–15
birele, 'cupbearer,' 66–7, 88–90
bishop: in law, 15, 44–6, 48, 61, 83–4, 155, 159, 164, 167–9, 174–6; of Bangor, 25; of Canterbury, 6, 23, 180 (*see also* archbishop of Canterbury); of London, 118; of Rochester, 6, 22, 153, 164, 180, 226n.10
bishopric: of London, 117; of Rochester, 6, 22
bismærwordum, 'with mocking words,' 27, 121, 130
blockade, 7
blood, 97, 102, 103, 133, 136, 138
blow, 32, 73, 99, 100, 102, 103, 104, 163, 179
boast, 137
bone, 15, 37, 71, 102
Boniface V, Pope, 10
book, 9, 10, 19, 24, 25, 36, 155n.c, 167
borders, 3, 40, 133, 138, 144, 157, 169, 170
borrowings, linguistic, 43–4, 51, 77n.b, 91, 166
Bosworth, Joseph, 129n.b, 152n.b
brain, 102
breaking and entering, 67, 69, 94, 96, 98
Bretha Déin Chécht, 43
bride-price, 79, 98–9, 107–8, 224n.112. *See also* marriage
Brihtwald, archbishop of Britain, 153, 164
bringing a charge, 131, 139–41, 143–4, 159, 161, 175–6

280 Index

Britain, 3–4, 8, 10–11, 16, 143, 148, 164
British Isles, 16, 41, 84, 86, 143, 168
British language, 3, 15. *See also* Welsh; Brythonic
British Museum, 24
Britons, 3–5, 93, 119. *See also* Welsh
Brokmer laws, 38. *See also* Frisian: law
Brooks, Nicholas, 8, 18
bruise, 32, 73, 100
Brunner, Karl, 28, 91, 123, 150
Brythonic, 14. *See also* British language; Welsh
bugan, 'dwell,' 78, 113
burg-bryce, 'breaking into a household,' 95, 98
Burgundian, 88; law, 109
buying, 11, 69, 79, 90, 106, 108, 135, 144, 178
byname, 226n.9

Cædwalla of Wessex, 147
Cælin. *See* Ceawlin
Caistor-by-Norwich, 15
Campbell, James, 123
canon law, 22, 98, 110, 155n.c, 166, 176
Canterbury, 5–6, 10, 13, 23, 47, 83, 98, 118–19, 142, 164–5, 167, 180
Canterbury Cathedral, 23
Cantium, 5–6. *See also* Kent
capture, 108, 163, 171, 178–9
caroline script, 21–2
Carruthers, Mary, 37
cattle, 143–4
ceapi, 'with a price,' 28, 78, 106
cearwund, 'grievously wounded,' 29, 74, 104
Ceawlin, 9, 10, 17
Celtic, 5, 14. *See also* Irish; Welsh;

language 3, 19 (*see also* Irish: Old Irish; Welsh)
ceorl, 'freeman, husband,' 27, 36, 42, 43, 51, 66, 67n.d, 68, 78, 79, 80n.a, 113, 114, 128, 132, 156, 157. *See also* freeman; husband
Chan, Jackie, 37, 38
chaplain, 13, 15, 24
Charibert of the Franks, 9
Charles-Edwards, Thomas, 75n.34
charters, 20, 27, 84, 119–20, 123, 147–8, 166–7. *See also under* Kent
Chessel Down, 15
children, 18–19, 47, 75n.d, 79, 82, 90, 99, 106–7, 112–14, 119, 129
Christ, 11–12, 117–18, 159
Christian, 11, 46, 118, 148, 169, 171, 180; era, 3; influence on law, 34; mass, 13; pre-Christian, 15, 44; religion, 5, 12–14, 117
Christianity, 9–10, 12, 14–17, 19, 45–6, 48, 92, 117–19, 167, 180
Christianization, 16–17, 46
church, 11, 15, 16, 19, 24, 36, 110, 117–18; in law, 17, 27, 33, 36, 44–8, 51, 53–4, 61, 82, 83–5, 93, 134, 153, 155–7, 159, 161, 164–7, 170–1, 174–6, 212n.125, 217n.193
churchman, 161, 176
church peace, 44, 54, 61, 84
ciricean, 'of the church,' 152, 153
ciriclicæs, 'of the church, churchly,' 27, 149, 154
clænsie, 'clear (oneself from accusation),' 149, 158
clergy, 12, 15. *See also* cleric
cleric, 12, 15, 44, 61 (*see also* clergy, ecclesiastic); laws dealing with, 45, 48, 84, 94, 155, 159–61, 168–9, 174–7
clitic, 54
Clofeshoh, Council of, 83, 166

Index 281

clothing, 73, 100
Clovis of the Franks, 9
Cnebba, 9
Cnut of England, 112
cognate, 7, 28, 30, 73n.a, 86, 93, 108
coibche, 'bridal gift' (OI), 107, 224n.100
coins, 16, 43, 82–3, 142–3, 208n.61, 209n.83, 218n.7
collarbone, 26, 71, 100
comitatus, 5, 89, 155n.a
commerce, 6, 7, 135, 141, 142, 143. *See also* market; merchant; purchase; trade
communicant, 161, 174–7
community, 41, 111, 155, 167, 174–7
compensation, 16, 29, 33, 42, 44–5, 48, 50, 61, 63, 69, 77, 81, 83–5, 93–4, 106, 108–9, 111, 114, 116, 123, 127, 163, 178
complicity, 99, 110, 115, 171
compound nouns, 27, 29, 31, 34, 54, 61n.a, 65n.a, 74n.a, 75n.a, 76n.b, 86, 87, 88, 91, 97, 103, 104, 106, 108, 129, 171
concubinage, 168
Constantinople, 165
Continent(al), 4, 7, 8, 16; laws, 25, 36, 83, 102, 109, 113–14, 169
conversion, 8, 10–16, 84, 119, 226n.10
Cook, Albert, 180
copula, 34, 45, 214n.145
copy(ist), 14–15, 22, 25, 34, 45, 55, 83, 116, 120, 122–3, 127n.b, 128n.c, 131n.b, 149, 162n.c, 172, 211n.101
Corpus Glossary, 91
Cotton, Francis, 24
counselor, 17, 25, 83, 164, 165, 180. See also *witan*
Cretan, 35
Crith Gablach, 46
Cromwell, Oliver, 24

crossroad, 144
cuma, 'he will come,' 122, 128
cumin, 'has come,' 122, 132
cup, 133, 135–7, 141. *See also* goblet
cupbearer, 67, 88–9
cure (from a wound), 104, 174
Cutha of Wessex, 9
cwyþ, 'says,' 150, 152
cyngæs, 'of the king,' 27, 29, 121, 132, 149, 154

Danish, 7, 86, 96
Dante, 4
Darius of Persia, 19
dative of quantity, 32–3, 42–3, 51, 66n.b, 70n.c, 121–2, 211n.101
daughter, 6
deacon, 44, 61, 84, 94, 159, 174–5
dean of Rochester Cathedral, 24–5
death, 163
debt, 179
deceased, 141
decree, 14, 17, 40, 46, 61, 83, 127, 134, 153, 155, 164, 167–8, 174
De Excidio Britanniae, 4
definite article, 34
deictic, 34
Deira, 11
de Laet, Johan, 52
deman, 'judges,' 130, 141
denns, 6
dental fricative, 26, 121, 148, 208n.71, 212n.123
deportation, 179
Dering, Sir Edward, 211n.108
Der Rosenkavalier, 107
devil, 94, 117, 157, 159, 170–1, 180
dialect, 26, 55, 122, 123, 139, 149, 161n.a
Die Gesetze der Angelsachsen, 23, 61n.a. *See also* Liebermann, Felix

digraph, 27–8, 212n.125
disfigurement, 73, 100
disturbance of the peace, 84, 96, 109, 136
divorce, 79n.a, 110, 113–14
Domesday Book, 219n.28
domum, '(with) decrees,' 126
doubling of vowels, 26, 88
Dover, 143
dower, 106–7. *See also* morning-gift
Drew, Katherine Fisher, 145
drihtenbeag, 'lord-payment,' 29, 62, 85
drinking, 48, 63, 85–6, 133, 135–7
drunkenness, 155, 168–9
dual kings, 7. *See also* joint rule
Duncan of Scotland, 86
dura mater, 102
dwell, 79, 113
dwelling, 13, 63, 67, 85, 89–90, 94–5, 98, 129, 145

Eadbald of Kent, 83, 117, 118, 119, 120, 143, 180, 227n.23
Eadberht, son of Wihtred, 148
Eadric of Kent, biographical information, 119–20. *See also* Hloþhere and Eadric, laws
ealuscerwen, 'pouring out of ale,' 228n.43
ear, 31, 37, 39, 71, 100–1
Early English Manuscripts in Facsimile, 25, 181, 210n.97
East Anglia, 18, 117, 119
Eastry, 6
East Saxon, 118, 142, 147
eaxle, 'shoulder,' 70, 105
ecclesiastic, 6, 164–5, 168 (*see also* cleric); laws governing, 155, 168, 174–5
Ecclesiastical History of the English People, 3, 48, 51, 148, 203. See also *Historia Gentis Anglorum Ecclesiastica*
edorbrycþ, 'hedgebreaking,' 69, 94
Edwin of Northumbria, 119, 206n.24, 226n.10
Egbert of Kent, 119, 120
Elstob, Elizabeth, 24, 211n.112
Elstob, William, 24
embezzlement, 111
end, 'and,' 213n.133
English channel, 6
English language, 20, 25, 53, 87, 173, 182; Middle English, 123; Modern British English, 95; Modern English, 57, 87, 103, 174
– Old English: borrowings from Latin, 43; hapaxes, 71n.a, 91, 101–3, 169, 210n.85; language, 11, 29–30, 33, 61n.a, 89, 93, 97, 102–3, 108, 114, 161n.a, 174; — Classical Old English, 26–8, 30–2, 55, 122, 149, 217n.3; — Early Old English, 55; — Late Old English, 120; laws, 36, 40–1, 216n.169 (*see also under* Anglo-Saxon); manuscripts, 20–2; poetry, 39, 82; texts, 21–2, 25, 55, 69n.f
English peoples and territories, 8, 11–12, 18, 118, 148
English synod, 166
enslavement, 93, 170–1, 179. *See also* slave; unfree
eodorbryce, 'hedgebreaking,' 95
Eorcenberht of Kent, 119–20, 166
eorl, 'nobleman,' 36, 82, 89, 90, 95, 155n.a, 165, 168
eorlcund, 'of noble rank/birth,' 155n.a
Eormenric, father of Æthelberht, 8, 207n.42
ēosago, 'scribe versed in Mosaic law' (OS), 35

Index 283

Eota (Danish peoples), 7
epilogue, 116, 146, 165
Épinal Glossary, 213n.133
episcopal, 6, 23, 46, 175
erasure, 21, 56, 70n.b, 76n.g, 78n.g, 126n.d, 130n.c, 152n.d, 154n.b
Eric (of the Jutes). *See* Oeric
Ernulf, bishop of Rochester, 22–3
escape, 25, 42, 50–1, 97, 114, 127
esne, 'servant (labourer),' 36, 42–3, 51, 78–81, 94, 114–16, 126, 156, 158, 160, 163, 171–2, 221n.54, 234n.52. *See also* servant
Essex, 5, 117, 123
estate, 63n.a, 133n.a, 176
etymology, 28, 91, 104, 113, 127n.b, 134
Eucharist, 176
Europe, 20, 41, 91
Eusebius (Frankish moneyer), 83
evidence in law, 129, 138, 142–3, 146
excommunication, 168–9
exculpation, 127, 140, 145, 159, 166, 174–7
execution, 178
exemplar, 22–3, 27, 29, 55, 123, 127n.b, 131n.b
Exeter Book, 35
exile, 178
Exodus, 105
eye, 31, 38–9, 55, 71, 81, 99, 114, 115

facsimile, 20, 25, 56, 78n.b, 181, 212n.120
False Judgments of Caratnia, 40
family, 9, 88, 90, 107, 112, 115, 141
fast, 159, 170, 172, 174
father, 8, 9, 47, 91, 107, 118, 148; legal position of, 112–14, 129
feaxe, 'by the hair,' 105
feaxfang, 'seizing of hair,' 29, 70, 105

fedesl, 'feeding,' 29–30, 64–5, 86, 166. *See also* feeding, *feorm*, food-render
feeding, 29, 65, 85–7, 109, 166. *See also* *fedesl*, *feorm*, food-render
Fell, Christine, 107–11
fellowship, 161, 175–6
female slaves, 67, 89–90
feorm, 'food-render,' 65n.g, 138, 219n.28
feud, 16, 50, 97, 105
figura etymologica, 49, 51
fine, 32, 46–7, 49, 51, 57, 65, 75n.d, 84–5, 88–90, 93–100, 102–5, 108–9, 111, 115, 133–8, 140–1, 146, 157, 163, 167–8, 170–3, 178–9, 219n.33
finger, 36–9, 72–3, 77, 99, 101, 104; *goldfinger*, 'ringfinger,' 37, 39, 72–3, 101; little finger, 37, 39, 73, 101, 223n.78; middle finger, 37, 39, 73, 101
flet, 'house,' 95, 130, 132
flogging, 47, 115, 157, 159, 161, 172–3, 175–7
folcy, '(with the) populace,' 28, 150, 152
food, 5, 86, 89, 96, 100, 133, 138
food-render, 86. *See also fedesl*, feeding, *feorm*
foot, 26, 31, 37–9, 55, 77, 80–1, 99, 103–4, 108, 114–15
force, 137
forefinger, 36, 73, 101
foreign, 5, 26, 30, 87–8, 91, 93, 145, 147–8, 155, 167–8, 179. *See also fræmde*; stranger
forgelde(n), 'pay,' 50, 54–5, 66, 68, 76
fornication, 117, 167, 221n.55
foundation myth, 7
fræmde, 'foreigner,' 149, 162. *See also* foreign
Francia, 8, 12

284 Index

Frankish: influence on Kent, 7–9, 12–15, 82–3, 91, 118–19 (*see also* Merovingian); law, 17, 35–6, 37, 41, 50, 63n.a, 93, 104, 139, 144–5, 157n.a (*see also* Salic law). *See also* Merovingian
fraud, 144
free, 159, 170, 179
freedman, 69n.b, 82, 85, 91–3, 96, 169–70, 220n.45
freeman, 28, 33, 36, 42–5, 48, 50–1, 63, 65, 67, 69, 77, 79, 82, 84–5, 87–99, 103, 106, 109, 111–15, 127, 129, 133, 135–6, 138, 140–1, 144–5, 155, 157, 159, 163, 167–70, 172, 174–5, 177–9, 219n.33, 220n.45. *See also* ceorl
free woman, 29, 77, 88, 105, 110–11. *See also* 'free woman in charge of the locks'
'free woman in charge of the locks,' 77, 105, 110–11. *See also friwif locbore*
French: Modern French, 69n.f
freolaeta, 'free-given,' 91
freols, 'free,' 156, 171
freolsdome, 'freedom,' 153
freond, 'friend,' 74–5, 145. *See also* friends
freum, 'from a freeman,' 28, 64
frialsgiafi, 'freedom-giver' (ON), 220n.45
friends, 49, 75, 141, 145, 175
frioleta, 'free-given,' 91
Frisia, 4
Frisian, 5; Brokmer laws, 38; coining, 142; law, 30, 97; Old Frisian, 30, 37–8, 40, 103, 213n.143; slave, 143
friþ, 'peace,' 60, 84
friwif, 'free woman.' *See friwif locbore*
friwif locbore, 'woman in charge of/bearing locks,' 29, 63n.b, 76–7, 105, 110–11. *See also* 'free woman in charge of the locks'
funereal inscriptions, 19

gængang, 'return,' 29, 78, 108–9
gang, 49, 96
gang, 'path, journey,' 21, 108. *See also gængang*
gathering, 84–7, 137, 139–40, 164. *See also* assembly
Gaul, 3, 7, 9, 12, 118
Gaulish, 12, 19
gavelkind, 6, 113
gebicgan, 'buy,' 106
Gebmund, bishop of Rochester, 153, 164
gebrengen, 'bring,' 122, 132
gebrocen, 'broken,' 70, 74, 102
gedes, '?of a community,' 160–1
gegen, 'against' (MG), 108–9
gehwæder, 'each of two,' 27, 148, 154
geligeþ, 'lies with (sexually),' 43, 54, 64, 66, 68, 78. *See also* lies with (sexually)
gemacene, 'of equals,' 149, 158
genealogy, 7–8, 17–19, 206n.35
George III of England, 8
Germanic: conversion to Christianity, 114; kingship, 18–19, 45; kinship, 16, 82; language, 15, 27–8, 30–1, 82, 91, 140, 215n.157; — Modern German, 69n.f, 82, 102; — Old High German, 35, 86; — West Germanic, 32, 63n.a; law, 15–17, 25, 33–6, 38, 40, 49, 61n.a, 93, 97, 99, 102, 108, 114, 139, 157n.a, 169, 180, 209n.82, 221n.45, 222n.62; literature, 39–40, 51, 88, 108; masonry (lack of), 229n.56; mythology and tradition, 7, 87, 117, 153n.a; peoples as pa-

Index 285

gans, 12–13, 15; warriors/peoples, 4–5, 17, 19, 43, 86, 153n.a
gesecæn, 'seek out,' 122, 130
ge[s]elle, 'give,' 54, 128
gesith(-cund), 'noble,' 155, 165, 167–8
Gifts of Men, The, 35
Gildas, 4
girdle-hangers, 110–11
goblet, 136–7. *See also* cup
God, 11, 44–7, 61, 83–4, 144, 148, 161
gold, 16, 67n.d, 82–3, 142–3
goldfinger, 'ringfinger.' *See under* finger; *see also* James Bond
goldsmith, 88
goods, 7, 65n.d, 79, 84, 93–7, 108, 110, 112–13, 129, 133, 141–5, 155, 163, 167, 177–9
gospel, 11, 167
Gothic, 28, 30, 79n.c, 213n.143
grandfather, 91, 180
grandparents, 91
grave-goods, 111
graves, 49, 53, 67, 96, 97, 110, 111, 143, 171
great-grandfather, 91
great-grandparents, 91
Greece, 18
Greek: law, 34, 92, 108; indiction system, 165; Mycenean Greek, 19
Green, D.H., 75n.e
Gregorius, 225n.121
Gregory I, Pope, 10–13, 15, 46–8, 83, 164, 207n.53
Gregory of Tours, 8–9. *See also History of the Franks*
Grendel, 95, 105
Grierson, Philip, 16
grievously wounded, 29, 75, 104
Griffith, Bill, 65n.d
Grimm, Jacob, 73n.a, 98, 103, 107

'grinding slave,' 65, 89
guest, 65n.c, 108, 133, 138. *See also* hospitality; host
guide, 29, 65, 87, 181. *See also* herald/guide
guilty, 90, 110, 167, 176–7
gwestfa, 'food-render' (OW), 86
gyfe, 'if,' 28, 43, 76
gylde, 'let him pay,' 44, 45, 48, 60, 61, 62, 123, 126

hair, 4, 10, 29, 71, 101, 105, 110. *See also feaxfang*
hall, 81, 86, 88, 93, 95, 116, 129, 133, 137, 141–3, 155, 167
halsfang, 'fine in lieu of imprisonment,' 150, 171
ham, 'home,' 48, 62, 68–9, 78, 97–8. *See also* home; homestead; house
Hammurabi of Babylonia, 19, 37–8
handspan, 101
hanging, 172
hapax, 28–9, 91, 109, 161n.a, 169, 210n.85
Hartman von Aue, 225n.121
Haðubrand, 86
Hawkes, Sonia, 110
healsfang, 'fine in lieu of imprisonment,' 150, 157n.f, 159, 170, 171, 172
hearing, 37, 100
heathen, 11, 118, 226n.10. *See also* pagan
Hebrew, 18
hedge-breaking, 95–6
heirs, 11, 47. *See also* inheritance
Hengist, 7, 8, 17–18, 206n.36
Henry I, 20
heom, 'him, them,' 62, 123, 150, 162–3, 178
Heorot, 89

286   Index

herald/guide, 26, 48, 65, 85, 87–8. *See also* guide
Herring, Thomas, archbishop of Canterbury, 25
Hickes, George, 44
hide (= skin), 157, 159, 170
highway robbery, 29, 52, 54, 67, 81, 93–4, 116
Hildebrandslied, 86
hio, 'she,' 53, 64, 78, 130, 150, 154, 156
hiom, 'him/them,' 123, 130, 150
hion, '?skull,' 30, 70, 71, 101, 102
Hirn, 'skull' (MG), 102
Historia Brittonum, 206n.35
Historia Gentis Anglorum Ecclesiastica, 25. *See also Ecclesiastical History of the English People*; Bede
History of the Franks, 8. *See also* Gregory of Tours
Hittite (laws), 37–8, 105
hlæfdige, 'lady,' 69n.a
hlafæta, 'loafeater, dependent,' 68–9
hlaford, 'lord,' 69n.a
Hloþhere of Kent, biographical information, 119–20. *See also* Hloþhere & Eadric, laws
Hloþhere & Eadric, laws: content, 125–46; — compared with other Kentish laws, 42–3, 51, 83, 86–7, 89, 95, 106, 112, 114–15, 152, 164–6, 219n.28, 221n.54; dating, 120; editorial practice, 52–7; linguistic analysis, 120–3; — compared with other Kentish laws, 21, 26–9, 31, 34, 42–3, 106, 148–50; scribal abbreviation, 34, 43, 55, 120–1, 123, 172
home, 4, 12, 15, 48, 63, 68–9, 79, 85, 90, 97, 106, 108–9, 117, 133, 138, 168, 175. *See also ham*; homestead; house

homestead, 95, 97. *See also ham*; home; house
Horsa, 7
horse-servant, 87
horswealh, 'horse-servant,' 87
hospitality, 138, 155, 168–9. *See also* guest; host
host, 133, 137, 138. *See also* guest; hospitality
Hough, Carole, 79n.a, 109, 113–14
house, 6, 8, 13, 86, 95, 97, 110, 111, 131, 133, 135, 136, 137, 138, 144, 161n.a, 174. *See also ham*; home; homestead
household, 33, 36, 65n.a, 69n.a, 79, 86, 87, 88, 89, 111, 112, 113, 159, 170, 172
householder, 95, 138, 169, 172
Hrafnkels Saga, 49
hreowe, 'repentence,' 27
hrif, 'abdomen,' 54, 74–5, 103
hrif wund, 'abdominal wound,' 54, 74, 103
Humber, 8, 10, 19, 83, 117, 148
Huns, 4
husband, 43, 69, 79, 90, 98, 107, 109, 110, 112–14, 157, 171. *See also ceorl*; wife
hwæder, 'whether,' 26, 121, 130
Hwyel Dda of Wales, 41
hyd, 'hide/skin,' 102, 156, 158
hyr, 'here,' 123, 126, 150, 152

Iceland, 35
idol, 94, 119, 166, 171–2, 174
imperator, 10, 17, 117. *See also* overlordship
imperauit, 17, 207n.49. *See also* overlordship
imprisonment, 150, 157n.f, 171
in capillo, 110

incest, 167
incisors, 100. *See also* teeth
India, 18
indiction, 147–8, 153n.b, 164–5
Indo-European: language, 31, 63n.a, 134, 139, 213n.143; lawgivers, 18; laws, 38, 40, 92, 105, 108; poetics, 40
Ine of Wessex, laws of, 32, 87, 92–3, 112, 137, 147, 155n.a, 166, 171–3, 177, 179. *See also* Wessex: West Saxon laws
informant, 9, 18, 173
informer, 129, 145
Ingoberg, mother of Bertha, 9
inheritance, 6, 43, 50, 79, 105, 110, 112, 113, 146, 157, 169, 170, 180. *See also* heirs
injury, 33, 37–8, 41, 51, 56, 77, 85, 99–104, 106, 135–6, 173
innocence, 140, 144–5, 174
in sceat, 'with money,' 78, 107
inscriptions, 15, 19. *See also* runic
insertion (scribal), 21, 42, 126n.b, 130n.a, 132n.c, 158n.a, 160n.c, 162n.a
insular, 15, 21–2, 44, 181
insult, 99, 115, 136–7
interpolation, 21, 78n.g, 175
Ireland, 15, 179
Irish, 4
– language, 3; Middle Irish, 140; Old Irish, 15, 40, 43, 46, 77n.b, 91, 101, 105, 107, 209n.71; — law, 40–1, 43, 46, 77n.b, 91, 101, 105, 107, 216n.171; — sagas, 143
Iron Age, 5
Isle of Thanet, 12–13
Isle of Wight, 6–7, 147
iuxta exempla Romanorum, 18, 35

jawbone, 71, 100, 108

Jewish, 18, 35
Johnston, Sir Henry H., 180
joint rule, 6, 120, 205n.23, 226n.11, 231n.5
judge, 22, 47, 131, 139, 141
judgment, 140
Julius Caesar, 3, 5–6
justice, 20, 49, 133, 138, 144, 166
Justinian, 84
Justus, archbishop of Canterbury, 10, 118, 142
Jutes, 5–6, 220n.45; Jutish (language), 5–7, 13, 93

Kent: charters, 167, 231n.5; church, 46, 84, 166; coins, 67n.d, 82–3; dialect, 26, 28, 55, 91, 121–3, 148–50, 169, 212n.126, 213n.132; history, 5–14, 17–18, 117–20, 147–8, 168, 226n.10; inscriptions, 15; *læt*, 92–3, 221n.45, 221n.54; laws, 6, 20, 22–3, 25, 27, 29, 31–2, 38, 49, 63n.a, 83, 93, 110, 113, 121–2, 127n.b, 142, 144, 155n.a, 157n.i, 164, 171, 173, 177, 221n.45; peoples, 6–7, 10, 20, 63n.a, 118, 127, 131, 133–5, 139, 141, 143–4, 153, 164–5, 170; scriptorial practice, 28, 209n.71
Kentish Glosses, 123
Ker, Neil, 23, 210n.97
key, 110–11
killing, 9, 42, 48–51, 53, 63, 65, 67, 69, 79, 82, 85, 89–91, 94–7, 109, 114–15, 122, 127, 135, 144, 161, 163, 170, 177–9, 219n.33. *See also* murder; slain
kin(ship)/kin-group, 16, 50–1, 53, 75n.e, 79, 89, 91–4, 96–7, 106–7, 110, 112, 114–15, 129, 135, 141, 145, 157, 169, 170–1, 175, 178, 220n.45

288 Index

king: in history, 5–6, 8–14, 16–20, 34–5, 41, 46, 82, 117–20, 147–8, 226n.10, 231nn.1, 5, 232n.18; legal rights, 33, 36, 45–6, 48–9, 52–3, 79, 84–90, 93–7, 106, 108–9, 112, 134–9, 141–4, 163–70, 174–8, 180, 219n.33; referred to in texts, 27, 29, 62–5, 121, 126–33, 149, 152–9
kingdom, 6–14, 17, 35, 41, 117–19, 134, 138, 142, 147–8, 165
king-list, 83
kingship, 5, 9, 14–15, 101, 112, 120

laadrinc-mannan, 'herald/guide,' 26, 29, 48, 65
læng, 'longer,' 149, 154
lærestan, 'least,' 30, 72
læt, 'freedman,' 29, 68–9, 91–3
laetus, 'foreign bondsman' (L), 91, 93
laghsaga, 'lawspeaker' (OSw), 35
Lamacraft, Charles, 25
Lambard, William, 23
lame, 49, 71, 75, 99–100, 102–3, 140, 145
lathes, 6
Latin (see also Roman): borrowings from, 43–4, 210n.85, 213n.139; borrowings into, 91; canon law, 166; Germanic laws in, 25, 35–6, 139, 145, 215n.157; language, 3, 17, 60n.a, 86; literacy, 15, 23; manuscripts by Textus Roffensis scribe, 20–2; orthographic practice, 212n.125; texts, 17, 24, 230n.74
Laurence, archbishop of Canterbury, 118
lawspeaker, 35
Laws of Manu, 40
layman, 161, 175–7
leg, 100, 103

legislation, 18, 20, 35, 134, 165
Lehman, Winfrid, 16
Lendinara, Patrizia, 17, 213n.139
Lent, 119
leodgeld, 'person-price,' 29, 49, 65n.b, 66. See also leodgeld; man-price; man-worth; person-price; wergild
Leonard, Thomas, 24
lerest, 'least' (OF), 30
lest, 'least' (OF), 30
leswæs, 'act of dishonesty,' 27–8, 76
leud, 28, 63n.a, 149, 160
leudgeld, 'person-price,' 28–9, 74
Levardus, 208n.61, 209n.83. See also Liudhard
Lex Alamanni, 46, 223n.85
Lex Saxonum, 98
leysinga-son, 'son of a leysingi' (ON), 220n.45
leysingi, 'freedman' (ON), 220n.45
Liebermann, Felix, 23–4, 43, 53, 56, 61n.a, 64n.a, 65n.a, 66n.f, 68nn.b, c, 69nn.c, f, 70nn.c, d, 71n.c, 73n.a, 75n.d, 76nn.c, e, f, 78nn.b, d, 83, 87, 90, 92, 94, 96–8, 101–3, 108, 110, 115, 119–20, 128n.e, 129n.b, 130n.d, 131n.b, 139–41, 145–6, 150, 152n.b, 153n.e, 154nn.a, e, 155nn.b, c, 156n.b, 161n.a, 162n.c, 163n.d, 165–6, 169, 172–3, 178–9, 210n.97, 211n.101, 214n.150
lies with (sexually), 43, 52, 65, 67, 69, 79, 85, 89–90, 109, 114. See also geligeþ
literacy, 11, 14–15, 35–6, 42
little finger. See under finger
Liudhard, 13, 15, 209n.83. See also Levardus
loaf-eater, 29, 69, 90. See also hlafæta
locbore. See friwif locbore
locks, 29, 110, 111

lǫgsǫgumaðr, 'lawspeaker' (ON), 35
Lombard (law), 50, 110, 144, 157n.a, 215n.157, 225n.117. *See also* Rothar of the Lombards
London, 3, 10, 24, 83, 117–18, 129, 133, 135, 141–4, 203, 229n.56
lord, 69, 85–6, 155, 157, 161, 167–8, 170, 172–3, 175–7
lord-payment, 63, 85–6. *See also* drihtenbeag
Lovedon Hill, 15
Loyn, H.R., 175
Lyminge, 6, 226n.10
lyswæs, 'Act of dishonesty,' 27–8, 48, 62–3. *See also leswæs*

Macbeth, 86
mægþman, 'maiden,' 29, 78, 106. *See also* maiden
mæn, 'man,' 78, 123, 128, 132, 149, 154, 156
mæthl, 'assembly,' 26, 49. *See also* assembly
mæthlfrith, 'assembly-peace,' 54, 211n.108, 212nn.122, 125. *See also* assembly
maiden, 29, 52–3, 65, 77, 79, 85, 105–6, 108–10. *See also* virgin; women
Maidstone, 20, 153n.d
Maitland, F.W., 16, 129
mallberg (Frankish law court), 103, 139
man-price, 16, 42, 65n.b. *See also leodgeld*; man-worth; *manwyrð*; person-price; *wergild*
Manu, 18
manumissio in ecclesia, 92, 169
manumission, 29, 55, 93, 144, 149, 157n.a, 166, 169–70, 221n.24
manuscript, 11, 15, 20, 22–5, 28–9, 34, 41, 52–6, 60n.a, 64–6, 70n.c, 78n.d, 91, 121–2, 127n.b, 128n.e, 132n.a, 152nn.c, d, 153n.e, 154n.c, 156n.c, 158nn.a, b, 160n.a, 181–2, 212nn.120, 123
man-worth, 34, 42, 50, 51, 114, 115, 121, 123, 127. *See also leodgeld*; man-price; *manwyrð*; person-price; *wergild*
manwyrð, 42, 123, 126. *See also leodgeld*; man-price; man-worth; person-price; *wergild*
margin, 21, 128n.d, 132n.b, 158n.a, 162n.b
market, 10–11, 143. *See also* commerce; merchant
marriage: in history, 9, 12–13, 117–19; legal rulings, 79, 98–9, 106–10, 112, 117–19, 155, 166–8, 180; in literature, 225n.120
marriage portion, 112. *See also* morning-gift
Martin, Saint, 205n.19
master, 79, 81, 91, 94, 114–15, 144–5, 170, 172–3, 177–8, 220n.45
Maxims I, 106
Maxims II, 106
Mayr-Harting, Henry, 11
McKitterick, Rosamund, 35, 41
mead, 88, 137
meadhall, 136
meal, 89, 137
medder, 'mother,' 123, 128
mediation, 99
medical fee, 104–5
medle, 'assembly,' 26, 121, 130
medume, 'ordinary,' 49, 66, 219n.33
Medway River, 6
Meillet, Antoine, 30
Mellitus, bishop of London, 10, 118, 142
meoduscerwen, 'pouring-out of mead,' 228n.43

merchant, 133, 138, 144. See also commerce; market; trade
Mercia, 83, 143, 148
merkismaðr, 'standard-bearer' (ON), 88
Merovingian, 38, 105, 215n.157. See also Frankish; Salic law
meðel, 'assembly,' 131, 139, 140, 145
meðle, 'assembly,' 26, 121
middle finger. See under finger
Mildreth, Saint, 227n.16
minster, 159, 166, 174–5
mint, 83
mission, 10–14, 16–17, 207n.53
missionary, 13, 119
mnemonic, 36–8, 40
mocking words, 27, 121, 131, 135–7
modernizing (linguistic), 22, 25, 34, 122, 148–9
molars, 100. See also teeth
monastery, 11, 23, 112, 118, 169, 176, 206n.24, 226n.10. See also monastic; monk
monastic, 155, 168. See also monastery; monk
monetary payment, 65n.g, 86
money, 16, 47, 67n.d, 79, 82, 90, 96, 97, 106, 107, 109, 115, 144
monk, 12, 23, 169, 176. See also monastery; monastic
monotheistic, 14
Moore manuscript (of Bede), 203
Morgay Farm, 107
Morgay Wood, 107
morgengifu, 'morning-gift,' 107, 110
morning-gift, 79, 98, 107, 110
Mosaic law, 217n.193
mother, 79, 105–6, 112–13, 123, 129
mouth, 71, 100
Mul of Wessex, 147
mund, 'protection,' 76, 89, 136–7, 219n.25. See also protection

murder, 90, 97. See also killing; slain

nede genimeþ, 'takes by force,' 78, 108
Nibelungenlied, 88
Nimrod, 4
noble(man), 33, 36, 50, 56, 57, 67, 77, 87–90, 94, 111–12, 114–15, 127, 138, 168, 175
non-free, 115
Norse, 73n.a, 107; Old Norse: — language, 7, 49, 65n.a, 86; — law, 40, 86, 157n.a, 171, 220n.45
Norðleod, 92
Northumbria, 11, 27, 46, 119, 123, 226n.10
nose, 32, 37–9, 70–1, 73, 100–1

oath, 29, 40, 50–1, 114–15, 127, 129, 131, 139–41, 144–6, 159, 161, 166, 170, 174–7 (see also swearing); oath formulation, 29, 166, 170; oath helper, 29, 50–1, 114, 127, 129, 144–5, 161, 176–7. See also witness
Octa, 8, 206n.35
Oeric (of the Jutes), 7–8
of-aslagen, 'struck off,' 31
Offa of Mercia, 166
offerings (sacrifice), 94, 136, 140, 157, 159, 170–2, 180
official smith, 54, 65. See also ambihtsmið
Oisc, 7–8, 17, 206n.35
oiscingas, 8
ond, 'and,' 21, 55, 70, 72, 106, 179
open a, 214n.150
oral transmission/tradition, 11, 14, 17–20, 33–6, 38, 40–1, 121, 135, 157n.a, 170, 215n.157
orthography, 14, 15, 22, 26, 27, 150, 212n.125, 227–39. See also vowel length
Oslaf (Kentish ealdorman), 9

Oswine of Northumbria, 46, 120, 147
overlordship, 12, 15, 18, 83, 119, 142, 148. See also *imperator*; *imperauit*
ownership, 40, 42, 50–1, 65n.d, 79, 108, 114–15, 127, 129, 131, 133, 135–7, 141–2, 144–5, 157, 161–3, 169–70, 172, 177–9. *See also* possession; purchase
ox, 82

pagan(ism), 3, 5, 11, 12, 13, 14, 46, 94, 117, 118, 119, 167, 171, 180, 226n.3. *See also* heathen
papacy, 12. *See also* pope
parchment, 14, 37, 56
pastus, 'banquet, food-render' (L), 86. See also *fedesl*; *feorm*
paternal, 79, 107, 112
Patriarch of Alexandria, 13
Paulinus, bishop of Northumbria, 226n.10
peace, 5, 44–5, 65n.c, 84, 86, 136
Pegge, Samuel, 24
Pelteret, David, 11
penalty, 48, 50, 84, 86, 94, 96, 98, 102, 146, 163, 172, 178
penance, 167, 168–9, 176. *See also* repentance
Penda of Northumbria, 226n.10
penis, 37, 75, 90, 99, 108
Penitentials of Theodore, 47, 146, 165, 167, 168, 171, 174, 176, 179, 221n.55, 232n.26. *See also* penance; Theodore of Tarsus
penny, 83
perjurer, 131, 135. *See also* perjury
perjury, 136–7, 141. *See also* mocking words; perjurer
Persia: Old Persian, 19
personal injury, 32–3, 35–9, 41–3, 49, 51, 56, 71, 75, 77, 82, 90, 99, 101, 104–5, 136, 138, 209n.82. *See also* injury

person-price, 28–9, 48–9, 53, 65, 67, 75, 96. See also *leodgeld*; man-price; man-worth; *manwyrð*; *wergild*
Peter, Saint, 118
Peterborough, 23
phonology, 26–9, 44, 55, 91, 120–3, 148–9
pia mater, 102
Picts, 3–4, 18
pierce, 71, 97, 99
pig, 143
pillory, 171
plague, 226n.3
Poetic Edda, 87
point(ing), 16, 21–2, 34, 46, 53–4, 56, 76n.f, 128n.b, 160n.b, 182
poison, 89
Pokorny, Julius, 139
Pollock, F., 129
pope, 10, 11, 47–8. *See also* Boniface V; Gregory I
possession, 19, 65, 85, 93, 95, 107, 129, 133, 141–2, 146, 149, 155, 157, 163, 167–8, 170–1. *See also* ownership
post-Conquest, 23, 28
pre-Alfredian laws, 15
pre-Christian, 8, 15, 44
pre-conversion, 14, 15
preliterate, 35, 41, 42, 215n.157
prickings, 20
priest, 11, 14, 44–6, 61, 84, 94, 155, 159, 166, 168–9, 174–5
primogeniture, 6
procedure, 49, 121, 134. *See also* process
process (legal), 29, 41, 49, 92, 121, 129, 131, 139–42. *See also* procedure
pro-drop, 214n.145
prologue, 6, 28, 38, 46, 82–3, 121–3,

134–5, 148–50, 153, 164–5, 180, 209n.77
property, 44–5, 47, 61, 69, 79, 82–4, 94–6, 102, 107, 112, 129, 131, 133, 136, 139, 141–5, 163, 172, 177–8. *See also* ownership
protection, 46, 56–7, 65, 67, 77, 79, 85, 88–90, 94, 97–8, 108, 111–12, 129, 133, 136, 138, 157, 167–70. *See also mund*
Provence, 11
public coffer, 134, 166, 172. *See also* Appendix IV
public order, 144
public peace, 85, 155, 168. *See also* Appendix IV
public safety, 136
punishment, 47, 115, 171, 177, 179
purchase, 133, 142–4. *See also* commerce; ownership; sale; selling
Pushkin, 105

rade, 'counsel,' 149, 156, 173
Rædwald of East Anglia, 117, 119
Ralf d'Escures, archbishop of Canterbury, 23
ransom, 178
rape, 108
recompense, 33, 46–7, 84, 90, 92–4, 96, 100–1, 103, 105, 109, 112, 115, 135, 141, 144, 161, 163, 173, 176–8
recording (of laws), 5, 7, 14–19, 22–3, 25, 34–6, 41, 45–7, 104, 122, 135, 149, 180
redeem, 163, 172, 177–9
reeve, 142–3, 234n.62. *See also* town-reeve
Renaissance, 7
reparation, 43, 137–8
repentance, 155, 167–8. *See also* penance

restitution, 15, 32, 42, 44–8, 51, 56, 63, 70n.d, 71, 73, 77, 84–6, 88–90, 92, 94, 99–100, 105–6, 116, 135, 144, 155, 167–8, 180, 212n.125
retribution, 101
reward, 86, 95, 173, 178
Rhine, 3
rib, 39, 76–7, 100
Richards, Mary, 20, 23
Richardson, Henry G., 15
right, 131, 133, 136, 139, 155, 167
rihthæmed, 'legitimate matrimony,' 98
rihthamscyld, '?protection of legitimate matrimony,' 29, 70–1, 97
ring, 82, 86, 101, 103, 106
ringfinger. *See* finger: *goldfinger*
ritual, 169, 174
Rivers, T.J., 145, 224n.111, 224n.112
robbery, 46, 69, 94–6, 109, 177–8. *See also* theft; steal; *wegreaf*
Rochester, 6, 10, 20, 22–4, 28, 119, 142, 153, 164, 180; Cathedral Library, 20, 23; scriptorium, 23, 28
Rodulfus. *See* Ralf d'Escures
Roman: Church, 176; coins, 16, 82; Empire, 3–4, 12, 18, 35, 93; indiction system, 165; mission to Kent, 11–14, 17, 119, 206n.37; peoples, 11–13; Roman Britain, 3–6, 142–3, 229n.53; Roman Gaul, 41. *See also* Latin
Rome, 7, 10, 12, 14, 84, 153n.b, 206n.37
Romney Marsh, 6
Romulus and Remus, 7
Roskilde, 4
Rothar of the Lombards, 214n.151
rubric, 14, 83–4, 120, 134, 152n.a, 164, 209n.77
Rudiments of Grammar for the English-Saxon Tongue, The, 24. *See also* Elstob, Elizabeth

Rugern (autumn harvest), 153, 164–5
runic, 15, 21, 26. *See also* inscriptions
Rushworth Gospels, 123
Ruslan and Ludmilla, 105
rustling (of cattle), 95–6
Ruthwell Cross, 28

Sabbath, 172–3, 180
Sachsenspiegel, 40. *See also* Anglo-Saxon: laws
sacrament, 167, 180
sacrifice, 94, 117
Sæberht of Essex, 117–18
St Martin. *See* Martin, Saint
St Martin's Church, Canterbury, 5, 13, 205n.19, 208n.61
St Mildreth. *See* Mildreth, Saint
St Paul's Church, London, 117
St Peter. *See* Peter, Saint
sale, 10, 129, 133, 142–4. *See also* purchase; selling
Salic law, 102–3, 139, 145, 214n.151, 217n.197. *See also* Frankish: law; Merovingian
Sanskrit (law), 40, 92, 107, 108
Sarre, 15, 143
Sawyer, Peter, 20, 23–4, 27, 181, 210n.97
Saxon: Old Saxon, 30, 35; peoples, 3–5, 34, 88, 147; settlements in England, 6, 142–3
Sayles, G.O., 7, 15
Scandinavia, 7
scar, 104
scearwund, 'wounded in the groin,' 223n.90
sceatt(as) (unit of money), 67n.d, 71, 73, 77, 82, 89–90, 100, 142, 157, 170, 172–3, 218n.7
Schmid, Reinhold, 97, 171
scilling-, 'shilling,' 21, 32, 39, 42–3, 49, 55–6, 64, 66, 68, 70, 72, 74, 76, 78, 80, 102, 130, 132, 211n.101, 214n.150
Scotland, 18
scribe/scribal, 15, 20–3, 24, 28–9, 34–5, 53–6, 65n.a, 66n.d, 70nn.a, c, e, 71n.c, 72nn.b, c, 73n.a, 76n.d, 78n.a, 120–1, 123, 128n.g, 129n.b, 130n.e, 131n.b, 137, 161n.a, 172, 217n.2
scriptoria, 23, 121–2, 212n.125
scrotum, 39, 75n.d, 99
Scyld Sceafing, 86
Sebbi of Essex, 147–8
Seebohm, Frederic, 220n.45
seizing of hair. See *feaxfang*
seller, 142, 144. *See also* purchase; sale; selling
selling, 12, 17–19, 107, 163. *See also* purchase; sale; seller
seman, 'arbitrate,' 54, 74, 141
servant 31, 33, 36, 42–3, 50, 55, 79, 81–2, 85, 87–8, 94, 99, 114–15, 118, 127, 144, 146, 157, 159, 161, 170–7. See also *esne*
Shabbat, 18
sheep, 118, 143
shilling, 32, 36–7, 39, 42–3, 49–50, 52–3, 55–7, 63, 65, 67, 69, 71, 73, 75, 77, 79, 81–2, 84–97, 99–104, 108–12, 114–16, 127, 131, 133, 135–40, 153, 155, 157, 159, 163, 166–8, 170–3, 177–8, 211n.101
ships, 4
shoulder, 37–9, 71, 99–100, 102, 105
sick maintenance, 105
Siegfried, 88
Sievers, Eduard, 27–8, 121, 150
siexg-, 'sixfold' (OHG), 61n.a
silver, 6, 83, 142
simony, 12
Simpson, A.W.B., 16

294   Index

sin, 155, 167
sinew, 37, 39, 77n.c, 103. See also *wælt*
sio, 'let (him) be,' 32, 53, 64–5, 123, 126, 130, 132, 150, 154, 156
sio, 'the,' 70
sion, 'let them be,' 150, 156
Sisam, Kenneth, 123
Sixtus, martyr, 205n.19
skin, 39, 102–3
skul, 'covering' (OF), 97
skull, 30, 38, 71, 101–2
slain, 88–90, 96–7, 106, 115, 171. See also killing; murder
slave, 11, 27–8, 33, 36, 53, 65, 81–2, 85, 87–94, 110, 114–16, 129, 143, 145–6, 149, 157, 159, 163, 169–73, 177–9, 221n.55. See also enslavement; *þeow*; unfree
slave-work, 157, 170, 172
sleeping with (sexually), 98, 109, 114
smell (sense of), 100
smith, 48, 54, 65, 85, 87–8
Smith, James, 24
sold, 11, 129, 133, 141–4, 179
solidus (Roman coin), 82
Solomon and Saturn, 161n.a
Solon, 18
son: in history, 6–9, 83, 117–19, 147–8, 180, 206n.35; in law, 107, 112, 141, 143, 220n.45; in literature, 86
Sophie, 107
speech, 37, 71, 100, 136
Spelman, Henry, 34, 41
spina dorsa, 103
spinal column, 103
stabbing, 99
Stanley, E.G., 105, 139
steal, 15, 45, 48, 63, 65, 81, 85, 93, 116, 129, 141, 145, 163, 177. See also robbery; theft; stolen

Stenton, Sir Frank, 93
stermelda, '?informer,' 128–9
stipulation, 47, 49, 52–3, 85, 96–7, 101, 104–6, 110, 112, 115, 121, 134, 138, 145, 177
stolen, 47, 53, 65, 79, 84, 93, 108, 111, 133, 142, 144–5, 163, 177–9. See also steal
stomach, 39, 75, 223n.85
Strand, 142
stranger, 149, 159, 163, 174–5, 179. See also foreign
striking off, 31, 55, 71, 81, 84, 99–101, 104, 114
Stubbs, William, 119, 169
Sturry, 6
surety, 112, 129, 131, 139–41
Sussex, 5, 107, 120; South Saxons, 17
Swæfheard of the Saxons, 147–8
swearing, 137, 140, 142, 144–6, 174, 177. See also oath
Sweden, 5; Swedish, 35
swine, 6
sword, 15, 137
sylfæs, 'of self,' 27, 149, 158
synod, 10, 164, 166–7. See also Clofeshoh, Council of
Synod of Hertford, 169
syntax/syntactic 30–2, 34, 42–3, 45, 48, 61n.a, 121–2, 181, 209n.82, 212n.125, 214n.145

taan, 'toe,' 26, 76
Tacitus, 13, 16
Tate, daughter of Æthelberht, 119, 226n.10
Tate, Francis, 24, 60n.a, 119, 212n.122
tax(ation), 153, 165–6
teeth, 37, 39, 71, 100, 104
Textus Roffensis, 20, 22–7, 55–6, 120–1,

127n.b, 134, 181, 209n.71, 210n.97, 212n.120; scribe, 29, 55, 123
Thames, 6, 20, 25, 142, 203
þane, 'the,' 21, 68, 122, 126, 128, 130, 132
Thanet, Isle of, 12–13
þare, 'the,' 56, 66, 76, 122, 128, 149, 156
theft, 15, 45, 47, 63, 82, 84, 90, 93–4, 96, 106, 109, 111, 115–16, 129, 142–3, 145–6, 161, 163, 166–7, 177–8, 221n.55. See also robbery; steal
thegn, 87, 143, 159, 174–5
þegnunæ, 'service,' 27, 149
Theodore of Tarsus, archbishop of Canterbury, 47, 119, 165, 167, 169. See also Penitentials of Theodore
þeow, 'slave,' 36, 79–80, 115, 158, 172–3; þeowne esne, 116; þeuw(ne), 28, 149
thigh, 39, 43, 49, 75, 77, 99, 103, 140
þing, 'assembly,' 131, 139, 140
Thoresby, Ralph, 24
threat, 136–7. See also assault
þridde, 'third,' 64–5
throat, 71n.c
thumb, 31, 36–7, 39, 73, 84, 101, 223n.78; thumbnail, 36, 73, 77, 100–1
tindscra, 'brideprice' (OI), 107, 224n.100
toe, 26, 36–9, 41, 77, 98–9, 104; toenails, 104
toll, 142
Toller, Northcote, 98, 223n.90
tonsured, 155, 168
town, 106, 119, 133, 135, 141–2. See also township
town-reeve, 133, 141–2. See also reeve
township, 145. See also town
trade, 7, 8, 138, 142, 143. See also commerce; merchant

transcription, 24, 41, 54, 56, 60n.a, 181, 212n.122
treasure, 5, 82, 111
Treasury, Whitehall, 143
Tschernamor, 105
tun, 'estate,' 27, 63n.a, 95
twam manwyrþum, 'with two manworths,' 33, 42, 121, 126
Twysden, Sir Roger, 24

uinge, 'inch' (OI), 44
uncia, 'inch' (L), 43, 44, 77n.b
uncial, 22
unfree, 51, 87–8, 94, 115–16, 161, 175, 179. See also enslavement; slave
unlægne, 'incontrovertible,' 150, 158
unlegnæ, 'incontrovertible,' 150, 158
unmarried, 43, 79, 110, 114
unrihthæmed(e), 'unlawful union,' 98, 154
uterre, 'outer,' 70, 102

vellum, 20, 24, 25
vendetta, 171
verb-final, 31, 214n.149
verb-initial, 214n.149
verb-second, 214n.149
vernacular, 14, 25, 35–6, 40–1, 63n.a
Verner's law, 213n.143
vestments, 159, 174
Victoria, queen of England, 8
Viking, 11
violation, 44, 46, 57, 65, 67, 69, 77, 84–6, 88–90, 98, 111, 112, 133, 136, 138, 153, 166, 168
virgin, 106–8, 110. See also maiden
Visigoth, 45
Vǫlundr, 87
von Amira, Karl, 88
Vortigern, 4, 8
vouch, 129, 133, 141, 142, 144, 175.

296   Index

See also evidence in law; warrantee; witness
vow, 137. See also oath
vowel length, 26, 208n.71, 121

wadfalt, 'blow' (F), 103
wælt, '?welt,' 29, 30, 39, 76, 102–3
waldsine, 'spina dorsa' (OF), 103
Wallace-Hadrill, J.M., 7, 16, 19, 20, 46, 47, 63n.a, 83, 97, 119
warrantee, 129
warrior, 4–5, 17–19, 38, 65n.c, 86–7, 95, 137
war band, 89
war leaders, 17
water mill, 89
water stain, 20, 25
Watkins, Calvert, 105
Weald (forest in Kent), 6
wealh, 'servant,' 79n.c, 87–8, 93
wealtan, 'roll,' 104
weapon, 52, 67, 87, 94, 96, 101, 133, 136
Wecta, ancestor of Hengist, 7
wegreaf, 'highway robbery,' 29, 54, 66, 80, 221n.52. See also robbery
Welsh: conversion, 15; language, 3, 14–15; laws, 41, 48, 84, 86–7, 91–3, 108; peoples, 4 (see also wilisc)
welt, 29–30, 39, 77, 103–4
wergild, 'man-price,' 16, 49–50, 65n.b, 69, 87–90, 92–3, 96–9, 102, 109–10, 115, 127n.c, 135, 140, 150, 156–7, 161, 163, 168–72, 177, 178, 219n.33, 221n.52, 224n.112, 234n.52. See also leodgeld; man-price; man-worth; manwyrð; person-price; wyrgelde
Wessex, 5, 9, 147; West Saxon language, 22, 26, 31–2, 122–3, 217n.4; West Saxon laws, 87, 92–3, 98, 112n.a, 137, 155, 166, 179 (see also Alfred of Wessex; Ine of Wessex); West Saxon peoples, 10, 17
Whitelock, Dorothy, 63n.a, 65n.d, 67n.b, 87, 113, 128n.c, 129n.c, 155n.a, 157nn.e, i, 161n.a, 163n.b, 171, 173, 177–8, 233n.52
Wibbandum, 9
wicgerefan, 'town-reeve,' 132, 142. See also reeve; town-reeve
widobane, 'collarbone,' 26, 70
widow: in history, 206n.24; in law, 56–7, 77, 89, 105–8, 111–13, 141
Widsið, 82
Wieghelmestun, 27
wife: in history, 8–9, 13, 15, 117–18; in law, 43, 69, 79, 90, 98, 107, 109–14, 128–9, 157, 167–8, 170–1, 179, 224n.112
Wight, Isle of, 18
Wihtgisl, ancestor of Hengist, 7
Wihtred of Kent:
– biographical information, 119, 120, 147–8
– laws: content, 6, 152–80; — compared with other Kentish laws, 46, 83, 92, 94, 98, 115–16, 127n.b, 144, 145; dating, 165; editorial practice, 52–7; linguistic analysis, 21, 26–8, 148–50; — compared with other Kentish laws, 26–9, 31, 121–3
wilisc, 'Welsh,' 92–3
William de Corbeil, archbishop of Canterbury, 23
wills, 86, 114
wine, 143
witan, 'counsellors,' 165, 180
witness, 129, 133, 141–2, 144–5, 148, 174–5, 177. See also oath; vouch
Witta, ancestor of Hengist, 7
Woden, 7, 10, 17–19

women, 9, 24; in law, 33, 36, 42, 67n.a, 69, 77, 79, 82, 88–90, 99, 105–7, 109–13, 167, 171, 174. *See also* maiden; widow; wife
word division, 34, 54
work, 157, 173, 180
Wormald, Patrick, 16, 18, 34–5, 41, 46, 49–50, 97, 180, 228n.42
worship, 13, 118, 166, 174
wound, 17, 29, 37, 39, 43–4, 51, 54, 75, 77, 95, 99–100, 102–4, 118, 120, 136, 140. See also *wund*
writing, 14, 16, 17–21, 26, 28, 31–3, 35, 38, 40–1, 51, 63n.a, 121, 135, 169
Wuffa of East Anglia, 18

Wuffingas, 18
Wulfgar, 89
wund, 'wounded,' 39, 74, 75, 76, 102, 103, 104
wuntana baugas, 'wound rings,' 86
Wyatt, Sir Thomas, 7, 206n.29
wyltan, 'roll,' 104
wyrgelde, '(with) wergild,' 28, 150, 160

Xerxes, 19

ynce, 'inch,' 17, 43, 44, 51, 76
York, 164

TORONTO MEDIEVAL TEXTS AND TRANSLATIONS

General Editor: Brian Merrilees

1 *The Argentaye Tract* edited by Alan Manning
2 *The Court of Sapience* edited by E. Ruth Harvey
3 *Le Turpin français, dit le Turpin I* edité par Ronald N. Walpole
4 *Icon and Logos: Sources in Eighth-Century Iconoclasm* translated by Daniel J. Sahas
5 Marie de France *Fables* edited and translated by Harriet Spiegel
6 Hetoum *A Lytell Cronycle* edited by Glenn Burger
7 *The de Brailes Hours: Shaping the Book of Hours in Thirteenth-Century Oxford* by Claire Donovan
8 *Viking Poems on War and Peace: A Study in Skaldic Narrative* by R.G. Poole
9 François Villon *Complete Poems* edited with English translation and commentary by Barbara N. Sargent-Baur
10 Guillaume de Machaut *The Tale of the Alerion* edited and translated by Minnette Gaudet and Constance B. Hieatt
11 *Prions en chantant: Devotional Songs of the Trouvères* edited and translated by Marcia Jenneth Epstein
12 *Fishers' Craft and Lettered Art: Tracts on Fishing from the End of the Middle Ages* by Richard C. Hoffmann
13 Thomas Usk *The Testament of Love* edited by Gary W. Shawver
14 *The Beginnings of English Law* by Lisi Oliver